Transitional Justice and the Politics of Inscription

Taking Northern Ireland as its primary case study, this book applies the burgeoning literature in memory studies to the primary question of transitional justice: how shall societies and individuals reckon with a traumatic past? Joseph Robinson argues that without understanding how memory shapes, moulds, and frames narratives of the past in the minds of communities and individuals, theorists and practitioners may not be able to fully appreciate the complex, emotive realities of transitional political landscapes. Drawing on interviews with what the author terms 'memory curators', coupled with a robust analysis of secondary literature from a range of transitional cases, the book analyses how the bodies of the dead, the injured, and the traumatised are written into – or written out of – transitional justice. The author argues that scholars cannot appreciate the dynamism of transitional memory-space unless they first engage with the often silenced or marginalised voices whose memories remain trapped behind the antagonistic politics of fear and division. Ultimately challenging the imperative of national reconciliation, the author argues for a politics of public memory that incubates at multiple nodes of social production and can facilitate a vibrant, democratic debate over the ways in which a traumatic past can or should be remembered.

Joseph S. Robinson is a Ph.D. candidate in the Department of Geography at Maynooth University, Maynooth, County Kildare, Ireland. He is an Irish Research Council Fellow and a Research Fellow at the Glencree Centre for Peace and Reconciliation in Glencree, County Wicklow, Ireland. The research and first drafts of this book were written when he was a Researcher with The Junction, a community relations and peacebuilding non-profit located in the city of Derry, Northern Ireland.

Transitional Justice
Series Editor: Kieran McEvoy
Queen's University Belfast

The study of justice in transition has emerged as one of the most diverse and intellectually exciting developments in the social sciences. From its origins in human rights activism and comparative political science, the field is increasingly characterised by its geographic and disciplinary breadth. This series aims to publish the most innovative scholarship from a range of disciplines working on transitional justice-related topics, including law, sociology, criminology, psychology, anthropology, political science, development studies and international relations.

Titles in this series:

Transitional Justice and the Politics of Inscription
Memory, Space and Narrative in Northern Ireland
Joseph Robinson

Resistance and Transitional Justice
Edited by Briony Jones and Julie Bernath

The Reparative Effects of Human Rights Trials
Lessons from Argentina
Rosario Figari Layus

Amnesties, Pardons and Transitional Justice
Spain's Pact of Forgetting
Roldán Jimeno

Forthcoming titles in the series:

The Judiciary and the Politics of Transition
Police Brutality Cases in Chile, Northern Ireland and South Africa
Marny Requa

The Trouble with Truth
Dealing with the Past in Northern Ireland
Kieran McEvoy

Transitional Justice and the Politics of Inscription

Memory, Space and Narrative in Northern Ireland

Joseph S. Robinson

Routledge
Taylor & Francis Group
LONDON AND NEW YORK

First published 2018
by Routledge

2 Park Square, Milton Park, Abingdon, Oxfordshire OX14 4RN
52 Vanderbilt Avenue, New York, NY 10017

Routledge is an imprint of the Taylor & Francis Group, an informa business

First issued in paperback 2018

British Library Cataloguing-in-Publication Data
A catalogue record for this book is available from the British Library

Library of Congress Cataloging-in-Publication Data
A catalog record for this book has been requested

ISBN: 978-1-138-29151-5 (hbk)
ISBN: 978-0-367-19174-0 (pbk)

Typeset in Galliard
by Out of House Publishing

I am thy father's spirit,
Doomed for a certain term to walk the night,
And for the day confined to fast in fires,
'Til the foul crimes done in my days of nature
Are burnt and purged away …
… Adieu, adieu, adieu. Remember me.

W. Shakespeare, *Hamlet*, Act I, V, 9–13, 91

For I have learned
To look on nature, not as in the hour
Of thoughtless youth; but hearing oftentimes
The still, sad music of humanity,
Neither harsh nor grating, though of ample power
To chasten and subdue.

W. Wordsworth, 'Lines composed a few miles above Tintern Abbey'

The past is never dead. It's not even past.

W. Faulkner, *Requiem for a Nun*

Contents

Figures

Acknowledgements

This book was written with the aid and support of a number of wonderful individuals. I had the privilege of being employed by the incomparable Maureen Hetherington while writing this book. She was my host, supervisor, and collaborator, and without her, this book would never have been written. Shaul Cohen offered excellent insights, criticisms, and support throughout the length of the project. I must also especially thank the family and friends of Terry Enright, in particular his brothers Feargal Mac Ionnrachtaigh and Niall Enright. Their powerful testimonies fundamentally re-cast the arguments of this book and the graciousness with which they shared them is beyond my limited powers of description. The Conflict Archive on the Internet (CAIN) website maintained by Ulster University is an invaluable resource for anyone interested in any aspect of Northern Ireland's history, culture, and social realities. I wish to thank especially the director of CAIN, Martin Melaugh, who has generously allowed me to reproduce CAIN copyrighted images in this work. CAIN is an incredibly valuable public resource in Northern Ireland for scholars and laypeople, and should be protected. Other people who provided contacts and perspectives on this work for which I am extremely grateful are: Eamonn Baker, Julieanne Campbell, Liam Campbell, Eamonn Deane, Gerard Deane, Jacqueline Erwin, Seamus Farrell, Maureen Fox, Susan Glass, Brandon Hamber, Catherine McColgan, Sara McDowell, Alison Murray, Anna Murray, Brendan Murtagh, and Karen Till. Love to my parents, Kevin Robinson and Martha Scott, my brother Reid Robinson, my sister-in-law Brittney Deibert, and my baby niece Marian. Finally, I wish to thank each and every one of the respondents who took time out of their lives to sit down and selflessly share their insights, perspectives, and memories with me.

This book is dedicated to the memory of my grandmother, Marian Robinson, and all those times we made the time to drive out west.

Glossary of terms and acronyms

32-County Sovereignty Movement: An organisation formed out of a split in Sinn Féin in 1997. It is commonly referred to as the political wing of the Real IRA, although spokespeople for the group deny this (Horgan, 2013). It is currently classified as a terrorist organisation by the United States.

Alliance Party: A small, liberal, officially non-sectarian party in Northern Ireland formed in 1970. Originally funded to represent moderate, non-violent unionism, the party has sought to attract Catholic support since the 1990s. The party was represented in the British Parliament until 2015, and is represented in the Northern Ireland Assembly[1] and local Northern Irish political bodies. The party supported the Good Friday Agreement. It is currently led by Naomi Long.

Anglo-Irish Agreement: Not to be confused with the Anglo-Irish Treaty of 1921. A negotiated agreement signed on 15 November 1985 by the British and Irish governments. In exchange for granting the Irish government an advisory role in Northern Irish affairs, the Irish government agreed that no change in the constitutional status of Northern Ireland could be secured without the approval of a majority of Northern Irish citizens. The agreement was and is bitterly opposed by conservative unionists.

Anglo-Irish Treaty: Not to be confused with the Anglo-Irish Agreement. A treaty signed in 1921 that ended the Irish War of Independence. It established the Irish Free State as a self-governing dominion within the United Kingdom. It also partitioned the six counties of Northern Ireland, which remained under the direct administration of the UK. Negotiators for the Irish Republic, Michael Collins and Arthur Griffith, signed the treaty plenipotentiarily, and their action was bitterly opposed by other elements within the republican movement. The treaty was ratified by the Dáil, but those

1 As this book went to press, in February 2017, there was no Northern Ireland Assembly pending an election on 2 March 2017. Even after the election, it is unclear if the Northern Ireland Assembly will be able to re-form. Therefore, I indicate if a party was represented in the Northern Ireland Assembly prior to its dissolution on 26 January 2017.

opposed to ratification walked out after the vote. The Irish Civil War of 1922–1923 followed shortly thereafter. Collins, Griffith, and the pro-treaty faction viewed the Partition of the North as temporary. It was not.

An Phoblacht: Also known as 'Republican News', *An Phoblacht* was a weekly newspaper published by Sinn Féin in Ireland that served as the official mouthpiece of the IRA during the Troubles. Currently, it is published by Sinn Féin in Ireland on a monthly basis.

Belfast Agreement: See Good Friday Agreement.

B Specials: See Ulster Special Constabulary (USC).

Continuity Irish Republican Army (CIRA): A splinter group that opposed the Good Friday Agreement of 1998. It was responsible for the murder of PSNI Officer Stephen Carroll in 2009 and has been involved in a number of bombings and shootings (Independent Monitoring Commission, 2008). It is classified as a terrorist organisation by both the United States and the United Kingdom.

Criminalisation: The British policy, which began around 1975, of treating members of republican and loyalist paramilitary organisations as ordinary criminals and not political prisoners.

Dáil Éireann: The lower house of the Parliament of the Irish Republic.

Democratic Unionist Party (DUP): Both the largest unionist party and the largest party in Northern Ireland until the dissolution of the Northern Ireland Assembly in January 2017. Formed in 1972 by the Rev. Dr Ian Paisley, the DUP attracted a more conservative strain of unionism and was a key player in the UWC general strike that brought down the Sunningdale Agreement of 1974. The DUP was the only major Northern Irish party to oppose the Good Friday Agreement and refused to share power in the Northern Irish Executive with Sinn Féin until 2006, when it dropped its objections after the St Andrew's Agreement. The party is currently represented in the British Parliament, the Northern Irish Parliament, the European Parliament, and local Northern Irish political bodies. Currently the party is led by Arlene Foster.

Direct Rule: The term given for the administration of Northern Ireland directly from Westminster, as opposed to the Stormont assembly in Belfast. The Northern Ireland executive was suspended on 28 March 1972 and was only reinstated after the signing of the Good Friday Agreement. Subsequently, Stormont was suspended a number of times but was reinstated after the St Andrew's Agreement of 2006. Direct rule has not existed in Northern Ireland since spring 2007; however, it may be reinstated if the 2 March 2017 Northern Ireland Assembly elections fail to reconstitute the Northern Ireland Assembly.

Dissident Republican: Generally speaking, a term for a self-described republican who opposes the Good Friday process. In popular parlance, however, the term is generally used to refer to republicans who seek to continue the republican campaign by violent means. A significant minority of self-described republicans embrace the term 'dissident' even if they do not openly advocate violence to show their opposition to, and displeasure with, Sinn Féin.

Easter Rebellion: Also, Easter Rising. A seminal moment in Irish history. Begun on 24 April 1916, members of the Irish Republican Brotherhood and Irish Volunteers seized key points around the city of Dublin in an armed insurrection. The insurrection was chiefly led by Padraig Pearse and James Connolly. The British quickly suppressed the Rising and executed those whom they deemed to be the 16 leaders. The insurrection was one factor leading to the Irish War of Independence from 1918 to 1921.

First Dáil: An Irish assembly convened from 1919 to 1921 during the Irish War of Independence. Sinn Féin won 73 out of a possible 105 seats in the House of Commons during the 1918 general election and established the First Dáil as part of their campaign promise to establish an independent parliament separate from Westminster.

(Irish) Free State: The term for the 26 counties of the Republic of Ireland from 1922 to 1937. After 1937, it became the Republic of Ireland. The terms Free State and 'Free Staters' are used today by republicans to refer in a derogatory way to the Republic of Ireland because the terms imply abandonment of the claim to the six counties comprising Northern Ireland.

GAA: Gaelic Athletic Association. This is the largest amateur sporting organisation in Ireland. It organises and promotes Gaelic games such as Gaelic football and hurling. The GAA is also a community organisation and often serves as a focal point for community activism and cohesion within Catholic/nationalist/republican communities in Northern Ireland. Gaelic games and Gaelic life are almost exclusively the province of Catholics.

Garda Siochana (Gar-da Shiu-kana): Irish for 'defenders of the peace', the Gardai are the police force of the Republic of Ireland.

Good Friday Agreement: The consociational, or power-sharing, peace treaty that marks the semi-official end of the Troubles in Northern Ireland. It was signed on 10 April 1998. In two referendums held on 22 May 1998, in Northern Ireland and the Republic of Ireland respectively, voters approved the Good Friday Agreement by a wide margin.

Hunger strikes: A watershed moment in republicanism culminating in 1981. Begun by republican prisoners in the Long Kesh/Maze prison, the hunger strikes were the final stage in a lengthy protest against the British policy of criminalisation. Eleven members of the IRA and the INLA, led by Bobby Sands, starved themselves to death in protest at the circumstances of their incarceration. Sands was elected MP for the Fermanagh constituency and died shortly after his election.

Interface: Also interface area. Generally, a border area between a Protestant-dominated and a Catholic-dominated community in urban areas such as Belfast and Derry/Londonderry. Interfaces are generally thought to be focal points of inter-community violence and tension and they are often separated by 'peacelines', walls, barriers, or other defensive architecture that physically separate the two communities.

Irish National Liberation Army (INLA): Originally a breakaway group from the Official IRA, the INLA was known for being a particularly extreme manifestation of violent republicanism. The INLA and the IRA engaged in several republican feuds and three members of the INLA died in the 1981 hunger strikes. The INLA was responsible for 127 deaths (McKittrick et al., 2008, p. 1560). The INLA opposed the Good Friday Agreement but in 2009 declared an end to its armed campaign. It was deemed to have decommissioned in 2010.

Irish People's Liberation Organisation (IPLO): Formed as a consequence of an internal split in the INLA, the IPLO had ceased to exist by the early 1990s. The IPLO was responsible for 23 deaths (McKittrick et al., 2008, p. 1560).

Irish Republican Army (IRA): The predominate republican paramilitary organisation in Northern Ireland during the Troubles. The IRA has existed in some form since 1913 and traces its formation to the Irish Volunteers who initiated the Easter Rising in 1916. Following the signing in 1921 of the Anglo-Irish Treaty that partitioned the six counties of Northern Ireland, the republican movement split between those who supported the treaty and those who opposed it. The modern IRA is descended from the anti-treaty IRA, who fought and lost a civil war against the pro-treaty faction from 1922 to 1923. The IRA split again in 1969 into the Provisional and the Official IRA. The Official IRA ceased to exist as a paramilitary force after 1975 and its rump members formed the INLA. The Provisional IRA (or 'Provos' as they are often known) was responsible for 1,768 deaths during the Troubles (McKittrick et al., 2008, p. 1560). The leadership of the IRA supported the Good Friday Agreement in 1998. It announced an end to its campaign in 2005 and was declared to have decommissioned its weapons in September 2005. In 2011, Sinn Féin President Gerry Adams declared the IRA had ceased to exist.

Irish Republican Socialist Party (IRSP): The political wing of the INLA.

Long Kesh: See Maze, The.

Loyalist/loyalism: A Northern Irish person/ideology that believes in loyalty to the British sovereign. Loyalists generally believe that violent action is justified to defend the union of Great Britain and Northern Ireland.

Loyalist Volunteer Force (LVF): A breakaway organisation from the UVF that opposed the UVF ceasefires of the mid-1990s. It killed 19 people during the Troubles (McKittrick et al., 2008, p. 1553), most in the aftermath of the assassination of its leader Billy Wright in the Maze prison in 1998, including that of Terry Enright (McKittrick et al., 2008, pp. 1423–1424).

Maze, The: Her Majesty's Prison Maze, formerly known as Long Kesh. A prison used to house primarily paramilitary prisoners during the Troubles from 1971 to 2000. The prison played a pivotal role in the Troubles and is perhaps best known as the site of the 1981 hunger strikes. Republicans generally refer to the prison as Long Kesh to avoid any reference to the British Crown.

MLA: Member of the Legislative Assembly. Elected member of the Northern Ireland Assembly.

MP: Member of Parliament. Elected member of the Westminster (British) Parliament.

Nationalist/nationalism: Not to be confused with nationalism more generally, in the Northern Irish context this term refers to a person/ideology that supports the peaceful reunification of Northern Ireland and the Republic of Ireland.

NORAID: An American organisation dedicated to raising funds for the families of republican prisoners. It also funnelled money to the IRA (Holland, 2001).

Northern Ireland Assembly: The devolved legislature of Northern Ireland. See also: Stormont.

Northern Ireland Civil Rights Association (NICRA): An organisation first established in 1967 and modelled after the civil rights struggle in the United States. The NICRA was a non-violent advocate for equal civil rights for Catholics. Subjected to often brutal repression, the NICRA largely ceased to exist after 1973.

Northern Ireland Executive: The executive branch of the Northern Irish devolved government. Prior to the dissolution of the Northern Ireland Assembly in January 2017, it was a joint office held by the largest Catholic/nationalist/republican party and the largest Protestant/unionist/loyalist party. From 2006 to 2017, that was Sinn Féin and the DUP, respectively.

Northern Ireland Office (NIO): A cabinet-level position within the British government that was established to administer direct rule. After Spring 2007, and the return of devolved rule, it is no longer the chief governing authority in the province. The head of the NIO is the Secretary of State for Northern Ireland. In 2017 that position was filled by James Brokenshire.

OFMDFMNI: Office of the First Minister and Deputy First Minister of Northern Ireland. Another name for the head of the Northern Ireland Executive. See: Northern Ireland Executive.

Official Irish Republican Army (OIRA): A product of the intra-IRA split of 1969, the OIRA declared a ceasefire in 1972 and largely ceased to exist as a paramilitary force from that point. Those opposed to the 1972 ceasefire formed the INLA. Its members were colloquially known as 'sticks' or 'stickies'. It was responsible for 57 deaths during the Troubles (McKittrick et al., 2008, p. 1553).

Orange Order: A fraternal and cultural organisation existing primarily in Northern Ireland, but also in the Republic of Ireland, Britain, and Canada. The Orange Order is the largest organiser of parades in Northern Ireland and its attempts to parade through Catholic-dominated communities continue to cause controversy. The Orange Order does not admit Catholics or those of Catholic parentage into its organisation. Women must join a parallel, women-only order.

Partition: The separation of the six counties of Northern Ireland from the Irish Free State in 1921.

Police Service of Northern Ireland (PSNI): The successor organisation to the RUC formed in response to the Patten Report of 2003.

Progressive Unionist Party (PUP): The political wing of the UVF, active primarily in Protestant/unionist/loyalist neighbourhoods of Belfast. Its official political orientation is left wing, which differentiates the party from other unionist parties, which are right wing. Its most prominent members are David Ervine (deceased) and Billy Hutchinson. Hutchinson is the current party leader. The party has been represented in the Northern Ireland Assembly in the past, but currently is only represented at the local level in Northern Ireland.

Provisional Irish Republican Army (PIRA): One of the two factions of the IRA to emerge after the 1969 split. By 1972 it was by far the largest republican paramilitary organisation.

Real Irish Republican Army (Real IRA): A splinter republican group that opposed the Good Friday Agreement of 1998. The Real IRA perpetrated the Omagh bombing of 1998. It is classified as a terrorist organisation by the United States and the United Kingdom, and as a proscribed organisation by the Republic of Ireland.

Republican/republicanism: General term for a person/ideology that supports the reunification of Northern Ireland and the Republic of Ireland. Most self-described republicans do believe that violence can be a justifiable means to achieve reunification, but this is not universally the case.

Royal Ulster Constabulary (RUC): The civilian police force for Northern Ireland first established in 1921. Overwhelmingly Protestant in make-up, the RUC was directly responsible for 51 deaths during the Troubles (McKittrick et al., 2008, p. 1553). In 2003 it was renamed the Police Service of Northern Ireland (PSNI).

St Andrew's Agreement: An agreement signed by the British and Irish governments as well as all five major Northern Irish parties (Alliance, DUP, Sinn Féin, SDLP, UUP) that ended direct rule in Northern Ireland and returned power to the Stormont assembly. Its major accomplishments were an acceptance of the PSNI by Sinn Féin and a commitment to power-sharing by the DUP.

Saracen: An armoured combat vehicle used by the British army.

Sinn Féin: Formerly the political wing of the IRA, currently the second-largest political party in Northern Ireland and the third-largest party in the Republic of Ireland. Irish for 'ourselves alone', Sinn Féin was formed by Arthur Griffith in 1904. Modern Sinn Féin traces its ancestry to that time period. Sinn Féin's elected representatives practise abstentionism; they do not take the seats they are elected to in the Westminster Parliament. There have been a number of splits in the party over time. Sinn Féin currently contests elections in the Republic of Ireland, Northern Ireland, Westminster, and the European Parliament. They have taken their seats in the Republic of Ireland since 1986, the European Parliament since 1985, and local government elections in Northern Ireland since 1981. Many Sinn Féin members were also members of the IRA (Moloney, 2002). The party is represented in Dáil Éireann, the European Parliament, the Northern Ireland Assembly, and local Northern Irish political bodies. They continue to abstain from taking their seats in the Westminster Parliament. Sinn Féin supported the Good Friday Agreement. The party is currently led in the North by Michelle O'Neill and in the South by Gerry Adams.

The six counties: The term for Northern Ireland preferred by many republicans because they argue that the term Northern Ireland legitimises the separation of the Republic of Ireland and Northern Ireland. The six counties are Antrim, Armagh, Derry (also known as Londonderry), Down, Fermanagh, and Tyrone.

Social Democratic and Labour Party (SDLP): The main nationalist party in Northern Ireland. It was established in 1970 to promote the peaceful reunification of the Republic of Ireland and Northern Ireland. Currently, it is represented at Westminster, the Northern Irish Assembly, and local Northern Irish political bodies. It supported the Good Friday Agreement. Its then leader, John Hume, received a Nobel Prize for his efforts at securing the Good Friday Agreement. The party is currently led by Colum Eastwood.

Special Air Services (SAS): A special forces unit of the British military first deployed to Northern Ireland in 1976. Throughout the Troubles, the SAS was involved in a number of controversial actions and killings of both IRA members and civilians (Murray, 2004).

Stormont: A building that is the seat of the Northern Ireland Parliament. The name of the building is coterminous with the Parliament. It is located in East Belfast.

Sunningdale Agreement: An initial attempt at a negotiated solution to the Troubles. The Sunningdale Agreement proposed a Northern Irish government with power-sharing between the UUP and the SDLP. It was brought down by Protestant resistance spearheaded by the UWC and the DUP. It was also opposed by Sinn Féin.

Taig: A derogatory term for a Catholic, generally an Irish Catholic.

Taoiseach (Tee-shuh or Tee-shukh): The title of the Irish Prime Minister. The current Taoiseach is Enda Kenny.

Teachta Dála (TD): An elected member of the Dáil.

Unionist/unionism: A term for a person/ideology that supports the continued union of Great Britain and Northern Ireland. Unionism historically and in general is internally divided by what legitimate means can be used to protect the union.

Ulster: Historically, one of the four regions of the island of Ireland comprising the six counties of Northern Ireland and Counties Cavan, Donegal, and Monaghan. Currently, Ulster is used as a toponym for Northern Ireland mainly by the Protestant/unionist/loyalist community. Nationalists and republicans object to using Ulster to describe Northern Ireland because it is not coterminous with historic Ulster.

Ulster Defence Association (UDA): One of the two largest loyalist paramilitary organisations active during the Troubles. The UDA was established in Belfast in 1971 and proscribed in 1992. The UDA declared a ceasefire in 1994 but continued to carry out sporadic attacks and killings. The organisation declared an end to its armed campaign in 2007 and was deemed to have decommissioned in 2010. It remains classified as a terrorist group by both the governments of the United States and the United Kingdom. The organisation was responsible for 431 deaths during the Troubles (McKittrick et al., 2008, p. 1553). It has been implicated in subsequent killings up to 2009 (BBC News, 2009).

Ulster Defence Regiment (UDR): An auxiliary wing of the British army composed of part-time Northern Irish volunteers formed in 1970. Overwhelmingly Protestant, the UDR primarily functioned as border guards and supplementary forces for police and regular army action. It was merged with the Royal Irish Rangers in 1992 to form the Royal Irish Regiment. It was directly responsible for eight deaths during the Troubles (McKittrick et al., 2008, p. 1553).

Ulster Freedom Fighters (UFF): A cover name for the UDA.

Ulsterisation: A policy undertaken by the British government in 1975 that sought to shift the onus for security provision back onto local Northern Irish actors, especially the RUC and the UDR.

Ulster Special Constabulary (USC): The precursor to the UDR, also known as the B Specials. Overwhelmingly Protestant and implicated in the repression of the civil rights movement, the USC was abolished in 1969 and replaced by the UDR in 1970.

Ulster Unionist Party (UUP): The only unionist party in Northern Ireland from 1920 to 1972, it remained the largest unionist party until it was superseded by the DUP in 1999. The party is currently led by Mike Nesbitt. It is currently represented in the Northern Ireland Assembly, the European Parliament, and local Northern Irish government. The UUP supported the Good Friday Agreement and its then-leader, David Trimble, was the recipient of a Nobel Peace Prize for his efforts at securing the Good Friday Agreement.

Ulster Volunteer Force (UVF): One of the two largest loyalist paramilitary organisations active during the Troubles. The UVF traces its lineage to a militia group formed by Edward Carson and James Craig in 1913 to oppose Home Rule for Ireland. The modern UVF was formed in 1966. It was proscribed from 1966 to 1974 and again from 1975 onwards. It was responsible for 550 deaths during the Troubles (McKittrick et al., 2008, p. 1560). It declared an end to its armed campaign in 2007 and was deemed to have decommissioned in 2009. However, individuals associated with the UVF continue sporadic violent actions up to the current day (BBC News, 2013b). It is deemed a terrorist organisation by the British government, the Irish government, and the United States.

Ulster Workers' Council (UWC): The umbrella organisation that organised the general strike of 1974 that brought down the Sunningdale Agreement. See also: Sunningdale Agreement.

Introduction: A short history of the Troubles

Transitional justice and Northern Ireland

On 22 May 1998 voters in Northern Ireland overwhelmingly approved the Good Friday/Belfast Agreement (hereafter, the Agreement). Voters in the Republic of Ireland simultaneously agreed to excise the irredentist claims to Northern Ireland from the Republic's Constitution to the tune of 94.4 per cent. The 30-year conflict known as the Troubles had claimed up to that date approximately 3,600 lives (McKittrick et al., 2008). While there has been no agreed-upon measure of the number of people wounded in the Troubles, conservative estimates of direct injury as a result of the Troubles cluster around 50,000 people (Breen-Smyth, 2013). While the total number of casualties in Northern Ireland is quite small in comparison to contemporary bloodbaths in Syria, Yemen, Sudan, Afghanistan, and Iraq, these figures suggest just under 3 per cent of the total population of Northern Ireland was a direct casualty of the conflict. In one survey, approximately half of the population Northern Ireland reported 'knowing someone' who had been killed, though that number dropped to around 30 per cent when asked about close friends or relatives (Hilyard et al. 2003, p. 61). While conflict-related casualties in Northern Ireland are geographically clustered, leaving an uneven distribution of suffering across the small territory of Northern Ireland (Cunningham & Gregory, 2014), it is still safe to say that the conflict left a deep-rooted legacy of victimisation and wounding in the province as a whole and a significant number of people directly affected by death, violence, and traumatic injury. Beginning with the IRA and loyalist ceasefires in 1994 and continuing through to the signing and ratification of the Agreement in 1998, it became increasingly clear that something must be done to address those legacies.

Yet the truth of the matter is that very little has been done in the intervening 18 years, at least very little at the political or institutional level. More than 3,000 killings remain officially unsolved (indeed it would be safe to say there has been a de facto amnesty for all Troubles-related crimes since the signing of the Agreement), and there has been no serious or in-depth official truth recovery process. Victims and survivors of the Troubles have, in the majority of cases, been left in the dark about who specifically harmed them or their loved ones, or gave the orders to harm them and their loved ones, or who is ultimately responsible for protecting those who harmed them or their loved ones. If transitional justice is defined as the "conception of justice associated with periods of political change, characterised by legal responses to confront the wrongdoings of repressive predecessor regimes" (Teitel 2003, p. 69), then the question must be asked, has transitional justice had *any* relevance at all to the Northern Irish situation?

The answer may be a bit of a mixed bag, and will no doubt depend on a scholar's preference for narrow versus broad definitions of transitional justice (see Roht-Arriaza, 2006). In this book, I am deeply sceptical of narrow approaches to transitional justice, and believe that if transitional justice is to be of any relevance to societies such as Northern Ireland, it must expand its scope beyond purely legalistic philosophies and mechanisms. It must take into account a burgeoning, interdisciplinary literature on how the past is utilised in the present, how memories are socially constructed and geographically emplaced, and how new, creative forms of placemaking and inscription have challenged and will continue to challenge and unsettle the justifications for violence and the supposed imperative of social reconciliation. To that end, this book is more indebted to memory studies, progressive human geography, and critical theory than it is to transitional justice. But it is written in the hope that it can provide theorists and scholars of transitional justice, as well as peace practitioners in transitional societies, a signpost towards a form of transitional justice that takes memory, space, place, and the politics of inscription seriously and expands the universe of transitional possibilities and potentialities.

Stan argues, "*Memory* relates directly to only a subset of the methods and practices that legal scholars and political scientists recognise as part of transitional justice – that is, to the so-called backward-looking, not the forward-looking processes" (2013, p. 6, original emphasis, referencing Offe, 1996). Stan may be correct, but only correct inasmuch as she accurately but ironically describes the failings of transitional justice in relation to its treatment of memory. How individuals, groups, and societies remember a difficult, contentious, and traumatic past is of the utmost significance in accurately tracing the contours of present and future possibilities.

The Troubles in Northern Ireland

This section hardly purports to reinvent the proverbial wheel. Many readers will be aware that there are a litany of excellent histories of modern Ireland, Northern Ireland, and the Troubles, and for those interested in more detail, context, and analysis of the Troubles and the history of modern Ireland, I do not hesitate to direct them elsewhere (for general histories, see Jackson (2014), Cochrane (2013), McKittrick & McVea (2001), Ó Dochartaigh (1997); for modern Irish republicanism/nationalism, see Bean (2007), Murray & Tonge (2005), Moloney (2002); for modern loyalism, see the perspectives in McAuley & Spencer (2011), Spencer (2008); and for unionism's relationship with loyalism, see Southern

(2007)). This section is intended purely to provide readers unfamiliar with Northern Ireland with a context and a backdrop for my arguments throughout the book.

Writing history in modern Ireland can be a fraught endeavour. History in Ireland is often used as an ideological or political weapon, as a means to discursively reproduce an antagonistic, violence-producing, or violence-justifying narrative. By emplacing such a narrative within the realm of historical 'objectivity', the production and reproduction of these histories lays claim to unbroken lines of nationhood, oppression, threat, siege, and/or class struggle. In Northern Ireland, these discursive reproductions tend to take three major forms: nationalist (green) histories, unionist (orange) histories, and Marxist (red) histories (Perry, 2013). The first argues that there is a coherent, historical polity called Ireland/Éire, and a people describable as Irish/Éireannach, that was severed by British colonialism. The second argues that there are two distinct political, ethnic, and/or religious communities on the island, and that the conflict has historically been caused by the refusal of one community (nationalists) to recognise this. And the third sees British imperialism and policy as stemming from its inseparability from the imperatives of capital and capitalists and, generally, sees greater hope for a socialist state under an Ireland free from British imperialism. However, Marxist perspectives on Ireland tend to view both nationalism and unionism as 'false consciousness' (for example McCann, 1993). These frames are all ubiquitous in Northern Ireland and they provide a reservoir from which 'chosen traumas' and 'chosen glories' can be selectively recalled as a means of political mobilisation and social cohesion (Volkan, 1997).

Key events in a highly punctuated nationalist historiography include the savage seventeenth-century Cromwellian reconquest of Ireland, the United Irishmen Rebellion of 1791 led by Theobald Wolfe Tone (which is often pointed to as the 'birth' of republicanism (Bew, 2007; Smith, 2000)), the Irish Famine of the mid-nineteenth century, during which approximately one million people died of starvation and one million people emigrated (Gray, 2014), the Easter Rebellion of 1916, and finally the Partition of Northern Ireland in 1921. The nationalist historiography essentialises to an Irish nation brutally conquered, colonised, and starved by its larger neighbour of Britain, but always seething in a state of unrest and rebellion, culminating in a glorious, if failed, 1916 Rebellion that galvanised the Irish people as a whole to finally rise up against their colonial occupiers. The partition of the six counties now comprising Northern Ireland means that the struggle is unfinished, and what separates Irish nationalism from Irish republicanism is the question of what methods and means are, have been, and will be legitimate in the ongoing struggle.

Key events in an also punctuated and selective unionist historiography also include the Cromwellian reconquest, but the historical scenario is flipped to emphasise the massacres of Ulster Protestants that preceded (and presumably justified) the reconquest. As Ian Paisley, the firebrand Free Presbyterian Minister-cum-First Minister of Northern Ireland stated with typical bellicosity in 1969: "In 1641, the Roman Catholic Church decided to exterminate the Protestants in

Ulster ... [the massacre] was led by priests of the Roman Catholics and the rivers of Ulster ran red with Protestant blood" (in Rea & Wright, 1998, p. 6). But there are also three major 'chosen glories' of a unionist historiography that function as an emotive parable of the Protestant situation in Northern Ireland, which again is presumed to be constant throughout history: the Siege of Derry, the Battle of the Boyne, and the Battle of the Somme. The unionist historiography is one of perpetual siege and threat, of a minority people on the island of Ireland who have always defined themselves as British, in spite of British ambivalence towards them, surrounded on all sides by a majority people and a hated Church that will divest them of their rights and identity given any opportunity. The unionist historiography believes that the British state and the British empire was sustained by the blood and sacrifice of (Northern) Irish Protestants, especially on the battlefield of the Somme in the First World War.

Turning now to Northern Ireland after Partition, the Anglo-Irish Treaty of 1921 granted the 26 southern counties of the island the status of a 'Free State' within British dominion, but left the six north-eastern counties (Antrim, Armagh, Derry,[1] Down, Fermanagh, and Tyrone) directly under British rule. In the North, the first Prime Minister of Northern Ireland, James Craig, immediately set about consolidating a one-party government and institutionalising religious segregation. Northern Ireland was to be governed by, in Craig's words, "A Protestant Parliament for a Protestant people" (cited in Bardon, 2005, pp. 538–539). There were three major forms of social and political discrimination against Catholics in the North: housing, employment, and politics. Catholics were not permitted equal access to housing and clustered into tenements on the peripheries of productive space, they were subject to formal and informal exclusion from certain trades and industries, and finally, Northern Ireland was risibly gerrymandered to produce a parliament with a comfortable unionist majority, even returning Protestant majorities in cities such as Derry where the majority of the population was Catholic. Entrenched discrimination was justified partly by simple sectarianism but also by the fear of Irish irredentism; Catholics were seen as a population inherently anti-unionist and thus disloyal en bloc.

The social pressures that would lead to the Troubles began to build most visibly in Derry in the 1960s. One major precipitating event was the decision

1 The official name of both the county and the main town/city is Londonderry. The original English name Derry is more commonly used. One's choice of name can be an indicator of one's ethnopolitical persuasion. Some unionists insist on Londonderry; virtually all nationalists would use Derry. The clumsy moniker Derry/Londonderry is sometimes used by those not wishing to give any offence, but many residents find this tiresome. I use Derry throughout this book for both the city and the county. This is not a political statement in the slightest, merely a reflection of my experience living in Derry City for three years and the fact that Derry is the commonplace toponym used by members of both/all local communities in everyday speech. I invite the reader to refer to and think of the name of the county and town howsoever they please.

to site Northern Ireland's second university in Protestant-majority Coleraine instead of Derry, Northern Ireland's second city that was and is predominately Catholic. The mobilisations and pressures surrounding the university decision dovetailed with ongoing mobilisations around the chronic housing shortages in Catholic areas of the city. Most scholars date the beginning of the Troubles as 5 March 1968, when the Derry Housing Action Committee (DHAC), a more-militant strand of the larger civil rights movement engulfing the city, applied to stage a protest march directly on the route of the annual Apprentice Boys' march (the Apprentice Boys being a Protestant-only fraternal and commemorative organisation that performs one of the three central founding glories of unionist historiography, the Siege of Derry). The DHAC protest march was of course a transgressive provocation designed to challenge the geographical and symbolic ownership of the city claimed by the Apprentice Boys, and to challenge the Protestant community's power-based demarcation of public space (Cohen, 2007). The DHAC protest march was predictably banned but staged anyway. The police counter-response was vicious and brutal, and unlike other instances of repression directed at nationalists in the past, the beatings were captured on television cameras, including the beating of the MP Gerry Fitt, one of the founders of the SDLP. Television coverage of the event dominated the news cycles in Ireland, Britain, and the United States. The next year's (1969) Apprentice Boys' parade saw intense violence, and residents of the Catholic neighbourhoods of the Bogside and the Creggan essentially closed those neighbourhoods to the police and their auxiliaries, known as the B Specials. Residents set up barricades at key entry points to the Bogside and fought running battles with the police and B Specials predominately using stones and petrol bombs. This would become known as the Battle of the Bogside. In response, the British government removed the police and the B Specials and called in the army in an attempt to restore order. The government of the relatively moderate Terrence O'Neill quickly toppled and was replaced first by the ineffectual James Chichester-Clark and then by Brian Faulkner. Within unionism, the more militant and less conciliatory voices of William Craig and Ian Paisley pulled Faulkner's government steadily away from compromise and self-evaluation. In 1971, in what was viewed as the ultimate weapon in the arsenal of the unionist and British authorities, Faulkner called for the reintroduction of internment without trial. The brief honeymoon period between the residents of working-class nationalist areas and the British authorities was irreparably severed. The British launched Operation Demetrius on 9 August 1971; this was a massive series of home raids across Northern Ireland designed to arrest the leaders of the Irish Republican Army, the IRA. It was largely unsuccessful in its primary objective and resulted in the arrest of many Catholics who were not in the IRA and the wrecking countless homes. Furthermore, 20 people were killed, 12 of them massacred by one group of British paratroopers in Ballymurphy, West Belfast.

But the IRA, as I shall discuss in more detail in Chapter 3, became the singly most dangerous and violent armed group of the Troubles only after Operation

Demetrius, the Ballymurphy Massacre, and another massacre of unarmed, peacefully protesting civilians *by the same group of paratroopers* in Derry on 30 January 1972, which came to be known as 'Bloody Sunday'. It needs to be stressed here that physical-force republicanism was not the most proximate cause of the outbreak of the Troubles in the late 1960s/early 1970s. There have been three major post-Civil War attempts by anti-treaty[2] republicans to put an end to British sovereignty in Ireland, and later Northern Ireland, by armed means. The first was the 'Northern Campaign' of 1942–1944, the second the 'Border Campaign' of 1956–1962, with the third being the Troubles themselves. All three campaigns failed, at least if the oft-stated goal of the reunification of Ireland is taken to be the most appropriate measure of success. However, only one of the three campaigns, the Troubles, engendered the requisite community support necessary to carry on a sustained guerrilla war, namely the Provisional IRA campaign of 1969–1998. Both the Northern and Border campaigns were abysmal failures, and one of the chief causes of those failures was the inability of the IRA to move beyond a small, secretive, and insular network of anti-treaty republican families and mobilise the support of a larger 'host community' (Flynn, 2009; Moxon-Browne, 1981). The historiography of anti-treaty republicanism had been available as an ideological mechanism of mobilisation since 1921, but it was only in 1971–1972 that the Provisional IRA was successfully able to legitimate its proclamation of an existential crisis state to Northern Ireland's Catholic/nationalist/republican (hereafter, CNR) minority community (Ó Dochartaigh, 1997). The proximate cause of the Provisional IRA bursting violently onto the scene when it did is thus internment, Operation Demetrius, Ballymurphy, Bloody Sunday, and the vicious internecine displacement occurring throughout Belfast. Internment may have been the beginning of the end for the peaceful civil rights struggle for many nationalists, even those nationalists who harboured no love for or allegiance to the PIRA. Writes Ó Dochartaigh (1997, p. 265): "Internment made it clear that the British government was prepared to repress the Catholic population at large in order to preserve Unionist rule. It demolished the last vestiges of trust in the British government's intentions." If internment was the beginning of that end, then Bloody Sunday, and the subsequent whitewash of the massacre by a horrendous British judicial inquiry known as the Widgery Tribunal, was the blood-soaked Rubicon.

Organised loyalist killings, and the rise of the UDA and UVF, the two major loyalist paramilitaries, also cannot be thought of as a proximate cause of the Troubles. Although again I will displace much of this to Chapter 3, organised loyalist paramilitary killings track with the rise of the IRA, and it should come

2 This term means republicans who rejected the Anglo-Irish Treaty of 1921 and Partition. Some of those in turn would eventually join the Irish Dáil (Parliament) after the Irish Civil War (breaking from Sinn Féin to form the political party Fianna Fáil), thus tacitly accepting the Treaty and the Partition of Ireland. I am not referring to those *dissident* republicans who reject the Good Friday/Belfast Agreement.

as no surprise that many high-profile loyalists trace their embrace of violence to reactions to specific IRA atrocities in the early 1970s, including Bloody Friday, the Balmoral Showroom bombing, and the Claudy bombing (Cusack & McDonald, 2008; Wood, 2006). Thus, I argue we should understand the origins of the Troubles as a cycle of escalating violence that ultimately drowned out, co-opted, or outright destroyed non-violent alternatives such as civil rights and trade unionism.

I shall return to the, as Simpson (2009) puts it, 'master narratives' of the primary belligerents in the Troubles in Chapter 3. But it is important to put some numbers on the table here, especially considering how an ethos of collective victimisation can skew perceptions of culpability and innocence (Vollhardt, 2012; Bar-Tal et al., 2009). Using McKittrick et al.'s (2008) data, 3,720 people lost their lives as a consequence of Troubles-related violence, of whom 2,087 (56 per cent) were non-combatants. The PIRA killed 1,768 people and other republican paramilitaries 384. All told, 58 per cent of the total number of victims of the Troubles were killed by republicans. A further 1,112 people were killed by loyalist paramilitaries (30 per cent) and 361 by the security forces (10 per cent). In light of the consistent evidence of security force collusion with loyalist paramilitaries (McGovern, 2015; Cadwallader, 2013; Cory, 2010), it can be problematic to separate the latter two percentages.[3] I will do so here out of a belief that the majority of the security force victims were not the architects of collusive policies or the handlers of informants.[4] But when we compare the numbers of deaths caused with deaths suffered by organisations, a more accurate picture of the conflict begins to emerge. Members of republican paramilitaries suffered 395 deaths and killed 2,152 people (1:5.4), members of loyalist paramilitaries suffered 167 deaths and killed 1,112 people (1:6.7), and members of the security forces suffered 1,012 deaths and directly killed 367 (2.8:1). What emerges, tellingly, from this admittedly crude metric is two interrelated things. First, if victimhood in Northern Ireland is understood collectively, paramilitaries were perpetrators, not victims, and claims to collective victimisation on their behalf should be treated sceptically; and second, Northern Ireland seems to have been a war fought, especially by loyalists, but *also* by republicans, the British army, and collusive elements in the security forces, either directly against civilians or without any sort of adequate discrimination or care towards civilians.

3 The security forces also colluded with and protected informants within republican paramilitaries (McSmith, 2016). Security force informants within republican paramilitaries were also involved in killings (BBC Panorama, 2017). However, the prevalence of agents and informers within loyalist paramilitaries was much higher and more systematic than the prevalence of agents and informers within republican paramilitaries (BBC Panorama, 2015).

4 While certainly MI5, the SAS, and the RUC Special Branch bear an organisational culpability for collusive Troubles-killings, individual RUC and UDR men and women who were killed bear on the whole significantly less of that organisational culpability.

The first major political attempt to end the Troubles was the 1974 Sunningdale Agreement, a power-sharing framework that bears no small resemblance to the 1998 Agreement. The 1998 Agreement is sometimes caustically referred to as 'Sunningdale for slow learners'. Sunningdale was brought down by sustained Protestant/unionist/loyalist (hereafter, PUL) opposition, including a general strike by the ad hoc Ulster Worker's Council (UWC). The UWC marked the rise of a more-militant unionism personified by men like Paisley. In the late 1970s the British government attempted to roll back the tacit arrangement of special treatment for paramilitary prisoners ('criminalisation') and attempted to shift the burden of security provision away from the British military and onto local police and the UDR, the auxiliary force that had replaced the B Specials ('Ulsterisation'). Margaret Thatcher's hard-line imposition of criminalisation led to a wave of protests amongst republican prisoners in the Long Kesh/Maze prison, culminating in a series of hunger strikes in 1980–1981. Ten prisoners starved themselves to death, led by Bobby Sands, who was elected an MP for Fermanagh during his protest. Sands' funeral was attended by over 100,000 people and resulted in the emergence of Sinn Féin as a major political force in Northern Ireland.

The Anglo-Irish Agreement of 1985 represented the tentative beginnings of the current Peace Process. Essentially, the British government acknowledged the interest of the Republic of Ireland (ROI) in the governance of Northern Ireland, and in exchange the ROI adopted the principle of consent, that no change in the constitutional status of Northern Ireland could occur without the support of a majority of the Northern Irish people. The agreement was bitterly rejected by Paisleyite unionists and less bitterly by Sinn Féin.

But between 1986 and 1993, a series of horrible attacks and murders sapped the legitimation of violence-producers in Northern Ireland. These include (but are not limited to) the Enniskillen Bombing of 1987, in which the IRA killed 11 Protestant civilians during a Remembrance Day ceremony, the Milltown Cemetery attack by loyalist killer Michael Stone in 1988, the Teebane bombing by the IRA in 1992, the Sean Graham's Bookmakers murders of Catholic civilians perpetrated by the UDA, the Shankill bombing by the IRA in 1993, and the retaliatory attack on the Rising Sun pub in Greysteel, County Derry by the UDA of the same year. These murders represented such a cascade of brutal savagery that many Northern Irish, Irish, and British citizens and organisations began to demand a sustained push for peace. This was aided by significant changes occurring within the leadership structures of the paramilitary organisations themselves. Gerry Adams, president of Sinn Féin and allegedly in control of the IRA's Army Council as well, shepherded a secret decision through the IRA Council in 1988 that stated that the IRA could agree to a ceasefire even in the absence of a British withdrawal from Ireland (Moloney, 2002). Adams would lay out his arguments publicly as early as 1989 (Adams, 1989). On the loyalist side, men like David Ervine, Billy Hutchinson, and 'Gusty' Spence of the UVF were also beginning to explore the possibilities of a ceasefire (Moloney,

2008). The decisive moment came on 31 August 1994, when the IRA declared a unilateral ceasefire. They were followed later in the year by the UDA and the UVF. The peace process was derailed over decommissioning and a contentious Orange Order Parade at Drumcree, Portadown, County Armagh. In response, the IRA ended its ceasefire and exploded two massive bombs in England, in Manchester and London's Docklands. But in spite of this, multi-party talks led by the US diplomat George Mitchell continued, resulting in the Agreement of 1998.

The Peace Process since 1998 has been plagued by fits and starts. But there has been no return to widespread, organised violence. The Agreement broke down in 2003 and the British reinstituted direct rule, but the St Andrew's Agreement of 2006 re-established Stormont and brought the last political holdout, Paisley's DUP, into government. In exchange, Sinn Féin recognised the Police Service of Northern Ireland (PSNI), the successor of the RUC, as the legitimate law-enforcing authority in the province.

However, violent splinter groups (known collectively as 'dissidents') still exist in Northern Ireland. The single worst atrocity of the Troubles (in terms of total deaths) was carried out by a dissident group known as the 'Real IRA' three months after the signing of the Agreement in 1998 in the town of Omagh, County Tyrone. A bomb killed 29 people, including one woman pregnant with twins. No doubt intending to derail the peace process, the bombing revulsed Ireland, North and South, and confirmed the lack of legitimacy of dissident groupings.

Up until January 2017 Northern Ireland was led by a consociational executive jointly led by the Democratic Unionist Party and Sinn Féin. The First Minister was Arlene Foster of the DUP and the Deputy First Minister was Martin McGuinness of Sinn Féin. However, as this book was going to press, the Northern Ireland Executive broke down as Sinn Féin withdrew from government in response to a scandal over a renewable heat incentive programme. The dissolution of Stormont shocked many observers from outside Northern Ireland; however, those with expertise in Northern Ireland had long realised that everything was far from rosy. Northern Ireland remains a deeply segregated society, and though patterns of segregation are shifting, the "two main communities live largely segregated lives, in which the basic daily routines and practices are structured by the dominant sectarian divisions of Northern Irish society" (Hamilton et al., 2008, p. 11; see also Knox, 2011). Communities that both produced and bore the brunt of Troubles violence remain highly deprived (Nolan, 2014). Paramilitary, or at least paramilitary-style, violence still lurks in the form of so-called 'punishment' beatings, kneecappings, and killings carried out by groups with more than tacit linkages to former and current paramilitaries. Internal feuds within paramilitary groups have claimed the lives of several other people. The killing of two prominent former members of the IRA rocked Belfast in 2015, as did the allegation that the identities of the killers were known to high-placed members of Sinn Féin. An ongoing stand-off over an Orange Order Parade in Ardoyne, North Belfast has only recently been tentatively resolved.[5] The 2016 Brexit vote in the United Kingdom promises to disproportionately and negatively affect Northern Ireland and has thrown the state of the border with the Republic of Ireland into uncertainty. And, perhaps most importantly for this book, there has been no agreed-upon way forward when it comes to issues of justice and accountability for past crimes. The latest proposals, contained within the Stormont House Agreement (SHA) first published in December 2014, call for a dedicated Historical Investigations Unit to investigate 'legacy' crimes and recommend prosecutions, but most victims and survivors groups and those seeking justice and accountability are deeply sceptical of its potential. Since the collapse of Stormont in January 2017, even the cautious mechanisms of the SHA are not merely stalled, but potentially off the table completely.

Plan of the book

The first three chapters lay out the major theoretical frameworks of this book. In the first chapter I group questions about how the past will be represented and reproduced in the present into three larger categories. I refer to these categories as 'victimhood', 'placemaking', and the 'inscription', respectively. All transitional societies must confront *who* exactly is worthy of social memory (victimhood), they must examine *where* those bodies can be remembered and how such a place can be made (placemaking), and they must examine *how* memory of the past is written into the present: what mnemonics, narratives, and ideologies are written into a place of memory and how and why they change, expand, contract, or disappear (inscription). In Chapter 1 I use the two primary commissioned legacy reports, the Bloomfield Report and the Eames–Bradley Report, as stepping stones to illustrate how these efforts attempted to deal with these crucial questions in Northern Ireland and why their responses were misguided, overly simplistic, or simply ineffective.

Chapter 2 moves on to look at the vast theoretical work in the field of what has become known as 'social memory studies' (Misztal, 2003; Olick & Robbins, 1998). Rather than a traditional literature review that strives for comprehensiveness, I instead attempt to genealogically trace the origins of social memory studies' burgeoning interdisciplinary impact on the social sciences. I begin by looking at the approach to memory of four major modern European thinkers and then provide a typology of the five major avenues by which I argue memory studies entered the social sciences in the latter half of the twentieth century. The chapter is concerned with how memories of the past (and often a traumatic past) are constituted, collated, and narrated in the present.

5 Just before this manuscript was submitted, a tentative agreement was reached over the future of the parade, though it was rejected by the Greater Ardoyne Resident's Committee, a largely anti-Sinn Féin group. It remains to be seen whether violence at the flashpoint has truly been abated in the long term.

In Chapter 3 I outline the Italian political theorist Giorgio Agamben's famous concept of the 'state of exception', or the suspension of individual rights of citizenship during a period of supposed political crisis (Agamben, 2005; 1998). I argue that all major belligerents operational during the Troubles utilised a state of exception to suspend the very legitimating discourses of a polity they hoped to produce or protect through violence and war. In Northern Ireland, I argue, exception became a permanent state of existence, a state in which the bodies of victims were transformed through legitimating discourses focusing on the inevitability of death in war, or transformed into justifiable 'targets'. I argue that violence-justifying narratives dehumanised Northern Irish, Irish, and British bodies by transforming them from complex individuals into performative political objects. However, the crux of this argument lies in the space between the operational hegemony of the state of exception prior to 1998, and its cracking, splintering, and leaking facade post-1998. In post-conflict Northern Ireland, former belligerents still depend on legitimating discourses rooted in the state of exception, and still reference it in their claims of de facto immunity, in spite of the fact that their claims are increasingly unmoored from an operational present. In the 18 years since the Agreement, a singular opportunity has emerged for using the power of place to inscribe the humanity that was severed from bodies existing in the thrall of the Troubles.

Chapters 4 to 6 take on the three fields delineated above: victimhood, placemaking, and inscription. Chapter 4 begins with the concept of a 'hierarchy of victims', a concept no doubt common to all transitional space. Those who employ the concept allege that certain victims of political violence garner disproportionate access to social attention, public resources, and/or public memory. The term is generally used negatively, to imply that 'these' or 'our' victims are marginalised, silenced, forgotten, ignored, and 'those' or 'their' victims are not. It can also be used to resist moral ambiguity and affirm the value of innocence. I delineate several social discourses that alternately reaffirm and challenge the hierarchy of victims in Northern Ireland and discuss their resonance in public space. I use this discussion in turn to bring in the work of the theorist and survivor Primo Levi (1989), arguing that the politics of memory in transitional societies demands a new approach to victimhood – a confused, unsettled, dissonant, and humane treatment of the lives and bodies that were lost. Following Dominick LaCapra (2001), I argue for 'empathic dissonance' regarding victimhood – the creation of critical spaces between victim and witness, representation, and audience that are necessary to maintain an ongoing, unsettled dialogue about the memory of traumatic pasts. This argument explicitly rejects the 'full stop' – the discourse that seeks to 'draw a line' between the past and the present – and it rejects any subordination of the complex voices of survivors to a supposed imperative of national reconciliation or a shared moral catharsis.

Chapter 5 takes on the potential of places of memory. It begins with a short survey of some major geographical thinkers, seeking to outline why 'space' and 'place' are central to understanding the complex power constellations operating in transitional space. I lay out and closely examine Henri Lefebvre's (1991, p. 416) famous concept of 'trial by space', in which he argues that no individual, group, or class can establish themselves as subjects unless they generate a space for the visible, audible, and symbolic transmission of their ideas, identities, and values. To that I also add their narrations of the past – their memories. I argue that places of memory can give shape and voice to the ghosts of the past and can stand as resistant 'irruptions' of wider attempts to both draw a line under contentious pasts, and to defend the recourse to past violence and killing. These contentions will be illustrated by looking at several places of memory in Northern Ireland that disrupt and challenge dominant forms of space.

Chapter 6 takes on the politics of inscription. I begin by briefly surveying the politics of inscribing contentious pasts elsewhere, dwelling particularly on the experience of subaltern people as represented in public space in North and South America. Returning to Northern Ireland, I seek to provide a new set of frames to understand the ubiquity of paramilitary imagery in public space. I look at a number of practices that groups and individuals have employed to resist and reframe violence-producing and violence-justifying imagery and inscribe new social memories into Northern Ireland's contentious spatial fabric.

Chapter 7 focuses closely on the dissonance between remembering a loved one as a complex, fallible human being and remembering a loved one as a politicised object. I argue that the bodies of those killed during the Troubles are far more complex objects than as they are often read and that each body contains within it the potential for multiple, variegated memory performances. I also focus on the human toll of this dissonance, looking closely at the way in which the body of one murdered victim of the Troubles, Terry Enright, is remembered by his family, friends, and community.

In the concluding chapter I argue that any discourse promoting a consensual or cathartic inscription of past violence risks domesticating, controlling, or depoliticising a traumatic past. I argue that a 'controlling consensus' (Teeger & Vinitzsky-Seroussi, 2007) can in fact prevent an ongoing, critical, and dynamic remembrance of the past. Consensus can facilitate a failure to reckon with the bodies of the dead and the living, can prevent a rigorous social discussion of the role and morality of violence, and can prevent the type of empathic unsettlement I have suggested is so crucial to social rehumanisation. I argue for memory that incubates at multiple nodes of social production and can facilitate a vibrant, democratic debate over the ways in which a traumatic past can or should be remembered. To make this case, I look at two places of memory from outside Northern Ireland that I argue are microcosms of the larger closing off of critical discussions of the past, namely the US Holocaust Museum and Memorial and the Vietnam Veterans' Memorial, both in Washington DC.

Largely, this book makes the following broad argument: only through rehumanising the victims of political violence can we truly undercut the tautological and vicious internal logic of the state of exception. Only by demonstrating the vibrant qualities of a human life, and making the places through which that vibrancy can be communicated, can we truly challenge and resist the recourse to violence, past, present, and future. But I am not merely satisfied with the notion that we must resist. I wish also to discuss and examine how we must resist, and how we can resist empathically, humanely, and in such a way as to not demand that others, and often very different others, adhere to our own assumptions and the baggage that we all bring to the proverbial table.

Interviews and ethics

In this book I rely heavily on the testimony of 52 memory curators in Northern Ireland I interviewed between 2014 and 2015. The term memory curator is my own creation and I define it as those individuals who are actively engaged in retaining, collecting, selecting, presenting, or caring for particular strands of narrativised memory. These memory curators naturally include representatives of victims and survivors groups, community relations workers, justice campaigners, ex-combatants, artists, and memorial curators, but they also include 'ordinary people' who had been victimised in some way, participated in victimisation in some way, or lived some combination of both perpetration and victimisation, but generally keep a low profile.

Scholars conducting narrative research and narrative interpretation around and about the Northern Irish Troubles all do their work under the shadow of the Boston College debacle (for further information, see McDonald, 2016; Moriarty, 2016; McKee, 2014; McMurtrie, 2014; Moloney, 2008) and I took significant care to protect my respondents' confidentiality. No information that could by any stretch of the imagination be conceived of as legally actionable has been retained in any records, notes, or transcripts. All respondents have been given a unique pseudonym, indicated by inverted commas (i.e. 'James'). These pseudonyms were generated randomly using past lists of the most common Northern Irish baby names, with one exception: I did not give Irish or Gaelicised pseudonyms that came up randomly (i.e. 'Seán', 'Siobhán') to respondents who I speculated may not prefer them. In some cases, participants requested to be named and I respected their wishes. I also requested that any politician serving in an elected capacity at the time of the interview speak for named attribution. Where possible, I provide the respondent's general primary location, but sometimes I choose to omit that data out of concerns for confidentiality. I also provide the affiliation of any former security force personnel (i.e. ex-RUC, ex-UDR, etc.) where appropriate, as long as there is no risk to a respondent's confidentiality.

Chapter 1

How will 'we remember them'?

Revisiting the reports

The fallacy of the full stop

In 1997 then Secretary of State for Northern Ireland Mo Mowlam appointed Sir Kenneth Bloomfield as Northern Ireland's Victim's Commissioner. Mowlam tasked Bloomfield with producing a report designed to "Look at the possible ways to recognise the pain and suffering felt by victims of violence arising from the troubles of the last 30 years … [and] to examine the feasibility of providing greater recognition for those who have become victims" (Bloomfield, 1998a, p. 8). Bloomfield's subsequent report, entitled *We Will Remember Them*, was published in April 1998 to coincide with the adoption of the Agreement. It remains arguably the most important official effort to deal with the traumatic legacy of the Troubles, and to recognise its impact on Northern Irish, Irish, and British individual victims and survivors.

Bloomfield's 'Summary of Recommendations' is an interesting and revealing text. The specific language used seems to couch the recommendations in the form of polite suggestions, and where the words approach an issue of political volatility, they dissolve into frustrating equivocation. In some sense, this should come as no surprise. The Agreement itself contained no concrete mechanism for confronting the legacies of past violence; indeed, it seems to have conveniently sidestepped these issues and essentially shunted them into Bloomfield's lap (Bell, 2002). Of the mere three points regarding 'victims of violence' in the Agreement's text (6.11–6.13), one is especially telling: "The participants believe that it is essential to acknowledge and address the suffering of the victims of violence as a necessary element of reconciliation. They look forward to the results of the work of the Northern Ireland Victims Commission" (i.e. Bloomfield and his staff). The crafters of the Agreement believed that issues surrounding the past in Northern Ireland were so volatile and so divisive, any inclusion of them in the Agreement would potentially derail the entire Peace Process (Powell, 2009). The solution seems to have been to put them off to the side in the hope that Bloomfield could 'sort that all out'.

Bloomfield's prose is robust and confident when he stands on the firmer ground of advocating for financial support, resource allocation, psychological care and rehabilitation, and increased access to trauma services for victims and survivors. However, when the Report's recommendations approach questions of justice, accountability, and truth recovery, they tend to vaguely gesture towards a future context when such questions could begin to be explored ***and*** to suborn such questions to an alleged social imperative of 'reconciliation'. But here is the paradox: reconciliation in a transitional society is rarely (if ever) realistically achieved, to say nothing of the essential emptiness and malleability of the term itself; and the notion of a truly post-conflict and post-sectarian future in Northern Ireland is consistently thwarted by the policies and actions of those perpetrators (and perpetrator-victims) who have enjoyed a de facto immunity from any type of social, legal, or political accountability. De facto immunity in Northern Ireland in turn allows former violence-producers the freedom to inscribe their particularistic conflict narratives into public space and public discourse relatively unfettered, though not, as we shall see, unchallenged.

But this may not be entirely the fault of the Agreement, Bloomfield, the pseudodemocratic and overtly anti-pluralist consociational structure of the Agreement, or any of the parade of civil servants and foreign academics who also tried (and failed) to reckon with Northern Ireland's violent and traumatic past. It may also be laid at the feet of a failure of transitional justice as a paradigm to move beyond thinking of memory, victimhood, placemaking, and inscription as peripheral to or less important than the 'puzzlingly irreconcilable' goals of institutional design, national reconciliation, and justice and accountability (Leebaw, 2008). It may also be laid at the feet of a transitional justice imagination that consistently dichotomises between 'good' survivors and 'bad' survivors. The former are those who accept and work within the unfolding transitional reality, make places that conform to the supposed imperative of 'moving on', 'looking forward', 'forgiveness', and 'reconciliation', and inscribe said places with the narratives of hope and harmony. The latter are those who resist such a consensus being imposed upon them, who create places of irruption, melancholia, and indignation, and inscribe them with a narrative focused on the festering and undressed wounds still scoring and pockmarking transitional space (for a closely related argument, see Acorn, 2004). Writes Brewer (2010, pp. 166–167):

> Honouring the sacrifice of dead/survivors, however, does not involve them becoming such a weight that they preclude the living from moving on … a redirection of society's public gaze seems appropriate, with sights set determinedly on the future not the past … the cult of the dead harbours conflict not peace.

Brewer's epistle finds its closest approximation in the German concept of *Schlußstrich* – 'to draw a final line' under the past (Till, 2005, p. 1)[1] – and

1 See also Levey (2016), McGrattan (2013), Fulbrook (1999).

ironically seems to misapprehend the field of social memory studies from whence it draws its ostensible support. It also hearkens back very closely to Marx writing in the *18th Brumaire* and his denunciation of memory as false consciousness. Memory, according to Marx, was fundamentally reactionary, the 'reactionary cult of the past', that prevented the French populace from learning the new language of socialism (Marx 1999 [1852], p. 6, cited in Misztal 2003, p. 42). Brewer argues that memory is only of use in transitional societies if it is "functional for post-violence societies" (Brewer, 2010, p. 192) and, presumably, only recounted by those who inhabit "socially functional public victimhood" (Brewer, 2010, p. 166). For Brewer (2010, p. 193), functional memory is that which is resolutely forward-looking; he refers to it as "re-remembering, turn[ing] the past into something pivotal for the future", a process in which social memory is manipulated into something which does not interfere with the business of moving on through sound public policy.

Writing with his lens completely focused on Northern Ireland's uneasy relationship with social memory, Brewer fails to see how his call for 'socially functional memory' carries with it totalitarian undertones. "Socially functional memory", writes Brewer citing Michael Ignatieff (1993), is that which "releases society from the cult of the dead" (Brewer, 2010, p. 166). He goes on to suggest that this does not mean that victims/survivors should be silenced, but then exposes his preference for such a silencing by clearly advocating the use of public purse strings (i.e. to starve oppositional victims and survivors groups of public funding) to force victims/survivors to move on from the past and be accountable to and for the future. But who decides what is 'socially functional'? And how, in a supposed modern democracy, does seeking justice for murders in spite of the weight of a regressive peace architecture run counter to social functionality? The fact that mass murders, bombings, and maimings have not been addressed in any modicum of fashion in Northern Ireland, coupled with the presence in government of political parties both directly and indirectly responsible for such widespread violence, suggests perhaps that the blame for what is socially ***dysfunctional*** in Northern Ireland does not lie exclusively with victims and survivors' groups.

Brewer also seems to replace the 'cult of the dead' with the 'cult of the future'. Looking briefly at other examples, Bogdanov (2010, p. 79) suggests the:

> psychological orientation of Soviet people towards the future was a crucial aspect of Soviet ideology that was constantly reinforced. Whatever reservations one might have … future developments were all pre-scripted, and all that was needed for the realisation was the ability to wait and the strength to endure.

Rene Lemarchand (2005, 2006) argues that the Kagame regime in Rwanda has ruthlessly suppressed any social memories or narratives that run counter to their narrative of national unity, justifying its draconian memory laws on the supposed functional necessity of the future and the unifying Banyarwanda project. Brewer's argument also eerily echoes the attempts of transitional politicians in a wide variety of contexts to impose a 'full stop' on politically uncomfortable remembrance of past violence and inscribe the *pacto del olvido*, the 'pact of forgetting'.[2] The crux of the *pacto del olvido* was that certain remembrance practices, including those demanding justice and accountability for past crimes, would get in the way of the difficult work of the post-authoritarian future. If we truly wish to understand the central role of memory in post-conflict societies, we as scholars must engage with it honestly, and not confine those whose memories do not conform with our futurist visions to the pathologised peripheries, or read them as wholly the unwitting dupes of the antipluralist projects of instrumentalist political elites.[3] If this book succeeds in its central arguments, I intend to show how and why perspectives in Northern Ireland reminiscent of *Schlußstrich*, socially functional victimhood, or the *pacto del olvido* are misguided, oppressive, and paradoxically run counter to 'reconciliation', whatever that term may in fact be said to mean. In doing so, I see 'reconciliation' in Northern Ireland (and in other transitional societies) as one of the 'master narratives' so cogently criticised by Kirk Simpson. He writes (2009, p. 57):

> Governments or policymakers that seek to induce collective political, cultural, or social amnesia through the use of conformist 'master narratives' of the past … risk repeating the offences of despotic groups by revictimising, objectifying, and restigmatising victims of conflicts.

Bloomfield's Report attempted to grant victims and survivors better access to care, support, and financial aid. In these respects, while its recommendations remain only partially realised (O'Connor & O'Neill, 2015), it is hard to find fault with its intentions. However, there are important reasons why the Bloomfield Report, in terms of serving as a pathway to either justice or reconciliation, has largely fallen by the wayside, along with similar reports, similar findings, and similar recommendations made by Archbishop Robin Eames and Dennis Bradley (2009) and the aborted efforts of the US academics Richard Haass and Meaghan O'Sullivan. All fundamentally underestimated the need to address the difficult memories of the Troubles in public space. Transitioning to a new political or social order partially lifts the veil of silence surrounding the past and confronts political actors and citizens with the problem of representing the past. And Northern Ireland, like all transitional societies, will have to find some way to reckon with the bodies of the dead and the living, and the traumatic and disruptive 'spectral traces' they leave on societies and space (Jonker & Till, 2009).

2 For Spain, see Davis (2005); for Latin America, see Levey (2016), Collins, Hitte & Joignant (2013, Jelin (2003).

3 Patricia Lundy and Mark McGovern have consistently provided a welcome corrective in Northern Ireland; see especially Lundy & McGovern (2008).

Victimhood

Jeffrey & Candea (2006, p. 287) provide an excellent brief summation of the difficult victimhood questions facing transitional societies:

> Why might people seek to be recognised as victims? How do claims to passive victimisation come up against counter-claims of agency or perpetration? How should we relate to claims of subalterneity when such claims are also deployed by states and powerful groups? How should we attend to expressions of suffering when such expressions obscure or deny others' suffering?

McEvoy and McConnachie (2012, 2013) argue that victimhood in transitional societies is often a dialectic that constructs victimhood as the obverse of the dominant group representation of the perpetrator (see also Christie, 1986). Victimhood becomes innocence, innocence becomes defined as the categorical rejection of a dominant perpetrator, and all of the unsettling complexities inherent in transitional space are written out and suborned to the unambiguous line between victim and perpetrator, guilt and innocence. It may be almost trite to say it, but clearly transitional societies struggling to emerge from civil wars, dictatorships, ethnic cleansings, and/or widespread internecine atrocities do not render themselves neatly into such simplistic categories, and individuals and groups who deploy such categories often flounder logically when their protective logic is pierced by disconfirming information. To construct such a duality invariably requires that certain Northern Irish politicians and victims and survivors groups gloss over, ignore, or selectively not see a complex web of moral culpability and traumatic fragmentation. McEvoy and McConnachie are certainly correct to say this occurs regularly in transitional societies like Northern Ireland; however, an analytic focus on this prominent dialectic at the expense of other potentialities often forgets that the victims and survivors of the Troubles are a diverse population whose needs, rights, and desires do not always overlap. Many may stridently advocate for justice, truth, vengeance, accountability, and demand that they be recognised as categorically 'innocent' and those who harmed or are alleged to have harmed them categorically 'guilty', but many others in turn may deploy narratives that question the innocence/guilt dialectic in its entirety. And still others simply wish to be left alone, to work through their pain, to move on, or to grieve privately and draw at least a personal line under the trauma of the past.

This is the divisive social reality that first Bloomfield, and later Eames–Bradley, nervously waded into. In Section 2.14 of his report (1998a, p. 14), Bloomfield first attempts to bridge the divide between a morally unambiguous distinction between guilt and innocence and the ambiguous realities of post-Troubles space:

> One of the most sensitive issues I have been obliged to confront is that of blame. Many people feel that any person engaged in unlawful activity who

> is killed or injured in pursuit of it is a victim only of his own criminality and deserves no recognition for it ... I would, however, make the point that any individual's involvement in unlawful activity does not lessen the grief and loss of close family who mourn him or her.

Here, while Bloomfield clearly resists a purely relativistic stance on victimhood (which should be unsurprising considering Bloomfield himself escaped an IRA assassination attempt), he seeks to soften this by empathising the shared experience of grief and loss of those left behind. Later in the Report, his prose sways towards the elegiac (1998a, p. 23).

> We need to truly remember those who have suffered, to grieve at this side of the communal grave, to reflect on the truth of what occurred and to move forward from there. Above all, we have to persuade our children how costly and counter-productive it would be to pursue the animosities of the past.

Bloomfield thus seeks to break out of the dialectic through a rhetorical appeal to shared experience and the necessity of a shared future. But in doing so, he cannot adequately confront questions of justice, accountability, or truth recovery. All he can do is plant his flag firmly on the much less controversial ground of advocating for better financial and psychological support for victims and survivors. But the Report's inability to even engage with these questions is troubling, especially for a document expected (unrealistically) to fill the gaping holes in the Agreement around how to reckon with the past (see Bloomfield 1998b). And by eliding the complex modalities of victimhood and perpetration, it paradoxically strengthens the dialectic it hopes to surmount. Behind the rhetorical flourish, many victims and survivors groups simply saw another attempt to foist an unacceptable equivalence on them – a moral and practical equivalence between those who took life in the service of a political cause and those who did not.

As such, many CNR and PUL victims and survivors groups used their responses to strengthen their particularistic and exclusionary legitimacy claims. A group representing CNR survivors of state violence and closely associated with Sinn Féin, Relatives for Justice, claimed that Bloomfield had side-stepped and disregarded their constituency's need to understand the circumstances of the killings of their loved ones and as such was merely another layer of an ongoing political minimalisation of the guilt of the British state (O'Tuama, 1998). PUL victims and survivors groups representing mainly victims of republican violence also vociferously rejected the Report, again because of what they perceived as an erasure of the unimpeachable moral delineation between perpetrator and victim (McDowell, 2007; Smyth, 1998).

Eames–Bradley takes a similar tack, suggesting that few lessons were learned (or the wrong lessons learned) in the intervening 11 years. When Eames–Bradley was released, one line from the lengthy report was immediately highlighted and vigorously assailed by a cross-section of politicians and victims and survivors groups. "The Group … recommends that the nearest relative of someone who died as a result of the conflict in and about Northern Ireland, from January 1966, should receive a one-off ex-gratia recognition payment of £12,000" (Eames & Bradley, 2009, p. 31). Despite being an almost 200-page document examining a range of issues relating to the past, Eames–Bradley is now largely reduced to that one clumsy, ill-conceived recommendation. For victims and survivors, this passage meant that the value of their loved one was priced the exact same amount as the person or persons who may have killed them. It meant that, for example, the life of Thomas Begley, the 19-year-old IRA man who planted the Shankill bomb and died in the blast, was worth the exact same amount as the nine other people he killed. It meant that the life of Lennie Murphy, the psychopathic head of the Belfast loyalist death squad known as the Shankill Butchers and killed by the IRA in 1982, was worth the exact same amount as the Catholics he randomly targeted and proceeded to torture and murder.

Yet for many, these criticisms of the Eames–Bradley Report as a whole are deeply unfair. One victims and survivors advocate who was and is close to a leading member of the Eames–Bradley Group related to me his understanding of how that recommendation came to be in the Report:

> The initial recommendation ahead of a process[4] was to award everybody that had lost somebody in the conflict over 75 years old or something like this. That went to the Victims' Commission[5] … and they said, look you can't do this, you have to make it either everybody or nobody. Now Mike Nesbitt didn't agree with that and voted against it but the other three Commissioners were in favour of it. Now I never saw the Commission, the old Commission, stand up and support that recommendation – they stood back and let Dennis Bradley and Robin Eames get it in the neck from everybody in relation to that recommendation … And of course when that recommendation came out, it was just a free-for-all down at the Europa [Hotel in Belfast, where the report was released].
>
> And I think that's the saddest thing about Eames–Bradley. Because Eames–Bradley I think was the best attempt to date on dealing with the past.
>
> ('Jack', North Belfast)

4 'Jack' is saying that the initial idea for the recommendation was as the outcome of a compensatory process, not a single *ex gratia* payment.

5 At the time, due to political squabbling, the post of Victims' Commissioner was held by four individuals jointly: Mike Nesbitt (who would become the leader of the UUP in 2012), Bertha McDougall (the widow of an RUC reservist shot dead by the INLA in 1981), Brendan McAllister, and Patricia McBride (the sister of an IRA man killed by the SAS in 1984). As one can no doubt see, the balancing act is very clear. McDougall and McBride were closely tied to someone killed on each 'side' of the conflict, with Nesbitt and McAllister serving as the balancing unionist and nationalist, respectively.

'Jack' makes the point that the suspect recommendation itself was a product of political wrangling between the Eames–Bradley Group, the Victims' Commissioners, and the Stormont Executive (the DUP and Sinn Féin), and reading the entire Report as tantamount to comprising merely that one clause is deeply misguided. 'Jack' is partially correct; indeed, many of the victims and survivors advocates I interviewed rejected the Report in its entirety, but had no qualms about confessing they had not actually read it. I have read the entire Report, and I suggest that this recommendation cannot be divorced from the Report's elision of the complex politics of victimhood in transitional societies.

The problems with the Report begin as early as its epigraph. Citing an early twentieth-century Christian spiritualist, Margaret Fairless Barber, it reads: "To look backward for a while is to refresh the eye, to restore it, and to render it more fit for its prime function of looking forward." Again, one cannot help but read this in terms of *Schlußstrich*: the past is suborned to its 'prime function' – building a usable future (McGrattan, 2013). Those aspects of the past which are ill-suited to a preferred future must be overcome. The Report also clearly signals this orientation at the outset, when it identifies the key ethical principle that came to guide the work: "The past should be dealt with in a manner which enables society to become more defined by its desire for true and lasting reconciliation rather than by division and mistrust, seeking to promote a shared and reconciled future for all" (Eames & Bradley, 2009, p. 24). This is a laudable goal, certainly, even if phrased in the form of a somewhat banal set of platitudes; but again, note who is implicitly to blame here for the fact that a shared and reconciled future has not emerged. It is those who see the past as an open wound, an unaddressed parcel of injustices, and see themselves and others like themselves as marginal, peripheral, silenced.

Peppering the report is phraseology such as "for all" above, or "common humanity" (Eames & Bradley, 2009, p. 96), "moral failures on both sides" (p. 53), and "mutual forgiveness" (p. 25, 53–55). The consistent repetition of this type of language frames the conflict as something for which all of Northern Ireland shares the blame, and for which all of Northern Ireland must shoulder the burden of creating a new future. But this is fallacious. For one thing, the direct responsibility for the vast majority of the killings, maimings, and bombings clearly rests with a comparably small number of individuals and the groups and state institutions they represented. Morally, these individuals, groups, and institutions bear a vastly disproportionate culpability, and thus a disproportionate responsibility to address the wounds of the past. Yet in Northern Ireland the elision of the complex politics of victimhood through shared responsibility and the forward-looking, reconciliatory imperative gives rhetorical cover to these groups and the British government, and allows for a political reality that would be farcical if it were not so disturbing. It is a reality where Sinn Féin President and current TD for Louth Gerry Adams can claim he was never 'in the IRA'. As one of my respondents puts it, speaking for a wide spectrum of Northern Ireland, and indeed the world at large, "Every man and his dog knows Gerry

Adams was in the IRA" ('Luke', County Tyrone) (see Moloney, 2002, 2008). It is a reality where for 45 years successive British regimes can avoid bringing any of the paratroopers who callously massacred unarmed, peacefully protesting, and in many cases fleeing civilians in broad daylight in Ballymurphy, West Belfast and the Bogside neighbourhood of Derry to any semblance of justice. It is a reality where certain former loyalist killers can receive hundreds of thousands of pounds of public monies in their new capacities as 'community workers' to intimidate communities, hoist paramilitary flags from lampposts, and saturate private gable walls with images of masked gunmen (BBC Spotlight, 2016). This is not a reality to be reconciled to (Curtis, 2014). As Edwards and McGrattan (2011) crucially point out, this reinvention of what peace in fact means in Northern Ireland is fundamentally status-quo protecting. Contentious victimhood, victimhood that fundamentally challenges *Schlußstrich*, the 'cult of the future', and the imperative to reconcile in the absence of social justice, is both dynamic and democratic. Yet it is fundamentally this contentiousness that has been repeatedly painted as harmful or out-of-step in Northern Ireland. Payne has penned perhaps one of the most eloquent treatises calling attention to the creative potentialities of contentious victimhood in transitional societies.[6] She writes (2008, p. 291):

> I advocate political participation to contest prevailing views that have impeded the promotion of democratic values like human rights and the rule of law … Both the 'fatal overdose of truth' and 'healing truth' theories suffer from the same utopian assumption that democracies can successfully gag contentious issues. Little evidence supports this assumption.

What is needed in Northern Ireland and other transitional societies is an approach to victimhood and truth recovery that is guided by a philosophy of empathic dissonance (LaCapra 2001), an argument which I will develop further in Chapter 4. But we must be very clear on where we stand. Both the Agreement and the subsequent efforts of Bloomfield, Eames, and Bradley to address its major lacuna, have envisioned a Northern Irish society where the memory of the offence is confined to those who do not disrupt the consociational consensus. This process has been supported by the British state, whose primary goal has been to avoid any disruption of the 'Peace Process' through contentious politics and any widespread disruption of its preferred narrative of being an 'honest broker' (see Ní Aoláin, 2000). Switzer and Graham (2009) refer to this as the British state's 'memorial agnosticism'. This refusal to confront the past, to suborn it to the future and the reconciliatory imperative, has helped to solidify a dominant visible geography of paramilitary justification in public space in Northern Ireland. It has ceded the space to former (and current, sometimes) paramilitary sub-state groupings to inscribe their particularistic historical narratives, notions of victimhood,

6 See also Phelps (2005).

and legitimating tropes into Northern Ireland's visible landscape relatively unchecked. Graham and Whelan (2007, p. 489) perhaps describe this best:

> It is difficult to escape the conclusion that the burgeoning landscape of commemoration represents an orchestrated process in which paramilitary organisations and their political parties are consciously creating these sites and their memorial practices as one means of perpetuating identity politics and territorial control.

In Graham and Whelan's perspective, memorial agnosticism on the part of the state renders public space vulnerable to paramilitary inscription. Alternative social groups and individuals seeking acknowledgement of their experiences are dwarfed by the oppressive aesthetics of paramilitarism. But their argument too quickly de-emphasises less visible and less audible voices, the discursively subaltern in Northern Ireland. Subalternity is a concept stemming from the work of the Italian theorist Antonio Gramsci (1971) and popularised further by the decolonial theorist Gayatri Spivak (1988). It refers to how political subjects can be emplaced *outside* of a cultural and political hegemony and denied access to the dominant means of social communication. Those in Northern Ireland lacking access to the well-oiled conduits of political and social communication are sometimes silent, but not always; often they merely lack the forum, the press coverage, or access to the dominant forms of discourse that are monopolised by former paramilitary groups and the Stormont establishment. Rather than overlook these discursively subaltern voices, I argue that we as researchers must seek them out and understand the often encoded milieus in which they circulate. We must pay attention in particular to what Marianne Hirsch and Leo Spitzer (2016) call 'small acts of repair' and resistance. To notice and appreciate these small imprints on landscapes of past violence, and thus attune ourselves to alternate possibilities and practices of remembering and reckoning with the past, we must adopt alternative spatial readings. We must reclaim those small acts of repair and resistance and see beyond dominating dialectics and the production of violence-justifying space.

Placemaking

Almost by their very definition, the discursively subaltern are out of place (Cresswell, 1996). This is not to say that subaltern memory does not circulate in physical and material places – these are often the ghetto, the slum, the *favela*, or the shanty town – but subalternity is more complex than social exclusion. Just by way of illustration, let us take the case of emergent loyalist identity and memory in Northern Ireland. Loyalism as an ideology incubates in relatively deprived, working-class Protestant communities in Northern Ireland (McAuley, 2015). These communities suffer from low educational attainments, especially in relation to their working-class Catholic counterparts (Borooah & Knox, 2015), they have significantly higher levels of unemployment (Tomlinson, 2016), and collectively suffer from poor mental health relative to the rest of UK society (Gallagher, Hamber, & Joy 2012). This suggests that loyalist communities in Northern Ireland could justifiably see themselves as socially excluded (see Hills, Le Grand, & Piachaud 2002). However, I have described subalternity as being denied access to a dominant dialectic. If we take loyalism within the world at large, or even within the UK as a whole, there may be some justification in referring to loyalist discourses as subaltern (Southern 2007; Graham 2004). Writes Graham (2004, p. 488):

> Seen by the world as oppressors themselves, the self-imaging of the UVF/PUP, for example, centres on the neglected memory of the Ulster working class, its interests suppressed by those of the Stormont Unionist government ... This is a discourse of betrayal and alienation, of being 'sold out' as the oppressed victims of unionism and the world opinion that bought the Sinn Féin message.

However, within working-class Protestant communities themselves, loyalism seems to retain a near monopoly to inscribe its preferred narrative of the conflict. Writes McDowell (2008, p. 340): "While almost every one of the 1,574 combatants ... killed throughout the conflict are commemorated physically in some way, only 30 per cent of the 2, 074 civilian deaths are marked in the public sphere." Considering that working-class civilians were victimised at far greater numbers than loyalists, and considering the sheer amount of academic material written about Northern Irish loyalism and loyalists, this suggests that the subaltern *within* Northern Ireland are those who lack or are denied the space to remember their loved ones in public, who lack the ability, means, or forum to challenge the dominant paramilitary narratives of the conflict.

For Cresswell (1996, 2014), the concept 'place' is far more than a topographical location. It relates to belonging and imaginative spatial ordering; what *belongs* here and why? Why does it not belong here and what is the relationship of the 'here' to the 'there?' To say, for example, that 'a woman's place is in the home' is to construct a particular form of patriarchal space-time – the man's place is in the public sphere, the workplace, the spaces of power, while the woman's place is in private life, domesticity, the spaces removed from power. This spatial dispensation over time becomes normalised and taken for granted, the natural order of things, what Pierre Bourdieu (1977) famously referred to as 'doxa'. When women transgress this dominant representation of the appropriate spatial order, they expose the social imaginary that holds the order together (or the 'orthodoxy' in Bourdieu's terms). But women's mobilisations are never uniform; they are in a complex dialectic with the material and ideational order that surrounds them and differs across space and time (Massey & McDowell, 1994).

The critical human geographer Doreen Massey has had a profound impact on how many scholars conceive of and articulate the concepts of space and place today. Drawing on Raymond Williams, Massey asks her reader to picture themselves on a train speeding through a countryside, looking out of the window. Every human face that flies by, every pockmark of human habitation in the landscape, contains a multiplicity of stories and a multiplicity of human trajectories, each chaotically sliced through by their complex and contemporaneous interrelationalities to those other stories and trajectories that surround them, all up to that particular point when the train speeds by and the reader herself encounters them in a fleeting instant (Massey 2005, pp. 118–120). Space, for Massey, is defined as the "simultaneity of stories-so-far" (Massey 2005, p. 12). Space is never empty, never flat, but constantly being produced and reproduced by the changing constellations of social relationships, each imbued with and shaped by different strands and tendrils of power. Unlike more traditional Marxist geographers like David Harvey (2009), for example, Massey does not conceive of the production of space as purely the product of capital flows, accumulations, mobility, and exploitation; rather, she describes space as "loose ends and missing links" (Massey 2005, pp. 11–12) – a set of relationships that can never be holistically described nor safely predicted, but a radical universe of potentiality.

Massey allows us to think of place as concatenations[7] of particular stories that coalesce with varying degrees of coherence at unique junctions in space-time. Places are thus better conceived of not as 'containers' with boundaries, locations on a map, edifices, brick-and-mortar structures, but as '*spatio-temporal events*' (Massey 2005, p. 130, original emphasis), events that are produced by mobilisations that result in shared trajectories within the larger power and chaos of space. When I speak, therefore, of 'places of memory', and the processes involved in their production, I draw on Massey and Karen Till (2005, p. 8) to define them as:

> Fluid mosaics and moments of memory, matter, scene, and experience that create and mediate social spaces and temporalities. Through place making, people mark social spaces as haunted sites where they can return, make contact with their loss, contain unwanted presences, or confront past injustices.

Northern Ireland is spatially dominated by two dialectics: one that justifies and legitimises past violence, and one that suborns the past to a shared future and the reconciliatory imperative. It should not be surprising, therefore, that both the Bloomfield and Eames–Bradley Reports examined the possibilities of surmounting the former with the latter, without recognising the power-geometries of Northern Irish space and the ways in which people deploy the memory of bodies within that space. Any quick perusal of the map of physical

7 Massey refers to places as "articulations within the wider-power geometries of space" (2005, p. 230). I prefer 'concatenations' to better emphasise the interrelatedness of the stories that hold a place together.

memorials on the CAIN website[8] reveals thousands of monuments, memorial plaques, statuary, and gardens dedicated to members of paramilitary forces, the state security services, and ordinary civilians who lost their lives in the Troubles. But what is striking about these places of memory is how exclusionary they are, how segregated, how they reify the existing spatial segregation so distressingly visible in Northern Ireland (Shirlow & Murtagh, 2006). Places of memory are especially significant concatenations of stories in transitional space because they are places where human beings can go to remember, mourn, grieve, and interact with those who have died. They are ghost-places, haunted places, places that blur the temporal lines between life and not-life. When places of memory are made, they are not made simply to put the ghosts to rest (a gravestone, a cairn, a shrine, or a private, meaningful location loved by the ghost in life many serve that purpose), they are *performing their haunting in public*, and the performance is designed to instruct an audience in *how* to remember the life that was lost. If the death was violent or unjust, the ghost-place may confront the audience with a violent or unsettled past, and the ghosts who haunt the place, like the ghost of Hamlet's father, may cry from within for justice and vengeance. But a paramilitary place of memory, as I shall develop later in this book, is not generally a place of haunting but rather a formulaic, standardised aesthetic which apes traditional sites of war remembrance to promote a narrative of violence justification. Though even within these highly circumscribed readings, citizens can repair, resist, and reclaim the paramilitarised space.

The potentiality for shared spaces of mourning in Northern Ireland is at least partially closed off by the unaddressed trauma and injustices of the past and the attempted spatial monopolisation over memory in working-class areas carried out by former paramilitaries. Thus, it is not sufficient to simply decry the segregation of places of memory in Northern Ireland or to opine wistfully for the making of a province-wide place of communal grief. To many, a British soldier, RUC, or UDR officer may have been unjustly killed and may have left behind a network of family and friends who grieve for him/her, but these memories cannot be publicly emplaced where the dominant narrative produced in space is one of collective victimisation at the hands of the security forces. To do so would be an unbearable affront to the other ghosts who may haunt the area. To erect a republican plinth near or around the site of an IRA atrocity, such as Enniskillen or Kingsmills, would similarly be an unconscionable violation of a space of communion with the dead. To have this other remembered next to our loved ones, or perhaps this 'guilty one' next to our 'innocents', would undercut and deny the warrants of the stories circulating in place.

8 The Conflict Archive on the Internet, housed at Ulster University, is one of the best resources for anyone interested in any aspect of Northern Ireland's troubled history and present (cain.ulst.ac.uk).

The Bloomfield Report misrepresents both the difficulty, and even the desirability, of conflating remembrance of all the bodies together in one communal place. In Section 7.13 of the Report, after considering and ultimately dismissing those who object to a province-wide memorial, Bloomfield suggests a memorial building that is a "striking work of architecture", constructed in a central location, "amidst beautifully landscaped gardens" (pp. 47–48). The rest of the Report's recommendations seem carefully calculated to provoke a bare minimum of recrimination and provide no thoughts on a specific location for such a memorial, except to suggest such a memorial should be "readily accessible" but also erected in "relatively undeveloped countryside" (p. 47), which is very much a geographical contradiction.

Areas of Northern Ireland that both produced and bore the brunt of Troubles-related violence are not shared space currently. The vast majority of the deaths attributable to the Troubles occurred in areas of high segregation and high deprivation, particularly North and West Belfast, though Cunningham and Gregory's (2014,) micro-geographical analysis of killings in Belfast clearly shows that only *particular* areas of segregation and deprivation bore the brunt of the deaths. Rather, their research suggests that the pioneering work of Allen Feldman (1991) remains largely correct: Troubles-related killings occurred primarily within specific neighbourhoods defined as 'sanctuary' spaces for either the working-class CNR or PUL populations of Belfast. Expanding out of Belfast, Troubles-related killings were not distributed evenly across Northern Ireland; they were not evenly distributed across areas of high deprivation, as is commonly believed. Rather, the trauma landscape of Northern Ireland is "small pockets of concentrated suffering" ('Patrick', West Belfast), areas such as the Ardoyne, New Lodge/Tiger's Bay, Shankill, Falls, Short Strand, and Lower Ormeau areas of Belfast, the deadly border areas of West Tyrone, South Fermanagh, and South Armagh, the so-called 'Murder Triangle' of the towns of Lurgan, Craigavon and Portadown in mid-Ulster, and the Bogside/Creggan areas of Derry. None of these areas is politically or geographically neutral; as sanctuaries, they are claimed, appropriated, and spoken for by a particular sub-population that suffered immensely during the Troubles at the hands of paramilitaries and/or the state. The deaths that occurred within those areas are imminently recognisable as part of a larger narrative, a larger story-concatenation, particular to a still-haunted place. The memory of the dead, while it may be internally contested, is closely guarded against outside imposition.

Eames–Bradley thinks slightly more creatively about the role of memory and place. However, there are still significant problems with its recommendations. Worth noting at the start is a much more ambivalent perspective around shared memorialisation, and indeed memorialisation in Northern Ireland generally:

> Many who engaged with the Group were positive about the healing quality of memorials; others considered the way in which memorialisation has taken place in Northern Ireland to be divisive, only serving to perpetuate

> sectarianism … The Group does not believe that a shared memorial can be agreed at this time. It remains a contentious issue for many and poses many challenging issues around which we could not see consensus.
>
> (Eames & Bradley 2009, p. 33)

After Bloomfield's vapid elegies, this pessimism is a welcome change. However, Eames–Bradley still presents 'consensus' as something to be celebrated and 'contention' as something to be avoided. This is again the reconciliatory imperative operating in a transitional space that cannot democratically, and should not morally, suborn the contentious past.

Both Bloomfield and Eames–Bradley also touch briefly on 'storytelling' as a means of creative conflict and memory transformation. Their brief sections are noticeably light on details; however, anyone working in or around peace in Northern Ireland would instantly recognise the contextual basis for the sections. Because the Agreement provided no means of reckoning with the difficult legacies of the Troubles, a number of important storytelling initiatives were undertaken by NGOs and community-based organisations in Northern Ireland. Beginning with the poet/activist Damien Gorman's project *An Crann*/The Tree, initiatives such as Towards Understanding and Healing based in Derry and *Healing through Remembering* based in Belfast sought to bridge the deep wounds and entrenched social distances left by the Troubles by bringing disparate individuals and groups together to recount their experiences of trauma, pain, and loss in public (Aiken, 2010; Shea, 2010; Hackett & Rolston, 2009; Senehi, 2009; *An Crann*/The Tree, 2000). The work drew heavily on the thinking of Dan Bar-On (1989; 2006) and Michael Jackson (2002), and psychologists of trauma such as Cathy Caruth (1996) and Judith Herman (1992). Storytelling, and having those stories socially witnessed, Jackson (2002, p. 16) argues, "allow[s] us to feel that we actively participate in a world that for a moment seemed to discount, demean, and disempower us". If trauma is the shattering of the self and the self's ability to narrativise what has happened to it, storytelling is also a form of traumatic healing, of learning to speak again, and reconstructing a just world (Caruth, 1996; Herman, 1992; Janoff-Bullman, 1992). Thinking of space and place in Massey's terms allows us to see how public storytelling and witnessing could potentially produce places that resist and counter dominant dialectics. It also allows perpetrators to witness the pain they have caused in human form. Fundamentally, it can alter the collective stories societies tell themselves about the past.

Unfortunately, little evidence exists on whether or not storytelling in Northern Ireland has actually led to the positive, psychotherapeutic, or reconciliatory outcomes its advocates claim. More importantly perhaps, the pervasive moral relativism in Eames–Bradley mutes the potentiality of their storytelling recommendations and in turn is reflected in many prominent storytelling initiatives. The notion that 'we all have a story to tell' or everyone has their 'own truth' allows violence-producers the forum to replicate and reify the 'truths' that allegedly produced the violence in the first place. Because storytelling has become so de rigeur as a substitute, less-threatening means of 'truth[s]' recovery in Northern Ireland,[9] public funding is routinely devoted to at least partially allowing this reification of violence justification. But fundamentally, peace advocates in Northern Ireland all too often fail to ask themselves how the ubiquitous narrative of 'multiple truths' – all worthy of respect and witnessing – can mute the power of the story-places they are seeking to create. Storytelling in Northern Ireland, in the absence of legitimate truth recovery mechanisms, can become a mere sop to victims and survivors, the political limit of what transitional space can provide them. And paradoxically, by infusing transitional space with the logic that all truths are equally accurate, it can strengthen and cement the places housing the legitimating stories of violence-producers and undercut the ability to actively resist and reappropriate public space.

Again, the Agreement, Bloomfield, and Eames-Bradley have failed to provide any compelling means to reckon with past and any cogent theories about how the diversity of stories could be mediated in public space, and have failed to challenge extant power constellations and mechanisms of violence justification. Because of this, they have facilitated a patchwork and oppressive spatial landscape in Northern Ireland. In Belfast, for example, it is a landscape in which working-class space is publically monopolised by paramilitary displays; yet as one approaches the borders of the City Centre, such displays abruptly end and the centre of Northern Irish capitalist and materialist consumption is carefully scrubbed clean of the past (Switzer & McDowell, 2009). Increasingly however, as the threat of organised, sustained violence recedes into the background of Northern Ireland, the role of places and placemaking is changing and diversifying. It is important, therefore, to examine how places are changing, how they are coming to be read, and what the politics of alternative spatial readings might look like.

The politics of inscription

I argue that perhaps the most important question in all of transitional justice is the question of *inscription*. How shall the bodies be remembered? How shall places of memory be read? An inscription is a mnemonic guide for a visitor or audience that indicates how places should be read or experienced. Inscriptions

9 Consider the immense number of storytelling projects sampled by Kelly (2005). Unfortunately, to my knowledge, nobody has updated her audit. In 2014 the University of Ulster unveiled what they hoped would be a central archive of storytelling material gleaned from community groups active in storytelling projects (accounts.ulster.ac.uk/repo24/index.php). From my personal experience working in community relations in Northern Ireland between 2014 and 2016, nearly *every* group I encountered it seemed was doing some sort of 'storytelling' initiative, ranging from collecting the stories of people from particular geographic locations, to restorative justice-type projects involving victims meeting perpetrators, to women's stories of the conflict, to stories of former paramilitary members and ex-prisoners.

can be (and often are) etched, soldered, physically written into stone, tablet, concrete, or affixed in the form of plaques. They can be present in dedications, place descriptions, artists' statements, but they need not be purely textual. Inscription is also aesthetic, imaginative, and symbolic; it is never settled, never solidified – signs are transient: they leak, they evolve, and they migrate. But in terms of victimhood and placemaking, memory curators can provide mnemonic inscriptions by choosing who to include and who to exclude at a place of memory; they can appropriate particular locations or articulate their inscription in certain genres. Through the text and symbols publicly presented, the aesthetic choices that are publicly displayed, the place and its curators impart messages to their audience (which may or may not be accepted or even understood) that construct and communicate a social memory of past events.

For Bloomfield, the question of inscription is quite simple. There must be one message, one narrative imparted above all else regarding the memory of the contentious past: "The costly and counterproductive" human toll of the Troubles and the absolute necessity of social and political reconciliation (Bloomfield, 1998a, p. 23). Eames–Bradley's preferred narrative is similar if not identical. It suggests that the absolute inscriptive imperative is "remembering for reconciliation" (Eames & Bradley, 2009, p. 24). Though this preferred narrative might resonate with a wide cross-section of Northern Irish society, it is again evasive and does not adequately encapsulate the dizzying variety of performative uses the bodies of Troubles victims and survivors can possess. For example, inscribing such a narrative seems to forestall questions of justice and accountability. For some of the families of the Enniskillen bombing, a primary focus on reconciliation is unacceptable considering the fact that none of the perpetrators of the atrocity have ever been 'brought to justice'. Any reconciliatory narrative at their places of memory would 'airbrush' out of 'the annals of history' the wanton cruelty committed on Remembrance Sunday 1987 (Ely Centre, 2016). Reconciliation is at the very least premature until the truth of the Enniskillen bombing is recovered and some measure of justice and accountability achieved. For these reasons, the proposed new Enniskillen memorial focuses directly on inscribing what for many families is the truth of the atrocity:

> This memorial is erected in loving memory to the 12 innocent civilians murdered by the IRA and in recognition to the scores of innocent civilians injured on Remembrance Day, Sunday 8th November, 1987.
>
> (Ely Centre, 2016)

Similarly, the politics of inscription was very prominent in the lengthy debate over the Omagh Bomb Memorial. The Omagh bombing was a very unique case, in that it was both the single worst atrocity of the Troubles and that it occurred three months after the signing of the Agreement and was attributable to the splinter republican group the Real IRA. Omagh and West Tyrone are majority CNR areas and have generally returned a reliable slate of Sinn Féin politicians to local, district, and provincial office. Thus, how to memorialise a terrible atrocity committed by people who just three months prior were in the IRA, and politically represented by Sinn Féin, posed a deeply unsettling conundrum (indeed, the debate over the memorial inscription took years to be 'resolved'). The main local victims and survivors group, the Omagh Self-Help and Support Group (OSHSG), alleges that their preferred inscription was not allowed by the Sinn Féin-dominated local Council (Stevenson, 2008). Their preferred inscription is the following: "To honour and remember 31 people murdered and hundreds injured from three nations by a dissident republican terrorism car bomb." The OSHSG claims that the Council baulked at both the tone of the statement and the adjective 'republican', arguing that dissidents were not (or at least no longer) in fact republicans, that Sinn Féin was the only true representative of republicanism, and that Sinn Féin had agreed to the Agreement and ceased its support for violence. The Council thus favoured an inscription that carried no direct attribution of blame and emphasised the necessity of rebuilding shattered lives. Their preferred inscription was: "Saturday 15 August 1998 at 3:10 PM. To honour and remember the 31 men, women, and children who were killed, the hundreds injured, and those whose lives were changed forever in the Omagh Bomb. The light shines in the darkness and the darkness has not overcome it (John 1: 5)." Eventually, after a lengthy process of outside mediation, a compromise was reached. The physical memorial itself contains a number of concrete plaques surrounding a reflecting pool (see Figure 1.1). One additional plaque faces outwards towards Drumragh Avenue and is visible from the footpath.

Figure 1.1 Omagh Bomb Memorial Garden, Omagh, County Tyrone. Photo by Martin Melaugh. Photograph © Martin Melaugh and © CAIN. Used with permission.

The compromise was for the OSHSG to inscribe one panel in the interior of the memorial with their preferred inscription while the rest of the panels in the interior would be devoted to the Council's preferred tonality. The Council's preferred inscription would be the most visible, on the plaque facing the footpath.

The spatiality of the inscription is clear; the OSHSG's panel, which works to splinter and disrupt the reconciliatory imperative contained in the place, is marginalised and rendered almost invisible. The mnemonic demand that the audience witness the 'truth' of what happened – the mnemonic demand for justice and accountability – is suborned and buried within the larger inscription. The larger inscription hews quite closely to the imperatives of Bloomfield and Eames–Bradley. It emphasises the human cost of the bombing and through the last clause with the biblical passage, guides the audience towards a prospective, forward-looking narrative, one in which the struggle of the larger Omagh/West Tyrone community to overcome the damage wrought by the bomb parallels the ongoing struggle of Northern Ireland to achieve a lasting peace and reconciled society. And this lasting peace and reconciled society, it is presumed, is threatened by a justice-seeking inscription on the place. As one person active in the extremely tense debate over the memorial in Omagh told me in a moment of candour:

> The sooner we accept it the better ... We as ordinary people on the ground, the sooner that we recognise that yes, we were hung out to dry for political expediency, but at the end of the day, what did they need us to do? There doesn't seem to be another choice.
>
> ('Emily')

Of course, communities of IRA or dissident republican violence are not the only people resisting the foreclosure of Troubles memory through reconciliatory inscription. Predominately Catholic victims of state violence and/or loyalist paramilitary violence do so too, employing the bodies of loved ones killed unjustly to insist that no reconciliation is possible without justice and accountability (see Figure 1.2). In addition, as I shall discuss in Chapter 3, not everyone in Northern Ireland shares Bloomfield's desire to represent the Troubles as 'counter-productive'. For many republicans, while their campaign may not have been successful in terms of achieving a united Ireland, it was successful in that it ameliorated the oppressed, second-class status of Catholics across Northern Ireland through the equality provisions and guarantees of the Agreement, for example. For many loyalists, their campaign prevented a united Ireland and preserved the sanctity of the union with Britain. Members of paramilitary groups who were killed in the service of such goals therefore should be remembered in much the same way as the Northern Irish, Irish, or British dead of the First and Second World Wars, as honoured soldiers in the service of a noble cause. Thus, paramilitary places of memory confound the reconciliatory imperative and inscriptions of the Troubles as unjust, counter-productive, or deviant.

Figure 1.2 Ballymurphy Mural, near Upper Springfield and Whiterock Roads, West Belfast. Photo by author.

Another, more complex means to mnemonically inscribe the bodies of the dead into Northern Ireland's social and material landscape is through what I refer to as *rehumanisation*. Rehumanising inscription demands acknowledgement of the dead as complex, multi-faceted individuals whose former life is more than the circumstances of his or her death.

In a narrative focusing on reconciliation, justice, or violence justification, a body is separated from its complex potentialities and suborned to a particular political purpose. As such, it is dehumanised, and by dehumanised I mean that the circumstances of a person's life are subordinated to the inscription the curator wishes the death to stand for. This is not to suggest that rehumanisation is apolitical or that dehumanisation is exploitative, though both may be true in certain contexts; rather it is to suggest that rehumanisation is a particular form of resistance to the dual dominating dialectics circulating in Northern Irish memory-space, a resistance that attempts to argue that a human life is worth remembering in and of itself, above and before it can be reduced to a politicised object.

To illustrate, consider a memorial to Terry Enright, a popular youth worker killed by the LVF in 1998 in Belfast City Centre (see Figure 1.3). Terry's case will be taken up in some detail in Chapter 7. Terry's family, friends, and larger community consciously chose to remember Terry at this place of memory

Figure 1.3 Terry Enright Memorial Mural, Gort na Mona GAA Club, Whiterock Road, West Belfast. Photo by Martin Melaugh. Photo © Martin Melaugh and © CAIN. Used with permission.

as, respectively, an outdoor enthusiast, an explorer, an Irish dancer, a footballer, and a boxer, and the written inscription above Terry's head in the centre frame reflects what these curators decided best reflected Terry's guiding ethos or philosophy in life. No mention here is made of the circumstances of his death, a brutal, unjustifiable slaying at his secondary employment at a nightclub in the City Centre. Rather, the inscription here attempts to flesh out Terry's young life and what it stood for. In doing so, a casual observer could be forgiven for not realising that Terry Enright was a victim of Troubles violence. The aesthetic of the memorial invites further inquiry. The aesthetic is designed to illustrate a human role model for the deprived youth of the Upper Springfield area. As such, it is certainly not apolitical; it is a constitutive object in a narrative of communitarian re-empowerment, and as such could be read as dehumanising. But because the inscription hews so closely to Terry's human qualities, even if such qualities are carefully selected and protected, it resists the foreclosure of Terry's memory or its reduction to a single narrative or mnemonic. Terry is not just a name on a plaque, garlanded by poppies or lilies, and used as an exhortation to remember the 'glorious fallen'. Nor is he an object suborned to a larger narrative of British injustice, loyalist murder, or collusion. *But nor does it completely foreclose those readings.* In performing rehumanisation, the place of memory subtly, deftly, and in a complex form of social encoding, challenges other memorial places in the larger Outer West Belfast area, places that have recruited dead bodies in the service of a political cause. Terry's brother Feargal clearly suggests as much in the quote below, but again, he does so subtly. A crucially important aspect of truly understanding the radical potentiality of memory-space in Northern Ireland lies in understanding why Terry's place of memory is a 'wee bit different':

> It's a very positive memorial, because sometimes memorials can be used negatively, memorials can be used for a certain political project or it can be used to promote a certain political agenda in the present. Well, this wasn't anything to do with that. It was about this club doing a memorial to one of its own members … in a way that could make a difference … and show people a ray of light or a ray of hope. And that's why it was so important, and that's why it's a wee bit different from some of the other memorials that you will see.
>
> (Feargal Mac Ionnrachtaigh, West Belfast)

By presenting above all a multifaceted human being, the memorial challenges the legitimating narratives that could justify the taking of his life, of the stripping of this complex man down to one particular defining facet: the fact that he was a Catholic.

This perhaps is what Bloomfield, Eames–Bradley, and the larger discipline of transitional justice have missed. Bodies in transitional space have too readily been stripped of their creative potentialities of inscription, stripped of their polyvocality, their fluidity, their movement, reduced to one inscriptive message – justice or reconciliation – out of their constellations of possibilities. This has often been done violently; but sometimes it has been done in the name of 'peace'. Peace without contention is not a healthy peace. The politics of inscription is a contest over the legitimate right to inscribe a particular strand or strands of social memory into the spatial politics of everyday life, to exert a degree of control over the speech of the bodies of the dead, bodies who have been robbed of the ability to speak for themselves (see Verdery, 1999, pp. 28–29). We need to understand that there is a vibrancy in letting those contestations play out in public space, and an oppressiveness in trying to shut them down or close them off.

Chapter 2

On social memory

Transitional justice and the politics of memory

Jay Winter (2001) and Andreas Huyssen (1994) both argue that twenty-first-century social science and historical studies are experiencing a 'memory boom'. To some degree, both are partially responsible for this, Winter for his groundbreaking historical work on war memory (Winter & Sivan, 1997; Winter, 1995) and Huyssen for his interdisciplinary masterpieces (1994; 2003). In the late 1980s and throughout the 1990s, a number of highly influential texts were produced in a variety of academic disciplines that challenged entrenched historicist and empiricist understandings of the past and promoted a central role for memory –collectively, socially, and culturally defined – in how individuals and groups constructed identities, mobilised politically, and cohered socially (see especially LaCapra, 1998; Hirsch, 1997; Sturken, 1997; Nora, 1989,1996; Irwin-Zarecka, 1994; Thomson, 1994; Connerton, 1989; Passerini, 1987). Writing in 2008, Guy Beiner noted that 936 books had been published from 1998 to 2008 that had an adjective (social, collective, cultural, public, or popular) plus memory in the title (Beiner, 2008, p. 107). Indeed, memory gained traction so rapidly within the social sciences and humanities that its rapid ascension has led to some scholars warning of a backlash (Beiner, 2008; Berliner, 2005). Radstone (2008, p. 35), writing in the first issue of the first journal exclusively devoted to the burgeoning discipline, *Memory Studies*, suggests that memory has become what Mieke Bal (2002) refers to as a 'traveling concept', a concept that by virtue of its fluid mobility across disciplines, ultimately comes to be seen to explain more than it can. The focus on memory in scholarly studies has paralleled what Erika Doss (2010, p. 2) has referred to as 'memorial mania' in public life in the United States, "an obsession with issues of memory and history and an urgent desire to express and claim those issues in visibly public contexts". Having passed the boom, we may now be living in an era of 'memory fatigue' (Langenbacher & Eigler, 2005), where the seemingly endless calls to remember and commemorate a version of the national past engender more of a hearty cynicism than a patriotic fervour. The Irish writer Samuel Beckett perhaps has the clearest literary statement on memory fatigue, in a vicious aside to the memory politics of his Irish homeland: "Wherever nauseated time has dropped a nice fat turd, you will find out patriots, sniffing it up on all fours, their faces on fire" (in Lloyd 1993, p. 41).

Yet this wave of scholarship in memory studies has rather remarkably made very little impact on transitional justice as a field, at least not until recent years. Within transitional justice, the role of memory has been largely two-fold. First, citizen memories have been conceived as a critical means of 'truth recovery', a tool to call attention to past wrongdoing and pierce the silence engendered by repressive political authorities and institutions. Memory has been contraposed to enforced forgetting and political amnesia (e.g. the *pacto del olvido)* (Levi, 1989; Jelin, 2003). Second, memory has been confused with commemoration and folded into reparative or restorative justice. The politics of memory have been conceived of as the struggle over public symbols, monuments, and how best to visibly mark sites of past violence, oppression, murder, or disappearance (Jelin 2007; De Brito, Aguilar & González-Enríquez, 2001).

But this treatment of memory is, on the whole, unsatisfying. It is important to note that transitional justice began in the ruins of defeated Germany in 1945 and the shadow of the Holocaust. Transitional justice was a radical attempt to apply embryonic international (read Anglo-American) human rights law to an unprecedented collective crime (Teitel, 2003). Transitional justice probably begins with the Nuremberg and Tokyo Tribunals (Teitel, 2002), though Elster (2004) has suggested its concerns began as early as Ancient Greece. But it was only in the late 1980s that it assumed the characteristics of a 'field', "an international web of individuals and institutions whose internal coherence is held together by common concepts, practical aims, and distinctive claims to legitimacy" (Arthur 2009, p. 323). Fields in Bourdieu's (1993) sense hang together through unifying *nomos*, and Arthur (2009) has presented a compelling argument that the essential *nomos* of the emergent field is contained in the adjective 'transitional'. Transitional is a temporal adjective; there is a prior space-time evoked by 'transition from' and a prospective space-time evoked by 'transition to'. But the traumatic 'transition from' is not psychoanalytically 'knowable' in the sense that it is an "event without a witness" (Laub, 1996).[1] Memory is thus a tool to recover a partial, fractured truth(s) in the spaces of obliteration and forced disappearance. The recovered memory-qua-truth in turn functions pedagogically; its presence in public space forces a confrontation with the realities of past evil (Minow, 1998, pp. 130–131). The bodies of victims and the memories of survivors become a text on which to write a new moral contract between citizen and state (Humphrey & Valverde, 2008). Only after this confrontation can a society move from 'from' to 'to'.

1 For counterargument, see LaCapra (1998).

In contrast, the 'transition to' is relatively well defined. Transitional justice as a field *knows where transitional societies should be going*. They are going towards democracy, and democracy rooted in a liberal, Western human rights ideal (Carothers, 2002). But the problem is that the oppressive regime, and the oppressive ideology(ies), rooted in force and violence, does not simply disappear or even go underground. The past regime's power to disseminate its own 'truth' maintains, undergirded by the memory of force in the past and the threat of force in the present. In Argentina, it can explain the destruction of the human rights movement that took root after the fall of the dictatorship. This destruction took the form of the ascendance of the Menem government's reconciliatory imperative under the Due Obedience and Full Stop proclamations of 1992. The Agreement in Northern Ireland was signed under the cloud of Gerry Adams' chilling 1995 statement, in response to a call to 'Bring back the IRA': "They haven't gone away, you know." Because 'to democracy' is the superordinate animating ethos of the field, the potentialities of bodies and memory narrows. Reconciliation takes precedence over justice, because the latter threatens to return the transitional society to widespread violence. Potentially transgressive memory, memory that disrupts the *nomos* of 'transition to' becomes suspect, out of place, socially *dysfunctional*, to draw again on Brewer (2010).

Survivors, denied justice, accountability, and, generally, monetary or land reparations and redistributive justice by the transitional paradigm, are left with the memorial, the site of remembrance, as a place to tell their story or inscribe their truth. It is assumed that by marking the landscape in some way, the transitional society can preserve the memory of the offence in the collective consciousness for posterity. It is for this reason that it seems that so many 'official' memorial sites to places of past violence are imbued with what White (2006) and Stone (1999) call 'the domestication of affect'. Official memory-places are generally bounded containers of quiet reflection, introspection, and quietude, and in being marked and policed as such, they close off the potentialities of alternative, non-reconciliatory memory mobilisations. Compare this with the noisy, justice-seeking spatial and political transgression of the *escrache* in the Southern Cone of South America, where memory and justice advocates would noisily converge on the house or workplace of an alleged perpetrator in an attempt to expose him and undermine his places of comfort and well-being (see Levey, 2016). I overstate the dualism here intentionally, as a gateway to exploring the politics of memory in some detail. The point that is to be made here, drawing on James Young (1993, p. 15), is that public memory is operationalised and emplaced within the power-geometries of space. Within those confines, we must ask: to what ends have we remembered? Transitional justice as a field has privileged 'remembering for the future' and in the process has created implicit, and sometimes explicit, hierarchies of memorialising practice with 'transition to' placed above 'transition from'. In doing so, transitional justice as a field has partially closed off memory's inherent 'multidirectionality' (Rothberg, 2009) and polyphony/polyvocality (Bakhtin, 1981).

Memory and history

When we employ the word 'memory', we tend to conjure a specific set of phenomena, learned, I think, primarily from Freud, though as a distorted and simplistic reading of his complex theories. I call it the theory of the *unconscious repository*, and its best articulation is by Arthur Conan Doyle's famous detective Sherlock Homes. " 'You see', he explained, 'I consider that a man's brain originally is like a little empty attic, and you have to stock it with such furniture as you choose' " (Conan Doyle, 1887/2016, p. 5). Events, once experienced, are catalogued and stored in our unconscious minds and available for recall should we, as individual actors, choose to, or are triggered to, or encounter a reminiscent object, image, or experience. But we understand with Freudian psychoanalysis that what is recalled from the unconscious mind is never an exact replica of what came before. We understand that recall from the unconscious can be plagued by distortion and misrepresentation; but still, we believe that memory is largely accurate (in the historical sense), and that memory that is inaccurate is generally a result of extreme circumstances or conscious dissimulation.

But this lay understanding of memory is misguided. Far from being a matter solely of individual experience, memory is a social phenomenon. What and how we remember is shaped and moulded by our experience and interaction with significant others, our participation in social discourse, and our interactions with meaningful symbols, surroundings, and landscapes. Nor is memory purely a record of the past. While memory is indeed *about* the past, perhaps memory's defining feature is its presentism. We deploy memories to make sense of present circumstances. Which memories we invoke or call forth and why we invoke those representations are our attempt to narrate a symbolic linkage between past and present. Memory is a guide through the present, or sometimes a justification for a particular action or set of actions in the present. Thus, memories are not static; they are not crystallised into an unchanging portrait, a set of images, or a film reel. They change, adapt, and morph, and they do so in response to social phenomena that we are experiencing in the present. Writes David Lowenthal (1975, p. 21):

> The tangible past is altered mainly to make history conform with memory. Memory not only conserves the past but adjusts recall to present needs. Instead of remembering exactly what was, we make the past intelligible in light of the present circumstances.

Both Lowenthal and Pierre Nora posit separate and distinct realms for history and memory, though both for radically different reasons. For Lowenthal (1985), history is the collective agent, produced through dialogue, discussion, criticism, and review, and thus superior to memory, which need not be collectively produced at all, and thus is fungible, alterable, and deeply anachronistic. Memory is how actors *use* (and misuse) history. Nora, however, relentlessly prioritises memory over history:

> Memory and history, far from being synonomous, appear now to be in fundamental opposition. Memory is life, borne by living societies, founded in its name. It remains in permanent evolution, open to the dialectic of remembering and forgetting, unconscious of its successive deformations, vulnerable to manipulation and appropriation, susceptible to being long dormant and periodically revived. History, on the other hand, is the reconstruction, always problematic and incomplete, of what is no longer.
>
> (Nora, 1989, p. 8)

For Nora, history's authoritarian project is to "suppress and destroy memory" (Nora, 1989, p. 9) which it is unable to tame, which threatens its temporal continuities, reinserts the realm of the sacred, and refuses to be bound by historical frameworks, standards, and debates. But both Lowenthal and Nora seem to be labouring under the weight of man made of straw. I have yet to read anyone who believes that history and memory are the same thing (LaCapra, 1998), yet both react to this constructed scholar who ostensibly does view them interchangeably, which in turn justifies their radical separation. By positing a separation between them, they fail to account for their complementarity and inbuilt interlinkage. Of course, history is forever incomplete, scored by absence and power, 'written by the winners', and plagued (but not defined by) by bad scholarship and pompous, Eurocentric scholars. Of course memory is biased, presentist, selectivist, and, being human, deeply fallible. Both the jurist and the psychologist have long understood that the most suspect form of testimony is eyewitness recall (Loftus, 1996). But the camera's lens can be damaged, the photograph altered, the archive destroyed, the records mismanaged, forged, or fabricated, the recording device selectively turned on, as well. Neither history nor memory has any claim to be authoritative, complete, or even in the process of completion. The past is always an object of social and historical interpretation. The truth is not 'out there', to paraphrase the tagline of my favourite television programme as a youngster (*The X-Files*); all pasts stand available for interpretation, appropriation, adaptation, and erasure.

But this is not to invite readers down the rabbit hole of total postmodern relativism. As Graham Dawson (2007, p. 47) has ably put it, "If all ... representations of the past are equally valid, we find ourselves in a postmodern world of relativism in which any notion of historical truth or ethical discrimination has been abandoned". But Dawson's salvo against postmodernism is also over-stated. As Hutcheon reminds us, "[Postmodernism] does not deny the *existence* of the past; it does question whether we can ever ***know*** that past other than through its textualised remains" (Hutcheon, 1987, p. 25, original emphasis, cited in Sturken, 1997, p. 17). Things happened, people were killed, the gas chambers existed, and to paraphrase a line from the film *Hiroshima mon Amour*, an entire city was lifted off the ground and fell back to the earth in ashes (Duras, 1959). And what we are left with after collective experiences that approach the limits of human comprehension are the 'spectral trace' (Jonker & Till, 2009), the 'memory of the offence' (Levi, 1989). Historians have helped us remember; indeed, many historians have answered the call of an indescribably immediate moral imperative and returned forgotten genocides and atrocities to the written record (see especially Dreschler (1980), and discussion in Olusoga and Erichsen (2010) and Crawford (2002)). Truth commissions have stood against oblivion and cried *Nunca Mas* (Jelin, 2003; Minow, 1998). But history could never have returned memory to us if memory had been completely obliterated or forgotten.

History as a larger discipline is also growing increasingly aware of the processes of its own creation. Nora (1989, pp. 9–10) argues that modern history has turned to *historiography*, or, as he puts it, 'the history or history', in response to critical challenges from memory that it cannot adequately deflect. Indeed, it may be this opening in history that has recreated the space to rediscover the great theorists of memory, such as Bergson, Freud, and Halbwachs, and to elevate memory to a central place in the historical, sociological, and philosophical imagination. Thus Nora's radical delineation seems almost belied by his own argument.

But perhaps we should take seriously his call to think *historiographically*. Thinking about how histories are created and produced allows us to become more aware of *silences* and *incompletes*. In the case of the latter, Trouillot (1997, pp. 14–15) asks his readers to consider what a 'complete' history might entail: all of the recollections of the actors present, their thoughts, underlying motives and motivations, actions, gestures, movements, changes to the *mise-en scène*. Any attempt to record or recreate this completely dissolves into, at best, a Robert Altman film, or at worst, a cacophonous, madcap farce. Both memory and history must interpret this, and through interpretation, they produce a narrative that is intelligible for readers and for audience (even if that audience is purely the monastic self). Yet this narrative is inherently incomplete. The process of narration places what (to its author!) is deemed irrelevant or unintelligible on the periphery, or writes it out altogether. This is Trouillot's silencing, a necessary yet oft-abused facet of the creation of any historical representation. And what is silenced is not merely the cacophony that strains and eventually overwhelms the boundaries of language and interpretation. Power silences, and power enters the equation at all stages of the production. In the United States and Canada, there are few histories written by Indigenous Americans, or at least few Indigenous histories that are taught to settler children.

And, as Trouillot (1997) and Sturken (1997; 2007) remind us, history is not produced merely by historians; it also a produced by significant cultural and political figures, forums, and artefacts. This facet of historical production lays far greater claim to the socialisation of its populace than weighty historical debates. And this form of historical production narrates and silences as well:

> Remember the Alamo? That was a history lesson delivered by John Wayne on the screen. Davy Crockett was a television character who became a significant historical figure rather than the obverse … Then as now, American children and quite a few young males elsewhere learned to thematise parts of that history by playing cowboys and Indians … Is it really inconsequential that the history of America is being written in the same world where few little boys want to be Indians?
>
> (Trouillot, 1997, pp. 21–22)

There is no such thing as an objective, authoritative, complete record of past events. While there are certainly more objective, more authoritative records than others – records with a greater claim to accuracy, facticity – all recordings are also narrations. And whether particular narrations are adopted, internalised, and inscribed into public space and the social imaginary depends on a number of questions, but most crucially questions of social and discursive power and proximity.

The evolution of social memory studies

This section is not intended to be a comprehensive review of the burgeoning sub-discipline.[2] Indeed, the voluminousness of the literature, and the often severe disciplinary entry costs to its various function rooms, cries out for more and more systematic review, analysis, and meta-analysis. This deficit is beyond the scope of this project. My intention in the remainder of this chapter is to provide a truncated genealogy of memory as an epistemological orientation. To do so, I will examine the work of four important twentieth-century thinkers of memory and then outline four partially overlapping but not wholly complementary 'intellectual traditions' that rediscovered memory in the latter part of the twentieth century. It is my hope that this section will serve to scaffold readers who are new to the study of social memory and signpost routes towards greater familiarity.

My first claim, building off the previous section, is that social values, group identities, and representations of the past possess no *ipso facto* 'reality' until they are inscribed into the social imaginary and produce a space for their visibility and transmission (Wright, 1997; Lefebvre 1991; Connerton, 1989; Castioradis, 1998; Berger & Luckmann, 1966). Inscription in turn is a political and politicised process shaped by different people and groups contesting what the right, moral,

2 See Olick, Vinitzky-Seroussi, & Levy (2011) generally. See also Nikulin (2015) for philosophy; Hirst & Echterhoff (2012) for social psychology; Erll, Nunning & Young (2008) for cultural studies; Moore & Whelan (2007) for heritage studies; and Misztal (2003) for sociology.

or appropriate image of *space* (the relationships of people, places, and things to other people, places, and things) should be. The politics of inscription will vary widely given the spatial, cultural, historical, and institutional power-geometries under observation. But what I am concerned with is a particular aspect of the politics of inscription, how a violent or oppressive past will be remembered and what sorts of narratives and speech genres will it use to mnemonically guide subjects and bodies through the present. This might be, holistically, albeit loosely, sought after in the realm of social memory.

Social memory is a trans-disciplinary concept used to explore the relationships and linkages between group identity in the present and a group's production of an inter-subjectively intelligible past. Still perhaps the best attempt at a definition is David Thelen's. While Thelen eschews specificity for broad reach, he perhaps best articulates how social memory could be understood and applied:

> The historical study of memory would be the study of how families, larger gatherings of people, and formal organisations selected and interpreted identifying memories to serve their changing needs. It would explore how people together searched for common memories to meet present needs, how they first recognised such a memory and then agreed, disagreed, or negotiated over its meaning, and finally how they preserved and absorbed that meaning to their ongoing concerns.
>
> (Thelen, 1989, p. 1123)

In arguing this, Thelen is drawing on memory as a concept enjoying the newfound prominence in historical studies allowed for by the historiographical turn. The historiographical turn was in part fuelled by emergent readings of four major European thinkers: Sigmund Freud, Marcel Proust,[3] Friedrich Nietzsche, and, most importantly, Maurice Halbwachs. It will not be possible to do justice to the entirety of the work on memory of these profound thinkers in this short review. Nor will I mention other seminal figures who could be discussed here, such as Henri Bergson, Emile Durkheim, or Marc Bloch, partially because I wish to set myself some limits, but also because these scholars' work on memory generally comes to the field in large part *through* Halbwachs.

In Freudian thought, the unconscious mind functions as an accumulative repository; past experiences lodge themselves in the individual brain and remain preserved deep within. This image of the unconscious mind as an attic or a storage space largely goes unproblematised in Freudian thought. What is significant for Freud is how memory is recalled (Misztal, 2003, pp. 140–141; Freud,

3 There are several modernist writers who could be held up here as representative, not least the Irish writer James Joyce. But Proust's voluminous *La Recherche du Temps Perdu* (In Search of Lost Time) is, I would hazard, the most well-known Western text absorbed with memory and recall of the twentieth century.

1899/1999). The subject recalls memory from the unconscious in a manner distorted by the passage of time but ultimately for functional needs. Some memories, however, can only be recalled through use of a 'screen', and for Freud, these 'uncanny' memories are rooted in traumatising or damaging sensory experiences in early childhood (Smith, 2000). For Freud, all memories of early childhood are screen memories; they are shields on which to project a representation of past events that protects the individual from the traumatising event that is the penultimate aetiological source of a given neurosis. Freud was one of the first scholars to question why memory was consistently inaccurate, consistently fungible. Screen memories were mechanisms of both repression and disassociation; they protected the psyche from further damage. When the individual encountered a parallel representation of the trauma-source, screen memories could falter and the individual could be plagued by the unintelligible and uncanny return and re-enactment of trauma. For our purposes, though, it is important to note that, for Freud, memory is uniquely rooted in individualised, experiential reality. Trauma is part of the unconscious repository, but unlike other sensory experience, it cannot be recalled or controlled by the conscious mind. The subordination of the unconscious and uncanny to the conscious and the intelligible was, for Freud, one of the main functions of psychoanalysis (Caruth, 1996; Herman, 1992). If uncontrolled, the uncanny return of traumatic memory would continually re-emerge to overwhelm the conscious mind and plague the somatic capacity of the body.

Freud was probably somewhat influenced by Bergsonian and Lamarckian ideas of 'embodied memory', or that the body itself was a memory container and specific sensory experiences were often triggered or recalled through a refractive encounter with meaningful or reminiscent symbols, senses, and places in the present.[4] Marcel Proust perhaps provides the best artistic illustration of these Bergsonian ideas, though it must be noted that there is no evidence that Freud and Proust were familiar with one another's work, despite being contemporaries. Consider the famous literary example of the 'episode of the madeleine' in Proust's celebrated *In Search of Lost Time* (1913/1981). A specific memory of childhood washes over the narrator as he reproduces a familiar childhood sensation, namely dunking a madeleine cake in his tea. The implication is that the original memory lies there, somewhere within the narrator's unconsciousness, but has tragically faded with the passage of time and the loss of an authentic childhood. In learning to become an artist, the narrator learns to mediate the fading memories, to reclaim them, and to recognise their true significance. For Proust, significant and refractory objects, places, and aesthetic forms mnemonically trigger the sense-memory stored away in our unconscious. Thus, Proust artistically reproduces the Freudian individualisation of memory, but also connects it to the subject's exterior milieu and

4 For a theory of embodied memory, see Connerton (1989); for a rejection, see Spillman & Conway (2007).

positions childhood not as a forum of violence and traumatic repression, but as an idealised return to beauty and innocence (though not unsullied by jealousy, heartbreak, and loss) that can be saved and preserved by art and artistic expression.

However, Nietzsche and Halbwachs are horses of a very different colour. Both theorists radically reject the individualistic frame of memory. Nietzsche is especially concerned with setting up memory as a utopian social device to transcend the enslavement of history (Huyssen, 1994). For Nietzsche, the 'natural' state of man is a state of forgetting. When societies begin to historicise themselves, they begin a process of domesticating their subjects. In his particularly iconoclastic language, Nietzsche compares humans to bovines and notes that cattle live an ahistorical life in prehistory, without any need for a realisation of different temporal states. In contrast, humans are animals that remember, but according to Nietzsche, this has not always been true. In prehistory, humans, like bovines, were concerned simply with immediate survival and had no purpose for the ritualistic recollection of the past. Rather, it was society, and a particular form of stultifying modern society, that relentlessly historicised and demanded that human societies learn their histories and accept the supremacy of the past. It is a society that fixes its subjects into a historical chronology and constantly "remind[s] [man] what his existence fundamentally is" (in Richardson, 2008, p. 88; see also Lemm, 2006). In other words, a slave remembers that he is a slave because his father was a slave, his grandfathers were slaves, and thus, through the forced connection to his past, accepts that his future is one of slavery. Historicism is also a vicious cycle: the more humans come to believe in the necessity of historicising the past, the more important it becomes to construct histories, and the more wounded, haunted, and infected by the past societies become. To achieve utopian freedom, humans need to escape from the thrall of history. Though we can never escape from it entirely, Nietzsche seems to be calling for a more invigorating, public, and creative means to represent the past, which he sees represented in memory, and especially memory's ability to 'selectively forget'. While Nietzsche's treatment of the past is scattered throughout *Untimely Mediations* (1873/1997) and some of his other works, what seems to emerge is a desire to construct a philosophy that can adequately delineate the ways in which history is constructed, used, and abused in order to put humans in their places and justify the recourse to violence and terror. Nietzsche's disjointed call would perhaps be most firmly taken up later in the twentieth century by Michel Foucault, as we shall shortly see.

The single most important text in the evolution of social memory studies is the hugely influential *Sur la Mémoire Collective* (*On Collective Memory*) by Maurice Halbwachs, first published in 1925 (1992). As with Freud and Proust, it is unfortunate that Halbwachs was not familiar with Nietzsche because they both share a clear social constructionist and collectivist understanding of memory. Where they differ is largely in the centrality of violence to their theses, with Halbwachs largely emphasising *pathos* – conceptualising memory as an emotive group appeal to love and social cohesion (Assman, 2005). But Halbwachs' primary argument is with Freud. In a direct riposte to Freud, he writes:

> Most of the time, when I remember, it is others who spur me on; their memory comes to the aid of mine and mine relies on theirs ... There is no point in seeking where [memories] are preserved in my brain or in some nook of my mind to which I alone have access; for they are recalled to me externally, and the groups of which I am a part at any time give me means to reconstruct them.
>
> (Halbwachs, 1925/1992, p. 38)

Memory was thus particular strands of constructed narrative, strands that social groups selected out of the past to privilege or valorise, to use as constitutive parables or cautionary dystopias. Equally as important was what collectives chose to forget, those strands of the past that for one reason or another were abandoned or erased. The construction of collective memory was in turn shaped by the collective context, especially its proximity to larger constellations of power and inscriptive potential. In Halbwachs, we see a turn towards the impermanence of memory, of treating collective memory as a product of changing social circumstances and contestations. Moreover, Halbwachs notes how individuals belong to multiple collective groupings at any one time, and the attachments or identities of which group(s) we wish to signify at any given moment in turn directs and shapes the recall of memory.

Functionalist theorists, such as Halbwachs' mentor Durkheim, argued that memory was purely a function of a given context; its nature could thus be explained by focusing on *why* it became necessary for a group to remember a particular strand of the past. But Halbwachs seems to have at least partially broken from Durkheim's functionalism by noting that there were important strands of memory that remained or emerged often *in spite of* a given context; that memory could sometimes be afunctional or work outside of collective imperatives or collective desires. In other words, there was something about collective memory that imbued it with power beyond its mere social function.

But one troublesome aspect of Halbwachs' approach is how he seems to merely 'scale up' from individual to collective memory. In doing so, he sublimates intra-group dynamics of memory by assuming that the collective is merely a larger representation of the individual. This leads to criticism that Halbwachs assumed an unproblematic 'group mind', in the sense of Gustave le Bon's infamous crowd hypothesis (1895/2009). While Halbwachs should not be accused of erasing the individual – "Halbwachs reminds us that it is only individuals who remember, even if they do much of this remembering together" (Olick, 1999, p. 335), – the more cogent criticism is rooted in Halbwachs' Durkheimian orientation in treating collectives as relatively cohesive aggregates (Wilson, 2005). Indeed this Durkheimian orientation is directly belied by the fact that some of the most fascinating contemporary studies of memory have looked at within-group dynamics, revealing dynamic and contested within-group memory-space (for example, Alderman, 2003, 2010; Conway, 2010; Doss, 2010; Burk, 2006; Till, 2005).

Largely for this reason, the time has come to abandon Halbwachs' term 'collective memory'. A cursory survey of the literature suggests I am late to the party. As far back as 1998, Olick and Robbins wrote: "Critics who charge that 'collective memory' over-totalises prefer a proliferation of more specific terms … official memory, vernacular memory, cultural memory, etc." (Olick & Robbins, 1998, p. 112). Of those terms, I argue that only *social* memory adequately refutes totalisation. For example, Marita Sturken (1997) uses the term 'cultural memory' (as indeed do other giants in the field such as Jan Assman (2005 (1992), Marianne Hirsch and Valerie Smith (2002), and Mieke Bal (1999)). Sturken defines cultural memory as "memory that is shared outside the avenues of formal historical discourse yet is entangled with cultural products and imbued with cultural meaning" (Sturken, 1997, p. 3). However, cultural, like collective, is also a potentially totalising adjective, and in employing it, scholars run the risk of making the same error as Halbwachs, as viewing cultural memory (the output) as something somehow distinct or superordinate to the intra-group cultural dynamics and contestations that are as much memory as any 'finished' product. Sturken's brilliant work makes a compelling case for considering the modern United States as a diffuse cultural community rooted in notions of 'Americanness', but I do not necessarily agree. The election in 2016 of Donald J Trump as president I think reveals a far more fractious 'America', one that is becoming increasingly unmoored from intersubjectively understood cultural signs and signifiers. While Sturken was writing in 1997, it would seem that Trump also belies her argument that cultural memory reveals "the demand for a less monolithic, more inclusive image of America" (Sturken, 1997, p. 13). Her error comes in putting the cart before the proverbial horse. Assuming cultural memory exists, even in a loose form, prioritises the finished product (cultural memory) that is always unfinished, never settled, always contested. Social memory in turn is a reorientation back towards the social processes over the social products, where one can see the politics of inscription at work. Indeed, Sturken's work is highly attuned to this. If the question is how cultural forms, symbols, and webs of meaning mediate and shape the possibilities of social memory, that is one thing (we might even call it sociocultural memory studies), but scholars must be cautious not to reify Halbwachian totalities and implicitly view memory as a cultural output; memory and culture are co-constitutive and always in a process of becoming.

An approach that makes a similar totalising error is the instrumentalist school of memory, arguably inaugurated by Eric Hobsbawm and Terence Ranger (2012) in one of the most cited books in the history of nationalism and memory studies. Misztal (2003, pp. 56–61) refers to their approach as *presentist*, but I disagree with this characterisation and argue that all major contemporary approaches to social memory studies accept the fundamental Halbwachian/Freudian notion that the manifestation of memories of the past is shaped in some way by presentist concerns. However, Hobsbawm and Ranger's approach is very clear as to the *how* of memory in the present; for them, group histories and memories are created and imposed by the state and by political and cultural elites in the service of consolidating power over the dominated classes. Again, we see the primacy of product over process; the traditions 'invented' by national elites operate in a particular way, to enforce national cultural cohesion, and the processual agency of those involved in their creation is written out of the analysis or confined merely to quasi-Marxist theories of dominance. Those who have tradition imposed on them are similarly robbed of agency, and treated as the unwitting dupes of elite machination.

The 'popular memory' approach promises a needed correction to the instrumentalist telling. The popular memory approach stems ultimately from the work of Michel Foucault (1977), but is also founded on an important criticism of Foucault and brings in the work of Antonio Gramsci (1971). Foucault coined the term 'popular memory' to describe the memory-work of those at the bottom – the dominated, those lacking the ability to construct dominant history. Contra to the instrumentalist approach, Foucault did not write out the agency of dominated peoples, viewing them as creating 'counter-memories' that provided space to resist the imposition of dominating discourses. But, as is perhaps common to much of Foucault's work, he was strikingly pessimistic about the potential of 'popular memory' to provide adequate resistance over the long term to dominant social imaginaries (Misztal, 2003, pp. 62–63). Popular memory theorists (see Dawson 2007; Ashplant, Dawson & Roper, 2006; Thomson, 1994; Passerini, 1987; Popular Memory Group, 1982) sought to correct Foucault's pessimism with a reading of counter-memories or resistant memories based more on a reading of Gramsci, and to also correct Foucault's tendency to see popular memory as unproblematically uniform (Misztal, 2003, pp. 62–63).

For the popular memory theorists, dominant and dominated memories are inexorably fused together in a complex interplay of power and resistance. In other words, they go together, and they need to be studied together; power and resistance are part of the same structure and mutually constitutive, very much in line with Gramsci's theories of hegemony and counter-hegemony. Dominated memories must reference and react to dominating frames for their very intelligibility, and in some cases, for example the Bolshevik Revolution, dominated memory can become dominant, though, most importantly, new-Soviet memories also appropriated and reinterpreted the signs, symbols, and forms of feudal power and Orthodoxy (Haskins, 2011; Yurchak, 2005; Jowitt, 1992). What the popular memory school does so skilfully is to marry the local and the institutional units of analysis, arguing that the contexts, intentions, and temporalities of individual *rememberers* cannot be disappeared into a nexus of theory and large-scale social processes. Yet, at the same, time, the popular memory school notes that large-scale social processes provide the boundaries of the remember-*able*.

They are also attuned to memory processes over memory products. For theorists such as Ashplant, Dawson, and Roper (2006, p. 37), the struggle to inscribe a site of memory is contained in what they refer to as the "micro-politics of the aesthetic form". This is similar to my approach in this book, but I shall subtly depart from the popular memory school in two ways. First, we need to bring geography into this analysis. The politics of inscription that play out at a given 'site of memory' are themselves processes conditioned not merely by institutional configurations, but are also concatenations of stories circulating and crystallising in public space. Memory studies must be liberated from the site approach, an approach that sees statues, parks, and war memorials as bounded sites of hegemonic contestation (see Till, 2006). While the commemorative site is certainly *one arena* where a form of the politics of inscription can be observed, thinking instead of 'places of memory' allows us to bring in other forms of politics, spatial alterations, transgressions, and accretions, and to see place-memory not as *topographical* (i.e. cemented into the site) but as *topological* (inherently fluid, capable of movement, stretching, disappearing and reappearing, etc.). Second, the Gramscian frameworks coupled with the site approach too quickly write subaltern voices of out of public memory dialectics. If the commemorative site is a process and product of hegemonic and counter-hegemonic contestation, then studying subalternity (the condition of being denied access to *both* hegemonic and counter-hegemonic narrative) can reveal how the memory of the subaltern is eclipsed and shouldered out by the commemorative site. A site-based approach in Northern Ireland is especially misguided, I argue, because so many of those killed and wounded during the Troubles lack access to *both* socially dominant forms of power *and* resistance, and counter-hegemonic space is often actively and ironically monopolised by a form of social memory whose boundaries are policed by former paramilitary groups. Being attuned to subaltern memories in Northern Ireland, I believe, shows an important limitation of analyses of memory focused on both the site and Gramscian dualities. First, what happens when the site of memory is monopolised, not just by the state (as in authoritarian/totalitarian regimes), but by sub-state actors enjoying near-total freedom do so in *their* geographical areas because of the 'memorial agnosticism' (Switzer & Graham, 2009) of the state and its enforcement agents? Where does memory go? What happens to the subaltern?

Four traditions

Barry Schwartz (1996) provides a helpful genealogic biography of the social memory studies after Halbwachs, which in turn is expanded by Olick & Robbins (1998). These scholars argue that interest in Halbwachs and the concept of social memory was rekindled in the latter half of the twentieth century by three major scholarly trends, which they name multiculturalism, postmodernism, and hegemony (Schwartz 1996, pp. 277–278), the latter category conflating what I have called instrumentalism and the popular memory school. While there are obviously significant disagreements between instrumentalists and popular memory theorists about the role and potential of counter-memory/counter-hegemony, having called attention to this above, I believe I can safely leave Schwartz's category intact as both see the production of social memory as the "contested product of differently empowered communities" (Schwartz 1996, p. 278). To my shorter reflections on these three traditions, however, I add a lengthy discussion of what I believe should be viewed as a tradition its own right, the post-Auschwitz corpus of literature regarding *traumatic memory*.

Briefly, the multiculturalist turn was spurred by often decolonial or postcolonial scholars who challenged dominant historiographies by pointing out the marginalisation and historical silencing of colonised cultures and ethnicities (Trouillot, 1997; Taylor, 1994; Kaye, 1991). By employing Halbwachs, Foucault, and others, they hoped to use colonised memories and traditions to challenge the legacy of the colonial project and usher in a new, postcolonial world rooted in the 'politics of recognition' (see Taylor, 1994). Many multiculturalists were critical historians who sought to rehistoricise colonised peoples by excavating their historical memories, narratives, and traditions. They were joined by feminist scholars (Hirsch & Smith 2002; hooks 1989, 1990) who pointed out a similar dehistoricising silencing of women's lives, narratives, and bodies.

The postmodernist tradition of memory studies also owes something to Foucault, but perhaps more to Adorno, Benjamin, and Lyotard. For Benjamin especially, studying memory is studying aesthetic fragmentation and historical 'traces', the *left behind* when macro-historical narratives are deconstructed or found lacking. For Benjamin (1992), history and memory are layers of sedimentation lying across the social landscape that can be excavated; the historian is more archaeologist constructing stories out of trace material, out of fragments of fossils in a space that has no fixed temporal topology, no inherently stable relationship with its surrounding lifeworlds. For Benjamin, the connection between the past and the present is not a temporal one but an interpretive aesthetic, an image, not a chronology. With Lyotard (1984), the postmodernist turn points out the fundamental unreliability of representation *generally*, and exposes the instability of histories and narratives that are taken to be timeless or at the very least, relatively stable. Many share a perspective like Andreas Huyssen's, that social memory has become a means of resistance:[5]

> Our obsession with memory functions as a reaction formation against the accelerating technical processes that are transforming our *Lebenswelt* (lifeworld) in quite distinct ways ... [Memory] rather represents the attempt ... to claim some anchoring space in a world of puzzling and often threatening heterogeneity, non-synchronicity, and information overload.
>
> (Huyssen, 1994, p. 7)

Having briefly discussed the popular memory tradition, here it may be important to provide a criticism of instrumentalism. For instrumentalists like Hobsbawm and Ranger (2012), social memory in the form of 'tradition' is grafted onto a given society by political and cultural elites interested in protecting and preserving

5 Compare Nora (1989).

existing arrangements of capital and control. Hobsbawm and Ranger's essays expose how national myths and cultural traditions are constructed and implemented over time to promote a false sense of national or cultural unity in the dominated classes. For Marxists, this should be readily familiar as 'false consciousness'; for quasi-Marxists like Pierre Bourdieu (1994), dominant history and hegemonic social memory are symbolic and linguistic productions that create the boundaries of the socially imaginable.

But instrumentalism in general has major internal problems. Because instrumentalists focus so much on elite machinations, they cannot fully explain Benedict Anderson's (1991) timeless question: why are men willing to kill and die in the name of the nation? They do not adequately interrogate how and why the dominant classes accept, incorporate, adapt, modify, and/or resist elite impositions of memory, history, culture, or tradition (Forest, Johnson, & Till, 2004; Winter, 1995). They also inadequately conceptualise power dynamics. As we have seen, the Gramscian power dynamics present in the popular memory school understand power and resistance as being locked in a complex, multidirectional interplay, each influencing one another and operating within mutually negotiated fora (see Hoare and Smith's introduction to Gramsci (1971)). Foucault's work on power has also exposed major flaws in instrumentalism. For Foucault, power is not centralised but dispersed, and not unidirectional but circular and relational. Relationships of power incubate at multiple nodes in any given social organisation. Foucault focuses on sites of 'discipline' that in turn produce 'knowledge' over the human subject. Both the hegemonic and the power/knowledge perspectives allow scholars to break from a simplistic notion of powerful elites dictating acceptable frames of memory to an oppressed, lower-class majority (who may or may not know they are oppressed), and opens the analysis up to questions of how layers of complicity, denial, textual and symbolic authority, grieving, and justice-seeking can influence the processes of contested social memories.

Social memory, and its role in creating larger social imaginaries and landscapes, is far too complex to be reduced to simplistic dichotomies and subjected to narrow understandings of power and control. Doing so blinds scholars to the multiple claimants of memories and the multiple places of memories that they may operate from. It blinds scholars to the diversity of memory curators' motivations, intentions, and practices in presenting memory for public encounter. We need an understanding of memory that is attuned to the continually unfolding nature of memory, to Benjamin's layers of sediment, and to memory's temporal and spatial unpredictability and instability. We need an understanding of memory that can speak to the social pressures and resistances that often spring up around attempts to delineate a controlling or domesticating narrative of past violence. We need to better understand memory's role in the production of space and identity.

In the following section, I discuss another scholarly trend that should be added to Schwartz's typology: the post-Auschwitz explosion of trauma studies, especially of 'traumatic memory'.

The memory of the offence

Sarah Kofman eloquently argues:

> About Auschwitz and after Auschwitz, no story is possible, if by a story one means: to tell a story of events that make sense ... There remains, nonetheless, a duty to speak, to speak endlessly for those who could not speak because to the very end they wanted to guard true speech from betrayal. To speak in order to bear witness. But how?
>
> (Kofman, 1998; cited in Edkins, 2003, p. 43)

Thomas Mann also explored similar themes in his novel *Dr Faustus* (1947/1999). In it, the devil describes hell as a place where horrible things happen that stretch beyond the confines of human imagination, everything "that you verily cannot do to a soul". But Mann's hell is not the torture itself, rather the fact that the torture occurs "in the soundless cellar, far beneath God's hearing". Hell is not the suffering itself but the lack of language or the lack of audience with which to communicate the traumatising experience. It is the terrorising voice of Marcelo Vignar's oft-cited torturer: "Go ahead, scream ... Nobody can hear you, nobody would dare hear you, nobody cares about you, nobody will ever know" (in Weschler, 1995, p. 495).

In the aftermath of widespread traumatic violence, war, genocide, ethnic cleansing, or mass atrocities, the scale and intensity of the suffering for both individuals and societies is bewildering. Kofman and Mann both harrowingly describe how the magnitude of such suffering outstrips the human capacity for both language and symbolic representation. Torture is ***beyond metaphor*** (see Caruth, 1996; Scarry, 1985; Kristeva, 1982). Yet never has providing a representation of the torturous experience seemed more imperative; even though the 'memory of the offence' cannot be articulated, there is a duty to bear witness, to speak of the unspeakable, and to acknowledge the experience of both the traumatised survivor (the 'saved', in Primo Levi's terms) and the murdered body (the 'drowned') (Levi, 1989). Scholars, therapists, and practitioners must all recognise that survivors of traumatic violence will never fully escape the past; they are bound to the experience of shocking violence. Writes Jean Amery (1998, p. 94): "Every morning when I wake up ... I can read the Auschwitz number of my forearm ... Every day anew I lose my trust in the world".

But for all of us, those who have experienced such trauma and those who have not, pain – one of the most basic human emotions – resists or overwhelms available forms of communication. This is one of the most central themes of the work of the Nobel Prize-winning South African author J. M. Coetzee, especially the novels *The Life and Times of Michael K* (1983) and *Disgrace* (1999). Coetzee routinely places his protagonists in spaces of such extremity that they lose the ability to communicate and are forced to turn to other forms, genres, and technologies outside of, or besides language, to attempt some measure of solace or rehabilitation. Writes Elaine Scarry (1985, p. 4): "Physical pain does not simply resist language but actively destroys it." Scarry is perhaps foremost in a psychoanalytic tradition that calls attention to the traumatic destruction of representation through torture (see also Caruth, 1996; Felman & Laub, 1992). Writes Dori Laub (1992, p. 69):

> The trauma is thus an event that has no beginning, no ending, no before, no during, and no after. This absence of categories that define it lends it a quality of 'otherness', a salience, a timelessness, and a ubiquity that puts it outside of the range of associatively linked experiences, outside of the range of comprehension, or recounting, and of mastery.

While Scarry (1985, pp. 11–19) clearly notes the political implications of pain's inexpressibility, other scholars point out that the construal of pain-as-inexpressible may be at best overstated, and at worst colonising. Because pain is conceived as inexpressible, the compulsion to eliminate pain often moves the third party to speak on behalf of those who are (or who are understood to be) in pain. But in doing so, the third party colonises the body that (supposedly) can no longer speak, or appropriates their voice to speak for them (Bennett, 2005). A complex criticism of Scarry, Felman, Laub, and Caruth can be found in Bennett (2005) and LaCapra (1998, 2001). For these two theorists, the construction of pain as inexpressible is a colonising construct, which ironically implicates the scholar or the activist in the processes they criticise. Writes Harry West in a devastating criticism of inexpressibility:

> The contradiction in this is readily apparent, of course, for *I* know of these things only because I was *told* them. Knowing then, that there is something communicable in the experiences of these men, I have been left to wonder to whom I might speak of them, and to what ends.
>
> (West, 2003, p. 345, original emphasis)

It is better thus not to think of pain as somehow outside of representation. It is perhaps better to see it as the breakdown of systems of *signification*, not the breakdown of the possibility of *representation*. The old forms, frames, and genres of expressibility prove unreliable in the face of the traumatic experience. That does not mean the survivor is unable to communicate or to express herself; rather, it means that those who have not been traumatised *no longer understand them*. Looking at trauma this way allows us to shift the focus of the analysis from the inability of a trauma survivor to communicate to the inability of a witness to hear. Trauma is a projection into liminality, into a state "betwixt and between all familiar lines of classification" (Turner & Turner, 1978, p. 2). Liminality is a state of disruption, especially of chronological time and linearity. Liminality and the breakdown of signification have profound consequences for survivors. In many societies, there is a fairly rigid understanding of chronological time – the past is past, the present is now – but this is simply not the case for someone who is (re-?)living trauma. The psychotherapeutic frameworks often imposed on the survivor emphasise a similar processual chronology, of moving linearly in time from the traumatic experience to mourning to healing and/or 'closure', and are signposted by widely available (yet often patently unhelpful) nostrums such as 'the stages of grief'. Because the survivor has become, to use Kurt Vonnegut's (1969) magisterial description of trauma, 'un-stuck in time', they are often rendered out of step with their own societies, even their own friends and families.

Thus, what the politics of witnessing demands is that we recognise the traumatised, and that we recognise them by recognising that they are in a liminal state that is not necessarily our own. Slavoj Žižek, building on the theories of Jacques Lacan, describes this space as approximating or approaching the 'Real'. For Žižek, the 'Real' is the total negation of systems of signification, the 'beyond' space where symbol, metaphor, and language have crossed the threshold, and have reached and surpassed their limit. In contrast, humans exist in the realm of social 'phantasy', where our own crude signifying systems shape the contours of the knowable world. But humans 'touch' the Real at the space where our systems of signification break down, where our symbols cease to symbolise. This we might call the 'traumatic Real'. It is not the 'Real' itself, but the place where we catch a horrifying glimpse of it (Žižek 1989,1991). Žižek's difficult, challenging ideas and often perplexing prose make for difficult application and analysis, and I personally remain agnostic on whether Lacanian Real/social phantasy is a helpful dualism. But I do believe that Žižek and other Lacanians have pinpointed something crucial in the study of trauma: that horrifying prospect of the complete breakdown of signification systems and the confrontation with what lies beyond humanity.

When read with Scarry (1985) and Julie Kristeva (1982), I suggest Žižek underscores the fact that the inscription of traumatic memory resists normal cognition; sometimes pain can only be represented and communicated *affectively*, through art, touch, tears, and placemaking. The duty of witnessing thus demands a new politics of inscription, both aesthetic and political. It demands that we excavate the past that has been buried, or is in the process of being buried, buried by silencing discourses and the imposition of amnesia. It demands we identify and face up to the silencing discourses operating within post-conflict or transitional societies. Writes Husanovic (2009, p. 103): "Political trauma uncovers a hidden dimension within the interlocking texture of political community and violence – we are faced with the inherently traumatic dimension of the political which various ideological technologies and disciplines mask, repress, or silence."

I find two major silencing discourses operating in many post-conflict societies, two ways to put survivors 'in their place' (or render them 'out of place', in Cresswell's (1996) formulation), and Northern Ireland is no exception. One such discourse may originate with Freud himself, particularly his dangerous dichotomy of 'mourning' and 'melancholia'. For Freud, there were positive and pathological reactions to trauma, grief, and loss: the former, mourning; the latter, melancholia. Mourning is the staged individual procession through grief, a process by which grief is "overcome after a certain lapse of time, and we look on any interference with it as useless or even harmful" (Freud 1917a/1999, p. 243). In contrast, melancholia is unmediated grief, a grief that cannot let go of the object; that allows loss of the object to become affixed to the identity of the self.[6]

Today it has become common to transmute melancholia-as-pathology into the pathology of 'post-traumatic stress disorder' (PTSD), though to be fair, this would be more common in lay people or armchair psychologists than those better trained. But the blurring of the lines between the two 'pathologies' also has political consequences. To pathologise something, to name it as a disorder, is a silencing technology that often masks the aetiological source of trauma, understates the agency of survivors, and colonises their representative potentialities. As Jenny Edkins argues:

> What the state attempts ... is a normalisation or a medicalisation of survivors ... The aim is recovery, or the reinsertion into structures of power. Survivors are helped to narrate what has happened to them, they receive counselling to help them accommodate once more to the social order and re-form relationships of trust ... If this fails, then the status of victim of post-traumatic stress disorder *serves to render the survivor more or less harmless to existing power structures.* In contemporary culture, victimhood offers sympathy and pity in return for the surrender of any political voice.
>
> (Edkins, 2003, p. 9, emphasis added)

In other words, the traumatised who do not fit into appropriate mechanisms for the progression through grief and pain (or who constantly demand that *trauma be recognised as traumatic!*) can be shouldered out of the politics of inscription, their bodies pathologised and subject to the classificatory mechanisms of authoritative knowledge, such as those found in American Psychological Association's *Diagnostic and Statistical Manual of Mental Disorders* (DSM).

But refusing (or perhaps being unable) to 'get over' trauma is still not necessarily a pathology. Often it is a powerful political statement. Erika Doss, citing Muñoz, points out that melancholia has been "constant, if not central" in the formation of subaltern and oppressed identities and social mobilisations, such as

6 Judith Butler points out that Freud seemed to have changed his mind on what constituted productive responses to loss between 1917, when he published 'Mourning and Melancholia', and 1923, when he published 'The Ego and the Id'. Butler argues he came to see melancholia as an integral process to mourning, so before Freud is criticised for the dichotomy he set up in 1917, it should be noted he altered his thinking (see Butler 2006, pp. 20–21).

African Americans in the United States and the LGBTQ (Doss 2010, p. 81, citing Muñoz, 1997). The continuous performance of public grief, in art, discourse, and placemaking, can constitute acts of political resistance that demand recognition and acknowledgement of traumas, past and ongoing, perpetrated on subaltern or oppressed groups. This argument has been taken up most prominently by Judith Butler, who argues that keeping the trauma alive through the restaging of public grief is potentially politically transformative: "Such mourning could effect a transformation in our sense of international ties that would crucially rearticulate the possibility of democratic political culture here and elsewhere" (Butler, 2006, p. 40; see also Rankine, 2015).

Freud's dichotomy, and its related offshoot of PTSD, creates a duality between 'healthy' and 'unhealthy' forms of grief. But the constant popular replication of this duality fails to appreciate that political trauma is caused by acts perpetrated by an individual, group, or institution, on another individual or group of people. Traumatic reliving certainly is 'real' in the sense that it exists and survivors suffer from it both psychologically and somatically. But unlike a pathology or a mental disorder such as depression or schizophrenia, it is not transmitted through the air or through bodily fluids, it is not a product of genetic predispositions, and it has no relation to our immune systems. Someone inflicted traumatic violence on someone else and pathologising survivors' memories of the offence allows post-conflict societies to elide the aetiological roots of the traumatic experience. For example, take a soldier who has returned home from an active war theatre and is then diagnosed with PTSD. The 'D' implies that it was *contracted* or that the subject was predisposed to it, as if the subject had consumed polluted water or possessed poor neural circuitry beforehand. It conceals the aetiological agent of trauma: the state (usually) sent that human to kill and be killed; the state decided that that human body, and the human bodies it encountered, were less important than an overarching *casus belli*.

In Freud's earlier work he seemed to partially recognise this problematic, but by 1917 he had largely desubjectified the traumatic event(s).[7] In his early explorations on the aetiology of hysteria, Freud argued that what he and his colleagues diagnosed as hysteria was actually the repressed memory of traumatic sexual abuse in early childhood, what he formulated as 'seduction theory' (1896/1999). However, he would subsequently abandon seduction theory in favour of the theory of 'infantile sexuality', which held essentially held that

7 Jeffrey Masson's immensely controversial book (1984) alleges that Freud had deliberately concealed and falsified his research on the aetiology of trauma because he was unable to countenance the ubiquity of traumatic sexual assault in his own Viennese bourgeois society. Judith Herman (1992) takes up this argument as well, but she argues Freud's 'crime' was less of a conscious distortion of the truth than an inability to believe his own evidence, i.e., the testimony of his patients. There is a much longer discussion of this point in Fassin and Rechman (2009, pp. 81–83).

symptoms of hysteria were not screen memories of trauma but childhood sexual fantasies rooted in the unconscious mind, what he referred to as an 'instinctual libido' (Freud 1917b/1999). Thus, what he initially perceived as aetiologically rooted in a traumatic event became aetiologically rooted in the fantastical and the unconscious. The aetiology of trauma thus had no subject; it was instinctual. The social results of Freud's shifting aetiology are brilliantly elucidated by Fassin and Rechman (2009, p. 55):

> From the 1930s onwards, Freud's writings were principal references for official psychiatry on the question of trauma. The dominant psychiatric paradigm has moved far from the idea of the traumatic neurosis caused by a violent event. Trauma had become a concept free from the event in the generic sense of the term ... From Freud's second theory of hysteria, trauma is neither the event itself nor the psychic consequences of the event.

Trauma was thus a guiltless, culpability-free phenomenon. In one sense, this represented a strikingly progressive paradigm shift in the field, as traumatised soldiers, rape and incest victims, or manual labourers injured through unsafe working conditions had long been seen as the aetiological source *of their own trauma*, aetiologies rooted in their own underdeveloped (sexual) characters, their conscious or otherwise malingering, their conscious or otherwise expectation of compensation, which sapped their will to work, serve their country, or care for their family. Freud and his disciples argued that they were no longer to blame for their own trauma, but their analyses were still unable (or refused) to recognise an active agent of traumatic violence. And while the work of Freud and his disciples made trauma an important object of both psychoanalytic and sociological inquiry, their exculpatory aetiology essentially wrote the agents of trauma out of their own societies, histories, and memories, where they would stay until Auschwitz.

The rejoinder of feminist psychoanalysts such as Luce Irigaray (1985) to Freudian-inspired desubjectifications was to read female hysteria as a nascent form of social protest. The symptomatology of hysteria was a somatic performance that challenged the patriarchal structures that hystericised women in the first place (Abdullah, 2016). Hystericised women were thus exerting the only form of control over their bodies that they could in the face of traumatic violence. The performance of hysteria in this reading is a demand to witness and acknowledge the trauma, oppression, and domestication inscribed brutally onto the female body. By fantasising hysteria, by subsuming it into infantile sexual development and the Oedipal complex, Freud failed to recognise hysteria as the attempted reclamation of the body as a political field for inscribing trauma (Grosz, 1994).

If the first silencing technology is the medicalisation or pathologisation of survivors coupled with the desubjectification of traumatic acts, the second technology I wish to discuss is what Hamber and Wilson (2002) term 'symbolic closure'. These scholars use South Africa's Truth and Reconciliation Commission (TRC) as their central case study (see also Brüdholm, 2009). Hamber and Wilson (2002, p. 36) define symbolic closure as the attempt by powerful memory curators "to construct memory as a unified, static, and collective object, not as political practice" (compare Tutu, 1999). These powerful actors aim to construct a consensual memory product that is largely *depolicitised*, a unified, coherent grand narrative of past violence that celebrates 'moving on', 'reconciliation', and 'forgiveness' as the 'correct' way of remembering a violent past. This is tantamount to Brewer's (2010) and Ignatieff's (1993) 'remembering for the future' that I criticised in Chapter 1. But by enacting or attempting to enact symbolic closure, the TRC commissioners led by Archbishop Desmond Tutu created an implicit (and sometimes explicit) dichotomy between the right way of speaking for the dead and the wrong way. Brüdholm (2009) backs up Hamber and Wilson through a rigorous and convincing discourse analysis of the commissioners' rhetoric and public pronouncements, coupled with an analysis of prominent media portrayals of the Commission's work. Teeger and Vinitzky-Seroussi (2007) also make a compelling case that 'consensual memory' in South Africa privileges a particular narrative of the anti-apartheid struggle, and in the process shoulders out other resistant, politicised narratives. Specifically, they argue that consensual memory in South Africa avoids marking the dreadful and instead emphasises hope at every opportunity, it constructs national heroes such as Mandela through which all collective agency is directed, and it is deeply tokenist in the way it accounts for the contributions of other social actors and movements outside of the African National Congress (ANC). While certainly being consensual, Teeger and Vinitzky-Seroussi also describe memory that has been *sanitised*, memory that disinfects apartheid and the anti-apartheid struggle of complex political questions and confines ongoing political repression and injustice firmly to a past era that no longer exists, that has been cleaned up.[8] Those who refuse to (or cannot) forgive their perpetrators are rendered out of step with an imposed memory consensus. The demands of victims and survivors who seek acknowledgement of trauma as traumatic (not to mention justice and reparations) are sacrificed on the altar of political expediency. One such example from South Africa would be the case of the well-known victims and survivors' organisation *Khulumani* (isiZulu for 'speak out'). Write McEvoy and McConnachie (2012, p. 532):

> *Khulumani* was once largely feted by liberation forces in South Africa, yet gradually came to be rejected by the new political elites, in large part because *Khulumani* continued to demand reparations for victims of human rights violations, and in doing so, challenged the dominant (and politically convenient) political discourse that the past had been 'settled' by the Truth and Reconciliation Commission.

8 For a similar argument regarding the United States' (ongoing) history of racial injustice, see Dwyer (2008).

Another example might be the Madres de la Plaza de Mayo in post-junta Argentina (Levey, 2016; Bosco, 2004; Malin, 1994) and the other looser groupings of first- and second-generation survivors and relatives known collectively as *los afectados directos* (the directly affected). *Los afectados* largely refused to accept the Menem government's 'Full Stop' and 'Due Obedience' Laws, which were the post-junta state's legal and symbolic attempt to close their traumatic experience, to confine them to the past and to history. Rather, *los afectados* remained, performing their trauma in public places, exposing alleged perpetrators, marking the places where trauma had occurred, holding pictures of their disappeared loved ones in the face of passers-by, demanding that they be recognised and officially acknowledged. Often tarred as *las viejas locas* (the crazy old women), they stand firmly in the way of attempts to confine their traumatic memories to the past.

Thus, traumatic memory in all of its forms can serve as a powerful and unsettling challenge to the imposition of linear time and the shaping of a domesticating social consensus (Payne, 2008). But it is traumatic social memory performed and represented publicly, not the traumatised memory of broken individuals, that can perform this function. And to become visible and resist, traumatic memory needs to emerge and become visible. It is in this visibility where social and political geography has made its most profound contributions to the study of social memory and I shall attempt to outline these in Chapter 5.

Chapter 3

State of exception

Jo Berry and Patrick Magee

In this chapter I will examine the narratives surrounding Troubles-related violence in Northern Ireland. It is imperative that we establish how belligerent parties[1] to the Troubles justified the taking of life and how they employed and continue to employ dead bodies in the service of political causes, before I can turn towards examining how much of those narratives are retained in post-conflict space and what discursive and aesthetic power they still hold. There is no single macro-narrative that can enclose or encapsulate holistically the perspectives of all belligerent groups or their sympathisers. Like any population, their narratives are diverse and complex; however, I argue that there are a primary set of reference points that can be examined and analysed.

My purpose in analysing these narratives is to outline and delineate how belligerent parties to the Troubles understood and justified the violent taking of life. Only by doing so can I then understand how they have subsequently performed this justification in public and how they have attempted to inscribe these justifications into space. Only through understanding this process of inscription can I begin to analyse how resistance to it might operate. Only by examining the dehumanising legitimations, justifications, and performances of violent memories can the potential power of rehumanising memory be appreciated.

Let me begin with former IRA-man Patrick Magee. Magee was one of a team of IRA operatives who blew up the Grand Hotel in Brighton, England on 12 October 1984. The bomb narrowly missed killing the then-prime minister of the United Kingdom, Margaret Thatcher, and did kill five other people, including Conservative MP Sir Anthony Berry. Thirty-four others were injured, with some left permanently disabled. Magee served 14 years in prison for the bombing and was released under the terms of the 1998 Agreement. Like many imprisoned

1 By belligerent, I simply mean a party to the conflict. Belligerent parties to the Troubles are republican paramilitaries (PIRA, OIRA, INLA, etc.), loyalist paramilitaries (UDA, UVF, LVF, etc.), and the security forces (RUC, British military, and auxiliary forces (USC/UDR/RIR)).

republicans, Magee spent much of his time in prison studying and earned a doctorate from the Open University. The book based on his dissertation, *Gangsters or Guerrillas*, argues that Irish republicanism is disfigured and demonised in popular literature and mainstream media portrayals. It argues that Irish republicans themselves are transformed into archetypes through a representational process that delegitimises and appropriates their voices and narratives in the service of maintaining British colonial power. Describing his work, Magee states: "It struck me that, in terms of genre studies, it's the old archetypal Wild West story all over again. The republicans are the Red Indians, of course; they have no voice, they are not allowed to tell their own story" (cited in Wilson, 2000; see Magee, 2001).

In a BBC documentary from 2001, Magee meets Jo Tuffnell, who has since returned to using her family name, Jo Berry; she is the daughter of Sir Anthony Berry. On camera, Magee informs Berry that: "Brighton, from our perspective, was a justified act. Your father was part of the political elite, the Tory government. In that sense, you know, it's that cruel word, cruel expression, he was a 'legitimate target'." Berry, who uses the opportunity to forgive Magee for killing her father, also states on camera that the way she explains to her daughter the reasons for Sir Anthony Berry's death is "because that was the only way [Magee] felt he could be heard" (Sharrock, 2001).

Since the documentary aired, Berry and Magee have formed a somewhat unlikely partnership. They have made joint appearances around the world speaking on topics such as forgiveness, peace, and reconciliation. However, Magee has not changed his underlying justifications for the Brighton bombing, at least not publicly, and his motivations for their joint work appear to differ from Berry's. He writes:

> I decided to meet Jo because ... I felt obligated as a Republican to explain what led someone like me to participate in the action. I told her that I'd got involved the armed struggle at the age of 19, after witnessing how a small nationalist community were being mistreated by the British.
>
> (The Forgiveness Project, 2010)

Berry's motivations are more difficult to discern; hers seems to be a process of seeking to understand, borne out of the belief that only through understanding the life experiences of men like her father's killer can she use her experience to prevent other lives being violently taken in the future.

Magee advances a two-part justification for the taking of another's life, not just the lives he was directly responsible for, the victims of the Brighton bombing, but also the other victims of IRA violence throughout the Troubles. And Magee is involved in the Forgiveness Project and with Jo Berry for many of the same reasons that he delineates in his book; for him it is imperative that the republican perspective be heard and not silenced or marginalised by British power. In no small part, by talking about his actions publicly, Magee continues the republican struggle by other means. But in doing so, Magee and other republicans are faced with the bodies of those they killed. Republicans and republicanism must construct a narrative that moulds those bodies into a particular form, and that form largely has two parts. The first part is that those human bodies killed by the IRA were unfortunate victims of war, either legitimate targets or unintended and unfortunate collateral damage, and the second part is that the Troubles and the Brighton bombing in particular were necessary acts because they helped ameliorate the oppressed situation of the CNR community in Northern Ireland. In other words, war may be hell, but it works, or perhaps war was the only way to end the oppression against the CNR community in Northern Ireland. In some sense, my own reservations on the analytic viability of these arguments are beside the point. What I want to do in this chapter is to show how these justifications can only be fully understood through the lens of *the state of exception*.

State of exception: dehumanised bodies

My use of the concept 'state of exception' stems from the highly influential work of the Italian political theorist Giorgio Agamben (1998; 2005). Agamben begins from the work of Carl Schmitt, a jurist and political philosopher now closely associated with the Nazi regime, on the concept of sovereignty (Schmitt 1922/1985). For Schmitt, the sovereign is the person or entity with the power to suspend the law, to decide on a given time when the law no longer applies. However, I agree with Thomas Lemke (2005) that Agamben's concept of sovereignty is far too legalistic and his criticism of Foucauldian biopolitics unconvincing (see especially Agamben, 1998, pp. 3–7 and 28–29). This is a far longer and more intricate debate than I wish to enter into here; rather, I will suggest that sovereignty is *more* than simply the power to proclaim the exception. For modern philosophers such as Jürgen Habermas, sovereignty is also the successful ability to legitimise a right-to-rule. That legitimation takes the form of a dialectic between ruler and ruled, a continuous circular transmission of social values, ideologies, and moral communication (Habermas, 1984). This does not, however, require that we abandon the concept. Rather, I suggest we see the state of exception as not merely suspending the law (though certainly often that), but also suspending the very normative underpinnings of the political order and being able to successfully alter the contours of that legitimating dialectic.

For Agamben, sovereign power (now reconceptualised as the power to both alter the dialectic of legitimation and suspend the law) asserts itself during a time of real or supposed political crisis. I say 'real or supposed' because the construction of a state of political crisis must be narrated into existence, it must be proclaimed and justified in readily intelligible languages and genres, and it must be accepted by a significant enough section of a population at whom the narrative is aimed to have effect. One might be reminded of the anti-war slogan popular in the United States during the Vietnam War: "What if they declared a war and nobody came?" A crisis state that would justify mobilisation to war on terms contained within its internal logic can be proclaimed by a political entity, but if that entity has no real capacity to influence a relevant citizenry to accept its narration of crisis, then the proclamation has no actionable authority – at least, no authority beyond bare force and coercion. This is the essence of the crisis dialectic. Agamben (2005) argues that an accepted crisis state creates the political space for the state of exception and that exception is not as simple as the unilateral suspension of law by the sovereign. Rather, it is an acceptance by the population that old norms no longer apply *because* of the constructed crisis. In such a crisis state, the state of exception renders previously objectionable political acts and decisions justifiable, but only as a response to the crisis itself and only because they have been deemed 'necessary' by sovereign power (and largely accepted as 'necessary' by the citizenry) to alleviate the crisis. But again, necessity is constructed and subjective: "Far from occurring as an objective given, necessity clearly entails a subjective judgment, and obviously the only circumstances that are necessary and objective are those declared to be so" (Agamben, 2005, p. 30).

Agamben's work is also concerned with the modern state's capacity to prolong indefinitely a supposedly temporary response to crisis. He argues that the modern Western state has proclaimed a supposedly temporary state of exception in response to the 'Global War on Terror' that is fast transmuting itself into a *permanent state of existence.* "The instruments of government depicted here as temporary 'crisis' arrangements have in some countries, and may eventually in many countries, become lasting peacetime institutions" (Agamben, 2005, p. 9). This is, for Agamben, an eerie and disturbing parallel to Schmitt's philosophy and its incorporation into the Nazi regime's legitimating ideology. Hitler's Germany was able to successfully proclaim a state of exception in response to an existential threat to German identity, society, and *Lebensraum* ('living space') from international socialism, world Jewry, and German defeatism. The proclamation of crisis-as-existential-threat in turn was accepted and refracted by the German population and horribly altered the moral boundaries of what actions were possible, justifiable, or necessary because of the constructed crisis. Thus, the Holocaust, and the deafening silence of 'ordinary' Germans cannot be explained wholly by anti-Semitism or a penchant towards obedience to political authority; rather, it is only explainable in that space where exception expands from a temporary suspension of laws and norms into a permanent state of existence.[2]

The state of exception rests firmly on two central paradoxes. The first is a temporal paradox; the state of exception is simultaneously temporary and indefinite.

2 There is an old and somewhat tired debate on why most Germans displaced, ignored, or passively accepted the mass exterminations of the Holocaust. For those interested, it probably begins with Christopher Browning's important book *Ordinary Men* (1992), which in turn inspired Daniel Goldhagen's (1996) misguided and polemical reaction to it.

For example, thus US detention facility at Guantánamo Bay, Cuba, exists in a state of legal indistinction, a black (or at least 'grey') site where neither US nor international law wholly applies. Guantánamo Bay was repopulated by the administration of George W. Bush and the passage of the USA Patriot Act in response to the terrorist attacks of 11 September 2001 on New York and Washington. The existence of Guantánamo Bay is obviously not in accordance with US laws, norms, or even the moral ethos of the vast majority of Americans (including, supposedly, the 8-year administration of Barack Obama), but because the United States is waging a 'war on terror', a significant enough portion of the US citizenry and government can narrate Guantánamo Bay as a 'necessary evil'. Presumably, this necessary evil would cease to be necessary after the Global War on Terror is over, but the Global War on Terror has been constructed in such a way as to have no ending (Butler, 2006). Thus, Guantánamo becomes both a temporary response to crisis and a permanent state of exception. Judith Butler also notes how the state of exception has become more diffuse. No longer is the state of exception implemented by a unitary sovereign; the modern state now seems to have multiple, overlapping sovereigns all with the power to suspend the law in response to their particular readings of government instructions and decrees (both secret and public). "The future becomes a lawless future, not anarchical, but given over to the discretionary decisions of a set of designated sovereigns ... who are beholden to nothing and no one except the performative power of their own decisions" (Butler, 2006, p. 65).

Jenny Edkins (2003) also provides an excellent reading of Agamben. As she notes, the sovereign exists both within and without a juridical order, within because it is produced by that order, but without because it has the power to suspend the order that created it. This for Agamben is the 'zone of indistinction', the temporal space where the state of exception can jump the borders of exception and subsequently stretch the boundaries of legality to reconstitute the order as inclusive of the transgression – to reconstitute transgression as the new normal:

> What happened in the 20th century in the west was the state of exception transgressed its borders and started to coincide with the normal order. The zone of indistinction expanded from a space of exclusion within the normal order to take over that order entirely.
>
> (Edkins, 2003, pp. 180–182)

Indistinction, in other words, is when we no longer know what is exception and what is not. The line has become inexorably blurred.

Permanence is perhaps achieved when the excepted population accepts the new order to such an extent that it normalises it and places extraordinary actors such as internment without trial and indefinite detention beyond the realm of cognitive reflection. They become 'just the way it is' (doxa) and the reasons for their creation and continued existence are no longer critically discussed or interrogated. The constructed reality trumps the former underpinnings of the legitimating dialectic rooted in the moral ethos of the Western, liberal, late-capitalist order, and thus (here is the second central paradox), *exception suspends our rights, norms, and laws in the name of protecting them.*

Bodies within the state of exception are at constant risk of having their rights as juridical subjects suspended; they are at risk of being reduced to what Agamben calls 'bare life', represented in his work by an archaic Roman legal concept known as *homo sacer.* Bare life might be better understood as "life and nothing but" (Comaroff & Comaroff, 2016, p. 182). The life of the body is understood to be valuable in the abstract, but the actual human possessing the life is a mere afterthought. *Homo sacer* was the man *banned* from enjoying the rights of citizens in the polity, including the right to life; he could be killed by anyone, *but only if his killing didn't matter*, only if his death was not the larger purpose of killing him. Thus, when we speak of life and nothing but in the state of exception, we understand that the killings of those trapped within exception are predictable, but paradoxically unavoidable, because of the larger political context. Political murders or 'unintended killings' outside of the state of exception are extraordinary, but at the zone of indistinction they become something between extraordinary and normal; they become 'regrettable' or 'unfortunate', but no less legitimate, no less inevitable. *Homo sacer* becomes a particular type of 'collateral damage', and like other forms of collateral damage, the victim should not have been targeted. But as Zygmunt Bauman (2013, p. 25) writes: "Indeed, he need not be guilty of hostile deeds or intentions; it is sufficient that he is the 'other', the stranger, something different and alien."

The preceding argument has a crucial caveat: there are times when the body is conflated with the threat itself. The non-Aryan body *was* the threat to German *Lebensraum*, purity, and pre-ordained political rights to rule. As such, the genocide of the Jews and other suspect races (*Untermenschen)* was not collateral damage but ideational and programmatic. Eliminating the body of the *Untermensch* was ideationally indistinct from ameliorating the constructed threat; thus the Holocaust went part and parcel with the state of exception. The end of the crisis could only occur when the *Untermenschen* were eliminated. In Northern Ireland, many hard-line loyalists also conflated the Catholic body with the threat, making it acceptable and legitimate to kill Catholics regardless of their status. This ideology was the source of the infamous slogan 'any Taig'll do', or as Gusty Spence described it: "The attitude was that if you couldn't get an IRA man, you shoot a Taig, he's your last resort" (in Dillon 1999, pp. 20–23). For republicans, as we shall shortly see, in official republican ideology the Protestant body did not constitute an existential threat and thus could not be legitimately targeted.[3] But because for many republicans unionism and the British state (the official source

3 This was not always true. Republican paramilitaries occasionally carried out purely and openly sectarian murders, such as the Kingsmills Massacre (see Chapter 5).

of the threat) were mutually constitutive, dead Protestants may not have been a cause for great concern. Writes Agamben (2005, p. 2):

> Modern totalitarianism can be defined as the establishment, by means of the state of exception, of a legal civil war that allows for the physical elimination not only of political adversaries but of entire categories of citizens who for some reason cannot be integrated into the political system. Since then, the voluntary creation of a permanent state of emergency (though perhaps not declared in the technical sense) has become one of the essential practices of contemporary states, including so-called democratic ones.

Thus, the state of exception is an institutional fiction with the power of performative reality that facilitates the suspension of the citizenship and humanity of a political subject in response to a constructed state of political crisis. In the state of exception, subject bodies can be stripped down to bare life and killed, imprisoned, or debased with impunity, but only if the bodies' debasement is *not the sum total of the meaning of the act*, that is to say, if debasement is an afterthought in a larger political context or in larger political concerns. But, as Agamben, Butler, and Edkins all show, the state of exception is only real if political subjects accept and internalise its reality (or refuse to acknowledge that is being wielded on 'others'). To demonstrate the immorality or the fiction of the state of exception is to deny it its reproductive power; to rehumanise a body is to deny that it was ever completely stripped bare.

I argue that focusing an analytical lens on the state of exception and the legitimating crisis dialectic helps to explain how and why belligerents, their sympathisers, and their 'host' populations justified the suspension of rights characteristic of the idealised political and social systems they purported to produce (republicans) or protect (loyalists, security forces) through war and violence. The incoherence between the supposed 'justice' of their causes and the violent, indiscriminate means they sought to achieve that justice can only be narrated through the lens of the state of exception.

Republican state of exception

> Foremost in my tortured mind is the thought that there can never be peace in Ireland until the foreign, oppressive British presence is removed, leaving all the Irish people as a unit to control their own affairs and determine their own destinies as a sovereign people, free in mind and body, separate and distinct physically, culturally, and economically … It is then that we'll have the rising of the moon.
>
> (Bobby Sands, 1981, n.p.)

For Patrick Magee and other members of the IRA, the Troubles were a state of exception because of the political crisis engendered by the ongoing British presence on the island of Ireland. The basic outlines of a republican historiography are widely understood and need only cursory mention here. The history of Ireland is largely presented as a colonial conflict between British colonisers and the native resistance, flaring up into bloodshed at punctuated moments throughout the chronology. Like all nationalist historiography, certain dates are emphasised and certain dates glossed over. Lowenthal's (1985) famous remonstration that 'the past is a foreign country' is largely forgotten and at least partially anachronistic history is cut to fit a modern narrative. The republican narrative is both revivalist and tragic. "To help forge a respectable national identity in the face of English suzerainty, the episodes, symbols, and styles of a distinctly Irish past were rediscovered and deployed in every aspect of life" (Lowenthal, 1985, p. 333). Irish revivalism couples with what Volkan (1997) calls 'chosen traumas', or those aspects of the imagined community's group victimisation that could be selected out of history and used to affix continuity between oppression in the past and oppression in the present. In short, republican history rediscovers an Irish nation 'kept down' by the oppressive institution of colonialism, with its idealised (and inevitable) future being a united 32-county Irish state ruled by a populist, moral, socially just economic regime of some sort, one largely presented in opposition to rapacious British and 'Free State' capitalism.

But here lies a puzzle: as I described in the introductory chapter, the republican historiography has been present in Ireland (and indeed around the world with the Irish diaspora) certainly since at least the birth of modern republicanism and the founding of Sinn Féin at the beginning of the twentieth century. Yet since the end of the Irish Civil War in 1923 and the tacit acceptance of the Partition of Ireland symbolised by De Valera's split from Sinn Féin in 1926, only the (Provisional) IRA campaign of 1969–1998 engendered the requisite CNR mobilisation and tacit/active community support necessary to carry on a sustained violent campaign. It was only the emergence of a tangible and visceral crisis that was deeply intelligible to the host community that legitimised the republican proclamation of the state of exception and provided the space for the Provisional IRA campaign to become what it became.

I have discussed briefly the history of the civil rights movement and its violent repression in the late 1960s and early 1970s. The introduction of internment in 1971, the Ballymurphy Massacre of that same year, and the Bloody Sunday Massacre of 1972, to say nothing of the intense street-to-street violence and serial displacement occurring in Belfast, was how the republican state of exception was finally rendered deeply intelligible to a significant enough section of the CNR populace in Northern Ireland. The republican declaration can be found written in the dried blood of Belfast's Whiterock Road or Derry's Rossville Street, where Catholics were callously gunned down by British paratroopers. It can be found in internment, the mass arrest and incarceration of 1,981 Northern Irish people, the vast majority Catholic, without a trial or any semblance of due process (number taken from Coogan, 2000). It can be found in the Widgery Tribunal, which proved to many Catholics in Northern Ireland that the British were prepared to gun down their own citizens (in this case unarmed civil rights protesters) in broad daylight, blame those murdered for their own deaths, lie about it, and publicly absolve and lionise their military murderers.

As we can see from sources such as Sands' diary, in the republican narrative this existential crisis can only be achieved by driving the British out of Ireland. What changed after April 1998 was merely the best means to achieve a British-free Ireland. Mainstream republicanism, shepherded by what some scholars have called Gerry Adams' long-term peace agenda or strategy (see Moloney, 2002; McGovern & Shirlow, 1998), now argues that the most appropriate means to achieve its political goals and Irish reunification is through non-violence. Argues Adams (2005):

> For over 30 years, the IRA showed that the British government could not rule Ireland on its own terms. You asserted the legitimacy of the right of the people of this island to freedom and independence. Many of your comrades paid the ultimate sacrifice. The struggle can now be taken forward by other means ... In the past I have defended the right of the IRA to engage in armed struggle. I did so because there was no alternative for those who would not bend the knee ... Now there is an alternative.

Both the IRA and Sinn Féin conceptualised themselves throughout the Troubles as the legitimate voice of an aggrieved political community. And while republicanism variously and with varying degrees of success utilised the discourses of economic justice, human rights, and political pluralism, it must be stressed that republicanism was and still is primarily a communitarian project (Bean, 2007; Murray & Tonge, 2005; McGovern, 2000). Sinn Féin claimed and still claims to speak for the community that considers itself Irish – not British and not Northern Irish – and it was this Irish community that was under existential threat by the ongoing British presence in Ireland. At the national scale, republicanism speaks as the politically legitimate voice of the island of Ireland, democratically legitimated, according to them, by the only all-island democratic election, the 1918 election to the 'First Dáil', won overwhelmingly by Sinn Féin. At the local level in Northern Ireland, republicanism defines, defends, and delineates the boundaries of a particular cultural identity, in this case an Irish identity artificially severed (through Partition) from its natural political community; a colonial vestige in a largely decolonised world. To mark its territory, republicanism utilises charged symbols and referents such as the Tricolour, the Irish language, illustrations of British atrocities, past and ongoing, interspersed with illustrations of republican glories, also past and ongoing. In doing so, it creates ethnic sanctuary spaces, generally personified discursively in feminine terms, and 'eulogised' in the service of violent protectionism (Cunningham & Gregory, 2014). These republican eulogised territories were intense loci of violence during the Troubles, from both internal and external sources. Internally, they were the subject of brutal policing by the IRA or the INLA, and externally they were the subject of loyalist murder campaigns, police and army searches, harassment, arrest, internment, and killing. As 'Patrick' describes growing up in such a sanctuary area:

> There's not a street in [this community] that hasn't seen somebody murdered or some aspect of armed conflict. There was [slightly more than 7 per cent] of this community imprisoned in a population of [...]. That's every family. So never has been so much given.

Republicanism during the Troubles operated under the legitimating ideology of the 'just war' paradigm (Walzer, 1977). It maintained that its violence was fundamentally defensive, a response to acts of aggression by the British state and loyalist paramilitaries, and rooted in defending CNR communities from pogroms and state atrocities (Shanahan, 2009). But crucially, the threat to CNR communities could never be alleviated until the British presence in Ireland was removed. Thus for republicanism, its state of exception was clearly subject to the temporal paradox of exception. Subject bodies were subordinated to the goal of victory over the British, and to achieve such a victory, Northern Ireland also had to be cleansed of the pollution of British dependence (Sinn Féin translates as 'We, ourselves' or 'Ourselves alone'). Working-class unionism and loyalism, in the republican perspective, have to be explained as false consciousness, as an inauthentic attachment that could conceivably one day be cured, and not as a legitimate expression of political ideals or national belonging.

For the IRA, legitimate targets were not only the active agents of colonial oppression (the British political apparatus, the military and its auxiliaries, the police, loyalist paramilitaries), they were also civilians who 'colluded' with the British by informing. However, what is crucial to point out here is that none of the categories listed above contain individual faces or perspectives; all contained within them are reduced to the sum total of their political/organisational status. We didn't shoot people, we shot the uniform, goes a common republican refrain. For Patrick Magee, Sir Anthony Berry may have been someone's beloved father, but that interpretation of Berry's body was not relevant, and indeed counterproductive, to the alleviation of the existential crisis; only his status as an agent of the British state mattered. Thus, Magee may genuinely feel that Berry's death was unfortunate even though it was legitimate; but it also seems clear that Magee, given a similar opportunity and a similar context, would plant the bomb again. The Brighton bombing, in the republican narrative, was a successful military action in the war against British colonialism. Sir Anthony Berry was an agent of colonial oppression; he was denied the right to be anything more complex than that. This is dehumanisation par excellence. Berry is stripped down to bare life; he can be killed with moral impunity. Dehumanisation is the most important narrative and ideational component of the maintenance and reproduction of the state of exception. It is the lynchpin on which it turns. There is no possibility of exception if collectively we are able to see the bodies trapped within exception as complex humans first.

But even within a widely accepted and socially internalised proclamation of crisis, the state of exception may leave cracks and traces. This can be illustrated by examining two acts of republican violence that generated widespread anger from *within* the communities and individuals who were otherwise at least partially sympathetic to the republican campaign. My purpose here is twofold. On one hand, I want to show just how far the legitimating narratives can be stretched when the threat is more perceptibly acute; but on the other, I want to illustrate how the state of exception is never absolute – it can break down and rehumanisation can creep back in, even in the most polarised and terrifying of contexts.

On 24 October 1990 armed gunmen burst into the Shantallow home of Patsy Gillespie, on the outskirts of Derry. While his wife Kathleen and his three children were held captive at gunpoint, Gillespie was shackled to the driver's seat of his van and forced to drive a massive bomb to the British military base at Coshquin on the nearby border with the Republic of Ireland. The bomb was triggered remotely by an IRA operative and before the soldiers could extricate Gillespie from the death trap. Gillespie was killed along with five soldiers: Stephen Burrows, Stephen Roy Beacham, Vincent Scott, David Sweeney, and Paul Worral. Gillespie was 42; none of the soldiers were older than 30.

The Coshquin attack generated more opprobrium, and from a wider diversity of voices, than the IRA was accustomed to. Within the local nationalist camp, the Catholic Bishop of Derry, Edward Daly, referred to the attack as "the work of Satan" (cited in Clarke, 2013) and the local nationalist newspaper, the *Derry Journal*, editorialised that anger in the city was higher than it had been since Bloody Sunday (cited in Moloney, 2002, p. 350)., Veteran reporters Ed Moloney and Peter Taylor both claim that within the republican movement itself the Coshquin attack immeasurably strengthened the hand of those within Sinn Féin who favoured opening ceasefire negotiations with the British (Moloney, 2002; Taylor, 1998). Gillespie was targeted to become a human bomb because, in the IRA narrative, he colluded with the British state merely by working in a canteen at an army base. If one adopts the IRA's loose legitimating ethos – just war theory – it would then become necessary to examine whether Gillespie was entitled to the principle of non-combatant immunity (PNCI). Basically, in just war theory non-combatants may not be targeted and all necessary precautions must be taken to avoid collateral damage; however, debates tend to turn around just who exactly gets to count as a non-combatant (see perspectives in Primoratz, 2007). In this case, however, clearly the IRA was unable to successfully argue that Gillespie had sacrificed his non-combatant status through his actions. Neither could they do so in the case of John McEvoy, forced to drive a human bomb in Newry because he owned a petrol station that occasionally sold soft drinks to British soldiers (Bloom & Horgan, 2008).

Even during the height of the terrible violence of the early 1990s, the republican proclamation of the state of exception was not absolute. Two narratives, both utilising Gillespie's body, seem to have been present. In the hard-line republican narrative, Gillespie was a traitor to his country, he was a threat to community survival, purity, and cohesion, and he was actively preventing the alleviation of the threat through his collaboration with the British. But a counter-narrative was much stronger in Derry. In this narrative, Gillespie was a man taking the only job he could find in a severely impoverished area to support his young family. And if this narrative was not dissimilar from the personal experience of a wide swathe of the CNR community in the northwest, it certainly was not unrecognisable. And this is where the state of exception broke down – in the ability of Gillespie's body to resist dehumanisation. Gillespie's body, according to the IRA's host population, was not a 'collaborator' but a complex and familiar human being, as was his widowed wife and his children who lost their father (Fitzpatrick, 2015). In the face of widespread rehumanisation, the IRA was allegedly forced to call a halt to their human bomb campaign. Write Bloom & Horgan (2008, p. 602): "The consensus at the time was that the IRA Army Council had seriously misjudged the mood and tolerance of even its own supporters."

But while the body of Patsy Gillespie was imbued with rehumanising potential, other IRA victims of the same time period were not, at least within the larger CNR host population. On 23 October 1993 two young IRA volunteers, 22-year-old Thomas Begley and 21-year-old Sean Kelly, entered Frizzell's fish shop on the Shankill Road in West Belfast disguised as deliverymen. Begley carried a bomb allegedly meant to assassinate the leadership of the West Belfast UDA, then led by the notorious sectarian murderer Johnny 'Mad Dog' Adair. However, the bomb missed its primary target – Adair and the West Belfast UDA leadership – and instead killed eight civilians, allegedly one member of the UDA,[4] and Thomas Begley. This would become infamously known as the Shankill Bombing.

In the Shankill Bombing, even though the IRA exhibited disregard for civilians that many would see as callous and cruel (and certainly outside of even the most permissive parameters of PNCI), they did not garner the same sort of opprobrium from within the CNR community as they had when they killed Patsy Gillespie and the five soldiers at Coshquin. Thousands of mourners turned out for Begley's ritualised republican funeral; Gerry Adams himself took a turn shouldering Begley's coffin (McKittrick & McVea, 2001). This presents another puzzle: what

4 Malcolm Sutton (2001) identifies one victim, Michael Morrison, as a UDA member. McKittrick et al. (2008) do not.

accounts for the divergent representations of non-combatant bodies in the larger minds and narratives of the CNR community in Northern Ireland? Why was Patsy Gillespie's body a candidate for rehumanisation and Sharon McBride's, one of the victims of the Shankill bombing, denied the same treatment?

Alan McBride, Sharon's husband, poignantly calls attention to her discursive dehumanisation: "I'm not suggesting for a minute my wife was the intended target, but she wasn't even considered, her life wasn't even considered that it was worth anything" (in BBC News, 2013a). Perhaps this is simply because Sharon McBride was a Protestant, unlike Gillespie; but I suspect it is more complicated than that. Part of it may have been that the victims of the Shankill bombing were not the intended targets, unlike Gillespie (though of course the IRA took no precautions whatsoever to ensure that civilians would not die in the blast); but what I suggest here is that it is absolutely crucial that we understand the two bodies' proximity to an immediate threat, and how one could be framed within the state of exception, stripped down to bare life, and the other could not.

Some time in the late 1980s, a large arms cache arrived for loyalist paramilitaries from the apartheid government in South Africa (Cobain, 2012). In the minds of republicans and many nationalists, these weapons were provided with the approval and facilitation of the highest reaches of the British government. What is beyond dispute is that the UDA and the UVF in particular used their expanded firepower to accelerate their campaign against Catholics, mainly in Belfast, but elsewhere as well, a campaign that Feldman (1991) suggests was designed to invade, transgress, violate, and terrorise CNR sanctuary space in North and West Belfast. Around the same time, Johnny Adair ascended to command status within the UDA's so-called 'C Company'. Adair probably was/is a sociopath; but regardless of any armchair psychological diagnosis, he was certainly a sectarian killer who targeted Catholics without any sense of discrimination (Lister & Jordan, 2005; McDonald & Cusack, 2004). Adair was allegedly shielded and aided by sympathetic elements within the British security forces (McDonald & Bright, 2003) and may have been involved in as many as 40 killings (McDonald & Cusack, 2004).

In addition, Belfast had been on edge since the Milltown Cemetery attack of 16 March,1988, when UDA killer Michael Stone attacked a republican funeral ceremony for IRA members Mairead Farrell, Sean Savage, and Danny McCann killed in Gibraltar by the SAS. Stone surprised the procession and killed three, injuring more than sixty. Two days later, two British corporals mistakenly drove into a funeral procession for one of Stone's victims and were dragged from their cars by incensed mourners, brutally savaged by the crowd, and later taken away and killed by the IRA. 'Patrick' describes the atmosphere in West Belfast between 1988 and 1993:

> Growing up, there's only one time I can remember when the atmosphere … the only other time I can think of it was when Mairead Farrell and Sean Savage's funeral was attacked by Michael Stone and a week later, the two

> corporals were murdered in Casement. With them, I think I was maybe 10 at the time, but I can remember their being a palpable atmosphere in the air of we're a community under attack. And sensing that as a ten and eleven year old, that it was really important to be on your toes.

'Patrick' recalls a community feeling trapped in a state of existential threat or crisis. Though his memory is that of a child, the atmosphere he remembers is confirmed by journalistic sources. McKittrick and McVea (2001, pp. 174–175) have this to say: "The sequence of events is still remembered, often with a shudder, as an almost unreal period of instability and polarisation. The violence was unremitting ... at this stage, Catholic civilians bore the brunt of loyalist violence." Threat and crisis justified the internal logic of the state of exception and facilitated the dehumanisation of subject bodies. Psychologists have long understood that there is a relationship between threat perception and recourse to violence, especially when the relationship between groups is characterised by segregation and a lack of mutual understanding (Correll, Urland, & Ito, 2006; Goodwin, Wilson, & Gaines, 2005; McLaren, 2003), as would have been and still is the case in Northern Ireland. In such a crisis state, any attempt to rehumanise an 'other' may be perceived as misrepresenting or glossing over the extent of the threat. *An Phoblacht* published an interview with an unnamed IRA representative illustrating exactly how violent republicans proposed to deal with the threat posed by Adair and like-minded loyalists: "There is no hiding place for those involved with the loyalist death squads. We are determined to exact a price from them. Those involved with the loyalist death squads will be held accountable for their actions" (in Rowan, 2016). It may be, then, that Catholic West Belfast largely decided that even a botched attempt to ameliorate the immediate threat by killing Adair and his colleagues was worth the inevitable possibility that civilians would die in the blast. Writes a former member of the IRA, Anthony McIntyre (2013):

> Wax ethical and sigh at the terrible loss of life, as we might today, three quarters of we who came up through the ranks of the IRA would have been queuing up to plant that bomb: the remainder, waiting to tell their handlers. The pot of gold at the end of the black rainbow – the pernicious figures behind the anti-nationalist killing machine – was a tantalising prospect. I would have been jostling for my place. Misgivings, if any, would have been confined to the suitability of the fuse and the runback. And that is how it was. We were part of a guerrilla army primed for something other than social work.

Here, McIntyre disparages those who would 'wax ethical' and 'sigh', or those who would argue that, given the campaign against the CNR community of Belfast, the Shankill Bombing was misguided or criminal. Instead, he clearly empathises with and humanises the bombers, Begley and Kelly, by analogising their experience to his own. Like Patrick Magee, he argues that a failure to understand the reality of the crisis, and as such the state of exception, is a gross decontextualisation of history. But McIntyre does not mention or acknowledge Sharon McBride and the other civilian victims, except obliquely, and they are quickly returned to their dehumanised invisibility through a rapid lexical shift to justificatory language. This is not surprising, considering the nature of the republican state of exception. McIntyre must re-emphasise the threat itself and render invisible the bodies of the victims; to do otherwise would shake the foundation of the state of exception, and with it, his ability to narrate his own actions, and those of his comrades, to himself and to others.

Loyalist state of exception

> I wouldn't try to justify my actions because I wouldn't expect middle-class unionists to agree with what I did, but what I will say to you is that we're not in a united Ireland … My view is that I was fighting a war and I fought it … The IRA left me with no option but to carry out the tactics we had; the IRA weren't in the back of Land Rovers with uniforms on and the UVF had a very clear policy at one stage that they would drive the IRA out of the community.
>
> (Billy Hutchinson, cited in McBride, 2014)

> Yabba Dabba Doo, Any Fenian will do.
>
> (Loyalist prison mural, cited in De Breadun, 1997)

On 21 October 1974 two young builders and half-brothers, 27-year-old Edward Morgan and 18-year-old Michael Loughran, were walking to work down the Falls Road in West Belfast when a car drew up alongside them and opened fire. Both young men were killed. Neither had any ties to republican paramilitaries. They were marked for death randomly because they were soft targets walking in a Catholic neighbourhood. Their mother, Mary Loughran, poignantly asks: "Why my two boys? They never did anyone any harm. They went to work together, came home together, and today they died together" (McKittrick et al., 2008, p. 485). The murderers were two 19-year-olds from the Shankill, Billy Hutchinson and Thomas Winstone. As Winstone was led away, he raised his fist and called out, "No surrender – Up the UVF!" (McKittrick et al., 2008, p. 485).

Hutchinson was released from prison in 1990, after serving 16 years of a life sentence. While in prison and continuing on after his release, Hutchinson became part of a cadre of men around the late David Ervine, one of the most central loyalist figures in the peace process, credited with helping to achieve the UVF ceasefires, decommissioning, and the founding of the Progressive Unionist Party (PUP). After Ervine's death in 2007, Hutchinson became the leader of the PUP, which he remains at the time of this writing, as well as an elected Belfast City Councillor for the district including the Shankill. Clearly, Hutchinson has undergone some type of personal transformation; however, he still seems unable to countenance the idea that the callous, cold-blooded murder of two youths walking to work was not justifiable. The reasoning behind Hutchinson's justification is contained within the loyalist state of exception, the threat and crisis that loyalists constructed to justify it, and why for many loyalists all Catholic bodies were justifiable targets for dehumanised death.

Loyalism lacked one central violent organisation; in the mid-1970s there were up to 35 documented potentially violent loyalist groups. While many of those organisations were fictitious, McKittrick argues: "Up to a dozen were real – that is, with at least a rudimentary command structure and access to weapons" (cited in O'Leary & McGarry 1993, p. 206). Two particular loyalist groups carried out the majority of Troubles killings – the Ulster Defence Army (UDA) and the Ulster Volunteer Force (UVF) – but certain cells were far more active and deadly than others. The UDA and the UVF were counter-insurgency organisations above all; their goal was to protect the union with Great Britain by any means necessary and their primary justification for near-total indiscrimination in their targeting seems to have been largely three-fold. First, many loyalists were (and some still are) nakedly sectarian – hard-liners saw/see Irish Catholics as lesser human beings and therefore unworthy of equal citizenship in Northern Ireland. But open sectarianism could be somewhat concealed by the second justification, namely that Catholic civilians had in the aggregate after 1981 sacrificed PNCI by voting for Sinn Féin. Because they supported the political wing of the IRA, the political party actively seeking to destroy the union, they could be terrorised until they ceased their electoral and social support (McAuley, 2010). This is a fairly common counterinsurgency trope and harkens back to Mao Zedong's (1937) aphorism that the guerrilla fighter is a fish swimming in the sea. The sea is of course the community that sustains the fish. Draining the sea, or finding a way to 'encourage' the community to abandon the guerrilla, exposes this fish. The final part of the justification for loyalists was that the 'legitimate' forces arrayed against republicanism were incapable of defeating it because they were bound by law and order. Loyalism was therefore an auxiliary force that could operate extra-legally, a necessary component for defeating the IRA that could not be achieved by legal means.

But once more, all of these justifications are only intelligible in the state of exception, which in turn depends on the widespread and at least tacit acceptance of an existential threat or crisis by a significant enough percentage of a 'host' community, in this case, working-class Protestantism. To construct the threat, loyalism was able to draw on both historical and contemporary frames, fusing the past and present together to illustrate a Northern Irish political entity always tenuously clinging to its existence in spite of a constant threat that republicanism could either bomb or convince the largely uninterested and ungrateful British state into abandoning Northern Ireland (Wood, 2003; Ruane & Todd, 1996). To understand violent loyalism, one must understand that loyalism in Northern Ireland generally imagines itself as perpetually under siege (Spencer, 2008; Southern, 2007; Finlay 2001; Graham, 1998). The most common loyalist slogan, 'No surrender', both produces and reproduces the siege mentality. Its historical referent is the siege of Derry in 1688–1689 and its contemporary referent is the siege of the union and the territory of Northern Ireland by increasingly assertive republicanism/nationalism. In the siege mentality, 1688 and 1988 fuse and become ideationally indistinguishable; the threat transcends temporality and becomes, like all states of exception, paradoxically temporary and indefinite.

Consider the text of the original Ulster Covenant, signed by almost half a million Ulstermen and women in protest against the proposed Government of Ireland Act, which would have granted Ireland 'Home Rule' within the British dominion. The signers pledged: "To use all means which may be found necessary to defeat the present conspiracy to set up a Home Rule Parliament in Ireland." Of course, those necessary means were an implicit threat of violence, backed up by the concurrent organisation of the original, armed Ulster Volunteer Force (UVF) in 1913 (McMaster, 2011). Modern loyalism lays direct claim to this legacy of legitimate resistance granted by the Covenant, even reappropriating the name and slogan ('For God and Ulster') of the original UVF.

But like a republican historiography, loyalist historiography is too diffuse to adequately impose an immediate crisis state. They too needed a more tangible threat. The escalating Provisional IRA[5] bombing campaign of 1971–1972 provided that threat, at least to many young, working-class Protestants growing up in loyalist estates. Three major incidences are often pointed to in the testimony of current or former loyalists as convincing them to 'join up': the Balmoral showroom bombing, the Claudy bombing, and Bloody Friday. On 21 July 1972 the PIRA exploded 26 bombs over 80 minutes in Belfast City Centre in what came to be known as Bloody Friday. The intent of the bombings seems to have been to demonstrate to the British government the extent, sophistication, and reach of the PIRA's arsenal and to bring the war to the commercial heart of Northern Ireland. Ed Moloney describes Belfast on Bloody Friday: "[It] resembled a city under artillery fire; clouds of suffocating smoke enveloped buildings as one explosion followed another, almost drowning out the hysterical screams of panicked shoppers (Moloney, 2002, p. 116). Eleven people were killed by the PIRA on Bloody Friday, and 130 were injured, and with many left permanently disfigured or disabled, and because so many of the bombs exploded in such close proximity, on several occasions the emergency services shepherded people directly into the blast radius of another bomb (McKittrick et al., 2008, pp. 229–230). Bloody Friday in particular confirmed to many in the PUL community the true extent of the threat posed by the PIRA and the republican movement and provided clear linkage to the legitimising narratives of the past. This PUL historiography includes not merely the Siege of Derry, but also chosen traumas such as the Irish rebellion of 1641 when scores of Protestant settlers were massacred in Ulster by

5 Both the Provisional and Official IRA were active before 1973. All references to the IRA after 1973 refer to the Provisional IRA. Some former members of the Official IRA would later be instrumental in the founding of the INLA.

their Irish neighbours (see Canny, 2001), and more modern events such as the alleged 'ethnic cleansing' of Protestants from the South of Ireland during the massive social upheavals of 1916–1923.[6] Many prominent loyalists, such as Billy 'Twister' McQuistan, David Ervine, Jackie McDonald, and Billy Hutchinson describe first joining either the UVF or the UDA directly in response to the three atrocities listed above (Cusack & McDonald, 2008; Wood, 2006). Their testimony supports Ruane and Todd's illustration of loyalism during the Troubles and provides a much more proximate and tangible cause of the decision to join loyalist paramilitaries:

> Contemporary events were seen in terms of images of the past: Protestants were being pushed out of their traditional areas and workplaces, they were under siege, subject to genocidal attack, forced to retaliate. Only loyalist organisation, vigilance, and militancy could defend the Protestant population.
> (Ruane & Todd, 1996, pp. 94–95)

Thus the upheavals in Belfast and Derry that resulted in the creation of highly segregated neighbourhoods and communities (see Darby 1986; 1997) also buttressed the loyalist historiographical narrative of existential threat and provided a historical frame of reference with which to view Troubles violence. The political union with Great Britain was not safe, had never been safe, and would never be safe until the IRA was destroyed and the cancer of republicanism and Northern Irish nationalism was stamped out. Within that temporal space, the space between the present and the culmination of loyalist goals, falls the loyalist state of exception, again, paradoxically temporary and indefinite. And within that space there is no palpable irony in the fact that the loyalist state of exception depends on suspending what loyalism was supposedly fighting for: the right to be a British citizen and all the concomitant legal and humanistic protections that such citizenship supposedly entails.

Because of the particular nature of the loyalist state of exception, for many loyalists *any improvement* in the political or social standing of CNR communities and individuals has threat-potential. Both Southern (2007) and Hughes and Donnelly (2003) point out that first the civil rights movement and then the peace process, have been understood by large segments of the PUL population as

6 This was perhaps most forcefully alleged by Peter Hart (1998). Hart alleged that 'ethnic cleansing' had occurred in County Cork from 1916 to 1923. His source material is now under significant dispute (Murphy, 2005). The term 'ethnic cleansing' is anachronistic and Hart would almost certainly not have used it had the Balkan not been raging while he was writing. To say his book is controversial would be an understatement. He was publicly accused by J. M. Regan of committing academic fraud in the service of an 'anti-Republican' historiography in 2010. David Fitzpatrick (2013) has defended Hart. This is not a debate I feel qualified to enter, nor is it the purpose of this book to try and provide an answer.

'one-sided'. Considering that the CNR community was systematically deprived during unionist rule (1921–1971), if one has been socialised into a zero-sum, ethnocratic logic regarding political distribution, transitioning to an 'equal' society necessarily means that the CNR community has 'gained' and the PUL community has 'lost'. Thus, even civil rights could be relatively easily reframed as part of a nefarious plot to destroy the union. Post hoc, the brutal repression of the civil rights movement in Derry could also be justified when set against the alleged 'putting out' of approximately 16,000 Derry Protestants across the River Foyle.[7] Much of the widespread sense of Protestant alienation in Northern Ireland, in spite of Protestantism's privileged social position and monopoly of power before and during the Troubles, can be traced to the zero-sum logic of the state exception facilitated by a widespread siege mentality – not only that Protestants were under siege, but that the siege seemed to be working, as across Derry and Belfast working-class Protestants were being driven from their homes. Of course, working-class Catholics were also being driven from their homes, but that reality was generally ignored or selectively not seen by loyalists. Thus, Protestant alienation, and especially the 'double alienation' of the Protestant working-class (see Southern, 2007), fused with the siege mentality, easily facilitated the imposition of the loyalist state of exception. And in the loyalist state of exception, as Billy Hutchinson and Gusty Spence both claim, republicanism and the Catholic body are conflated. Killing Catholics becomes not merely justifiable in the state of exception, it becomes a successful military tactic. In this light, Hutchinson's perspective becomes more intelligible (though certainly no less abhorrent). He may genuinely still believe, in spite of campaigning for the 1998 Agreement and renouncing violence, that murdering two young men in cold blood while they were walking to work on a Belfast morning prevented a united Ireland.

The final explanatory factor of the complicated loyalist state of exception lies in loyalism's uneasy relationship with the British state. Speaking generally, there are two main differences between unionism and loyalism. The first is a class

7 'Putting out' is the standard Northern Irish euphemism for a violent or coercive eviction. During the years 1968–1979, many from the PUL community left the west bank of the River Foyle, or the Cityside of Derry, where the historic city is located. Nobody knows exactly how many Protestants left the Cityside and why. Marie Smyth (1995) gives the figure as 16,000, and this seems reasonable and well researched, though it is far less than many in the PUL community claim. Many in the local CNR community downplay this internal migration, preferring to think of it as similar to 'white flight' in the post-apartheid states of South Africa and the United States. For the PUL community, however, 'The Exodus', as it is evocatively known, was an orchestrated campaign by republican paramilitaries and their sympathisers to drive them from their homes. A local, self-described loyalist playwright, Johnathan Burgess, has dramatised the impact of migration in his play *The Exodus* (2011). Again, this is not a debate I am qualified to enter, but the reader should be aware that it is a profoundly sensitive subject in Derry and its environs.

difference; those drawn to loyalist paramilitarism and sympathies tend to hail from the Protestant working class and areas of relatively high deprivation and low educational attainment (Hughes & Donnelly, 2003). The second, inter-related factor, is that although both unionism and loyalism constitute the threat to the union in a similar way, for unionists appropriate and legitimate means to counter the threat of republicanism exist and existed, namely serving in the police or the army. Loyalist use of force was thus illegitimate because recourse to legitimate force existed and the decision of loyalists to join illegal[8] paramilitary organisations rendered them little better than members of the IRA:

> To me, if you were a loyalist you were loyal to the Crown, therefore you supported the police force and/or army. Those people who claimed to be loyalists were not loyal to anything. They were terrorists, full stop.
>
> (Ross Hussey, UUP MLA, RUC (ret.))

> We've made a very, very clear pitch that whether violence is perpetrated by republicans, loyalists, or individual members of the security forces who dishonour the code to carry out criminal activities, that's all viewed the exact same way ... When Billy Hutchinson ... justified the act of killing two Catholics in the media, we would have gone very hard on him ... The point is he murdered and he took life in a premeditated way, so to justify that all those years on irrespective of whatever he thought was going on at the time, there's no place for that.
>
> ('Michael', County Fermanagh)

Both Minister Hussey's and 'Michael's' perspectives chime with mainstream unionism generally. But what mainstream unionism often conveniently forgets is the extent to which loyalism was actively encouraged by right-wing unionists, including many in positions of political power. For example, in 1974 rejectionist unionists led by Ian Paisley, Harry West, and William Craig helped to form a broad umbrella group known as the Ulster Worker's Council (UWC) that incorporated the representatives of loyalist paramilitarism. The UWC was established to force the British government to abandon the first negotiated attempt to end the Troubles, the power-sharing Sunningdale Agreement. Paisley and others

8 Membership in loyalist paramilitaries was not always officially 'illegal'. The British state did not declare the UDA a terrorist group until 1992. This is probably because the UDA used the fictitious moniker the UFF (Ulster Freedom Fighters) when laying claim to paramilitary killings. The UFF was proscribed from 1973. Though the UDA and the UFF were widely known to be the same organisation, for whatever reason the British state did not connect the dots until 1992, when the UDA was also proscribed. In the case of the UVF, the British briefly legalised the UVF in 1974 around the time of Sunningdale in an attempt to bring the organisation into the peace process. When that failed, they were proscribed again in 1975.

forged alliances of convenience with the UDA and the UVF in order to ensure that the UWC's call for a general strike was adhered to across PUL communities. Even those loyalists/unionists who might have been inclined to support Sunningdale or go to work were less inclined to do so with such violent enforcers guaranteeing the strike. The political representatives of unionism sat publicly at the same tables as commanders in the UDA and UVF, in no small sense legitimising violent loyalism and promoting a general sense that murders, bombings, and widespread intimidation were being tacitly condoned. Ian Paisley's uncompromising, violent, and zero-sum rhetoric throughout the Troubles would also have given that impression. In a 1986 speech in Newtonards, in the aftermath of the hated (by many unionists and loyalists) Anglo-Irish Agreement of 1985, Paisley thundered:

> We demand that the IRA be exterminated from Ulster ... There are men willing to do the job of exterminating the IRA. Recruit them under the Crown and they will do it. If you refuse, we will have no other decision to make but to do it ourselves.
>
> (Paisley, cited in Bruce, 2007, p. 227)

In this speech and so many others like it, Paisley legitimates the loyalist state of exception. The hands of the legitimate defenders of Ulster, the police and the army, are tied by law and procedure; they are hamstrung in their fight against the IRA. 'There are men' is a clear allusion to loyalist death-dealers, whose hands are not tied, and Paisley advocates making them auxiliary forces of the Crown in order to 'exterminate' the threat of republicanism. Thus, while many unionists did repudiate loyalist ideology and tactics, the signals emanating from right-wing political unionism were mixed at best and often offered support and succour to loyalist paramilitaries. Of course, Paisley and the DUP would eventually go on to 'betray' anti-republicanism by joining a power-sharing government with Sinn Féin in 2006, leading to charges by many loyalists that they and their movement have always been exploited by mainstream politicians interested only in political power and their own careerism.

In the perspective of many loyalists, mainstream unionism is completely blind to the stark realities of life in working-class Protestant enclaves, which Hutchinson alludes to. These unionists did not experience the Troubles directly and they were not driven out of interface areas by the IRA and their largely unsympathetic Catholic neighbours (Finlay, 2001; McAuley, 1999). It was working-class loyalists who shouldered the burden and answered the threat of violent republicanism. And in spite of loyalist contributions to maintaining the union and preventing a united Ireland, they continue to be denied a political voice and are demonised by republicans, unionists, and the media (Spencer, 2008).

Loyalism is also in a bind over the question of state violence. While loyalists themselves were sometimes the targets of state violence, to acknowledge that the British state can be an agent of injustice comes dangerously close to accepting republican conflict-framing (Graham & Whelan, 2007). Loyalism seeks to square the circle by proclaiming that if the British establishment will not recognise their contributions and their devotion to the Crown and the union, loyalism is entitled to act outside the state apparatus to achieve its political objectives and ameliorate the threat.

In the aftermath of the Shankill bombing, Billy 'Twister' McQuistan claimed that the sense of rage among residents of the Shankill was palpable: "Anybody out on the Shankill Road that day, from a Boy Scout to a granny, if you'd given them a gun they would have gone out and retaliated" (cited in Wood, 2006, pp. 170–172). For McQuistan, a commander in the UDA, this seems to have been a self-fulfilling prophecy. One week later, on 30 October 1993, two UDA gunmen walked into the packed Rising Sun pub in the quiet County Derry town of Greysteel and sprayed the bar with bullets. Over 200 revellers were present, many of them in Halloween costumes. As one of the gunmen, Stephen Irwin, entered the bar, he called out "Trick or treat". The two gunmen fired 45 shots from AK-47s and likely would have fired more if one of the guns had not jammed. In the aftermath, eight people were dead – six Catholics and two Protestants – and eleven more seriously injured. Photographs of the scene show the floor and walls literally coated in the blood of the victims. Their names are John Alexander Burns, Moira Duddy, Joseph McDermott, Samuel Victor Montgomery, James Moore, John Moyne, Steven Gerard Mullan, and Karen Thompson.

The UDA's justification for the Greysteel massacre is detailed in Ian Wood's history of that organisation and is consistent with the parameters of the loyalist state of exception. Wood quotes an unnamed loyalist:

> You must appreciate … that to the UDA and UFF this is their Alamo. They feel they have nothing left to lose. They are in a war situation, and as the Provos have told us for twenty years, sometimes innocent people get hurt. When politicians say that Loyalist violence hardly strengthens the Union with Britain, they're missing the point. 'Loyal' these days means something new. The Tories can't be trusted, so it's Loyalty to Ulster and its people. *No-one else counts.*
>
> (Wood, 2006, p. 172, emphasis added)

Wood continues to quote the killer Stephen Irwin:

> I've never felt any remorse about what I did. We were using IRA tactics against the IRA and the republican community. It was Old Testament justice, an eye for an eye, a tooth for a tooth.
>
> (Wood, 2006, p. 173)

These justifications are clearly fixed in the loyalist state of exception. They did not cause the precipitating crisis; the IRA and its supporters within the republican community did, and both the unnamed loyalist and Irwin conveniently conflate them with all Catholics (or apparently Protestants who drink in the wrong pubs). No mainstream unionist or British actor can be trusted to protect working-class PUL communities, such as those blown up in the Shankill bombing. In the state of exception, *no-one else counts*, loyalism has suspended everyone's rights to life and rights to political citizenship (which of course the 'taigs' don't respect anyway), and they can be killed with moral impunity, without any regrets. Random killings, soft targets, murders of convenience – these are all strategically justifiable as well. They force the British and mainstream unionists to pay attention to the demands of working-class Protestants (as articulated by loyalist terrorists) and they attempt to emasculate republicanism by proving that no member of the CNR community they purport to protect is, or will ever be, safe from horror until republicanism ceases its campaign to unite the island of Ireland. These demands are not negotiable and the UDA is the only organisation with the right to articulate them.

The security forces' state of exception

> We shall maintain the Union of Great Britain and Northern Ireland in accordance with the wish of the majority in the Province. Its future still depends on the defeat of terrorism and the restoration of law and order. We shall continue, with the help of the courage, resolution, and restraint of the Security Forces – to give it the highest priority. There will be no amnesty for convicted terrorists.
>
> (Conservative Party of the United Kingdom, 1979, sec. 4.5).

The British state and its Northern Irish auxiliaries have consistently attempted to represent themselves as neutral arbiters seeking a satisfactory and mutually agreeable solution to an internecine conflict between warring sectarian 'tribes' (McLaughlin & Baker, 2010). But this framing of the conflict and its aftermath actively misrepresents the actions of the British army in the early 1970s, the extent of state collusion with loyalist and (to a lesser degree) republican paramilitaries, and the unequal imposition of force and surveillance in CNR communities in Northern Ireland. For example, internment without trial, introduced in 1971, imprisoned almost 2,000 people, 95 per cent of whom were Catholic. Even those approximately 100 suspected loyalists who were interned following Operation Motorman were generally imprisoned afterwards and were widely perceived by the CNR community to be tokenistic (Coogan, 1996). Some internees were tortured, and when the Republic of Ireland brought suit against the UK in the European Court of Human Rights (the so-called 'Hooded Men' case) over the treatment of internees, the British withheld key evidence that would have substantiated the allegations of torture (McKay, 2015; RTÉ Investigations Unit, 2014).

Any attempt by the British political establishment or media to claim the British state was either neutral or impartial in the Northern Irish conflict is inherently suspect. Of course, only one belligerent orientation, republicanism, professed to be openly at war with the British state. But even in noting this, it must be said that British policy bears a significant responsibility for catalysing and legitimising the republican state of exception. I have briefly touched on the Ballymurphy and Bloody Sunday massacres; however, perhaps the clearest example of British policy in the region that contributed immensely to the radicalisation of the CNR population (and the most directly indicative of the state of exception) was internment. Internment was instituted in 1971 at the urging of the then (and last) Prime Minister of Northern Ireland, Brian Faulker. Faulkner justified reintroducing the policy in the following manner:

> Every means has been tried to make terrorists amenable to law. But the terrorist campaign continues at an unacceptable level. And I have had to conclude that ordinary law cannot deal quickly or comprehensively enough with such viciousness.
>
> (Faulkner, cited in Compton Report, 1971, n.p.)

Faulkner argues that the law must be suspended to uphold the law; a clearer statement of the second paradox of state of exception may be difficult to find. Considering that English jurisprudence stems from the Magna Carta, it might be helpful to cite that document here. The document is widely available online. I cite from Section 29: "No freeman shall be taken, [or] imprisoned … except by the lawful judgment of his peers." And in arguing as such, Faulkner ignores many of the illegal actions by the state that (also paradoxically) precipitated the crisis state necessitating the suspension of the law, this being the selective, often brutal repression of the civil rights movement and the discriminatory, exclusionist policies inherent in one-party unionist rule.

Internment was designed to target violent republicanism, but in practice it was highly indiscriminate and swept up many non-violent, ordinary Catholic-nationalists. This may have been at least partially due to the fact that the British Army, MI5, and the RUC Special Branch possessed extremely poor intelligence on republican paramilitaries at the time; but the fact that they still went ahead with internment anyway, without any clear idea of who exactly constituted a threat to Northern Irish security, should point to an institutionalised disregard for a politically and socially excluded minority population (Ní Aoláin, 2000). Thus, whatever the actual intent of internment, all residents of working-class CNR communities where the PIRA was believed to operate were collectively stripped of their foundational rights as British citizens and presumed to be active or potential terrorists. Being reduced as such to bare life deprived them of individual personhood and made them subject at all times to anonymous arrest and incarceration.

Internment is perhaps the simplest illustration of the state of exception underwriting British security policy in Northern Ireland. Fionnuala Ní Aoláin's (2000) magisterial work details British security policy throughout the Troubles and is a much better guide than this brief sketch. Ní Aoláin argues that state security policy in Northern Ireland throughout the Troubles was rooted in laying claim to a 'state of emergency' that legitimised and normalised the recourse to extrajudicial action, including the widespread and consistent suspension of the right to more-than-life. In the words of Margaret Thatcher, "You have to, in order to beat off your enemy in a way, to suspend some of your civil liberties for a time" (cited in Cadwallader, 2013, p. 360).

As I argued earlier, any imposition of a state of exception requires a seemingly immediate threat or crisis in order to be fully internalised and operationalised by a subject population. And British soldiers in Northern Ireland, policemen and women, UDR men and women, were confronted by such an immediate and lethal threat throughout the conflict in the form of republican (and occasionally, loyalist) paramilitaries. This threat provided the tangible, immediate impetus to accept the dehumanisation of Northern Irish bodies, especially Catholic bodies, and to perceive them as outside of standard legal codes and protections. It is important to note here that not all soldiers and police officers 'dishonoured the code' in 'Michael's' words (above); many resisted to varying degrees the dehumanising context in which they found themselves, and resisted suspending the rights, norms, and moral ethos of the liberal state. But this is not a 'few bad apples' argument. Rather, it is an argument that asserts that the state of exception proclaimed by the British state (and the policies that flowed from that proclamation) *guaranteed* that individuals and groups within the security forces would engage in dehumanising, even murderous acts on a widespread basis, though of course again I recognise that many did no such thing.

I begin with the British army. British soldiers in Northern Ireland resembled to a large extent the population they were 'restoring order to'. Predominately young, working-class English men, they were outsiders in Northern Ireland, a province that even though it was officially part of the United Kingdom, must have seemed like a foreign country. In analysing the narratives of British soldiers, I was immediately struck by the fear and hostility they find embedded in the Northern Irish landscape (see Arthur, 1987; Lindsay, 1998). Despite the convenient public narrative of the British government, they were not there to 'keep the peace' but to fight a war against the IRA. They could be shot or blown up at any time by a paramilitary force that was often well integrated into the local population and much more familiar with the local environment. Soldiers' memories of Northern Ireland display a sense of hyper-vigilance and extreme social alienation. In John Lindsay's collection of soldier testimonies, nearly all of the soldiers interviewed use the derogatory term 'Paddies' to refer to the Northern Irish, both Catholic and Protestant. This is not a coincidence; casual racism is often used to dehumanise perceived enemies in a war zone. Dehumanisation may function as something of a cognitive insulation mechanism, used to narrate away the psychological distress inherent in the act of killing (Grossman, 1996). But it is also, as many scholars have noted, enabled by the official discourses emanating from command structures and the state itself (see Steuter & Wills, 2009; Jackson,

2005; Vietnam Veterans Against the War, 1972). Some narratives may illustrate this point:

> On the journey back I felt a sort of anger at being surrounded by so much hostility. None of these people knew me, but as far as I could see lots of them already hated me – and wanted to do me harm. 'Fuck them', I thought, I wasn't going to let them; it was as simple as that … I just wanted to survive – and was determined to do so in the best way I knew how. I would survive by dealing ruthlessly with any potential threats. And as far as I was concerned, anybody I didn't know personally was a threat.
>
> (O'Mahoney, with McGovern, 2000, pp. 116–117)

> Stan Evans was in one house (I was searching another house) and was shot through a window. It was a clever trap and Stan did not stand a chance. He was hit twice in the head and died later in the hospital. He was 21 years old … The section that was with Stan were really angry and we all wanted revenge. After that there was no more 'please' or 'will you'; we told them what to do and they did it … Everyone in Unity Flats [a working-class CNR estate in New Lodge, North Belfast] knew who shot Stan but said nothing, and that is hard to take.
>
> ('Bob', in Lindsay, 1998, pp. 82–83)

> A guy on my left … said part of my history is being a soldier in the Creggan [a working-class CNR area of Derry] during these Troubles. And one of the things he went on to say was that his friend had been shot dead in Creggan … [later], they're summoned to the area, and he admits and he acknowledges that he wrecked houses, that he put his boot through things, 'My friend's been killed, fuck you.' And he wasn't saying this is right, he wasn't saying this is wrong, but emotionally he was charged, the men were charged.
>
> ('Oisin', Derry, interview with author)

Soldiers' narratives contain many similarities to both republican and loyalist narratives. Many identify a defining moment, often the death or injury of a friend or loved one, that displayed the cowardice, shamelessness, and facelessness of an external combatant, a constant threat. The threat is then cognitively extended to a supposedly 'host' population, with varying degrees of intentionality. The conflation of the threat with the population dehumanises the population and thus cements the state of exception emanating from a larger state or sub-state discourse.

RUC and UDR narratives are similar to those of British soldiers, but carry a different register due to the fact that these were local Northern Irish men and women, not outside soldiers brought in to fight a war. The RUC and UDR narrative coalesces around a portrayal of those organisations as stretched terminally thin and unable to fully contain the spiralling violence. Police officers and UDR men and women did their jobs as best as they were able in the face of extreme pressure and danger. If members of those organisations used excessive force, it was merely the actions of rogue individuals and could be explained but not condoned by the extraordinary circumstances in which the local security forces were operating. Ultimately, the preferred story of the RUC and UDR is one of 'untold heroism' and a highly significant but rarely acknowledged contribution to the Peace Process (Potter, 2001). In the words of ex-RUC man Roger McCallum, "The whole peace process was bought by the lives of police officers because I believe they were providing the time for politicians and the government to get their act together" (interview with author).

As noted earlier, republican and loyalist paramilitaries together accounted for a full 88 per cent of all the deaths attributed to the Troubles (3,257 total deaths) while suffering only 15 per cent of the total fatalities (562). In stark contrast, the British army/SAS killed 301 people and suffered 503 fatalities, the police 303 and 51, respectively, and the USC/UDR/RIR 206 and 8 (all statistics from McKittrick et al., 2008). Even when collusion with paramilitaries is considered, the simple fact is that paramilitaries were the primary perpetrators in the conflict and claims to a parity of victimhood are simply empirically false in the aggregate. One source of consternation to many former RUC and UDR men and women is the widespread belief in an official or semi-official 'shoot-to-kill' policy allegedly enacted by the RUC and UDR.[9] Consider two first-hand perspectives from a former member of the UDR and the RUC, respectively (both engaged me on this subject without any prompting, suggesting a deeply-held desire to 'correct the record'):

> They always said and I've heard it said, the IRA's argument, that the British government had a shoot-to-kill policy. And I served my full term in the UDR and never at any time had to fire *one single round*. And if you did discharge a round, there was paperwork above paperwork above paperwork to fill in. And you would have been dogged the whole way through, 'Why did you discharge your round?' But none of us [in my regiment] ever did.
>
> ('Daniel', UDR (ret.), County Tyrone)

9 There are almost certainly incidences where the British military, the SAS in particular, shot and killed IRA men, rather than attempting to arrest them, in particular during the Loughgall and Gibraltar incidents (Murray, 2004). And of course before 1975 and the advent of Ulsterisation the British army regularly used indiscriminate lethal force in densely populated neighbourhoods, resulting in many civilian casualties. I am aware of no evidence supporting a shoot-to-kill policy operating within the uniformed rank and file of the RUC or the UDR, however. That is not to say that encounters with the uniformed UDR and RUC were always pleasant and professional for Catholics. They were not. Many Catholics living in border areas have communicated shocking stories to me of non-lethal encounters with individuals from these organisations.

> For somebody to do that, for someone to actually blast somebody to eternity and then complain that somebody shot back, well the IRA never shot to miss, yet if a police officer shot back then it was a shoot-to-kill policy.
>
> (Ross Hussey, UUP MLA, RUC (ret.), County Tyrone)

There is certainly no cause to dispute 'Daniel's' assertion that neither he nor anyone in his regiment fired a round in over 15 years in the UDR. Yet we also know that elements within the UDR throughout the course of the Troubles moonlighted as loyalist killers, that weaponry traceable to the UDR and/or RUC semi-regularly found its way into the hands of loyalist killers, and that the upper echelons of the RUC Special Branch extensively protected informants (even to the extent of covering up murders or allowing murder plots to occur) (BBC Panorama, 2015). The PSNI's own Historical Enquiries Team (HET) concluded that "widespread evidence of collusion was not a significant concern at the highest levels of the security forces or government" (cited in Cadwallader, 2013, p. 367). Yet we also know that many if not most individual security force members were not responsible for collusive policies or actions, and were probably even unaware that they were occurring. But it is also clear that the state of exception operating within the British and Northern Irish security services facilitated and enabled the murder and maiming of hundreds (if not thousands) of people. Given the positioning of RUC and UDR men and women, this should not come as that big a surprise. They were constant targets for depersonalised death by republican paramilitaries. Many were blown up or shot off-duty, in their civilian employ, at their homes, or doing their shopping. The bringers of death were men, and rarely, women who were deeply integrated into republican sanctuaries. In many cases the killers would be known, but no member of the sanctuary community would come forward due to a combination of disinclination and terror. In such situations, a heretofore unknown portion of the local security forces internalised the dehumanising logic of the state of exception and suspended the citizenship and humanity of an entire population.

State of exception today?

Brian Graham's work suggests that the state of exception (he does not use this term) remains a powerful and actionable frame of reference for former paramilitary groups and their political representatives even today, 17 years after the signing of the Agreement. Graham argues that Sinn Féin and loyalism are engaged in an ongoing attempt to saturate Northern Ireland's memory landscape with violent and violence-justifying paramilitary imagery. Maintaining the presentist relevance of the state of exception in turn allows for the continuation of Sinn Féin and the DUP's 'antipluralist and arguably ethnocratic' project, and cements their respective hold on political power over an ethnically defined and territorially defined population. Graham calls this "an embittered human geography of territoriality that is supported by competing memory discourses and is fundamental to the prolongation of contested identities" (Graham, 2011, p. 88). Sara McDowell argues a similar point: "Commemorations thus serve as an extension of the tribal politics that continue to exist in Northern Ireland as they demarcate and contest Nationalist/Republican and Unionist/Loyalist boundaries" (McDowell, 2008, pp. 338). In the rest of this book I will pursue a more nuanced and cautionary approach. For now, I suggest the perspectives of scholars such as Graham and McDowell run the risk of overstating the uniformity of working-class memory-space in Northern Ireland. The scope and furore of paramilitary imagery, and its insistence on reproducing the internal logic of the respective states of exception, can also be read as an attempt to silence or paper over voices from within ethnic sanctuaries that would resist the continuing relevance of the state of exception, especially as the Troubles have been officially declared 'over' by the IRA and the UVF, at the very least.

Which begs the question, if the Troubles are in fact over and the immediate crises precipitating the imposition of the state of exception alleviated, then what place in post-conflict society is needed for former paramilitary groups and their political representatives? Consider a UVF mural adorning the Mount Vernon estate in North Belfast (see Figure 3.1): the slogan is extremely well known in Northern Ireland and has adorned other murals that have existed with varying degrees of permanency. The inscription claims that the crisis and threat that

Figure 3.1 UVF Mural, Mount Vernon Estate, North Belfast. Source: Wikimedia Commons: https://en.wikipedia.org/wiki/File:Glenbryne.jpg

justified the loyalist state of exception *could return* at any time. The body of the armed gunman thus remains, looming over the working-class spaces where social memory of the Troubles is produced, proclaiming its discursive ongoing relevance should the threat of republicanism or Irish unity reassert itself. Maintaining and reproducing the state of exception thus ensures that the UVF still has a purpose, a *raison d'être*, and it suborns and renders invisible the bodies of UVF victims, placing them outside of an allowable spatial narrative.

In the remainder of this book I shall focus more directly on the question of how much legitimacy and symbolic power the state of exception still retains in post-conflict Irish space. I will argue that the dominance of paramilitary groups and their political representatives of public memory-space is slipping; it is splintering and diversifying as other social actors have begun to assert their rights to remember in public, their rights to inscribe the bodies of the dead in different, more intimate, human forms. I shall also argue that even particular paramilitary memory-*places* are beginning to break down – they are becoming more open to internal challenge and contestation as dead paramilitary bodies become subject to multiple, competing interpretations and narratives.

Ultimately, the politics of inscription in Northern Ireland is a contestation over how the bodies of the dead should be remembered and which dead bodies should be afforded preeminent public visibility. Paramilitary groups might wish to prioritise their own dead 'volunteers', and through that prioritisation, perform the relevance, past and present, of the state of exception. But there are competing usages of both those bodies and the bodies of non-combatants that perform other narrations of Troubles violence. Can the ghosts of the Troubles be resurrected to challenge the brutal, self-replicating internal logic of the state of exception that facilitated their dehumanised death in the first place?

Chapter 4

Empathic dissonance and the hierarchy of victims

The next four chapters of this book, while not purely 'empirical', are heavily indebted to interviews with 52 memory curators across the six counties of Northern Ireland that I conducted in 2014–2015, as well as ethnographic field notes collected at places and times where memory is performed publically in Northern Ireland. Where appropriate, I have attempted to allow memory curators to speak for themselves and limit my own authorial interference. A good portion of the text in the subsequent chapters will therefore be devoted to the first-hand perspectives of memory curators in Northern Ireland, as communicated to me in interviews and in the field. The term 'memory curator' is my own creation, and I choose it instead of the more common 'memory choreographer' (for example Conway, 2009, 2010; Spillman & Conway, 2007) or 'memory entrepreneur' (Jelin, 2003) because I feel both connotations would imply a too-centralised notion of control by an agent or group of agents over a given memory performance. By memory curator, I mean a person who selects, presents, and cares for a strand or strands of social memory for the purposes of public display and/or archive. Whereas choreography would connote a performative set of steps, movements, blocking, and positions created by someone with some degree of authorial power, referring to agents as curators I believe allows for the possibility that memory performances may in some cases jump the boundaries of curatorial intent.

Chapters 4 to 6 take up each of the three challenges memory makes to transitional justice that I outlined in the introduction. This chapter looks at how memory curators in Northern Ireland perform victimhood in public. Chapter 5 looks at the creation of places of memory in post-conflict space, and Chapter 6 closely examines how those places are presented and what narratives and mnemonics are and can be inscribed into them. Chapter 7 attempts to look closely at the human toll of these challenges as written on the bodies of those killed and those who loved them.

The political lives of dead bodies

Katherine Verdery's excellent book *The Politics Lives of Dead Bodies* (1999) figured heavily in the inception of this research programme. In it, she argues that the study of nationalism(s) must be turned on its head. For Verdery, nationalism has too long been studied exclusively as "a matter of territorial borders, state-making, 'constructionism', or resource competition" (Verderey, 1999, p. 26). Rather than focusing scholarly energies on rational and rationalist explanations, Verdery argues that scholars need to return to Max Weber in order to 'enliven' the politics of the past. Nationalism is about the ways in which people connect themselves to meaningful symbolic narrations of a foundational past. It is about how people affix themselves into a cosmology; how they struggle to understand their shared place in the world and how they came to it. Dead bodies are rendered into statues or chiselled into stone, they meet our eyes in old photographs (see Hirsch, 1997), their voices are rediscovered in letters and archives. The memories of dead bodies and their material and spectral traces left on the land help to produce that cosmology, for they link and connect social actors to the significant figures of their pasts and serve as focal lynchpins of intersubjectively understood genres, and performances. They are our saints, sinners, heroes, martyrs, villains, traitors, or mothers, fathers, ancestors, kinfolk. Their bodies and their traces are not, however, purely historicised objects; they are texts that must be read in the present, inscribed (or perhaps, rebirthed) into memory in a particular form, though that form has the potential to be read in a number of different ways. In cases of unsettled pasts, they are potent political objects, their appropriate and inappropriate spatial usage subject to contests of control and ownership. Just who has the right to speak for the ghosts and why? Writes Verdery:

> I present the politics of corpses as being less about legitimating new governments (though it can be that too) than about cosmologies and practices relating the living to the dead. And I see the rewriting of history that is obviously central to dead-body politics as part of a larger process whereby fundamental changes are occurring in the conception of time itself.
>
> (Verdery, 1999, pp. 26–27)

Here, I seek to bring Verdery to Northern Ireland and illustrate how dead bodies, and specifically those bodies that lost their lives in the Troubles, are employed to create social memory and order post-conflict space. When political actors in Northern Ireland appropriate the bodies of the dead, they are seeking, consciously or otherwise, to affect how the memory of the past can inform and guide the politics of the present. Dead bodies in Northern Ireland can be used to perform the relevance of violence, to sanctify ethnicised space, to demarcate borders, to enact social martyrdom and a hegemony of collective, oppositional suffering. But dead bodies have other uses as well. For the subaltern or the traumatised, dead bodies can be used to demand inclusion and recognition in the 'new' Northern Ireland, the post-conflict spatial fabric; they can be objects employed to demand witnessing and acknowledgement; and finally, through calling attention to their complex, meaningful lives and their status as dearly loved and dearly missed, they can challenge and disrupt the legitimating frames of the state of exception that allowed them to be killed in the first place.

In Northern Ireland, as 'Heather' articulates below, "everyone's a victim of somebody else" (see Jamieson, 2016; Brewer & Hayes, 2013; Lawther, 2013). Republicans and nationalists are victims of British colonialism, unionist oppression, loyalist murders, and deadly and collusive attacks by the security forces (Rosland, 2009; Rolston, 2002). Loyalists and unionists are victims of Irish irredentism, IRA terrorism, Sinn Féin machinations, the ungratefulness of the British state, and unfair media portrayals (McAuley & Ferguson, 2016; Monaghan & Shirlow, 2011; Rolston, 2006). Other survivors of the violence are victims of having been blown up or injured; they may be victims of unfair treatment by the state or inadequate compensatory or reparative mechanisms, victims of a denial of justice, victims of a political and social reality that privileges paramilitary narratives, messaging, commemorations, over their pain and suffering (Simpson, 2009). The sense that 'everyone's a victim' can sometimes lend an immediacy to the need to claim direct victimhood, as social actors seek recognition of the proximity and priority of their pain and the suffering of their group (Graham, 2014). For others still, it can fuel a rejection of the term itself, as 'victim' may come to connote a lack of agency, an expectation of pity, or a suspect political status. But the utterance 'victim' is part of a complex morphology. The experience of being or knowing a victim or a survivor of violence can be subject to multiple understandings, even within groups of people victimised by the same violent act:

> They still have their victimhood, which is really important for them to hold onto, because whenever that starts to fall apart, your whole identity falls apart … In Northern Ireland, everyone's a victim of somebody else. So to let that fall apart, people just can't come to terms with that, they can't cope.
>
> ('Heather', Derry)

> Victims have more in common [with other victims from across the communal divide]. I've worked with victims' groups before from both sides of the divide. But it's living in that victimhood and that attachment they have sometimes, they don't want to give it up because they feel like that's who they are.
>
> ('Sally', Belfast)

> When I was young … I didn't see myself as a victim and I still don't see myself as a victim. I'm not saying [Bloody Sunday] didn't have an impact on my life but I don't have this sense of (which I think happens too often now, in my view) … that people cling to victimhood because it gives them identity. *I don't want to be a victim.*
>
> ('Colin', Derry, original emphasis)

Each of these three quotations illustrates in some way the victimhood-as-identity argument; yet in all three cases these are survivors and bereaved individuals identifying the problem, externalising it to 'others', and rejecting the category of victim that could very well apply to them. Thus, it becomes hard, if not outright inappropriate, to make generalisations about 'victims' of the Troubles or even members of 'victims' groups. Naming and adopting victimhood as a social identity can be a political act; it may very well be an act of resonant protest against a larger perception of injustice embedded in the spatio-political order. But *not* adopting victimhood as a social identity or a mobilisation mechanism can also be a political act. In 'Colin's' perspective, victimhood is conflated with political *inaction*, whereas in other cases, joining a victims and survivors' group is seen as an act of political protest and social solidarity.

The utterance 'victim' is a politically motivated speech act. In Northern Ireland, the term victim generally is used as part of a predominately PUL speech genre, and it connotes a moral hierarchy. If someone is a 'victim', they are guiltless or innocent, and as such, morally 'clean', in contrast to other groups or individuals (predominately republicans, but loyalists and the security forces as well in certain instances) whose experience of violent death might be similar, but whose actions, status, or organisational membership negates their claims to victimhood. In constructing this larger narrative focused on IRA perpetration, many victims, survivors, or bereaved employ a dead body, or bodies, as a potent political symbol. Verdery illustrates how well suited bodies are for such narratives, arguing that they are both intrinsically malleable and deeply resonant symbols:

> Dead people come with a curriculum vitae or resumé – several possible resumés, depending on which aspect of their life is being considered ... Their complexity makes it fairly easy to discern different sets of emphasis, extract different stories, and thus rewrite history. Dead bodies have another great advantage as symbols: they don't talk much on their own (though they did once). Words can be put in their mouths – often quite ambiguous words – or their actual words can be ambiguated by quoting them out of context. It is thus easier to rewrite history with dead people than with other kinds of symbols that are speechless.
>
> (Verderey, 1999, p. 29)

While Verdery is focused on how past figures are selected out of time for the purposes of creating nationalist *mythos*, I suggest that, at the local level, many victims campaigners are engaging in a smaller version of the process she describes. They are not so much 'rewriting history' as they are selecting and negotiating into existence one overarching and reductionist body-narrative. Certain corpses are sanctified and certain corpses are not, and my choice of biblical terminology is not accidental. An 'innocent' body in Northern Ireland connotes a purity, a cleanliness, that if pushed towards the most reductionist extremes, rewrites and reduces memory of the body into a dichotomous political parable of worthy victim and evil perpetrator. The famed criminologist Nils Christie refers to 'ideal victims' as those bodies best able to encapsulate socially constructed and learned ideals of purity and blamelessness. He suggests that reducing victims to idealised objects is both an attempt to write out any complexity and to create an operationalised dualism of innocence versus 'big and bad'. For Christie, white women, and especially children, are the most susceptible to idealisation and the racialised and sexualised duality in social idealisation helps to explain why the bodies of people of colour are disproportionately punished and surveilled (Christie, 1986).[1] But conversely, attempting to problematise victimhood or innocence, whether by observing that perpetrators can also be victims or that complex people and the lives they live/led do not always fit into neatly dichotomous categories, can be viewed as either an attempt to exculpate a violent perpetrator or to erode the space of moral superiority that innocent victimhood must occupy. As I argued in Chapter 1, this explains the visceral rejections of the Eames-Bradley report and the pervasive relativism that undergirded it. Referring to the £12,000 clause, 'Benjamin's' perspective here is highly indicative:

> To put £12,000 on the life of my [loved one]! … But take the money out of it, the fact is the perpetrator could get that money. You imagine the Loughgall[2] families … their families would be entitled to the same amount of money as the Enniskillen families, Teebane, other innocent families. You think the likes of McGuirk's Bar, carried out by loyalists … the McGuirk's people deserve it, but say if one of them terrorists in the course of planting the bomb was killed, his family would be entitled to the money as well. That's totally wrong. It's the fact that perpetrators of what happened here [in Enniskillen] would get the same money as the victims, it equates them the same, which is totally, totally, wrong!
>
> ('Benjamin', County Fermanagh)

'Michael' adds to 'Benjamin's' perspective here, describing what 'innocent' means to him and the victims and survivors group he is closely aligned with:

> Innocent – we understand it as someone who loses their life, whom had been essentially targeted by others, they had no choice in the matter. Those whom in our view are murdered by republicans or loyalist terrorists or, in our view, the criminal element within the security forces, those individual members who dishonoured the code, those individuals are all innocent in that sense. We would not view an IRA member or a UVF member who goes purposefully to take life and who dies as a consequence of that action, we would not consider that

1 Herman and Chomsky's (1988) 'worthy' and 'unworthy' victims is a parallel argument.

2 Loughgall, County Tyrone, was where a squad of IRA men attempting to bomb a police station were ambushed and shot dead by the SAS. For republicans, Loughgall is one of the prime examples of the security forces' 'shoot-to-kill' policy as no attempt was made to arrest the IRA attackers before they were engaged. Some of the family members of the IRA men have pursued justice in this case against the British state.

individual to be innocent because he subscribes to a code which believes that there is a justification for taking another human being's life to further his cause. That's where innocence breaks down.

('Michael', County Fermanagh)

The acute reader may notice how both 'Michael' and 'Benjamin' take special care to emphasise that, in their perspective, the category of innocence could apply to Catholic-nationalist victims as well. This is a discursive attempt to pre-empt an argument that innocence is monopolised by PUL victims and survivors groups. In my interviews with Protestant members of victims and survivors groups, many seemed genuinely not to comprehend why the discourse of innocence was problematic for many from across the communal divide.

The discursive priority of innocence cannot be thought of merely as being unique to Northern Ireland either. Cara Levey (2016) has noted a similar refusal to problematise discourses of innocence within victims and survivors groups in Argentina, for example, even in cases where the killed or disappeared may have been actively participating in violent anti-regime activity. In this case, establishing collective innocence refutes Carlos Menem's 'two demons' argument, that both the state and the anti-state forces were culpable, and thus the past should stay in the past ('Full Stop'). In Northern Ireland, *innocence is also a political refusal to accept the Full Stop.* This must be noted and appreciated by scholars, especially given ongoing attempts by former paramilitaries such as Sinn Féin (not to mention the British state) to proceed on a programme of peace and reconciliation in the context of a Full Stop, in the context of a thorough 'depoliticisation' of the past:

> Reconciliation … is the public space within which we can collectively engage with the key challenges of truth, justice, and acknowledgment *within the context of building for the future.* For the purposes of this policy we focus on the construction of reconciliation as a process: a process that is open and which seeks to *position the possibility of reconciliation outside of the thrust of daily politics …*
>
> For Sinn Féin reconciliation and healing is intrinsically linked to shaping a future that assists us all to move beyond historical antagonism … Reconciliation and healing must be the antidote to past conflict and hostility.
>
> (Sinn Féin, 2016, pp. 4–5, emphasis added)[3]

Much of the backdrop for this is a 2005 bill proposed by the Blair government in the British House of Commons, called the Northern Ireland Offences Bill, in which Sinn Féin was accused of collaborating with the British government to severely limit the legal possibilities of investigating and prosecuting Troubles-related offences. SDLP MP Mark Durkan referred to their conduct, for example, as an 'alliance of sleaze' with the British (BBC News, 2005). For Sinn Féin, up to

3 See also Hedges (2015).

150 former IRA members still wanted for past offences (known as 'On-the-runs' or OTRs) would receive assurance from the British government that they were no longer wanted for questioning. The affair is murky, as at some point it became clear that the Bill would also include legal amnesties for British soldiers who could potentially be accused of war crimes for massacres such as Ballymurphy and Bloody Sunday. According to the SDLP and Peter Hain, the Northern Ireland Secretary responsible for crafting the legislation under the Blair government, Sinn Féin were well aware that across the Bill was essentially a legal Full Stop – the practical equivalent of laws such as Menem's Full Stop in Argentina – and that it also applied to British soldiers and security force members accused of past crimes. Sinn Féin virulently denied this and accused Hain of pulling a bait-and-switch (Derry Journal, 2014). Who one believes tends to be indicative of one's prior political orientation and I do not offer a comment here. What is important is that many within the unionist and some within the nationalist community have come to view reconciliation as articulated by Sinn Féin and the British state as tantamount to enforcing an end to all claims for justice. Peter Hain in particular has been very clear that that was indeed his very intention (Hain, 2014). The discourse of innocence operates within that context; among other discursive uses, innocence is also a demand that the past be left open to recovery and excavation and a denial of an alleged political programme that uses reconciliation as a means to impose a legal, institutional framework of moral equivalence and impunity for past crimes on Northern Ireland's political space.

Thus, while it can be tempting to merely write out discourses of innocence as barely concealed sectarianism, the reality is that innocence is multifaceted and operates within a complex political landscape of memory. Innocence, and the hierarchy of victims it seeks to narratively create, is more complex than simply 'Protestant bodies matter, but Catholics don't' or 'Victims of the IRA, on one hand, or the security forces, on the other, are the only real victims of the Troubles'. These connotations are certainly present in Northern Ireland, but they are not monolithic. Thus the hierarchy of victims may be much more complex than it seems at face value.

Hierarchy of victims

Brian Graham and Yvonne Whelan provide scholars with an excellent starting point for examining the hierarchy of victims in Ireland. They write:

> The dead remain a potent and emotive means of legitimating and perpetuating the ethnonationalism and sectarianism characteristic of political debate in Northern Ireland. There is little sense of reconciliation through shared loss, but, instead, the commemorative landscape seems largely to form part of the competing claims for hegemonic victimhood by trenchantly opposed identities and spatialities proclaiming their irreconcilable differences.
>
> (Graham & Whelan, 2007, p. 480)

While there is much to recommend this analysis, Graham and his colleagues tend to over-totalise. Ethnonationalism and sectarianism is certainly characteristic of political debate in Northern Ireland, and if a scholar's primary sources of data on memory and the dead in Northern Ireland stem from contemporaneous Northern Irish political discourse, then the analysis is largely accurate. The 1998 Agreement was a consociational agreement, which rather than attempting to ameliorate existing socio-political division, accepted it as essentialist and permanent. Through mechanisms such as mandatory coalition, the Agreement calcified these divisions and created a pseudo-democratic reality where the two primary sectarian parties, Sinn Féin and the DUP respectively, cannot be (realistically) voted out of office (see Taylor, 2009; Tonge, 2004).[4] Thus, these two parties' share of votes and level of political power is disproportionate and not necessarily indicative of the entirety of social attitudes towards memory, victimhood, and the past in Northern Ireland. The contradictory thing about Graham's work is that he often seems to understand this quite well, and often exposes it in quite acrid prose. In one article, he writes:

> If it is assumed that Northern Ireland is not merely the exercise in postmodern irony that mandatory coalition suggests ... then one requires a much more dynamic understanding of identity ... and of the potential alternatives to the legacy of sectarianism and ethnic conflict that spawned the DUP and Sinn Féin.
>
> (Graham, 2011, p. 88)

He is absolutely correct and may be unaware at times of just how many people in Northern Ireland agree with him. In doing so, he fails to give adequate space to ongoing efforts to shape 'alternatives to the legacies of sectarianism'. In interviewing memory curators in Northern Ireland, I was quite surprised initially to find that while there is certainly a strain of social memory that squares with Graham and Whelan's somewhat bleak understanding of the symbolic usages and potentialities of dead bodies, this strand is far from absolute, even among victims and their advocates. This challenged my own presuppositions and rewrote my original research plan. I will outline some of this testimony shortly, but first I want to define more comprehensively what a 'hierarchy of victims' means in the context of Northern Ireland.

In Northern Ireland, the term 'hierarchy of victims' has entered the wider vernacular and is familiar to many. However, people in general and my respondents particularly deployed it in slightly different ways. I argue that the concept contains two separate but closely related discourses. The first discourse is a hierarchy of social visibility and resource allocation; in this discourse the speaker alleges

4 For the primary defenders of the Agreement and consociationalism generally, see McGarry and O'Leary (2004).

that certain victims, survivors, and their families garner disproportionate access to social attention and public expenditure. This understanding is common to members of PUL victims and survivors communities and is rooted in the belief that within Northern Ireland and countries perceived to be sympathetic to republicanism, such as the Republic of Ireland and the United States, only the victims of state violence seem to matter. Like 'Benjamin' and 'Michael' (cited above), it does not make an explicit moral pronouncement regarding the nature of victims and tends to cloak its PUL biases in the language of equality, saying that all victims should matter equally and be treated in the exact same manner as long as, of course, they were truly 'innocent'. One case that is often deployed in this discourse is the Bloody Sunday Inquiry chaired by Lord Saville, by far the largest, longest, and costliest British public inquiry into any Troubles-related killings:

> This last few meetings we've had, the Catholic families haven't come along and I remember that day when the results of the Bloody Sunday [Inquiry] came out … I watched the [Bloody Sunday] families and the joy and the happiness they have and I had to leave … They have got the justice they want, whether it's proper justice or not which I don't think it is … but we in Claudy,[5] we feel we are just forgotten.
>
> ('Isabella', County Derry)

> There's some'll say the Bloody Sunday people were a hierarchy of victims because they got a public inquiry, but they wouldn't have given them a public inquiry if Sinn Féin and the Irish government and all them hadn't got involved. And when they found out how much it cost, you can be sure we're not going to get another one. If they give Omagh a public inquiry, the people in Castlederg[6] whose 29 loved ones were murdered along the border, they need a public inquiry and they're quite entitled to get one.
>
> ('Luke', County Tyrone)

Both respondents are operating primarily within the hierarchy of resources discourse and this discussion is fairly ubiquitous when it comes to discussions regarding the Bloody Sunday Inquiry, especially among unionists, though it is not confined to them, as evidenced by the fact that 'Luke' is a Catholic and would not identify as a unionist.

5 See Chapter 6. The Claudy bombing of 31 July 1972 was universally understood to have been carried out by the Derry Brigade of the Provisional IRA. It killed nine civilians: five Protestants, and four Catholics.

6 See Chapter 5. Castlederg is a small town in West Tyrone on the border with County Donegal of the Republic of Ireland. The IRA staged a number of cross-border attacks, primarily targeting local members of the security forces, especially the UDR, throughout the Troubles.

The second major discourse in which the hierarchy of victims operates is a moral discourse. In this telling, a group or faction is unworthy of being considered victims (or at least unworthy of our level of victimhood) in the first place. Rarely is this perspective openly sectarian, at least now, but it is rooted in divergent and sectarianised social understandings of the roots of the Troubles. Rehumanisation and acknowledgement of other narratives and other traumatic realities shakes the cognitive taxonomy that sustains one's own social identity and social memories, and sustains the moral superiority of innocence. Thus the line between 'worthy' and 'unworthy' victims must be maintained. It has two sub-variants. In one, the harder-line version, republican, loyalist, or security force dead are totally unworthy of commemoration because of their status or actions. These memories should be symbolically obliterated (Foote, 2003) from Northern Ireland's memory-space whenever possible. Such is the perspective of Ross Hussey, who goes so far as to compare the IRA to Nazis, the perspective of 'Erin', who angrily reduces Sinn Féin to child-killers, 'Daniel', who draws a clear line in the sand regarding those worthy of memory in public, and 'Ronan', whose perspective on the British army and the memory of British soldiers is indicative of someone who experienced Bloody Sunday first-hand:

> See the difference with [republican] memorials and UDR memorials, them people [the UDR] was all murdered. The IRA, they wasn't murdered ... if they was shot, they were on their way to shoot somebody else.
>
> ('Daniel', ex-UDR, County Tyrone)

> Unionists view those who murdered our colleagues as terrorists. Sinn Féin views them as volunteers on active service. So you'll never be able to get terrorism and volunteers together ... People like that I'm afraid are the lowest of the low as far as I'm concerned and I wouldn't commemorate them, full stop. It's like asking the Jews can we now have a memorial to the Nazis.
>
> (Ross Hussey, UUP MLA, ex-RUC, County Tyrone)

> You cannot equate a perpetrator with a victim ... Yes, they lost their lives through the Troubles ... but they went out to murder, whereas [my loved one] and the others, they were just going about their everyday business and were brutally murdered. So the perpetrators, they had a choice to go out and do what they did, whereas the innocent victim didn't have a choice.
>
> ('Benjamin', County Fermanagh)

> That's why [Sinn Féin] don't deal with the past, because they're in it up to their armpits ... They're child-killers at the end of the day.
>
> ('Erin', County Tyrone)

> The British are not going to allow themselves to be depicted in the way they ought to be depicted: as ruthless killers, liars, perjurers, and all the rest of it.
> ('Ronan', Derry)

The slightly softer line to obliteration I refer to as 'consociational' memory. While consociational memory does not call for the suspect memories to be obliterated from public space, it is no less strict about the need to segregate and categorise the bodies of the dead:

> I could never hold the same regard for a RUC man as I could for Terry [Enright].[7] Because Terry for me was doing something positive; the RUC were doing something oppressive. So I can never envisage thinking of them on the same level.
> (Peter Hughes, West Belfast)

> By saying that, Peter [Hughes, above] isn't saying that the RUC man or the loyalist or their families or their families' families haven't got the right to commemorate them, they should, they're well within their rights to do it and they probably will do it … but what our [GAA] club did is the memorial here and it was our own way of doing it. *Put up your own monument.*
> (Feargal Mac Ionnrachtaigh, West Belfast, emphasis added)

What Feargal seems to suggest here is that those folks or that other group can remember their dead and we have no problem with it, as long as the bodies, and their symbolic potential, are kept separate. Any infringement on his brother's memory-place, the GAA club, or any larger intrusion of RUC or loyalist dead into the larger space the ghost of his loved one haunts, is a violation of memory. You take care of your dead, we'll take care of ours. The Belfast NGO *Healing through Remembering* solicited ideas from a wide cross-spectrum of society about what aesthetic form a Northern Ireland-wide memorial to the dead of the Troubles might look like. In perusing some of the sketches and ideas submitted, I was struck by how many utilised some aesthetic form of consociational memory, generally by proposing a place where the names of the victims and even the aesthetics of the memorial itself are spatially and symbolically separated and the status of the ghosts that would haunt within clearly indicated. Consider Peter Shirlow and Brendan Murtagh's example of Belfast City Cemetery:

> Within Belfast City Cemetery there is an underground wall that purposefully separates the Catholic and the Protestant dead … Even in death there is a desire to remain uncontaminated by the presence of the etho-sectarian other.
> (Shirlow & Murtagh, 2006, p. 13)

7 See Chapters 1 and 7.

Porter (2003, p. 267) argues that Northern Ireland is "a society that is accustomed to cultural and political attitudes being shaped by habit of self-interest, suspicion, and contempt of the other". While again this perspective over-totalises, the distressing fact is that many in Northern Ireland simply exhibit no wish to understand the historiography of the narrative of the 'other' community, and this parochialism is further enabled by the territorial enclavement so distressingly typical of Northern Irish space (Shirlow & Murtagh, 2006). Thus, consociational memory should not be seen as something distinct from the consociational arrangement of the Agreement and what the former director of the Community Relations Council for Northern Ireland Will Glendenning called in 2002 'self-imposed apartheid' (BBC News, 2002). Perhaps 'Jack' describes consociational memory best of all my respondents:

> People will really just remember in their own way. I don't know if there's ever been an attempt to bring people together, [to put] all of these different commemorations and events into one single memorial. I think that'd probably be too painful because people would say, 'Look, I don't want this person near me, if they're remembered here, I don't want to be remembered, because of what happened.' That's just the way it is.
>
> ('Jack', North Belfast).

But no discursive form of the hierarchy of victims in Northern Ireland is monolithic. Many of my respondents consciously and stridently problematised it, even those who had 'lost someone belonging to them', which is a particularly Northern Irish euphemism for suffering through the violent death of a loved one. This contradicts the totalising impulses we see so often in scholarly portrayals of Northern Irish memory-space.

Julieanne Campbell and Jeanette Warke both utilise the cross-communal experience of death and violence to challenge the hierarchy of victims. Julieanne especially points to what she believes is a wider desire within Northern Irish society to cut through the social divisions maintained by the perpetuation of a moral hierarchy of victims:

> My [relative's] role was to say a prayer for all the [Bloody Sunday] victims and then it was unanimously decided, no, not just for our victims, a prayer for all the victims of the Troubles. And it went down brilliant because they weren't just thinking about themselves, they were thinking about all of them. And it got a massive cheer after the minute's silence, for all of them, for all the victims. So obviously there is an appetite out there.
>
> (Julieanne Campbell, Derry, former chairperson of the Bloody Sunday Trust)

> *Jeanette*: I often thought it'd be good if we had a memorial dedicated to the people who came from [Derry], who were killed during the

Troubles. Everybody. And I mean everybody … You remember them, I mean you can't just brush them all under the carpet.

Author: When you say all the people who died, do you mean literally *all* the people?

Jeanette: I mean all the people who died. I mean *all* the people. No matter.

Author: Including IRA men?

Jeanette: Including everybody. Put them all up. They died for something they thought they believed in … be it right, be it wrong. UDA, UVF, they was the same, they died for things. Well, to me they was always led to the slaughter.

(Jeanette Warke, Derry)

'Conor' and 'Oisin' both argue that peace itself is enabled by dispensing with the moral hierarchy completely:

Conor: I think we should remember everybody. *People* were victims of the conflict as well.

Author: But you could conceivably see [your loved one] honoured on the same place as his killers.

Conor: I wouldn't worry about it. Because it's remembering everybody that died, it's about how it affected the families, it's about how it affected the communities, it's about how it affected this place … Peace, that's the lasting memorial. You're talking about moving away from the type of situation that caused people to think it was right to take up a gun and go out and shoot somebody, to shoot a soldier, to shoot a policeman, the same way the police'd be heavily armed and involved in killing people.

('Conor', North Belfast)

> Going back to that phraseology [we were using] the ghettoisation of memory. I was thinking, 'I'm living in a bubble'. That bubble is a nationalist bubble and I'm not hearing that other story and that other story is a powerful dissuader … [The stories] bring humanity, hopefully … So how do we memorialise in a way that does that? That orchestrates that still, sad music of humanity[8] so that people say, 'Stop! Put down the guns!' So people say, 'Let's find new ways'.
>
> ('Oisin', Derry)

'Patrick', not unlike Feargal and Peter, also categorises memory by status, but his perspective and his tone are different. His focus is on the polyphonic potential of memory in Northern Ireland and the humanising capacity of narrative and

8 I owe the Wordsworth epigraph to this book to 'Oisin', who referenced it several times during our interview.

storytelling. Though he maintains clear types and categories, instead of focusing on keeping them apart, he seems to suggest that they should be put together, to share a memory habitat, and that the Troubles is a story that must be heard holistically, from a diverse cross-section of different voices:

> But as I say, Joe, if we could even agree that there's two, there's five, there's ten narratives, *if we could even have a place where we could go*[9] where there's loads of different narratives, having some way of capturing those different narratives, that would be a good place to visit, wouldn't it? That's be a good place to go and see ... To go and get the narrative of a prison officer and a blanket man, to get the narrative of the RUC man and the IRA man and the loyalist and the UDR man. I think getting those narratives would be good and develops us all through that.
>
> ('Patrick', West Belfast)

'Heather's' challenge to the hierarchy of victims is also profound, not least of all because, like 'Patrick', her experience is that of someone directly and viscerally affected by paramilitary violence:

> I think that everyone has an absolute right to have their person, that person that they loved and was lost, to be at the forefront of their memory, and they have a right to place them where they want to place them in their memory ... So, given my background and my own story, and who [my loved one] is, I have every right to think that morally, and through my own lens, he was a better person than the person who shot him ... But it would never be my place to turn around and say to the mother of an IRA guy or a UDA guy or whoever, I have no right so say to her that [my loved one] is better than your terrorist ... If you're looking at a mother who's lost somebody, her grief is the same as anybody else's, it would be the same thing. And I have no right to undermine that.
>
> ('Heather', Derry)

At this stage, I must make a very important point in regard to my own positionality. The way my respondents' testimony is laid out may lead some readers to think that I am arguing that the moral hierarchy of victims is misguided or incorrect, that it is better to remember the dead as 'Heather' does, or to affix loved ones' bodies into a wider, holistic conversation about the nature of the Troubles, as 'Patrick' does. If I were arguing that, I would be creating yet another hierarchy, a hierarchy of perspective, and I emphatically do not wish to do so. In Chapter 2, I introduced Hamber and Wilson's (2002) concept of symbolic closure to argue

9 I would like the reader to note the similarities between 'Patrick's' words here Ariel Dorfman's poem 'Red Tape', which I will cite in Chapter 5.

against proclaiming that there is a right way and a wrong way to remember to our loved ones. I suggest that such a hierarchy of perspective alienates and isolates those who would employ their loved ones for other purposes besides, or perhaps in addition to, the goals of social reconciliation, goals such as justice, accountability, information retrieval, and/or lustration. Here is the point I am making: 'Heather's' or 'Patrick's' or 'Conor's' testimony is not *better* than Ross Hussey's, than 'Erin's', 'Daniel's', or Feargal and Peter's; it is however, *different* from them and refutes the notion that remembering the dead in Northern Ireland is purely an exercise in ethnocommunitarian one-upmanship.

But this is not to say that victims and survivors advocates in Northern Ireland are blameless in perpetuating their own restrictive memory regimes. My major frustration with the 'innocence' discourse in Northern Ireland is not that it seeks moral clarity (it has every right to, as I have every right to simultaneously engage with it dissonantly, through both empathy and criticism), but that it seeks, consciously or not, to monopolise memory, to instil in a wider public a right way of remembering (there are innocents and there are guilty) and a wrong way of remembering (ambiguity). A conversation with a friend of mine, 'Roisin', may serve to illustrate this point. While discussing a well-known victims and survivors campaigner, and one who operates within the discursive field of innocence, 'Roisin' argued: "It's like nobody ever lost anybody in Northern Ireland except [him]. He needs to get over it. People all over are moving on with their lives" (personal communication).

Perhaps sensing that her initial knee-jerk reaction could be perceived or as unsympathetic, cruel even, 'Roisin' wrote me an email some hours after our discussion and added an important clarification:

> I get really annoyed when people in NI, particularly 'victims campaigners', take ownership of grief and try to tell everyone how we should feel or how victimhood should be ranked. And because they are carrying the mantle of victimhood, it's like this sacred thing that allows them carte blanche to be heard and to dictate the narrative … I do think that a lot of the victims' representatives are totally grief- stricken and this is their way of addressing their loss. And that's heartbreaking. But it's still not a good enough reason to dictate to the rest of us.
>
> ('Roisin', personal communication)

Both 'Roisin's' initial, knee-jerk reaction, and her subsequent, nuanced one are deeply important. The frustration she feels with the victims campaigner is rooted in her perception that she is being told how she *should* feel, how she should remember the past and the bodies that were lost. Within this attempted monopolisation, she finds no space for her perspective and those who feel like her. In her clarification, she emphasises that she does not criticise the campaigner for his inability to 'move on' (i.e. move from melancholia to mourning), which she refers to as heartbreaking (thus demonstrating her internalisation of the Freudian duality); rather, her criticism is focused on the campaigner's drive to control the space of memory and the potential for activism around legacy-of-the-past issues. This drive, she argues, is undemocratic; it attempts to dictate a particular response to past violence that is reductionist and one-sided. 'Roisin' makes an important point, namely that symbolic closure can cut both ways: it is not merely survivors and the bereaved who struggle against symbolic closure. They may enact it as well; they may demand a unitary response to disparate and incommensurate strands of social grieving and political activism.

Yet 'Roisin' and many others may also underappreciate the therapeutic value of the innocent/guilty dualism. In assumptive- or just-world theory, the assumptions we build and construct from our social and interpersonal worlds function as a cognitive shield against randomness or senselessness of the world. For its progenitor, Melvin Lerner (1980), our primary shield assumptions are our belief in a fundamentally just world. Janoff-Bullman (1992), clarifying and extending Lerner, names three such assumptions: the world is meaningful, the world is benevolent, and the self is worthy of being in the world. But just-world theory does not hold that people are merely naive optimists; rather it holds that the baseline of psychosocial well-being lies in the psychosocial construction of assumptions that protect us from *anomie*, or the possibility that worlds we live in are merely senseless, random, vicious, or disordered. We might say in a sense they protect us from what Thomas Hobbes (1651/2001, ch. XIII) argued was the natural state of humankind.

Judith Herman's (1992) touchstone work also holds that the experience of trauma involves the faltering or outright breaking of protective assumptions. Thus for her, appropriate therapy for trauma survivors should focus on narrative re-empowerment and the reconstruction of protective categories, *such as guilt and innocence*. Without this moral clarity regarding the nature of the traumatic act, the survivor's world may remain shattered. Thus, criticisms of innocence dualism may be missing a critical component, namely how necessary therapeutically it is for an individual to understand that they or their loved ones were innocent and those who killed for a political cause were not.

But while innocence may be individually therapeutic, it can be socially problematic in post-conflict space. One perspective that may suggest a new way to think about the hierarchy of victims in transitional space is the perspective of the philosopher, critic, and Holocaust survivor Primo Levi, especially his rightly celebrated and classic essay 'The Grey Zone' (1989).

Empathic dissonance

Levi's primary subject in 'The Grey Zone' is the *Sonderkommandos* (also known as *Kapos*), Jews who were used by the Nazis as collaborators within Auschwitz and across the *Lager*, the network of concentration camps across East–Central Europe. The *Kapos* were responsible for terrorizing new arrivals to Auschwitz and for operating the crematoria and the gas chambers, for which they earned the sobriquet *crematorium ravens*. They did this for a few extra grams of soup or a few extra crusts of bread; they did this because perhaps they believed it might help them survive the *Lager* (it did not: the Nazis exterminated the *Kapos* with staggering efficiency); they did this because maybe there is something within many of us that tends towards collaboration and submissiveness to violent authority. Levi is not interested in trying to crawl inside their heads. For Levi, it is impossible to adjudicate their guilt or innocence. In one of the most powerful, resonant lines I have ever read in any text, Levi argues:

> It must be the Jews who put the Jews in the ovens; it must be shown that the Jews, the subrace, the submen, bow to any and all humiliation, even to destroying themselves ... [National Socialism] represented an attempt to shift to others – specifically, the victims – the burden of guilt, *so that they were deprived even of the solace of innocence.*
>
> (Levi, 1989, pp. 52–53, emphasis added)

The Grey Zone is the zone of moral ambiguity where there is no possibility of simple guilt or simple innocence. The essay is a meticulous, humanistic, and impassioned problematisation of those easy dualisms, a call for the rehumanisation of the bodies of the *Kapos* and other Jewish collaborators through a vigorous interrogation not only of their actions, but also of our own internal biases and assumptions. Yet, coming seemingly out of nowhere, and seemingly out of step with the larger theme of the essay, Levi imparts to his readers a truly devastating cry from the heart:

> I do not know, and it does not much interest me to know, whether in my depths there lurks a murderer, but I do know that I was a guiltless victim and I was not a murderer ... To confuse [murderers] with their victims is a moral disease or an aesthetic affectation of a sinister sign of complicity; above all, it is a precious service rendered (intentionally or not) to the negators of truth.
>
> (Levi, 1989, pp. 48–49)

Thus, in this magnificent text we find a seeming contradiction. Here we find Levi demanding a moral line between victim and perpetrator. I struggled personally for quite some time to reconcile this argument with the larger argument of 'The Grey Zone'. It could be simply that Levi refuses to allow us (especially we who were not in the *Lager*) to judge other Jews or other victims of the Holocaust. It could be that as a survivor of Auschwitz, a survivor so tormented by his experience that he would tragically take his own life, Levi will not, cannot, extend the same zone of moral ambiguity to Nazis, even to the so-called 'ordinary men' of the Nazi Party, of whom, like the *Kapos*, it might be possible to narrate an at least quasi-rehumanising story (Browning, 1992). That would certainly be understandable. But I think it is more complex than that. I think that Levi recognises the dissonance between moral clarity and moral ambiguity and purposefully leaves it in.

I suggest that Levi invites us, his audience, to sit with this dissonance and with the mental turmoil it causes us. I suggest he forces us to witness these two dissonant ideas at the same time, and in doing so, to try and understand that they may not in fact be contradictions, or if they are contradictions, they are necessary contradictions. There is space for innocence, space for recognising that a loved one was killed unnecessarily, immorally, and for no justifiable reason, that he or she was and is innocent and always will be, that he or she wanted no part of your cause or your methods and you killed him or her anyway, without a thought to the searing pain that act would cause in the people that loved him or her. There must be space to say *J'Accuse!* (Zola, 1898). I accuse the people and the groups who killed my loved one; I accuse the people and the organisations that supported them; I accuse those who gave them money and information and weapons and those who trained them in their use; I accuse the brutal logic of war, violence, and the state of exception. But Northern Ireland was, is, and will likely remain, a Grey Zone. And if people are open to, as 'Patrick' suggests, the multiplicity of social narratives that surround them, they may begin to rehumanise those who inflicted such violence and such trauma upon them – rehumanise *but not excuse*. And that partial rehumanisation may force people to begin to interact with their social memories in more critical ways, ways that might finally start to crack the veneer of the state of exception.

As an intellectual tradition dating perhaps as far back as Aristotle, but certainly to Erving Goffman, makes clear, politics is a form of performance (Butler, 1988, 1997; Phelan, 1993; Turner, 1988; Goffman, 1959), and dead-body politics is a particularly emotive political performance (Verdery, 1999). In Chapter 3 I argue that dehumanising body performances are essential to maintaining and reproducing the state of exception. I also argue that dehumanising performances, performances that suborn the complexities of a body and the life it led to a narrow political goal, are essential for force-wielders to maintain their relevance and their legitimacy in a post-conflict realm. However, I also suggest that the state of exception, and the dehumanising body performances that sustain it, no longer possesses the same degree of social control it had from 1966 to 1998, when a dialectic of existential threat was at its most acute in Northern Ireland. As the state of exception slips and cracks emerge in its facade, the potential for rehumanising performance creeps back in. Now obviously, dehumanisation and rehumanisation are not bifurcated categories – they exist on a theoretical spectrum – but there are common characteristics of body performances that are more dehumanising and some that are more rehumanising. I argue that dehumanising performance is towards the effective and communicative end of the spectrum, whereas rehumanising performance is affective and transactional (see Bennett, 2005). A more-dehumanising body performance employs a corpse primarily in the service of a symbolic political goal or ideal; the performance is didactic and closes off the potential for dialogue with an audience. It distils and reduces the intricacies of a human life or lives down to a single, prescriptive narrative. In contrast, a more-rehumanising performance is emotive, sensory, and experiential, and while it does not divine an essence of personal experience, it gives and in turn receives something from its audience. It speaks with its audience, not at it, but the script or choreography is not necessarily transcribed in a familiar orthography. It communicates the trace of the body, but resists the audience seeking to colonise or appropriate the body's pain for its own political purposes.

And this is the essence of Dominick LaCapra's 'empathic unsettlement', described by Jill Benett as "the aesthetic experience of simultaneously *feeling* for another and becoming aware of a distinction between one's own perceptions and the experience of the other" (Bennett, 2005, p. 8; LaCapra, 2001). Or perhaps as Paulette Regan (2010, p. 26) describes it, as when a witness to violence "fully embrace[s] the uncomfortable epistemological tension that comes with the realisation that they can never fully know the Other; nor should they aspire to do so". Or as Maurice Blanchot (1995, p. 82) hauntingly whispers to secondary witnesses to Auschwitz: "Know what happened, do not forget, and at the same time never will you know." As LaCapra himself puts it:

> The role of empathy and empathic unsettlement ... involves a kind of virtual experience through which one puts oneself in the other's position while recognising the difference of that position and hence not taking the other's place.
>
> (LaCapra, 2001, p. 78)

The opposite of empathic unsettlement might be what Bertolt Brecht famously called 'crude' empathy, or the gratuitous stimulation of empathy through an over-identification or outright assimilation into the traumatised body (Brecht, 1964). Crude empathy exploits the body; it is selfish, hedonistic almost. It is a performance in which we demonstrate to a real or perceived audience how much we care or how much we identify with and support the survivor or the victim, how vigorously we are devoted to the political cause to which we have suborned the body. Empathic unsettlement, on the other hand, recognises the interdependence of bodies, but may carry with it the potential for a radical reformulation of how we understand the relationship between ourselves and others. It is mourning that still allows for the necessary critical space for subjects to truly *encounter* one another, as Judith Butler puts it so eloquently. For Butler (2006, p. 49), it is only our not knowing, and more importantly that starting-point of not knowing the other but still recognising that the subject cannot be constituted without others, that allows for the necessary cross-subject and cross-cultural translation that breaks up our own particularistic discourses and opens our bodies to the possibility of a larger transformative community of grief:

> For if I am confounded by you, then you are already of me, and I am nowhere without you. I cannot muster the 'we' except by finding the way in which

> I am tied to 'you', by *trying to translate but finding that my own language must break up and yield if I am to know you.* You are what I gain through this disorientation and loss. This is how the human being comes into being, again and again, as that which we have yet to know.
>
> (Butler, 2006, p. 49, emphasis added)

Exploring Levi's contradiction, and with it the inherent tension between a morally clear hierarchy of victims and the fact that a state of exception *implicates everyone within it* – all are in the Grey Zone, is only possible when the urge to colonise the body in pain has been abandoned (Scarry, 1985) and the space between the body and the witness has been established. Empathy in this context becomes an unsettling aporia, an expression of puzzlement or doubt that serves as a spur to continue the dialogue and prevents dialectical foreclosure. But by suggesting that the empathy of the witness to traumatic violence should be aporetic, I am not suggesting in any way that the 'truth' or falsity of the survivor's narrative is what is at issue. Rather, the aporia of the survivor is Levi's dissonance, the tangled fusion of clarity and ambiguity, and the resistance to ending the discourse that that fusion invariably represents. A liminal, transitional space is unsettled by definition. Why should clarity be imposed, especially when such clarity either colonises the body or renders the body peripheral, out of place? What I mean by calling for aporetic empathy is that the witness should doubt herself: she is not the 'saved' and she is certainly not the 'drowned'. They have touched the Lacanian Real; we have not. It is not that the survivor cannot speak, but that we have become unable to hear. In such a context, we have a moral duty to allow our own languages and discourses to break down, their remnants to rest for a time in the spaces of complexity and dissonance, resisting the urge to narrate distressing dissonance out of the milieu.

Walter Benjamin has written a small fragment that I believe precisely, if by very definition abstractly, illustrates one example of what liminal, aporetic space can do:

> A generation that had gone to school on a horse-drawn streetcar now stood under the open sky in a countryside in which nothing remained unchanged but the clouds. In a field of force and destructive torrents and explosions was the tiny, fragile, human body.
>
> (Benjamin, 1992, p. 84)

The aporia is that 'fragile, human body' – that body so easily removed from political rhetoric and social memory in the tumult that surrounds it. Rehumanisation is an aporia; it is a pause in that chronology of destructive torrents to remember a human being. And in the process of pausing to remember and mourn that human being and his or her tiny (in the cosmic sense) body, we challenge the state of exception itself.

Victim hierarchies can unsettle and be unsettled, as long as the space is produced for subjects to encounter the Other and the Other's hierarchies and complexities. A hierarchy of victims is a constant in every transitional society, everywhere where subjects struggle to confront complex legacies of violence, from brutal legacies of war, dictatorship, genocide, mass oppression. I close this chapter with the case of 'Jack', whose testimony perhaps comes closest to illustrating what the prosocial impact of creating the space for dissonance and unsettlement may be. Navigating between moral ambiguity and moral clarity is unsettling; it means existing in a Grey Zone where killing challenges and problematises everything we perhaps thought we once knew.

'Jack's' loved one was killed by an IRA bomb; she was merely in the wrong place at the wrong time. In subsequent years, 'Jack' went to a bad place; he describes being unable to get out of bed in the morning, of suffering severe depression and a traumatic loss of meaning. 'Jack' was not and is not a violent person; he never sought violent retribution or flirted with joining paramilitaries in the wake of his loved one's killing. Rather, 'Jack' chose to confront the person he believed primarily responsible for the killing, Sinn Féin President Gerry Adams, with the memory of his loved one, repeatedly, whenever he could find the opportunity. 'Jack's' loved one's face is an aporetic object, an attempt to pause the republican chronology of justification, a refusal to let it reproduce itself until it has explained to him why she had to die. 'Jack' wrote Adams a string of letters trying to describe what his loved one meant to him, how much he had loved her, and enclosing pictures of her to show Adams what she looked like. To call 'Jack's' actions a 'campaign' would overstate his memory of his own intentionality; he describes it to me as not being a fully conscious undertaking, but rather being somewhat driven to it because of a feeling of helplessness and a lack of other outlets for his grief:

> I suppose for a while after the bomb happened, I would have taken placards and stood outside of Sinn Féin offices and really hounded Gerry Adams … The idea for the letters and the photographs came when I was thinking about [her], because I would have phoned [Sinn Féin] up and tried to talk to people to ask why did they murder [her]? And of course I got nowhere. Once they heard who it was they put the phone down or they'd give it to somebody else and I wasn't getting anywhere with that … So I suppose for me I wanted to confront Gerry Adams with who [she] was. I wanted him to know that she was of no real political significance at all, that the IRA had murdered just an innocent girl going about her lawful business. *I wanted him to know what she meant to me* … So that's why I started writing letters, sending stuff on her birthday, the anniversary of her death, Christmastime sometimes. I would have told him stories about us, about her, about me, what we got up to, just trying to get him to know who she was.
>
> ('Jack', North Belfast, emphasis added)

It was exceedingly difficult for me to hear 'Jack's' testimony and not break down in tears. His memory of his loved one's body is an immensely potent object, one that he wields to devastating effect against the republican state of exception. Her face, their memories together, delegitimises a cause that can narratively justify her killing and pierces the state of exception by the reinsertion of humanity. Doing so also seems to have prompted 'Jack' to begin inquiring into the republican mind-set in order to seek to understand what could have caused someone to undertake this act of violence that caused him such terrible pain. Yet even as his own perspective became more and more unsettled, his loved one's innocence remained. I cannot go into more detail lest I violate confidentiality, but 'Jack' knows that the man who detonated the bomb that killed his loved one also suffered a violent death. In the following testimony, he displays a startling generosity that nevertheless refuses to sacrifice a clear moral hierarchy of victims:

Author: Without drawing a moral equivalence, ***without*** doing that because I'm not trying to suggest anything of the sort, would you suggest that [the bomber] was also a victim?

'Jack': Yeah, I have no doubt about that at all … But I would have to qualify it and say that he was not a victim in the same way that [my loved one] was a victim … because to be quite frank with you, there is no moral equivalence to be made. I do believe that there's a hierarchy of victims, I do believe that people were innocent, I do believe that people were guilty, I do believe that people have more questions to answer than others, and you'll never persuade me or convince me other than that … But I think that it's only right that people say and state that at the end of the day, we are coming out of the conflict and we have to look at what's left behind and to me that means the [bomber]'s family as well as myself in terms of being looked after and helping us both to come to terms with what we've both lost. I respect the fact that [the bomber's mother] lost her son … I don't see that as being very noble of me or very generous or whatever, it just happens to be how I see it, I see us as human beings. *But that's not pretending that we were all just innocent people. We weren't. We very clearly weren't* (emphasis added).

Chapter 5

Social hauntings, places of memory

I grew up in a small town in Northern California, USA, on the edge of Humboldt Bay. In the middle of the bay there is a small island known as Indian Island, accessible only by boat. The island is uninhabited and empty, save for the remnants of a former Coast Guard station. But there is one small plinth stuck into the grass of the sand dunes. This plinth bears a small inscription which states that Indian Island is the site of the 1860 Wiyot Massacre, where white settlers murdered over a hundred Native men, women, and children (Crandell, 2005). I took advanced placement history courses throughout my schooling, yet I can recall no mention whatsoever of the massacre in my curriculum (nor any mention of the periodic anti-Chinese pogroms that eventually drove out all Chinese immigrants from the area in the late nineteenth century (Perry, 2005)). The Wiyot as a distinct tribe were all but exterminated by the beginning of the twentieth century. Their remnants were subsumed into their larger neighbouring cousins, the Yurok. The Yurok Indian Reservation now spans parts of Humboldt County and its northern neighbour, Del Norte County. Plagued by many of the problems so distressingly characteristic of the reservation system in North America (addiction, poverty, social disrepair), the Yurok tradition and language almost became extinct as the start of the twenty-first century. Currently though, it is enjoying somewhat of a small revival due to the tireless work of Indigenous activists, local historians, and linguists (Onishi, 2014). But I do remember the first time, 12 or 13 years old, I gazed on that small plinth. What would happen if it were to disappear, if someone dug it up and stole it, or it was destroyed by a winter storm and washed out to sea? Would the people and the families marked by it *have ever really existed?* Or would all traces of their cries, their pleas, their blood, be gone forever?

Primo Levi asks us to consider if the *Lager* inmate is a human:

> Consider if this is a man
> Who works in the mud
> Who knows no peace
> Who fights for a bit of bread
> Who dies because of a yes and because of a no …
>
> (Levi, 1995, epigraph)

In a similar manner, I would like us to consider if Indian Island is a place, because memory needs a place, as does grief, loss, and melancholia – a place to be expressed, a place to call its home, a place for its unsettled ghosts to haunt, and a place for 'the saved' to return to and speak to those who have been taken. Ariel Dorfman reflects on this relationship between traumatic memory and place in his haunting poem, 'Red Tape', and in the process, with the words barely seeming to leak from his pen, vivifies the shocking violence of forced disappearance, of the severing of the memory of offence from a place to call its home:

> just
> to be able to bury your body
> to have a place
> where your mother can go with
> flowers
> (you liked chrysanthemums
> but they cost so much)
> on Sundays
> and All Souls'
> Day.
> ('Red Tape' in Dorfman, 2002, p. 5)

Space and place

The two most central concepts in the study of human geography are space and place. Yet while seemingly relatively simple terms, the more one delves into them, the more one finds a maddeningly diverse and inconsistent operationalisation of them, even within the field of geography. Writes Yi-Fu Tuan (1977, p. 3): "Space and place are basic components of the lived world; we take them for granted. When we think about them, however, they may assume unexpected meanings and raise questions we have not thought to ask." Outside the field of geography, spatial metaphors are routinely utilised by theorists, but they tend to be used in such a way that strips them of their fluidity and complexity. Mathew Sparke (2005, p. xvi) refers to this as *anaemic geography*: "A geography that, like white chalk on slate, conceals the complex geographical palimpsest over which it writes a singular and supposedly coherent geo." Inside, outside, and in the between-spaces of geography, space and place can be unhelpfully reduced to their purely material or physical facets. However, there is no easy distinction to make between materiality and non-materiality. Writes Huyssen (2003, p. 7), "We have come to read cities and buildings and palimpsests of space, monuments as transformable and transitory, and sculpture as subject to the vicissitudes of time." Matter is felt, perceived, and understood through immaterial practices such as representation and relationality; we know a rock is a rock both because we hold the rock and feel its material form, but also because we have a signification system in place to represent the essential rock-ness of an object and what its relationship is to other forms of matter that surround it (Bennett, 2010; Latham & McCormack, 2004; MacKenzie, 2004; Guattari, 1995). If the material rock-ness of a rock can be problematised, what are we to make of the materiality of plazas, parks, shopping malls, cemeteries, museums, cities, landscapes?

I deploy this brief aside by way of commenting more approvingly on approaches to space and place in human geography that view these concepts more as the imaginative ordering of social relations than as named or nameable bounded containers of resonant matter. This is emphatically not to argue that there is no materiality to space or place – far from it – but it is to suggest that questions of human social behaviour should be best engaged with by looking at the ways in which humans derive meaning from their surrounding materiality, meanings that are formed through social interaction, symbolic interpretation, communicative performance, and relational ordering (Massey, 2005, Butler, 1997, Blumer, 1986, Berger & Luckmann, 1966). We navigate space-time using signs and markers laden with symbolic meaning. Sometimes these signs can be decoded; other times they can be illustrated, or studied, or traced, or partially explained. Castioradis (1998) sees these signs, and the interplay between them, as constituting a social imaginary. Castioradis' social imaginary read spatially becomes an intersubjective understanding of how space should be ordered – the right, the proper, the normative understanding of things and people in relation to other things and people. But the social imaginary is never uniform or monolithic; like the space in which it exists, it is fluid and layered, contested, claimed, and shaped by the imaginations of social groups and individuals located at varying distances from the levers of political and representational power.

Edward Said's concept of *imaginative geographies* has been absolutely critical in the development of humanistic and cultural geography and will help me tease out further my understanding and operationalisation of space and place, which is primarily influenced by Doreen Massey, Edward Casey, and Karen Till. Said begins developing his theories of imaginative geographies in *Orientalism* (1978), but they find their fullest realisation in *Culture and Imperialism* (1993). For Said, the project of imperialism was built upon an imaginative and artistic understanding of the space of the colony produced in the metropole. "For the enterprise of empire depends upon *the idea of having an empire* … then in turn imperialism acquires a kind of coherence, a set of experiences, and a presence of ruler and ruled alike within the culture" (Said, 1993, p. 10, original emphasis). What Said identifies is a spatial imagination of a *proper*, natural relationality between subjects and rulers dependent upon an aesthetic production of a social imaginary. In this understanding he is very clearly following Foucault, especially *The Order of Things* (1994), in which Foucault argues that epistemic communities produce, through their knowledge transmuted into and fused with power (power/knowledge), *how things ought to be in relation to other things*. There is also a significant complementarity here with the seminal work of Benedict Anderson (1991). Said focuses primarily on the literary text (novels, travel diaries, Orientalist philosophy) as a vehicle for the production of imaginative geographies, whereas Anderson examines aspects such as the map, the museum, and the colonial census, which are also instrumental in gradually crafting a dominating power/knowledge over the space of the colony.

Resistance to the dominating spatial imagination, according to Said, produces space in a similar, if mirror-image way. Said refers to the relationship between the two as *contrapuntal* geographies: spatial imaginations and renderings developed as a counterpoint to the dominating form, but still dependent on the form itself for the transmission of its imaginary. In the Irish context, he singles out the poet W. B. Yeats, writing "Think of what Yeats does for the Irish past, with its Cuchulains and its great houses, which give the nationalist struggle something to revive and admire" (Said, 1993, p. 17). Contrapuntal space is formed by "a simultaneous awareness both of metropolitan history that is narrated and those of other histories against which (and together with which) the dominating discourse acts" (Said, 1993, p. 36). Said also pays attention to colonised writers who break from the contrapuntal form; who "act on territory taken back from the empire", making clear that the hegemonic/counter-hegemonic, dominant/contrapuntal need not be the only imaginations at work in colonised territories (he approvingly cites Salman Rushdie, Derek Walcott, Aimé Césaire, Chinua Achebe, Pablo Neruda, and Irish/Northern Irish playwright Brian Friel) (Said, 1993, pp. 34–35).

Finally, no doubt in dialogue with the criticisms of *Orientalism*, Said is very clear to state that he views the text as *one vehicle* that is constitutive of imaginative geographies, a necessary but not, in and of itself, sufficient means of establishing the colonial project. Imaginations require lands to imagine, and actual possession of this land, expropriating its resources, sorting and ordering its inhabitants, is what imperialism/colonialism is all about. Said's contribution to geography is limited to those textual, imaginary forms of power/knowledge, of spatial ordering, but it is a powerful contribution, and one that I believe helps us understand that space and place are not purely matter-based phenomena. "The appropriation of history, the historicisation of the past, the narrativisation of society, all of which give the novel its force, include the accumulation and differentiation of social space, space to be used for social purposes" (Said, 1993, p. 93).

Said's influence is very clearly felt in the work of Derek Gregory (1994, 2004), especially in his interrelated concepts of 'world-as-exhibition' and 'scopic regimes'. For Gregory, the known world is a presentation, a performance, rooted in imaginative illustrations. Again, we see how imagining and illustrating how space should be or is ordered dictates the potentialities of how subjects can encounter, navigate, and develop relationships *in* space. Observers presume the exhibition is known and knowable reality, but it is only a subset of possible imaginaries within space. Scopic regimes are collections of institutions governing how it is possible to visualise space. Gregory also employs Neil Smith's (2008) concept of 'deep space' and Henri Lefebvre's (1991) timeless insight that all space is produced by human actors, and likewise always in the process of new productions. Deep space for Smith is: "Quintessentially social space; it is physical extent fused through with social intent" (Smith, 2008, p. 214). Smith, Gregory, and Lefebvre all add a mobility to Said's imaginative geographies which often feels under-theorised in Said's work.

I discussed Doreen Massey's work in the opening chapter; I revisit it here because it is her conceptualisation of space that I find the most compelling. For Massey (2005, p. 12), space is the "simultaneity of stories-so-far", the complex and fluid constellations of human relationships, narratives, and bodies being produced, adapted, accreted, and reproduced at any given moment. Though power is never far from the equation in Massey's work, she breaks decisively with those Marxist, hegemonic/counter-hegemonic, and/or dominant/contrapuntal perspectives that hold that the limits of space are also the limits of power arrangements. For Massey, there is always a chaotic element to space, always a 'thrown-togetherness' that resists predictability and challenges the limits of the geographical imagination. In many ways, she is in dialogue with Deleuze and Guattari's (1987) idea of space as *relational assemblage*, a heterogeneity of relationships and things that "jostle, co-exist, interfere, and entangle one another" (Allen, 2011, p. 154) but still hold shape and coherence. But again she is critical because she feels the assemblage does not account for the "co-existing multiplicity" of many stories, potentialities, and relationships, many *assemblages*, in short, that share space (Massey, 2005, p. 54). When I shortly turn towards looking at spatial relationships, performances, and public memory in Northern Ireland, my preference for Massey's metaphors of simultaneity and multiplicity will become clearer. For now, space in my usage has three major components:

(1) It is imagined, the ordering of things is both a product and a process of systems, regimes sometimes, of *illustration and description*. This process is necessary, but not, in and of itself, sufficient.
(2) While it is shaped by power arrangements, it is never bound to them; it always retains some element of the chaotic and the unpredictable.
(3) Space is the relationships between people and things, and the multiple layers of those relationships co-existing simultaneously.

Places exist within space, and indeed are inseparable from the space that surrounds them (Tuan, 1977). Like space, my reading of place is more abstractionist; it breaks from the limiting notion that places must be *wholly* matter-based formations, brick-and-mortar containers for some particular things and some particular peoples. The everyday usages of the term 'place' evince this more abstract reading (Cresswell, 2014), and human, social, and cultural geographers have long commented on the necessarily non-material readings demanded by a colloquialism such as 'a sense of place' (Massey, 1994; Tuan, 1975, 1979).[1]

1 For counter-argument, see Stedman (2003).

Crucially, a sense of place is never uniformly experienced, nor is it separable from the spatial relationships in which it is ensconced. Keith Basso writes:

> Sense of place is not possessed by everyone in a similar manner or like configuration, and that pervasive fact is part of what makes it interesting. Like all the other 'senses' we have invented for mankind ... sense of place is inseparable from the ideas that inform it ... Locked within the mental horizons of those who give it life, a sense of place issues in a stream of symbolically drawn particulars – the visible particulars of local topographies, the personal particulars of biographical associations, and the notional particulars of socially given systems of thought.
>
> (Basso, 1996, p. 144).

Place is not merely a particular meaningful location within space; this, I believe, is more properly referred to as a 'site' and I, following Casey (1996a, 1996b), want to make what I believe is a crucial distinction between a 'place' and a 'site'. The terms share some features, but place is deeper, it is more. Sites are things that have locations, and while they can be picked up and moved to another location, one of their primary features is their topographical fixity. Casey writes:

> A place is more an *event* than a *thing* to be assimilated into known categories. As an event, it is unique, ideolocal. Its peculiarity calls not for assumption into the already known – that way lies site, which lends itself to predefined predications, uses, and interpretations – but for the imaginative constitution of terms respecting its ideolocality (these range from placenames to whole discourses).
>
> (Casey, 1996b, p. 26, original emphasis)

He is followed down this vein of thought by Massey, who describes places as "articulations within the wider power-geometries of space ... Places not as points or areas on maps, but as integrations of space and time; *as spatio-temporal events*" (Massey, 2005, p. 130, original emphasis). In doing so, both Massey and Casey are rather abruptly departing from the place-as-site fallacy, place as fixed in space. They are both also departing from another misconception about place's fixity, namely the idea that place enjoys a relative stable trajectory *through time*. In a conventional understanding, a place is built, it exists, people interact with it, animals make nests or roost within it, over time the place falls into disuse, people forget it is there, it becomes ruins, the jungle grows over it, it is excavated by aliens or archaeologists. But it may be more helpful to think of places, or at least highly significant places, as 'paused' in time. Foucault (1984) identifies places such as cemeteries, museums, and monuments as heterotopias because they are places paused in time, whose symbolic resonance incurs from the temporal contrast between the pause and the fluidity of the surrounding space. Yi-Fu Tuan also describes place as 'pause', writing, "If we think of space as that which allows movement, then place is pause; each pause in movement makes it possible for location to be transformed into place" (Tuan, 1977, p. 3). For Bakhtin, places become *chronotopes*,"Points in the geography of a community where time and space intersect and fuse. Time becomes visible for human contemplation; likewise, space becomes responsive to the movements of time and history and the enduring character of a people" (Bakhtin, 1981, p. 7).

But these perspectives, as redolent as they are, are missing a fundamental mobility *through space* that Massey and Casey provide. If space is the simultaneity-of-stories so far, of chronotopic events, then place is *where those events occur*, where those stories cluster and concatenate. The place follows the stories (or is vice versa?), it moves with them: some places move languidly, some places dash across space. How else are we to conceptualise the place of the protest march, the occupation, the homeless encampment always being pursued, moved, and removed by the police (Wright, 1997), the graffiti erased from one wall and reappearing the next night on another (Cresswell, 1996)? Humans may pause at places, but places are not always idle. Sites – locations – are fixed; places carry with them the inherent capacity for movement.

Casey's Heideggerian roots show in two simple words: "Places gather" (1996b, p. 24). They are concatenations of stories in space through which humans make shared meanings. Resistance places, mobile places, are *irruptions of stories.* In biology, an irruption is a sudden and unexpected increase in an animal population; in an unspecialised usage, an irruption is a sudden breaking in or bursting through. Both usages are apt. They are significant gatherings, a rise in the population of stories. Places, once made and produced, stand not just as articulations; they are also rips or punctures or bursting-throughs in the folds of space-time formed by the gathering of stories and narratives, all with a referent, never with a uniform referent, to the multidimensional spot of that puncture. It is only with this theoretical understanding that we can better understand the potential of places of memory.

Ghost stories

For too long, geographers of memory have been what I call 'site-bound', which is to say that their analyses focus on a particular commemorative, memorial, and/or contested site or set of sites. Some of these studies are of incredible depth and insight; but this is often *in spite of* the limitations of the site approach (e.g. Alderman, 2003, 2010; Doss, 2010; Switzer & Graham, 2009; Sturken, 1997, 2007; Graham & McDowell, 2007; Teeger & Vinitzky-Seroussi, 2007; Foote, 2003; Dwyer, 2002; Vinitzky-Seroussi, 2002; Jorgensen-Earp & Lanziotti, 1998; Azaryahu, 1996; Winter, 1995). Karen Till refers to this approach, popularised by the popular memory school and Pierre Nora, as the 'biography-of-a-site' approach. She argues that the approach focuses on "describ[ing] the specific forms and locales of particular sites to examine how their meanings and settings were negotiated, received and interpreted by various publics" (Till, 2006,

p. 329). This analysis can be simultaneously prescient and limiting. Thinking instead of 'places of memory' allows us to bring in other forms of politics, spatial alterations, transgressions, and accretions, and to see place-memory as not *topographical* (i.e. cemented into the site) but as *topological* (inherently fluid, capable of movement, stretching, disappearing and reappearing, etc.). To subtly correct Basso (1996) and Escobar (2001), culture, wisdom, and memory do not just 'sit in places', they travel with them, are carried by them. As Till (2006) crucially points out, sites are not the sum total of social memories, nor even the containers or nexuses of a particular transmission of memory. Places of memory can transcend the site, places of memory can link a multiplicity of sites together, the site can shift meanings across time and generations (Hirsch, 1997), or memory can persist even in the absence of a site (Hirsch & Spitzer, 2011, 2016). The site approach, "turns pliant memory to stone" (Young, 1993, p. 15), and worse: while the fluidity of the site is *temporally* studied, or how the subjective and intersubjective meanings, mnemonics and perspectives are received, challenged, and reinterpreted across time, the site approach falls into the trap of spatial fixity. There is no space for the simultaneity of borderline-chaotic trajectories and events, no space for incoherence or unpredictability. And as bell hooks so presciently shows, it is the space marginal to our eye, our focus, our dominant *and* resistant power arrangements, our imaginations, that "offers to one the possibility of radical perspective from which to see and create, to image alternatives, new worlds" (hooks, 1990, pp. 149–150). A spatial coherence would write out that radical marginality and presume that a site would impart a static set of possible interpretations, and that subjects would react to or interact with the site in predictable ways. The limitations of the biography-of-site approach, I argue, are especially visible in Northern Ireland, where sites of memory (especially in working-class communities) tend to exhibit the body of the armed gunman and perform a narrative of violence. A site-based approach to these sites struggles to do anything except read dominant and resistant meanings, not complex and layered simultaneities of stories and relationships.

Places of memory are places where people feel the need to be haunted, and to perform that haunting in public. Ghosts are spectral traces of the past, and their essence is contained (perhaps trapped) in the material and non-material vestiges of the past that we preserve (and how we choose to preserve them); these vestiges in turn create a sort of temporal bridge, a linkage between the space of the present and the space of the past. The casual tourist or observer could be forgiven for thinking that on a given day there are no ghosts still haunting Belfast City Centre. Indeed, the traffic zips by, people hustle and bustle, construction and renovation seems to be happening on every street. Everywhere the City Centre manifests a new consumerist, cosmopolitan, neo-liberal spatial orthodoxy that promises to 'transcend' the past. But in order to create the space for Belfast to become a multifunctional, dynamic, and modern European city, the space had to be 'normalised' and 'demobilised' (Kelly, 2012; O'Dowd & Komarova, 2011; Nagle, 2009; Shirlow, 2006). The normalisation project depended on wiping clean the traumatic memory rooted in the heart of the city (Switzer & McDowell, 2009). Now, very few markers, monuments, or designated sites illustrating the traumatic experience of the Troubles exist in Belfast City Centre; they have been moved, displaced, and confined to the sectarianised neighbourhoods of the city's periphery, put into a place that conforms to what political and economic power-brokers imagine the appropriate spaces of Troubles memory to be – the demarcated sanctuaries of republicanism and loyalism. They belong to those places that Brendan Murtagh (2017, n.p.) argues are forever imagined and confined to "deviant, untreatable, and socially regressive" status. This is very much akin to what Kenneth Foote (2003, p. 23) calls "rectification" of violent or tragic landscapes, or "the process through which a tragedy site is put right and used again". But put right for whom? Used again for whom? The new cognitive cartography being forced onto the City Centre has not disappeared the old maps, scored by the places of wounding, murder, bombings, and mayhem; it has simply added a layer of sediment on top of them. This contemporary narration and performance of the City Centre is inscribing a new form of architectural and authoritative space rooted in social forgetting. Ghosts are disruptions of progress. They are socially, politically, economically, and spatially disruptive, especially for those who would recreate the space for capital, modernity, *and reconciliation*.

I was personally struck by this reading of the city as I sat in a coffee shop near Belfast's City Hall reading Karen Till's magisterial *The New Berlin* (2005). Like Belfast, Till's Berlin illustrates a complex memory-space in which different memory curators seek to make places to house the ghosts of the past in the space of a city careening towards a new, cosmopolitan order that will (it is promised) transcend the traumas of the past. But in spite of this materialist transformation of Berlin, the ghosts still remain. They will remain in City Centre Belfast too. Ghosts haunt places. People may leave, they may emigrate, they may establish a new life elsewhere, and they may carry their ghosts with them, but haunting itself will never allow the haunted to fully sever themselves from a place of memory. Ghosts are *returns to place*, as Till argues:

> Being haunted involves the desire and the repetitive practice of returning to a past time and self that never was. People create homes for their ghosts through telling stories about places and returning to the places that haunt them. Returning to places that haunt our imaginations folds and warps imagined times and selves (past, present, future), yet the ritual practice of returning creates a sense of temporal continuity and coherence. When someone goes back home (and each of us may have many homes), he or she may experience such vivid memories that it may appear (even momentarily) as though the place and the person returning are exactly the same as they once were.
>
> (Till, 2005, p. 13)

Ghost stories are also disruptions of a linearity of time and that linearity exhibited on a given landscape. Ghosts are melancholic spectres who prevent staged progression through grief and/or anger towards recovery and/or reconciliation. Writes Feldman (1991), p. 67), "Ghost tales map the history of death in local space, disrupting the linearity of time." Ghosts are spectral traces whose reason for existing (or perhaps, persisting) in the liminal space between death and not-death is to call attention to what happened in this place, to demand that the place not pass from memory. Again, we might recall Hamlet's father's ghost's famous speech that I cited as an epigraph: "Adieu, adieu, adieu. Remember me."

Social haunting, which Till adapts from Jacques Derrida (1994), is an excellent concept for illustrating the role of places of memory, for exploring how the remnants of the dead still inhabit and influence the space of everyday life and modernity:

> The process of selectively calling forth the dead and the past through place is one way individuals and groups try to fill absence and represent loss in the present. To talk about ghosts means to interrogate the reasons people feel haunted, or even the need to be haunted, in the present. It means to take affect seriously as a part of politics of place making, memory, and social identity.
>
> (Till, 2005, p. 23).

The major points here are that dead bodies may live on after they have perished, especially if the manner of their death is significant and social actors feel a need to be haunted by them. Additionally, a need to be haunted requires a place for ghosts to haunt, and vice versa. The study of transitional justice should be attuned to the powerfully affective role that placemaking plays in transitional memory-space, and transitional justice must also be attuned to the violence underlying the denial of places to remember, places to be haunted. And ghosts always haunt *places*. These places can be haunted houses or old train yards, but they are also Proust's "houses, roads, avenues", cast as "fugitive, alas, as the years" because the artist has yet to reclaim them, yet to adequately return to them (Proust, 1913/1981, p. 482). To haunt or be haunted in such a place is to be confronted with an unsettled, violent past, one that will not simply fade into history and disappear.

Trial by space

What incorporating geography into the study of social memory reveals is that relationships between political subjects, their memories, and their bodies play out in public space and this space is imagined yet forever incomplete and *thrown together*. Space is social relationships in all of their multiplicity and complexity. Different individuals and different social groups have differing capacities to produce the space for their memories, to emplace memory, its strands and traces, into the social imaginary and the built environment. Subaltern stories of the past, of heartbreak, violence, and loss, *for some reason find it more difficult to gather*, and these reasons are almost always underscored by relational power. To create places of memory, to emplace a particular strand of social memory into the larger imaginary, means making memory socially visible; it means irrupting a section of space-time in order to make social memory visible and intelligible within a wider power-geometry. The process of this irrupting and nexuses of contestation within that process are referred to famously by Henri Lefebvre (1991) as 'trial by space'. What Lefebvre argues is that all representations of ideas, values, and identities that are unable to produce a space can be marginalised and eventually erased from the larger societies the rememberer may inhabit. The successful production of space, or the production of a place of memory, in contrast, alters, transforms, adapts in some way the larger social environment in which it is emplaced. It is important here to quote Lefebvre at some length:

> Nothing and no one can avoid *trial by space* ... It is in space ... that each idea of 'value' acquires or loses its distinctiveness through confrontation with the other values and ideas it encounters there. Moreover – and more importantly – groups, classes, or fractions of classes cannot constitute themselves, or recognise one another, as 'subjects' unless they generate (or produce) a space. Ideas, representations, or values which do not succeed in making their mark on space, and thus generating (or producing) an appropriate morphology, will lose all pith and become mere signs, or resolve themselves into abstract descriptions, or mutate into fantasies.
>
> (Lefebvre, 1991, pp. 416–417, original emphasis)

In Northern Ireland (and indeed much of the United Kingdom) memorials to the dead of the First and Second World Wars have been successfully inserted into space. We see the names of the dead etched into sombre obelisks in virtually every community. A narrative of their death and its larger social meaning is ritually and regularly performed, culminating in Remembrance Sunday every November and the laying of wreaths and the widespread use of the red poppy as symbolic accoutrement. Particular groups of the dead invoke particular narratives, narratives that are not merely confined to the past but that function as mnemonics for groups in the present. The commemoration of the Somme in Northern Ireland, for example, as McMaster and Higgins (2014, p. 419) cogently argue, "is a foundational myth of identity and has more to do with a politics of identity than with a historical Somme".

Likewise, the widespread (even ubiquitous) production of space for paramilitary bodies killed in the Troubles has less to do with the bodies themselves than with an attempt to emplace a certain frame of memory. But if we use Lefebvre and Massey correctly, we see the production of space and places of memory as never wholly predictable, never totally uniform (see for example Edkins (2003) for a brilliant elucidation of the place of memory surrounding London's Cenotaph). Even the paramilitary-garlanded place and the spatially hegemonic Great War obelisks afford opportunities for creative social re-evaluation and symbolic accretion (Dwyer, 2004). Narratives of violence and/or narratives of 'heroic sacrifice', are certainly *resisted* in Northern Ireland, and resisted at multiple levels, as I shall argue in the following chapter; but to appreciate their multiple potentialities, we must also look to hooks' margins, where the site-qua-place might also exist in a multiplicity and simultaneity of other varied forms of social memory, where it might mean something to local communities that we may not expect or that surprises us. The problem is that as geographers and scholars of memory have too often taken the initial sited reading at face value and not bothered to inquire deeply about understandings and spatial readings that may challenge our initial presuppositions. Places of memory are imbued with multiple referents and can be spoken with in multiple voices, even if some voices are quite obviously quieter than others. Thinking geographically, especially in the tradition of Lefebvre and Massey, I believe, will excavate additional claimants to public space in Northern Ireland and elsewhere. It will reveal a splintered landscape of memory, where public space and memory have become complex pastiches capable of evoking multiple pasts. And one of the chief drivers of this splintering is the reclamation and reinscription of the bodies, the human bodies, of the dead.

Out of place

Tim Cresswell (1996), building again on our everyday usages of place, develops a helpful dualism he refers to as 'in place/out of place' to describe the relationships between subjects and spatial power. He describes socially marginalised individuals and groups as *written out* of the social imaginary, denied the ability to construct a meaningful place. Sometimes, this exclusion can take the form of direct oppression: the excluded protestors can be simply beaten off the streets, subjected to curfews, pass laws, and restrictions of where, how, and when they can congregate. But thinking imaginatively about 'out of place' reveals subjects whose bodies are simply not contained within our normative understandings of the proper orderings and potentialities of space. Consider the case of the homeless. As Talmadge Wright (1997) shows, homeless men and women are perhaps the quintessential out of place. This is not merely because they lack a brick-and-mortar dwelling where they can lay their head at night, but because the homeless body conflicts with the social imaginary. In the imaginative proper ordering of Western society, every individual unit-person has a place of their own. The visible presence of those without homes, without places of their own, conflicts with the dominant social imaginary. To overcome our own cognitive dissonance, the homeless body is easily rendered diseased, dirty, crazy, addicted, or a host of other pejorative epithets (Amster, 2003; Smith, 1996), which in turn allows us to place the blame for homelessness on the homeless themselves, on personal failings and personal choices. Thus we sidestep the guilt for more proximate and accurate causes of homelessness, such as declining real wages, income inequality, gentrification, and racism (Williams, 2016). According to Wright, the homeless body is out of place because it conflicts with the social imaginary; it must be written out of public space, rendered invisible, denied a place for homeless stories and life experiences to shelter, and confined to the material peripheries of the city.

Out of place refers to the lack of place; *it does not refer to the lack of site.* Possession of a site does not guarantee that a social memory has truly 'passed' trial by space and has been incorporated into the social imaginary. Sites can be marginalised, appropriated by others, or used as tokenist acknowledgements that stand as cynical gestures forestalling the production of genuine empathy or acknowledgement. Robert Musil writes, "There is nothing in this world as invisible as a monument … They are no doubt erected to be seen – indeed to attract attention. But at the same time they are impregnated with something that repels attention" (cited in Young, 1993, p. 13). We can see an example of what Musil describes at the Japanese–American Memorial on the National Mall in Washington DC. In spite of its official (albeit, indirect) memorialisation in the Mall, its incorporation into US history curricula, an official apology from former President Bill Clinton, and the payments of reparations to survivors, mass incarceration of Japanese Americans during the Second World War in the United States remains characterised by what Marita Sturken (2001) calls 'absent images', where a site or an image comes to appropriate and shoulder out the space for the production of memory. Sturken argues these sites facilitate the absence of the Japanese–American body in American social memory by curating an exhibition of mass incarceration as either benevolent, inevitable, or both. For proof of this, we need look no further than the unveiling of the site on the Mall. The Japanese–American memorial was unveiled almost simultaneously with the Franklin Delano Roosevelt Memorial, also on the National Mall (Roosevelt, of course, being the president who signed the order for mass incarceration). Kirk Savage (2009) notes that in choosing the dates for the unveilings, the curators simply gave no thought to Japanese–American traumatic memory; it was absent, invisible, unacknowledged.

Erika Doss (2010) also notes how sites of memory in the United States can work against or undercut meaningful Indigenous melancholic placemaking. She argues that Indigenous Americans can make and participate in the making of places of memory only in a manner that is non-confrontational with the idealised imaginary of the American West that surrounds them. One very telling example is the Little Bighorn Monument in Crow Agency, Montana. Doss argues that this site of memory is widely framed as the site of 'Custer's Last Stand', in which the US Cavalry force is reframed as the 'moral victor' and the battle itself reframed as a bump in the road on the way to American national unity. The actual historical record is far more ambiguous and far more cold-blooded. The American military response to their defeat at Little Bighorn, for example, was genocidal. In Doss' work, we come to see how the larger experiences of both Indigenous Americans and Mexican Americans, and their chronology of suffering at the hands of the expansionist American state, has been largely denied places of memory (even as it is given tokenistic sites) and removed from the social imaginary. For example, there is a specifically Indigenous-designed and Indigenous-curated sub-section of the site at Little Bighorn; however, it was forced to subsume itself into the larger aesthetic being promoted at the site, one that Doss argues perpetuates the myth of the unclaimed frontier. Thus, denied their own aesthetic form, Indigenous memory exists merely as a peripheral aside:

> Forced to be compatible with the 7th U.S. Calvary Monument, the new memorial is conflated with long-standing assumptions of national unity through violence and militarism. Restricted by the theme of 'Peace through Unity', it fails to reckon with myth of the Western frontier, and stereotypes about American Indians.
>
> (Doss, 2010, p. 238).

This chapter closes by looking at two examples of how moving from the site to the place can expand our understanding of the potentiality of space and social memory in Northern Ireland. These examples are sketches or fragments gleaned through geo-ethnographic work in Derry and Southeast Fermanagh/West Tyrone. They are descriptive and they offer no conclusions or easy answers. The intention is to challenge the predominant scholarly readings of public memory in Northern Ireland as zero-sum proxy battles for territorial control (e.g. McDowell, 2008; Graham & Whelan, 2007) and to illustrate alternative ways of looking that may allow for new potentialities of place to be excavated.

The wedding photograph

On 2 March 1984 Lance-Corporal Thomas Loughlin, a part-time member of the UDR and a Water Service Employee, was killed by an IRA bomb placed under his van in the Castlederg area as he left his home on his way to his civilian employ. Mr Loughlin had been turning to wave to his new wife and his three-month-old child as the bomb exploded. Loughlin's wife was the sister of part-time UDR corporal Heather Kerrigan. Ms Kerrigan had been a bridesmaid at her sister and Mr Loughlin's wedding in 1982. Mr Loughlin's best man was part-time UDR private Norman McKinley. A guest at the wedding was part-time UDR Private and full-time electrician Robert Gregory Elliot. Potter (2001, p. 262) says about this wedding party: "There is a group wedding photograph. Now all but the bride [have] been murdered."

Within seven months of each other in 1984, Loughlin, Kerrigan, McKinley, and Elliot would all be dead, all killed by the IRA's ferocious campaign against the UDR in West Tyrone. Because the UDR was an auxiliary arm of the British military, the Northern Irish men and women who served and died in the UDR have no official site of memory within Northern Ireland.[2] Instead, they are officially

2 There is a monument to the UDR unveiled in 2011 in the town of Lisburn, near Belfast. However, the Lisburn Monument was commissioned by the UDR Memorial Trust, a private organisation using private funds. The memorial was erected on public land, a source of some controversy, but it still cannot be called an "official' (i.e. state-sponsored, state-maintained) memorial.

commemorated at the UK National Arboretum near Lichfield, Staffordshire, England. Some unofficial memorials to the UDR do exist in Northern Irish memory-space, but they tend to be small, limited in scope, erected and maintained by private actors and institutions, and often located in the closed space of Protestant churches or Orange lodges. But for the ex-UDR members I interviewed, this failure to remember and acknowledge the role and contribution of the UDR where they lived and served feels very much like a betrayal by the British state they argue they served loyally for many years. This betrayal is especially acute when their dearth of memorial space is contrasted with the widespread proliferation of republican memorials throughout areas such as West Tyrone, South Fermanagh, and South Armagh, where so many UDR members were killed. These republican memorials are technically illegal, but local authorities generally do not molest or challenge their erection or maintenance to any great extent:

> When you go in-country, and I'm sure you probably come across them in Derry,[3] [you come across] these memorial stones to terrorists. So they're allowed to put their memorial stones up illegally, and there's a lot of them down where I live [*sic*] between me and the border. In a certain area, I think there's six. It's funny, one day I went around and just read the inscriptions on them. First of all, it's in Irish, and then below it says they were assassinated by the British war machine, the British state, executed. So they can use them words, but when it comes round to innocent victims putting up that they were murdered by IRA terrorists, politically you're not allowed to do that.
>
> ('Benjamin', County Fermanagh)

Switzer and Graham (2009) convincingly make the point that RUC memory is a subaltern discourse in transitional Northern Ireland both because the British state has refused to conceptualise the Troubles as a 'war', and has also refused to enter into the socially contested memory-space of Northern Ireland. They write: "The particular curiosity of the commemoration of the RUC is that – agent of the state that the force was – its memorialisation constitutes a subaltern discourse due to the state's elision of memory work" (Switzer and Graham, 2009, p. 157). These insights could perhaps be extended even better to the UDR, especially considering that the RUC does have a quasi-official site of memory within Northern Ireland – the RUC George Cross Memorial Garden, located in Knock, East Belfast, whose patron is Charles, Prince of Wales – and the UDR has no such equivalent. This makes the RUC and UDR quite fascinating case studies as the vast majority of scholarly work on subaltern memorialisation processes and practices has concerned itself with attempts by marginalised, colonised, or peripheral

3 I lived in Derry at the time of the interview, as the respondent is aware.

groups to contest the appropriation of power-geometries from which they are excluded or dwarfed by the power of the state. But if we briefly adopt Weber's notion of the state, the "human community that (successfully) claims the *monopoly of the legitimate use of physical force* within a given territory" (Weber, 1919, p. 1), then it becomes clear that in many areas of Northern Ireland, paramilitaries were far more of a state than the state itself (McEvoy & Mika 2001; O'Connor 1993; Sluka, 1989). The preceding statement was (and to a lesser extent, still is) more accurate in republican working-class communities than in loyalist working-class communities, but even in loyalist estates it was clear to whom you went if you needed to avail yourself of the enforcement or contractual power that is generally the province of the state (Gambetta, 1996):

> To be honest with you, and I'm going to be perfectly honest about this, this area was policed by the UVF. If there was any noisy neighbours, any anti-social behaviour, people knew the police weren't doing anything for them so they knew who to go to to sort it out, if I can put it like that.
>
> ('Sophie', County Derry)

Like many subaltern memories, UDR public commemoration tends to operate in either an unsupportive, uncaring, or openly hostile atmosphere. To some degree, ex-UDR members have found some outlet for their memories and their commemorations through the type of story-telling initiatives I discussed in Chapter 1, but these initiatives tend to be limited and to circulate primarily within ex-UDR communities. Attempts to create places of memory for the UDR in public space are often cruelly violated, which no doubt partially explains why UDR-memory often feels so 'underground' in Northern Irish border areas.

Heather Kerrigan and Norman McKinley were killed by a roadside bomb planted by the IRA on 14 July 1984 while on patrol outside of Castlederg along the border with the Republic of Ireland. McKinley died instantly. Kerrigan, only 20 years old, passed away in a helicopter while being transported to the hospital next to her brother David, also seriously injured. On the thirtieth anniversary of their deaths, a small party of family members, friends, and local band members travelled by car to the site to erect a small memorial and hold a private ceremony, before returning to Castlederg to lay a wreath at the town cenotaph in their honour. Sometime after, the roadside memorial was vandalised, the poppies pulled down and scattered across the road, and a homemade sign claiming 'IRA 2 – UDR 0' was tacked onto a nearby post.[4]

4 The reader may view photographs of both the small memorial and the desecrating sign at A. Ferguson & A. Rutheford (17 July 2014). 'Family's Agony over Sick Sign at Memorial to UDR Soldiers.' *Belfast Telegraph*. Retrieved 15 January 2017 from www.belfasttelegraph.co.uk/news/local-national/northern-ireland/familys-agony-over-sick-sign-at-memorial-to-udr-soldiers-30437795.html.

'Daniel' (West Tyrone) comments on the impact of the desecration: "Makes it feel like the heart's been ripped out again … the heart's been ripped out of them people. And it retraumatised everything back again." It is imperative that we note the *spatiality* of this desecration, not merely the content of it. It is not merely that it trivialises the killings of Kerrigan and McKinley and the effect that had on their families and friends, nor that it reduces their lives and their deaths to some perverse competition. The essence of the desecration is in how it denies the right of their memory to be exhibited in public space, how it denies them the right to build a place of memory, denies them the place to commune with the ghosts. As such the desecration is a deeply political desecration, not an act of mere vandalism; it is a proclamation that you shall not remember here, your stories and your memories do not belong in *our* space.

Judith Butler (2006, pp. 33–34) argues that bodies that cannot be mourned in public, that are de-placed from the politics of public mourning, have been *derealised*. Rendering certain bodies unreal is achieved through dehumanisation through omission, as in the case of 200,000 Iraqi children killed during the course of the Gulf Wars and their aftermath. They receive no obituaries, but the *New York Times*' well-known 'Faces of the Dead' series provides a picture and obituary of every US serviceperson killed.[5] There is simply no space provided to mourn these bodies, no 'frame' for their memory, as Butler calls it. To truly *know* the bodies of the unreal requires an 'insurrection at the level of ontology', a fundamental alteration of the spatial politics of mourning.

The fact that the memorial outside of Castlederg was desecrated and desacralised thus may suggest a different, more hopeful analysis than one that focuses on the act of violence itself. Bodies do not need to be ruthlessly policed in space unless the insertion of those bodies, and the potentiality of their mourning, *threatens* an imaginary. Public violence against memory-places is itself an acknowledgement that the bodies cannot be omitted, that they still exist. This is cold comfort, I am sure, to the loved ones of those depicted in that stiff, black-and-white photograph at the wedding. But the desecration itself *acknowledges the reality of the bodies* and acknowledges the reality of the work of mourning (or melancholia) taking place.

In 2015 I attended the opening performance of a play written by the Derry-based playwright Johnathan Burgess called *Inconspicuous Gallantry* (2015) in Castlederg. The play premiered in the local Orange Hall, to an audience of approximately 40–50 people, most if not almost all ex-UDR men and women and their partners. To my knowledge, it is one of the only artistic efforts to depict the realities and toll of traumatic violence on the lives of border UDR men, women, and communities. The title of the play is a reference to The Cross of Conspicuous Gallantry, the second-highest gallantry honour awarded by the United Kingdom. It was awarded collectively to the UDR in 2006, and awarded

5 See www.nytimes.com/interactive/us/faces-of-the-dead.html.

posthumously considering the UDR ceased to exist in 1992, having been amalgamated into the Royal Irish Regiment (RIR).

The play is told in a series of sparse vignettes; the only setting is a kitchen table with two chairs and a sink in the background. In one vignette, a young wife sends her husband out to an all-night shift on the border and describes to her friend the effects of not being able to sleep, of hoping the phone doesn't ring but being unable to call anyone for fear it will. In another, in what my opinion was the most powerful vignette, a woman in her fifties or sixties carefully, silently, and meticulously irons a dress uniform, before placing it on a hanger and zipping it neatly into a dust bag. She says no dialogue, and in the Orange Hall where the play was being performed, only the occasional smoker's cough cut though the emptiness and tension. A younger man, clearly one of her sons, pokes his head in and off the stage worriedly but also does not speak. A gaunt looking man in a dark suit then enters, takes the proffered uniform respectfully, and says the only dialogue in the entire vignette: "Thank you. My deepest sympathy." The mother turns away. The other son shows the undertaker out. There is silence one more. The piece ends. In another vignette, this time set in the present day or thereabouts, an injured ex-UDR man discusses the inadequate compensation being offered for his injury while on duty with his wife. In the penultimate line of the vignette, he angrily says:

> The government sold us out! The same way they sold out the [Royal Irish] Regiment, the RUC, and the law-abiding people of this country. Now they won't even acknowledge the suffering of the people who lived through it. I'll tell you, Joan, sometimes, I don't know who I feel worse about, the people that I was fighting, or the ones I was supposed to be serving!

I was sitting off to the side and happened to look around the room when the actor delivered the line. Everywhere, I saw heads nodding. One elderly man could not control himself and let out a loud interjection of assent. This group of men and women, far from being the unquestioning soldiers of the Queen, collectively felt ill-treated, misused, betrayed by the British state, their contributions and intense pain rendered invisible. After the conclusion of the short play, I wandered around outside talking to the men smoking, asking what they thought of the play. While not verbatim, I have recorded in my fieldnotes several men saying versions of the same thing: *It's wile hard to watch. It's too real. Your man* [Burgess] *gets it.* By aesthetically rendering the out-of-placeness of the UDR memory, *Inconspicuous Gallantry* was helping UDR stories irrupt and gather, helping to create a place of memory.

What I observed in that performance was a room full of people hearing their stories depicted on stage, and indeed in public space, for the very first time. I knew these stories, or knew caricatures or conglomerations of them, because I had asked and they had told me (I paraphrase West, 2003). They were stories of perpetual vigilance, of decades of looking under cars for bombs, of never hanging any piece of your uniform on the washing line lest it be seen, of cracking under the constant and almost unimaginable strain, of the temporary absence of a family dog serving not as an everyday inconvenience but as a harbinger of terror, of cars driving slowly by the farm at night with their lights off, of intimate-partner violence – mental and physical, of alcoholism, insomnia, and the bodies of friends and colleagues butchered and blown up.

However, the performance of *Inconspicuous Gallantry* I witnessed occurred behind the doors of an Orange Hall – not the most welcoming or hospitable place to enter in Northern Ireland for Catholics, nationalists, women, sexual minorities. I myself had never been inside one before and have not been since. To truly create a place of memory in Northern Ireland for border UDR communities may require the stories that gather there to emerge into public, contested, and *unsafe* space, as opposed to concatenating under the wall displays of British military honoraria and under the shadow of portraits of the Queen. It would require it, in Lefebvre's terms, to 'make its mark', to 'constitute itself', and crucially, to 'recognise the other'. But what others should be recognised? If Butler is correct and the transformative politics of mourning requires languages and discourses to break down before they can reconstitute, UDR memories must encounter the stories of men and women like Eugene Reavey in the simultaneity of space, a simultaneity where both can coexist, side by side, in the same public space.

Fear in the hedges, fear in the bushes

On 4 January 1976, in the small village of Whitecross in County Armagh, armed gunmen threw open the door of the Reavey household and murdered three brothers, John Martin, Brian, and Anthony Reavey. The same party of gunmen then travelled 15 miles up the road to Ballydougan, also in County Armagh, and broke into the O'Dowd home, where the family was having a reunion. They sprayed the room with bullets, killing Joseph, Barry, and Declan O'Dowd (McKittrick et al., 2008, pp. 609–611). All were Catholics, and none had any links to violent paramilitaries. The evidence to date has become increasingly overwhelming that these horrid killings were perpetrated with the collusive aid, and even the active participation of, the UDR, specifically a group of UVF men who counted part-time UDR reservists serving RUC officers among their members centred in and around the so-called 'Murder Triangle' of Craigavon–Lurgan–Portadown in Mid-Ulster (Cadwallader, 2013; Cassel Report, 2006; Barron Report, 2003).

The next day, 5 January 1976, in retaliation for the Reavey/O'Dowd killings, members of the Provisional IRA, using an organisational alias (The South Armagh Republic Action Force), stopped a van full of workmen returning home from work just outside of the tiny village of Kingsmills, County Armagh. The workers were taken off the van and lined up. A masked man asked them their religion. The lone Catholic was told to 'get running'. The workmen were then strafed with gunfire, including at least one automatic weapon. Ten men were killed: their names are John Bryans, Robert Chambers, Reginald Chapman, Walter Chapman,

Robert Freeburn, Joseph Lemmon, John McConville, James McWhirter, Robert Walker, and Kenneth Worton. Alan Black was hit with 18 bullets and miraculously survived (McKittrick et al., 2008, pp. 611–613).

In a shattering coincidence, Eugene Reavey, brother to John Martin, Brian, and Anthony was on his way to the Daisy Hill hospital in Newry to collect the bodies of John Martin and Brian, and to visit Anthony (still fighting for his life), when his car was stopped by a neighbour just before he reached the physical site of the Kingsmills Massacre. Eugene Reavey describes mounting the small hill separating where his car was stopped on foot and looking down at the site. He describes the experience: "I look down and seen all these bodies lying on the road … steam rising out of those bodies. The smell of death, I'll never forget it to this day … [weeps]."[6] At the hospital morgue, he met the families of the arriving dead Kingsmills men and according to Alan Black, offered his deepest condolences and wept with them. Reavey and Black remain close friends to this day (McKay, 2009). On the way back from Daisy Hill that day, Reavey reports his car was stopped by the RUC. They forced him and his mother out of the car, opened the boot, took out and rummaged through the bags of his dead brothers' clothes, and according to Reavey, danced on them in the road and verbally abused his mother. The next day, Ian Paisley stood up in the British Parliament and, using Parliamentary Privilege, proclaimed that Eugene Reavey was a 'well-known Republican' who had orchestrated the Kingsmills Massacre. He claimed to have received this information from a police file. In all probability, he was quoting from a fraudulent document leaked to him by someone in the UDR or the RUC, probably by someone who had accused Reavey due to his coincidental passing-by of the massacre site and perhaps wished to allege that the Reaveys were an IRA family, and thus 'legitimate targets' for a loyalist massacre. Reavey and his family would spend the more than two decades living in terror from this false allegation (Mullins, 1999). Even four decades later, Mr Reavey cannot recount or remember what Paisley did to him without breaking down and shaking with anger: "[weeping] I'm thinking about that *bastard* Paisley and what he said about me and Kingsmills!" Alan Black claims that one of his first acts on being released from the hospital was to go straight to the Reavey house in Whitecross and tell them he knew they were innocent. Ian Paisley would never retract or apologise for the false allegation and refused repeated requests to meet with the Reaveys, up until his death in 2014.

The UDR, as an organisation, has skeletons in its closet. The Cassel Report (2006) examined 76 killings by loyalists in Northern Ireland and concluded that 74 of the killings involved the active collusion of members of the RUC, the UDR, or both. UDR weaponry seems to have consistently found its way into the hands of loyalist killers throughout the 1970s (Cadwallader, 2013). What

6 All of Mr Reavey's direct testimony is taken from his talk at a Bloody Sunday March Event in Derry, 26 January 2017, as recorded by me as a member of the audience.

are we then to make of those men and women in that Orange Hall in Castlederg when the soft voice of Eugene Reavey must also speak in the same space, and speak of his decades-long search for answers, frustrated at every turn by the security forces, and by some of his neighbours who continue to view him and his family not as grieving survivors, but as IRA murderers who got what was coming to them (McKay, 2007)?[7]

For Mr Reavey, the place where he lived became, after the massacre, a place of profound terror: "There was fear in the hedges, fear in the bushes." Crucially, Mr Reavey now believes that his family was targeted for murder because they were Catholics who did not know their place in the local sectarian hierarchy of South Armagh. They were or were in the process of starting a successful building company, and the family was comparably well off and comfortable. Again, according to Mr Reavey, their attempted transcendence of the place of a Catholic family, their move from labourer to owner, caused their execution. For Mr Reavey and his family, the idea that they could be murdered for this, and murdered with the participation of the security services, was truly unbelievable for them until the evidence became, to them, incontrovertible, that such was the case. "If someone had told me it was the police and UDR shot my brothers, I wouldn't have believed it." One can only imagine that Eugene Reavey's family's terror is similar to the stories told to me, and documented in *Inconspicuous Gallantry*, of being out shopping in Strabane or Enniskillen and seeing someone, your neighbour even, who you know is a republican sympathiser, miming a gun with his thumb and forefinger, and mouthing 'boom'. Or those poppies pulled down and scattered across the road outside of Castlederg. These are intersections in the folds of space for transformative encounters. The question then becomes how they are built, cultivated, and maintained.

The ghost of George McBrearty

Near the junction of the Cromore and Iniscairn Roads in the heart of Creggan, in Derry, there is an IRA/PIRA memorial garden (see Figure 5.1). Inscribed on the three tablets are the names of Creggan men and women identified as members of the PIRA/IRA who died during the Troubles. The area around Iniscairn

7 One of the most well-known and thoroughly sectarianised victims and survivors campaigner is Willie Frazer and his organisation of Families Acting for Innocent Relatives (FAIR). Mr Frazer emphatically does not speak for all PUL victims and survivors, but has a devoted following within a sub-section of that population (Dawson, 2007). Mr Frazer's father was in the UDR and killed by the IRA. His uncle, also in the UDR, was wounded. Four other members of his family were in the RUC and killed by the IRA (McKay, 2009). He has consistently maintained that the Glennane Gang is a 'myth' and casts doubt on Eugene Reavey's innocence; for example: http://victims.org.uk/frazer2/?p=640. Mr. Frazer and his organisation are based in Markethill, County Armagh is a mere 6 miles from the Reavey farm in Whitecross.

Figure 5.1 Cromore Park IRA/PIRA memorial, Derry. Photo by author.

Road during the 1970s was such a locus of violence that it was dubbed informally 'The Gaza Strip' (McGuinness & Downey, 2000). The near-perpetual violence in Creggan during these years solidified already dense intra-community networks and informal social surveillance; even to this day, if you walk around Creggan, you will be struck by how everybody knows everybody else: they know where they live and who their families are.

Thus, on one hand the Cromore Park memorial exhibits a violent, violence-justifying and exclusionist PIRA memory, a memory that valourises the bodies of killers or potential killers, and performs the 'valour' and 'nobility' of members of a group responsible for killing 1,768 people during the Troubles and injuring tens of thousands more. Memorial sites such as these are routinely used as stages for republican pronouncements, commemorations, colour ceremonies, and shows of force, especially at specific anniversaries of deaths. Resistance to these republican mobilisations of public space is common, with editorials in major newspapers like the *Belfast Telegraph* decrying the 'hurt' or the pain that these celebrations cause in families of IRA victims. A sited analysis of the site would look at the ethno-sectarian antagonism and one-upmanship contained in these mobilisations and counter-mobilisations, and at the routinised violence, exclusionism, and parcelisation of public space that takes place at these times, and would conclude, as Graham and Whelan (2007) do, that sites of paramilitary memory are merely forums or backdrops for a self-serving politics of antagonism that perpetuates systems of ethnic territorial control. There is a great deal of accuracy to this analysis;

however, if we move beyond a sited analysis to a placed analysis, we can observe multiple concatenations of stories operating in public space, stories that offer alternative readings of even the most banal of paramilitary sites.

The faces and bodies depicted on the Cromore Park Memorial carry the inherent potentiality for alternative readings, and if one lived most of one's life in Creggan, like 'Oisin', walking past their names and photographs might evoke something different than merely the proclamation of belligerent narratives:

> There's a lot of names on that memorial. Jim Friel's on there, Jim Friel's on that memorial that I mentioned earlier with a sort of sadness … Ethel Lynch is on that memorial, she's I think in Crawford Square, she's in a flat with a guy that I knew, that I went to school with, and they're making bombs. She and [*sic*], the bombing officer, the same class as my brother [*sic*], sitting beside him, he would have been up in our house, his [relative] taught me. There's a list there of about 40 people that could have been alive. George McBrearty, Pop Maguire, I know George McBrearty's wife, Pop Maguire taught two of my children. So there's a sense of [sighs] did it have to be like that? …
>
> … They enlisted. There was an emotional zeitgeist after Bloody Sunday, join the IRA … After Bloody Sunday, I went down into the Bogside and Máire Drumm was speaking and saying: "We've got to take up arms. This is the British state at work" …
>
> … And George McBrearty, how much sense and savvy had he? I would have a guess that he loved being a hero about Creggan because he had something to eat himself … He was such a range of things, such a range of things going on.
>
> ('Oisin', Derry)

One way of reading 'Oisin's' testimony would be to see him resisting the belligerence of the site and republican hagiography generally by recasting the 'martyrs' as ordinary so-and-sos, even, in the case of McBrearty, as a comparatively small individual interested more in his own self-importance than any overarching political cause. His words certainly seem to do that, but this monologue is not a conscious act of political resistance; rather, it is a wistful reflection on human life, on frail, fallible human beings, who died and who did not need to have died. And the recasting of republican semiotics in 'Oisin's' testimony seems only possible with a reference to a place, a place where stories can gather. And that place is not the site of Cromore Park, the overbearing stone obelisk, fixed in location; it is the larger chronotopic place of the Creggan and the memories, faces, relationships, and ghost stories encrusted in its fugitive streets. The name George McBrearty, and the photographs of him deployed at relevant anniversaries and events, is a stripped-down, dehumanising splinter of itself, affixed to the Cromore Park memorial. There, he is only an IRA man, a 'volunteer', a 'killer', a 'terrorist', a stultified trace of his life's complexity, frozen in time and space. But thinking of

George McBrearty as a spectral trace, a ghost haunting the streets of Creggan, still very much present in 'Oisin's' mind and the people who knew him, knew his family, reveals the people who engage in a complex social dialectic of guilt, justification, recall, and memory, set against the space that produced George McBrearty, the place that gave him life, the space and time that are irreparably bound up in his death, and the deaths of others he may have caused or helped to cause.

In another conversation in Derry, I spoke with two community workers who had seen their work honoured with a prestigious award for removing visible signs of sectarianism and promoting shared space. As we discussed how they had been able to make such compelling progress towards ameliorating their neighbourhood's reputation and public appearance, I asked them if they had ever thought about removing a central IRA memorial garden. The conversation, which had been clicking along, suddenly stalled. It is not fear that guided their words; I know for a fact that both workers have consistently and publicly stood up to violent force-wielders operating within their communities. What is clear to me now is that during that whole discussion of changing the aesthetic image of the neighbourhood and ending visible signs of sectarianism, they had not associated the memorial garden with sectarianism or sectarian imagery. While this may seem unbelievable to members of the PUL community, or at least initially to outsiders such as myself, the memorial seems to be chiefly viewed by the community as a repository for the ghosts of that area. Like 'Oisin', many members of the community may not have 'taken up arms', but all knew those who did, and all knew them as people, neighbours, relatives, humans, whose choices and actions were deeply resonant of the shared past circumstances of the larger community.

> '*Catherine*': No, [taking down the memorial], that was never ... never would have been in the cards.
>
> '*Darragh*': You look at it and you wouldn't think of it as something that was just thrown up. It wasn't just a big, ignorant thing that was thrown up.[8]
>
> '*Catherine*': Out of respect for the price they paid.
>
> '*Darragh*': And so many people here, even if they weren't in the IRA, they would have been interned so they find some comfort and identification in that.
>
> ('Catherine' and 'Darragh', Derry)

It is in the same vein that I came to witness the stories and accounts of border UDR men and women. I came with questions about memories and the places where they lingered; all I heard were the shocking stories of violent deaths, listed

8 'Darragh' is explicitly contrasting the cultivated and maintained memorial space with 'ignorant' displays of sectarian graffiti or sloganeering, associated in his mind with violent dissident republicanism.

one after another. They wanted me to understand the ubiquity of terror, and to document it, to make sure that it was known to the wider world of space, a wider world of space from which they were terrified of being erased. As names cascaded around me, and the terrible circumstances of their deaths, I recognised names I knew stood accused or suspected of the collusive or active killings of Catholic civilians. In some cases, the respondents were ignorant of this; in some cases, their status as 'bad apples' did not supersede the fact that they were violently killed. Or that their memories, and the lives they lived, like those of those IRA men on the Cromore Park memorial, were also more complicated when they were returned to humanity and bound up in a disconcerting and disorienting web of culpability and traumatic fragmentation.

All of these stories point us back towards the work of Jay Winter, who positions his well-known study of war memorials largely in opposition to Foucauldian analyses of spatial biopower. He argues that while such analyses are useful in that they call attention to discursive and contextual power frameworks that mould sites of memory, they forget the historical purposes and social understandings of war memorials themselves:

> What this interpretation lacks though is a historical sense of the meaning ascribed to war memorials at the time they were constructed. That meaning was highly personal. It used collective expression, in stone and in ceremony, to help individual people – mothers, fathers, wives, sons, daughters, and comrades-in-arms – to accept the brutal facts of death in war … This is not to suggest that war memorials were pacifist; a few were; the overwhelming were not. ***But the attitude to the war they represent reflects their local character and their sensitivity to the needs of the bereaved***, whose identities were in ***no sense*** a mystery to those who … stopped for a moment's reflection or just passed by.
> (Winter, 1995, pp. 94–95, emphasis added)

Ashplant, Dawson, and Roper, speaking from the popular memory tradition, criticise Winter's tendency to draw so stark a line between 'ordinary people' and 'state memory', and to depoliticise the historical practice of mourning at sites of memory. They write, "Wherever people undertake the tasks of mourning and reparation, a politics is always at work" (Ashplant, Dawson, & Roper, 2006, p. 9). This criticism is correct and I agree that there is much to Winter's larger analysis that is needlessly reductionist. I also agree with a subsequent criticism in the essay that Winter assumes a relatively unproblematic group psyche when it comes to local mourning practices (Ashplant, Dawson, & Roper, 2006, pp. 40–41). These are important criticisms. However, Winter is also correct to demand that scholars and historians acknowledge and understand the everyday usages of sites of memory – their performative functions for and within the local communities in which they are situated – and, though this is less central to his analysis, how that local character has altered at different junctures and why. In doing so, he is expanding his analysis away from the site of memory and towards the place of memory. These are the best parts of Winter's work, when he reminds us that sites of mourning (or more properly, places of melancholia) can signal multiple, overlapping readings that can still 'hang together' within the multiplicities and simultaneity of space (polysemy). That they can be spoken of (spoken *for*) in multiple voices, what Bakhtin (1984) called polyphony: multiple interweaving and interlocking voices gathering and coalescing together, multiple stories and narratives, making place.

Creating then truly transformative places of mourning/melancholia, in Butler's sense, would require a renewed focus on the 'place of the wound' (Till, 2012). The place of the wound is at these interstitial pinpricks in space where multiple ghosts haunt simultaneously. They create the opportunity for entrenched and polarised discourses to break down in the face of the other's pain, for human lives to be returned to reality through recognition, rehumanisation, and a refusal to allow their lives to be reduced to only one particular aspect of their humanity (ethnicity, status, guilt, innocence). Where the exclusionary claiming of the dead body is *or could be* contested, and contested from multiple angles. Where Heather Kerrigan's and Anthony Reavey's ghosts can haunt and exist in simultaneity with a place where George McBrearty's ghost could be simultaneously a killer or potential killer and a complicated human being. Where 'Oisin' and others can go to reckon with their own guilt, their own failures to adequately resist violence and the 'emotional zeitgeist' that enabled it. Where they may "confront and take responsibility for the failure of the democratic state and its violences" (Till, 2012, p. 7).

This is not a place to be reconciled to; nor does the place exist in a space where reconciliation, commonly understood, is even possible. It is a place that provokes contention, re-evaluation, and crucially, dissonance. The dissonance is in the multiplicity of stories that surround us and our attempts to witness and acknowledge them simultaneously, in fluid and changing space.

Returning to Indian Island

To be out of place is to be spatially excluded, to be denied the right to make places and curate memories within or accreted to the dominant social imaginary. But there are more complex social mechanisms at work than simply hegemonic/counter-hegemonic processes or dominant forms of space. For example, Kenneth Foote (2003, pp. 175–181) cites the houses where serial killers lived in the United States as places deemed unworthy of memory; often, they are simply bulldozed and obliterated to ensure that no mark or reminder will remain of what happened at that site. Eichstedt and Small (2002, pp. 175–181) argue that many Southern Plantation Museums in the United States simply ignore or refuse to acknowledge the presence of black slaves and slavery, a process they term 'symbolic annihilation'. The erasure of black bodies, black personhood, and black experience from the site thus "[meets] the need of whites to create a vision of the nation and themselves as noble and disassociated from racialised atrocities" (Eichstedt and

Small, 2002, p. 15). But neither obliteration nor annihilation is wholly 'successful'. They both leave behind spectral traces: the forced disappearance (the empty lot, the details glossed over and minimised by the helpful tour guides) itself is a cause of speculation, reflection, voyeurism, and analysis (Jonker & Till, 2009). But in extreme marginality, the spectral trace is buried or disappeared to such an extent that its absence is no longer even recognised or remarked.

Edward Relph (1976, Preface) argues that placelessness is the "casual eradication of distinctive places and the making of standardised landscapes that result from an insensitivity to the signification of place". Similarly, Augé (1995) calls attention to what he describes as 'non-places', places that exhibit no wider social or historical significance (i.e. airports, bus terminals, shopping malls) and thus cannot be affixed with narratives, or genres by which actors might recount narrative histories and social memories – places whose hyper-modern transience allows no bodies to 'stick' to them. Relph's placelessness is broadly similar; place becomes placeless through an 'insensitivity' rooted in commodification and the subordination of place's deep social significance to questions of governance, functionalism, organisation, and profit.

Augé's hypothesis has been justifiably criticised. Marxist-oriented scholars have pointed out that the places he cites as non-places are all actually places where the state is performed. An airport, for example, is a place of surveillance, categorisation, social differentiation (Korstanje, 2015). The non-place of an American shopping mall is hard to reconcile with qualitative, ethnographic research into the production of youth selves and everyday spatialities of significance that transcend mere banal consumerism (Thomas, 2005; Chin, 2001). But perhaps we might say that if out of place is being unable to pass trial by space and is thus excluded and confined to the periphery, being rendered placeless or non-placed would be to simply be invisible or unintelligible and to have no capacity to make oneself or one's story visible or intelligible. If out of place is the inability to make a mark on space, then placeless or non-placed is not even having a marker in the first place, a visceral subalternity. Relph (1976, pp. 119–121) approaches questions like this in a brief section on 'place destruction', which he sub-heads with the Heideggerian term *Abbau* (unmaking or dismantling), and another on place abandonment, but neither *Abbau* nor abandonment really fits what occurred and is still occurring on Indian Island. Here, another form of placelessness or non-placing is occurring. It is the placelessness or non-placing of terrible forgetting, of an amnesia intrinsically bound up in an imaginary that cannot provide the space for these Wiyot men, women, and children, lest it be forced to confront the dark recesses of its past that can still not be spoken in public and the bodies that cannot be grieved for. Nor is it even indifference to place; indifference would imply at least some degree of agency – the social or collective agent could be troubled to remember, but just doesn't care. On Indian Island, the ghosts cannot be cared for because, quite simply, they seem to no longer exist.

What I have described in Castlederg and Derry is people in the processes of gathering stories to make places of memory that challenge or circumvent a dominating but forever incomplete social imaginary that confines their experiences, perspectives, and memories to the peripheries of the social imaginary. What I have described on Indian Island is where traumatic memory has been erased from public space, where no stories circulate. In that regard, Indian Island retains only the last and most desperate tendrils of a place, that small plinth (which may have easily disappeared by now), a Master's student's rarely read thesis at the local university, a Wikipedia stub, my own memories of visiting long ago. It is where (and how) memory gets destroyed. In speaking with victims and survivors in Northern Ireland from all walks of life, I have concluded that for many of them, this is the fundamental terror lurking behind the labours of memory. It is why many of them are so resistant to discourses that stress the need or necessity to 'move on', which they claim are tantamount to 'rewriting history', and why they are so insistent that the ghosts of the dead continue to interrupt the 'transition to'. They cannot bear to countenance the possibility of their memories being disappeared, non-placed, rendered placeless, to have nowhere they can go, nowhere to return to, with a wreath, a prayer card, or nothing at all save their selves and their memories.

Chapter 6

The politics of inscription

In Northern Ireland and other societies struggling to confront difficult pasts, places of memory – realised, latent, or under construction – are crucial loci of symbolic contestation as different actors and groups lay claim to a right to speak through a place. This is especially acute in the arena of what Verdery (1999) refers to as 'dead-body politics', where actors essentially are contesting the right to speak for the bodies of the dead, bodies that can no longer speak for themselves. In Chapter 4 I examined which bodies are conceived of as having a right to speak and why. In Chapter 5 I examined where those bodies can speak and how such a place is or could be created. In this chapter I wish to move towards the questions of how bodies are permitted to speak, what are the forms, genres, and narratives available to them and their claimants, and how are those limits socially constructed. Before turning to Northern Ireland, I want to first look at some excellent research in other contested memory-space in North and South America to provide context and comparison.

Splintered memory

There is a fascinating and growing literature on the politics of inscribing the African-American body into public space in the United States (Alderman, Butler & Hanna, 2016; Dwyer, Butler & Carter, 2013; Small; 2013; Alderman & Campbell, 2008; Modlin, 2008; Hoelscher, 2003; Shackel, 2003), much of it influenced by Kirk Savage's (1996) brilliant work examining the divergent and changing means in which artists, sculptors, and photographers sought to humanise or marginalise black Americans in the late nineteenth century, how representations of the black body through commemorative monument drove and shaped the United States' changing and, ultimately, retrenching view of racial history and race relations. Other compelling work has examined naming and inscribing the civil rights struggle in the United States, especially through the body of the slain civil rights leader Martin Luther King, Jr. King's body is especially central to memory inscription due to his unique status as the 'face' of a massive and multilayered movement. Owen Dwyer (2002; 2008) argues that the maintenance, care, and location of memorials buttressing the 'traditional' places of civil rights memory in the United States is part and parcel with a larger project to re-imagine the civil rights struggle as unified, subdued, and black patrician, thus minimising the chaotic and often quite radical strains of the movement. This sanitisation of civil rights memory does not directly challenge the established understanding of fundamental American concepts of freedom, justice, and exceptionalism (Lipset, 1996) and thus does not challenge the ongoing legacy of racial inequality in the United States (e.g., Alexander, 2010). Derek Alderman and his frequent co-authors have continually called attention not only to the spatial exclusion or marginalisation of black narratives that challenge white dominance, but also to the vibrant and contested intra-community politics of inscription that surround King's body and the naming of King's body in public space (Alderman & Inwood, 2013; Alderman, 2003).

For example, Alderman's excellent essay on the politics of remembering in Savannah, Georgia illustrates how the struggle over the aesthetic form and written inscription on Savannah's monument to slavery functioned as a sort of proxy battle over competing visions of the historical institution of slavery and the role of the past in the present. The struggles were not merely between Savannah's black and white communities, though there were some tensions there; rather, Alderman uses the Savannah case to illustrate how the contested politics of slavery are written into public space and how those inscriptions refract competing understandings within the black community over how the memory of slavery should properly be invoked and narrativised.

Another quite compelling case study is Adrienne Burk's (2003; 2006) work on the visual politics of inscription in Vancouver's Downtown Eastside. Burk begins with the case of the 'Montreal Massacre' of 6 December 1989, when a murderous misogynist entered a university building on the campus of the University of Montreal medical school, separated the men from the women, and proceeded to mercilessly murder 14 young women, or 'damn feminists', as he chose to dehumanise them. Initially, a Vancouver women's group claimed the right to memorialise the slain women in public space and procured funding to erect a memorial in Vancouver's Downtown Eastside (DTES) CRAB park. Initially, the appropriation of public space was uncontroversial; however, that quickly changed when the women's group proposed to inscribe into the memorial the phrase 'women murdered by men'. Predictably, this provoked a backlash because it broke a patriarchal social taboo and upset the comforting and domesticating public narrative in the process of being shaped. But the subsequent challenge from *other women's groups* is even more revealing. Local feminist activists pointed out that the site chosen to remember 14 primarily white, middle-class women from Montreal was being emplaced into a larger community, the DTES, notable for its extreme levels of poverty, homelessness, mental health problems, addiction problems, and open-air sex trade, vis-à-vis the rest of the city (Campbell, Boyd, & Culbert, 2009). Activists also pointed out allegations that the DTES was where an alleged serial killer, who had at that point not been caught, had claimed the lives of at least 29 sex workers. The serial killer, since caught (though many cases remain officially unsolved), was allegedly able to operate with relative impunity for so long because the bodies of these missing and murdered women simply were of no great concern to law enforcement. These activists claimed that by creating a site of memory for the victims of the Montreal Massacre in the DTES, these memory curators were creating a hierarchy of victims of male violence, with young, white, professional students at the top and poor sex workers at the bottom.

But there was also a third and further challenge, a third larger claimant to speak in the name of women murdered by men. Indigenous or First Nations people make up approximately 15 per cent of the DTES population, compared to only 2–3 per cent of Vancouver's population as a whole. And 40 per cent of the population of sex workers is "immigrant or visible minority women", of which most would be Indigenous or First Nations women (City of Vancouver, 2013, p. 43). Indigenous or First Nations women are also drastically overrepresentative of the victims of serial killers in Canada, and the victims of the Vancouver serial killer were no exception. For Indigenous and First Nations activists, the discourse surrounding speaking for women murdered by men in the DTES starkly paralleled the systematic exclusion of the stories of Indigenous and First Nations women from Canada's history and social fabric.[1] In response to these multiple challenges, each reflective of simultaneous social narratives demanding access to a place of memory, CRAB park now holds *three separate memorials*, each uneasily co-existing in the same site, each irrupted with different stories. Despite the fact that the stories all 'hang together' and speak (in part!) the same challenge to dominant patriarchal violence, the place of memory is splintered and contested and bears the visible splintered memory of that contestation.

Erika Doss' (2010) study of the spontaneous memorials that sprung up in the aftermath of the Columbine High School massacre in the United States is also particularly instructive. In Columbine, the 'innocence' of all of the schoolchildren was completely unassailable, but even in such a case, a visual semblance of a hierarchy of victims seemed to emerge. Columbine, situated on the outskirts of Denver, Colorado, is at the edge of the United States' so-called 'Bible Belt'. Protestant evangelicalism plays a large role in the lives of many Columbine residents. In the aftermath of the massacre, the bodies of two victims in particular were used in an attempt to affix a particular, highly evangelicised, narrative of the massacre into public space, a narrative which quickly mushroomed into a redemptorist parable told in a hyper-evangelical speech genre readily familiar and open to evangelical political movements that emphasise an omnipresent threat to Christians and Christianity from unspecified forces within and outside the United States. One of the victims, 17-year-old Cassie Bernall, reportedly had

1 See the Canadian Broadcasting Company's Project: 'Missing and Murdered: The Unsolved Cases of Indigenous Women and Girls' at www.cbc.ca/missingandmurdered/.

been murdered "because she affirmed her faith in Christ at gunpoint". The body of another young woman, Rachel Scott, was reclaimed as a "Christian martyr". The bodies of these two young women were rapidly transformed into divine manifestations of evangelical faith in a situation of ultimate precarity and elevated to a more visible position in the local community's spontaneous mourning rituals. Doss writes that their bodies were transformed from schoolchildren into sacralised objects, that they "were viewed less as victims of a terrible crime than as modern day martyrs with post-corporeal power to spark a 'potential religious revival' in America" (Doss, 2010, pp. 104–105).

Fernando Bosco's (2004) work is also a compelling case study of how competing claims to inscribe places of memory, to exert a degree of control over the legitimate speech of the dead, can splinter and disrupt social movements and the memory-places they seek to build. Bosco's case study is the Madres de la Plaza de Mayo in Argentina and illustrates how the Madres movement splintered over control of the appropriate political speech of the bodies of the dead. In this case, these were often bodies that were not corporeally present, the bodies of the *desaparecidos* (disappeared), those tens of thousands of men and women disappeared by the junta. For one faction of the Madres, the Línea Fundadora, the logical culmination of the struggle for memory around forced disappearance is the answer to the question *¿Dónde están?* (Where are they?). Their struggle, or at least the struggle devoted to forced disappearance, ends when they are able to know the truth about what happened to their loved ones, to know where their loved ones are buried, or if they were dumped in the Río de la Plata, to return the bones of their loved ones to their preferred resting place or to create a place of memory on shores of the river. Thus, the Línea Fundadora focused their activism on accelerating the pace of forensic excavations of mass graves and demanding the truth of their loved ones' deaths and the return of their bodies. But the other faction of the Madres, the Asociación, uses the same disappeared bodies for a much different political purpose. For the Asociación, the bodies stand as powerful symbols for the continued necessity and relevance of the human rights movement, not just in Argentina or the Southern Cone, but throughout transitional memory-space elsewhere. Thus, the preferred inscriptive form the bodies take is as constitutive objects in an ongoing and perpetual struggle against state violence and terrorism that has no logical culmination.

Cara Levey's (2016) work provides a larger portrait of the movements against oblivion in the Southern Cone and her crucial contribution is to illustrate how these splintering memories contest and disrupt the emplacement of monuments to historical violence. One of her most interesting examples is the major 'official' memorial to the victims of state terrorism during the Argentinian junta, Remembrance Park (Parque de la Memoria). She describes a sustained grass-roots movement in post-junta Argentina to provide official places for memory that pitted grass-roots placemakers against the *pacto del olvido* forced on public space by the Menem government. As an unintended result of changes instituted in Menem's 1994 Constitution, citizens were able to elect a local government in the Buenos Aires district that could exert notable independence from Menem's government, and the local government changed from resisting the memorial project to supporting it in 1997. But groups like the Asociación and others boycotted the memorial project, claiming that any state involvement in the process of official memorialisation was immoral and unjust, considering the judicial immunity for perpetrators granted under the Menem government's imposition of the Full Stop, the laws preventing further prosecutions and investigations of past crimes. Levey argues that resistant memory was 'relocated' away from official sites and towards new, more combative, mobile, and transgressive places of memory such as the *escrache* and by returning to mark the 'shadowed ground' (see Foote, 2003) of torture sites that had been rectified and non-placed by the transitional regime. As the reader sees in Levey's work, the biography-of-a-site approach is untenable because it would fail to link multiple places of memory and potentiality, and fail to understand their combative and contested relationship to one another in the fluid and dynamic memory-space of the Southern Cone.

These cases are certainly a whistle-stop tour through a selective secondary literature based on transitional memory-space in North and South America. However, I argue that they provide us with some interesting beginnings to examine the politics of inscription in Northern Ireland. I suggest this literature illustrates one of my broader arguments, that when it comes to creating places of memory in landscapes of past violence and terror, there is no set, fixed, or even wholly predictable interpretive understanding of how transitional memory-space can be ordered, and no set, fixed, or even wholly predictable set of mechanisms regarding *how* dead bodies will perform the work of memory. In the *thrown-togetherness* of transitional space, a crucial question is *how* the dead bodies will speak to and narrate a contested past, and who will emerge to claim or contest their legitimate, post-corporeal speech and the genres in which they are capable of speaking.

In Northern Ireland, I begin by providing a close examination of the contested politics of inscription surrounding two larger memory-places in the Northwest of Northern Ireland: the small village of Claudy, County Derry, and the larger living landscape of Derry's Bogside. Next, I will turn towards an examination of paramilitary places of memory and the violent inscriptions that underwrite them. These paramilitary places exhibit what I refer to as a strict hegemony of form, a standardised aesthetic learned (perhaps aped) from British war memorials that would seem, at face value, to belie alternative readings and rigorously police the potentialities of possible challenge. However, I hope to show that in spite of the ubiquity of these paramilitary places in working-class space, with the saturation of violent imagery seeming to drown out resistance, memory in working-class space can be and is resisted and re-imagined. But like the examples above, that resistance often takes the form of a splintering of memory rather than a wholesale overhaul, and it often operates beneath the surface of the stultifying Northern Irish macro-narratives and sectarianised discourses.

Inscribing Claudy

On 31 July 1972 three car bombs ripped through the small village of Claudy, located approximately 15 km southeast of Derry. Six people were killed immediately and three more died subsequently from their injuries. Their names of the adults who were killed are Arthur Hone, James McClelland, Joseph McCluskey, Elizabeth McElhinney, Rose McLaughlin, and David Miller. While these deaths were indescribably terrible, the additional deaths of three children – 8-year-old[2] Kathryn Eakin, 15-year-old Patrick Joseph Connolly, and 16-year-old Billy Temple – were especially brutal.

Though the PIRA never officially claimed responsibility for the bombing, the South Derry Brigade of the PIRA is universally understood to have been responsible (McKittrick et al., 2008, pp. 240–241). Up until the bombing, Claudy had been a relatively peaceful village, but the spillover from the chaos engulfing nearby Derry had led to a rise in local tensions. Speaking generally, rural areas of Northern Ireland experience slightly different divisions and segregations than the urban or semi-urban areas of Belfast and Derry. Sectarianism in rural areas is often imperceptible to the outsider, even the outsider from other areas of Northern Ireland, in contrast to urban areas with their marked interface lines and visible territorial markings (though the flying of Irish, British, or other paramilitary flags in some rural areas is prevalent, giving the outsider a general understanding of where he or she is). But in rural areas of Northern Ireland, during the Troubles and its aftermath, an invisible cartography of fear rooted in secure/insecure places and landmarks tended and still somewhat tends to operate. As one of my respondents, who had relocated to Belfast from a rural area after the Agreement, put it to me: "A bend, a corner, dictates geographically where you feel safe" ('Sally', Belfast). In the South and West of Northern Ireland, villages are often inhabited nearly exclusively by members of either the CNR of PUL communities and sit side by side with villages inhabited nearly exclusively by members of the other community, for example Coagh and Ardboe near the border of County Tyrone and County Derry. However, in the 1970s Claudy was a mixed village and the bombing killed Protestants and Catholics indiscriminately. Five Catholics and four Protestants were killed in the bombing. None of the victims had ties to belligerent groups.

Nobody has ever been brought to justice for their role in the Claudy bombings. One particularly chilling aspect of the bombing revealed in subsequent investigations was the central involvement of a Catholic priest, Fr James Chesney, who allegedly acted as quartermaster for the South Derry Brigade (Bowcott, 2010; Cowan, 2002). A damning report by the Police Ombudsman for Northern Ireland Al Hutchinson in 2010 alleged that Chesney's involvement was covered up by the Northern Ireland Office in collusion with the Catholic Church, probably due to the fear that if it became widely known that a Catholic priest was centrally involved

2 *Lost Lives* (McKittrick et al. 2008) incorrectly lists Kathryn Eakin as nine years old.

in the atrocity, Northern Ireland would descend further into sectarian chaos. Thus, the Report alleged, then-Secretary of State for Northern Ireland William Whitelaw enlisted the aid of the Church to quietly move Chesney to a remote parish in County Donegal, where he could supposedly do no more harm (Police Ombudsman for Northern Ireland, 2010). Chesney died of natural causes in 1981.

The years 1972 to 1976 were by far the worst years of the Troubles in terms of total deaths, accounting for 44.2 per cent of all deaths attributable to the Troubles, according to *Lost Lives* (McKittrick et al., 2008). Claudy's ghosts were rapidly displaced from the media spotlight and public attention by a spiralling escalation of violence and murder. But the larger community of Claudy struggled on and, in the immediate aftermath of the bombing at least, actually seemed to draw closer together in their shared grief, even across the ethnosectarian divide. David Temple, brother of 16-year-old Billy killed in the bombing, testifies to this: "Everybody called to our house – Protestant and Roman Catholic. We had great support from all the community and it was one of the biggest funerals ever to take place [in the nearby hamlet of] Donnaghmonery" (Shared City Project & Omagh Self-Help & Support Group, 2011, p. 22). But as it became clear that no justice was forthcoming and that a Catholic priest may have been centrally involved, Claudy, in the words of 'Callum', "was left to lick its own wounds and the downside I think when communities lick their own wounds is they lick them on their own. All that grief turned into Catholic and Protestant, they both went back into their own."

In 1972 neither the British government nor the local authorities had any effective programmes for or insights into dealing with serious injury, bereavement, and trauma. The directly affected of Claudy received no additional trauma provision beyond what was already available through the National Health Service (NHS). The seriously injured of the bombings received ongoing help and financial support, but the bereaved families received only a small, one-off payment to help bury their loved ones. These payments generally arrived in the form of letters that prescribed a fixed amount to their loved one's current and future value. Unsurprisingly, the grieving families of Claudy found this approach needlessly callous, painful, and dehumanising. Mark Eakin (2010), brother of 8-year-old Kathryn, speaks poignantly to this reality:

> As for me? I couldn't even cry about it, and for years I didn't cry. It was as if some kind of paralysis came over me. This was 1972, mind, and there was no talk of counselling then. You wonder how you didn't go mad.
>
> [Billy and Merle Eakin, Kathryn's parents] were told that £56 would cover their funeral expenses and they were not entitled to any more as Kathryn was eight years old and now would not need further schooling
>
> (Jeanette Warke, quoting Mark Eakin, interview with author, Derry)

In 2000 a full 28 years after the Claudy bombing, a bronze memorial sculpture (see Figure 6.1) by the Irish sculptor Elizabeth McLaughlin (no relation

Figure 6.1 Claudy Bombing Memorial, Claudy, County Derry. Photo by Martin Melaugh. © Martin Melaugh and © CAIN. Used with permission.

to Rose McLaughlin) was unveiled in a car park off the main town square in Claudy. The memorial drive was spearheaded by community worker Jeanette Warke of nearby Derry, who was inspired to work for a lasting memorial to the victims of Claudy by her close friendship with the Eakin family and David Temple. Warke at the time was the head of the Shared City Initiative in Derry and although her initial application for public funding was turned down, the memorial working group and the Shared City Initiative managed to raise £25,000 in contributions for the erection of the statue. Intended to be unveiled on the twenty-fifth anniversary of the bombing, the project suffered delays and the memorial was unveiled three years later in 2000. For Warke, the memorial project is a demand for Claudy's inclusion in Northern Irish memory-space, a demand that the traumatic experience of the victims, survivors, and bereaved be inscribed into public space and with a certain degree of public visibility. It is a claim that, in spite of the fact that Claudy's bereaved and Claudy's survivors have been shunted aside, mistreated, and denied justice, the memorial will ensure that posterity will not forget them. Claudy's trauma will remain inscribed into Northern Ireland's social and material landscape, a trauma that, as Warke avers, is *entitled* to be materially present:

> The Claudy victims were entirely left out and they had a real cry for help … They felt they wanted a memorial so they could see something in memory to their loved ones … This memorial is for the people who were blew up, and this is a point where you can look at it and you're remembering and you're not being brushed under the carpet. *They're entitled to have something there*, regardless of who they were.
>
> (Jeanette Warke, interview with author, Derry, original emphasis)

However, in spite of the lofty goals and rhetoric of Warke and others, the process of erecting the memorial and the final product have proven controversial. The working group did not garner much cross-community participation and many people in Claudy are uncomfortable with the finished product. Rightly or wrongly, my research revealed a significant perception that the memorial aesthetic was imposed from outside the community, so it lacks full community ownership, and that it may have even exacerbated existing divides between the two communities in the region. Why that perception may exist provides a compelling case study of the tangled politics of inscription in rural areas of Northern Ireland.

As 'Callum' recalls, after the bombing the two communities of victims' families and survivors in Claudy gradually drifted apart, mirroring the larger intercommunal separation and segregation so deeply entrenched by the Troubles. When Warke's group proposed the memorial project, the working group attracted the participation of politicians from the SDLP and a community group generally recognised as representing a swathe of the local CNR community, but the families of Catholic victims did not participate directly. Within the Protestant community of victims and survivors, the families seem to have been internally split in terms of their relative attachment for or close affinity with the memorial project. A number of families were still actively involved in the justice campaign and viewed the memorial project as a bit of a distraction. 'Isabella' additionally argues that the design submitted by McLaughlin and championed by Warke and others:

> seemed to be pushed on pretty quickly; it was more or less decided on before any of us objected and I think we were all still hoping we would get some results [from the justice campaign] … so getting results … was more important than that and [the memorial project] just seemed to go ahead.

As 'Callum' recalls, the families in the region he contacted expressed concerns that were not incorporated either into the process or the outcome, in part because of their reluctance to participate in the working group:

> We were approached by a couple of the families who told us, "We just don't want the memorial". So at that stage we said, "Look, people in our [CNR] community are telling us that they don't want the memorial so we're going to remove ourselves from this conversation". We can't roughride the concerns [of these families], but the Shared City Initiative went ahead.

The completed memorial depicts a young girl on a stone pedestal, kneeling, her head in her hands (Figure 6.1). She seems to be in a state of anguish, her body contorted into a defensive position. She is clearly depicted as witnessing something awful or deeply traumatic. This is a statue focused on depicting the act itself and its effect on the young girl's body; it traps the viewer in the young girl's state of anguish: she lives the trauma over and over with each viewing. The age and the appearance of the young girl bear a clear resemblance to Kathryn Eakin, and although both Warke and McLaughlin vigorously deny the young girl was intended to be a representation of Kathryn Eakin,[3] the reality is that most viewers of the memorial, both within and outside Claudy, associate the young girl with the youngest victim of the bombing. There is no reason whatsoever to disbelieve Warke's testimony that the young girl was not intended to be Kathryn Eakin, but shortly I will suggest how the two bodies came to be bound together and why the aesthetic choice of the memorial all but guaranteed that they would.

The comments of both 'Isaballa' (PUL) and 'Callum' (CNR) clearly demonstrate the reservations both communities had regarding the choice of memorial aesthetic:

> The majority [of the working group] wanted that wee girl, the wee statue or the wee girl, but I didn't really like it because I think it's very sad and I always think its Kathryn.
>
> ('Isabella')

> We were kind of saying, "Well, we're not the ones who need to pick this [design], but we can tell you categorically, *do not pick that one*, the one with the young girl on her knees holding her head because to everybody in Claudy, that's Kathryn Eakin." That's just too emotive, too personal, get something new.
>
> ('Callum', original emphasis)

I believe both respondents implicitly identify something aesthetically oppressive in the memorial's form. It forces the viewer to participate in the repeating narrative of traumatic disruption and it forces them to experience it through

3 Warke insisted in our conversation that the young girl was 'too old' to be Kathryn Eakin.

the eyes and ears of an 'ideal victim', namely the young girl/Kathryn Eakin. The aesthetic promotes empathic arousal, but it does so gratuitously by erasing LaCapra's necessary separation between the viewer and the depiction of trauma and encouraging an outright assimilation into the traumatised body (LaCapra, 2001). As such it promotes Brecht's 'crude empathy' more than LaCapra's 'empathic unsettlement' (Bennett, 2005). In addition, because the memorial is closely identified with the body of Kathryn Eakin, it funnels empathic arousal away from the larger place of the wound, Claudy, and towards the figure itself, thus aesthetically marginalising the other victims and their families. This marginalisation parallels the larger media treatment of the bombing, a media treatment that focused their eye disproportionately on the youngest, 'most innocent' victim, and subsequently and quite quickly 'forgot' about Claudy and allowed the bombing to fade from the public eye, thus eroding any hope for the perpetrators to be brought to justice. Finally, if the viewer interprets the statue as a representation of Kathryn Eakin, there is a natural and shocking interpretation available, albeit this interpretation is certainly unintended: the viewer is witnessing Kathryn Eakin's last moments of life, the last moments before her horrible death.

In Chapter 4 I touched on Nils Christie's (1986) provocative concept of the 'ideal victim', a victim who most closely embodies shared understandings of vulnerability and innocence. I mentioned the relationality inherent in that concept, which is sometimes missed when it is adapted elsewhere. The body of the ideal victim is not a stand-alone vehicle; it is formed out of the victim's relation to the perpetrator. Christie's work suggests why it was inevitable that the young girl and Kathryn Eakin would fuse, regardless of McLaughlin or Warke's intentions. The memorial aesthetic, as we shall shortly see, is bound up in evoking the ideal of innocence and vulnerability, an innocence and vulnerability that is violently severed not simply by the act, but by the evil people who carried it out, people that most closely epitomise, according to Christie's somewhat childish language, the socially constructed 'big and bad'.

Consider Warke's testimony below. She dichotomises between a 'natural' childhood characterised by purity and innocence and the traumatic experience that stripped that childhood away. In Warke's reading, the young girl/Kathryn Eakin is not witnessing the bombing itself, but grieving for a girlhood she was never allowed to experience:

> The symbol there was innocence. It was this wee girl with her head in her hands and just this feeling of hopelessness at the same time for the future. And this innocence was being taken away. And that tended to[4] a lot of young people, their innocence was taken away. There was a lot of young people's lives destroyed. And then to expect everyone to forget and get on, it's not that easy, the Troubles has had a severe cost on people's lives.

4 In the northwest of Ireland dialect 'tended to' means 'applied to'.

If the young girl/Kathryn Eakin is the vehicle for innocence, then it becomes clear that the 'big and bad' perpetrators, the people who destroyed that innocence, are the PIRA and the larger republican movement. However, this discourse of idealised purity is characteristic of the innocent victim rhetoric so pronounced within victims and survivors groups and networks of a PUL orientation across Northern Ireland, which I also discussed in Chapter 4. Adopting and emplacing innocence into the aesthetic of the memorial promoted the severing of the shared trauma of the two communities and implicitly, again albeit unintentionally, made the members of the CNR community unwelcome at the site of memory. Many Catholic victims and the larger CNR community would no doubt prefer to view the Claudy bombings against the backdrop of Bloody Sunday and Operation Motorman in nearby Derry, where Catholics were being murdered and tortured by the British military, and many may even have sympathised with the larger republican movement at the time, even if they were tragically affected by the bombing and more generally objected to the PIRA's campaign of violence. Whatever the motivations of its authors, rendering the young girl/Kathryn Eakin's body a repository of innocence at the memorial site did not promote shared grief; rather, it promoted the further sectionalisation of social memory.

An inscription is not just a written inscription, a message, mnemonic, or narrative, etched, soldered, attached in prose to a site of memory. Moving from a site approach to a place approach allows the viewer to become aware that an inscription is also an aesthetic choice, the larger process by which a social memory is emplaced into a landscape, and dependent on how it is situated within a larger viewing community. Whether the viewer is a member of that viewing community, and her relationship to existing schisms or fractures within that community, colours how the performance is presented and received (Marschall, 2009; Savage, 1996). An outsider, someone observing a particular site at a particular moment in time, may not be able to decode the complex inscriptive process or may decode it in a manner drastically different from that of a localised audience. When we read the Claudy bombing memorial with this in mind, we find that the memorial remains bound to its contested inscriptive process, its particular aesthetic, and its mode of transmission.

Dead children are a potent emotive means to advance a preferred social narrative. Katherine Verdery (1999, p. 5) argues about statues of people: "By arresting the process of that person's bodily decay, a statue alters the temporality associated with that person, bringing [her] into the realm of the timeless, of the sacred, like an icon." As the young girl/Kathryn Eakin is transfixed into stone, she becomes a sacralised object and claims the space of the icon, the space of the saint or the angel. The purity of the image is unassailable and it neither provokes nor allows for any further space for the contentious politics of inscription.

Two children

Annette McGavigan was a 14-year-old schoolgirl from the Meenan Park housing estate in Derry's Bogside, where she attended St Cecilia's secondary school.

On the evening of 6 September 1971 she was shot dead, almost certainly by a British soldier, on Abbey Street in the heart of the Bogside. The exact details of her killing will probably never be confirmed, but the most likely explanation of the events is as follows. Shortly after 6:10 in the evening, two nail bombs were thrown at a British army patrol on Abbey Street. The soldiers returned fire using rubber bullets but switched to live fire when they were allegedly menaced by a PIRA sniper. Annette McGavigan, according to her friend, had begun collecting riot souvenirs (a testament to just how normalised urban violence had become in Derry at that point) and had broken cover in an attempt to add a rubber bullet to her collection. Though McGavigan may not have been targeted, her killing was part of a pattern of the callous and reckless use of deadly force by the British army in densely populated areas. In 1999 a large mural was unveiled on a gable wall at the junction of Lecky Road and Westland Street near the well-known Free Derry Corner by a three-man collective known as the Bogside Artists (see Figure 6.2). The mural is entitled 'The Death of Innocence'. Here is the Artists' statement:

> In telling this story, [the Bogside Artists] have served a pressing need for their community and Derry people in general to acknowledge with dignity if not pride the price paid by those who became victims of the struggle for democratic rights ... The artists are pledged to continue to express this spiritual dimension on the gable walls of the Bogside ... We believe that only when both communities of Catholics and Protestants have confronted the wounds they have inflicted on each other, and on themselves, can there be the possibility of healing or forgiveness.[5]

A close reading of this statement reveals why Annette McGavigan's body is selected out of the past 'to stand for all the children' (see Figure 6.2) killed during the Troubles and why the aesthetic presentation of her body takes the form it does. The 'Death of Innocence' mural is massive – my own eyeball estimate suggests it is around 6–7 metres high and 5–6 metres wide, and it dominates the intersection, staring across at the Free Derry Wall. For a young, slight girl, the representation of her body is not of corporeal fragility but spatial domination. The written inscription at the site (see Figure 6.3) imposes an ideational blueprint on its audience for how to read the mural. Each unsubtle symbol or metaphor, from the broken gun, to the colourful butterfly, to the broken glass, to the crucifix, to her school uniform, is painstakingly broken down for the audience to forestall any non-prescribed interpretation. The inscription exudes a claim to represent her body, to impose ownership over it. Note the final line beginning with 'our challenge'. Why should it be their challenge and not somebody else's? What gives them the right to impose a representation of this scale? And are there other possibilities for interpreting the violent death of Annette McGavigan at the chronotopic place of the Bogside, ones that do not demand that her death be

5 Available at cain.ulst.ac.uk/bogsideartists/statement.htm.

Figure 6.2 'Death Of Innocence': Memorial to Annette McGavigan, Derry. Photo by Martin Melaugh. © Martin Melaugh and © CAIN. Used with permission.

read as the sum total of 'innocence and rebirth?' The written inscription, coupled with the image's scale, and read in light of the other murals that dominate the aesthetic memory-space of the Bogside, seeks to exert control over not only Annette McGavigan, but also the social memory of the Bogside itself.

It is not particularly difficult to decode the Bogside Artists' underlying motivation for the appropriation of aesthetic memory-space. The Artists have sought to inscribe a particular strand of social memory into the Bogside that suits their particular social and ideational imperatives. These imperatives are perfectly readable in their statement. They aim to present a larger narrative that casts the Bogside as a community that bravely stood up for civil rights, whose members were beaten down and killed but who persevered, and eventually emerged or will emerge into a place where forgiveness and reconciliation will be possible through

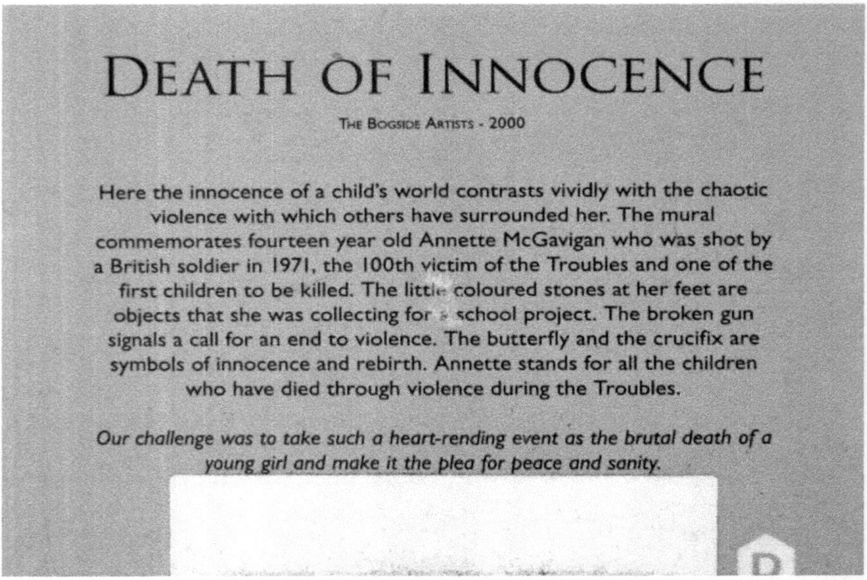

Figure 6.3 'Death of Innocence': Inscription, Derry. Photo by author.

a confrontation with past wounds. They are 'pledged' to do this with a 'spiritual' dimension, a statement that suggests a religiously inspired pacific imperative, and they intend their work to facilitate 'healing' and 'forgiveness', terms which also carry a clear religious connotation, especially in the larger context.

It is difficult to read the Artists' statement without reference to Foucault's (2004) concept of 'pastoral power'. Pastoral power is a form of biopower that exerts control over social groups through claiming the legitimate right to articulate the salvation of the group, and the means and processes through which salvation is achieved. The Bogside Artists claim the role of the shepherd of the Bogside, leading the flock through the noble civil rights struggle, covering its eyes to the intensity and complex culpability of the IRA campaign, and emerging into the new pasture of reconciliation, democracy, healing, and forgiveness.

My major criticism of the Bogside murals is not directed at any aspect of the Artists' 'calling' or their inscriptive imperative; rather, my criticism is with the way the Artists impose this vision over the social memory of the Bogside, the way they attempt to drown out other stories and narratives that swirl about the wounded place of the Bogside simultaneously. They are not successful at imposing a hegemony of inscriptive form; the Bogside is also a place that aesthetically houses the ghosts of IRA men and women and the narratives of dissident republicanism, but any attempts to alter the murals are strenuously resisted and attempts to symbolically accrete other social memories to them are carefully policed and wiped clean.

The notion championed by the Artists, that the Bogside is the 'People's Gallery', is quite ironic in this sense.

I suggest that what the Bogside Artists and their allies are attempting to do is to impose a 'carefully-controlled consensus' onto the Bogside as a place of memory (Conway, 2009; Teeger & Vinitzky-Seroussi, 2007) through the exercise of pastoral power. Consider how 'Ronan' frames the Artists' memory-work:

> Well the murals … in the Bogside are all about the civil rights movement and they all present the people of the area as *victims* rather than perpetrators, and that's true, overwhelmingly. But of course, that's not all that happened in the Bogside. There's no representation of the IRA campaign … The biggest murals in the Bogside *tell a story that everybody in the Bogside can be comfortable with.*
>
> ('Ronan', Derry, emphasis added)

As 'Ronan' presciently argues (and I very much agree with him), a carefully controlled consensus is not a blatant imposition, a narrative that is rejected by the inhabitants themselves that is imposed by force or coercion; nor it is a narrative that is even out-of-sync with a larger strand of the Bogside's social memory. But it is to suggest that the use of Annette McGavigan's body could be read as part and parcel of a larger, quasi-programmatic foreclosure of other narrative possibilities that could be written on the Bogside's gable walls, of other ghosts whose essence may still haunt the Bogside's fugitive roads. This inscription process is underwritten by focusing only on the stories we want to tell ourselves, stories that we are already, as 'Ronan' suggests, comfortable with, stories that do not challenge us to look outside of our narrow lenses and encounter other stories and bodies swirling in the simultaneity of space. Carefully controlled consensuses often take this hegemonic form, and the macro-narratives they espouse are often told in the stories of uncritical victimhood and uncritical heroism. And to problematise this imposed consensus compromises the alleged need for a social catharsis. Thus, the Artists make the same error as Bloomfield, Eames, and Bradley: their pastoral mission to emplace consensus through public imagery forestalls the production of dissonant empathy, forestalls the dialogic *aporia* that allows for the inclusion of other voices and other bodies in the multiplicity of space.

This reading allows us to see another role for the body of Annette McGavigan, and her body's strident insertion into public memory nearly 30 years after her death. Dawson suggests that the timing of the 'Death of Innocence' mural (including the timing of another mural depicting civil rights leader Bernadette Devlin McAliskey) may have been a direct response to a well-publicised charge by local feminist author Nell McCafferty that the Bogside Artists had written women out of the Bogside's social memory (Dawson, 2005). The Bogside Artists stridently denied this charge, but the murals depicting McGavigan and McAliskey went up soon after the charge was made and widely read. However, the true pastoral value of McGavigan's body is that she, like the young girl/Kathryn Eakin in Claudy, functions as an ideal victim rooted in the discourses of purity and innocence, though in this case the 'big and bad' becomes the British army and not the PIRA. Northern Ireland, not unlike many other transitional societies, remains quite a patriarchal society, both politically and socially (Potter, 2014), and in highly patriarchal societies the role of ideal victim is most adequately filled by young girls. Young girls can easily be inserted into public space as symbols of fragility, vulnerability, purity, and chastity, ideals that require the protection of men. In contrast, young boys can be imagined as rambunctious or mischievous, and thus not the ideal symbol of innocence and not the ideal victim. Idealising victims is a process of stripping down their complex characters into easily managed, easily projected, and easily controlled symbolic reductions. These reductions limit the space of contention through carefully controlled consensus. And when it comes to carefully controlled consensus, it should come as no surprise to see representations of young girls figuring prominently as dehumanised objects in social memory-space (Borzello et al., 2013).

Annette McGavigan was not the only child killed in the Bogside, and not the only child killed by British soldiers in the Bogside. Nor are there, as far as I am aware, reliable estimates of the number of children shot or kneecapped by republican paramilitaries in the Bogside as 'punishment' or 'anti-drug' measures (Lindsay, 2012). You will see no memorials to the victims or survivors of cruel, vindictive 'punishment' attacks in the Bogside, nor anywhere else in working-class memory-space in Northern Ireland. On 19 April 1982, 11-year-old Stephen McConomy was fatally injured by a plastic bullet fired by a British soldier during a riot in the Bogside. McConomy was probably watching a group of youths stone a Saracen, an armoured crowd-control vehicle often deployed by the British army in Derry and Belfast. The soldier who killed Stephen McConomy later testified that he was firing at another youth holding a cardboard box he feared contained an explosive device. No evidence was submitted that Stephen McConomy was throwing stones or doing anything to threaten the safety of the soldiers. Again, his death must be seen as part of a pattern of the reckless use of deadly force in densely populated areas by the British army (McKittrick et al., 2008, p. 901). On the thirtieth anniversary of his death, Stephen McConomy's family unveiled a small memorial plaque just yards from where he was fatally shot on the gable wall of his former home (Figure 6.4).

There are a number of differences between Stephen McConomy's memorial and the mural depicting Annette McGavigan. First, it is smaller and unobtrusive; I personally walked by it numerous times before I even realised it was there. It would be virtually impossible to miss the Annette McGavigan memorial, which is clearly visible from the city walls. The written inscription is different as well; the verb 'murdered' on the Stephen McConomy plaque prevents the memorial from being read in a manner conducive to discourses of reconciliation or forgiveness. 'Murdered by a plastic bullet' directly refutes the British army's narrative of the event, that Stephen McConomy's death was a tragic accident. It is a phrase

Figure 6.4 Stephen McConomy Memorial, Derry. Photo by Martin Melaugh. © Martin Melaugh and © CAIN. Used with permission.

carefully selected to draw attention to both the deadly nature of the projectile and the family's larger campaign to secure justice for Stephen's killing and end the ongoing use of such projectiles by the British army, police, and security services. And justice, for Stephen McConomy's family, is the prosecution and subsequent conviction of the soldier or soldiers directly responsible for his killing (Derry Journal, 2012).

Both places of memory tell the same larger story of an unjust death of a child at the hands of the British army in the Bogside. But they tell the story in vastly different ways. The first and most important difference is the 'scale' of the memory performance (Bosco, 2004; Burk, 2003). Derek Alderman defines the 'scaling of memory' as a "socially contested process of determining the geographical extent" of a given memory (Alderman, 2003, p. 164). The Annette McGavigan mural claims a wide scale; it directly purports to represent and speak for the deaths of all children during the Troubles ('Annette stands for all the children …'; see Figure 6.3). The Stephen McConomy memorial speaks to a much smaller scale; it memorialises only Stephen and is placed near his former dwelling, the place he and his family physically occupied.

The bodies also differ in *how* they are inscribed into memory-space. Stephen McConomy's body becomes a constitutive object in a narrative of the ongoing search for justice and is positioned as part of a narrow (comparatively speaking) human rights campaign: the end to the use of plastic bullets. His family's legitimate curatorship of his body in this way is relatively unassailable and stems from their direct, tragic experience. But the Annette McGavigan memorial is much less tangible, much less limited in scope and scale. It inscribes Annette McGavigan's body into public memory-space as a constitutive object in a larger pastoral narrative of an entire community, the Bogside. But a closer reading reveals that the Bogside Artists are not limiting their narrative to the geographical extent of the Bogside; rather, Annette McGavigan's body and the other bodies depicted in the 'People's Gallery' are part of a larger pastoral project of speaking for *all of Northern Ireland*. The Artists employ the bodies to claim a narrative consensus over how the Troubles should be remembered and how the deaths of innocents should be performed, and they attempt to impose this through the inscriptive process and the scale of their symbolic projection. It is thus no accident that the Annette McGavigan mural and the other Bogside murals loom over the place of memory, trying to shoulder out other forms of inscription and alternative, competing, or challenging narrative usages of the bodies of the dead.

Inscribing violence

Northern Ireland is saturated with paramilitary imagery, with images of the armed gunman, or depictions of historical injustices that justify and legitimate the armed struggle and the state of exception (McDowell & Switzer, 2011; McDowell, 2008; Graham & Whelan, 2007). Paramilitary public imagery, iconography, and places of memory also seek to inscribe a particular social memory into Northern Irish memory-space and the built landscape. They are cultural and symbolic artefacts that can be interpreted and analysed, a task made easier by their aesthetic uniformity and relative lack of variance (Jarman, 1997, 1998). The performative dimension of violent imagery in Northern Ireland is three-fold. First, it seeks to inscribe the core conflict narratives I identified in Chapter 3, narratives dependent on the proclamation of a state of exception. Second, they are mnemonic devices in an *intra*-community ideological struggle over the range of acceptable representations of Troubles violence. In this sense, paramilitary iconography is a power projection and a show of force that claims the authority to exclusively speak for a given working-class community. And finally, paramilitary iconography performs what political geographers call borderwork: commemorative sites demarcate and inscribe a boundary, both territorial and ideational, into the working-class landscapes and topography.

As I argued in Chapter 3, paramilitary conflict narratives are firmly rooted in the state of exception. If that state of exception has been lifted or the threat of existential crisis is no longer translatable or intelligible to a subject community, then paramilitary organisations (and maybe even ideologies) have no reason to continue to exist in post-conflict Northern Ireland. Violent iconography is used by former and current force-wielders to publicly justify their continued existence;

thus the legitimating frameworks of the state of exception must be curated and maintained. The function of paramilitary iconography is to retain recourse to the legitimating discourse provided by the state of exception. This retention in turn replicates the ongoing *raison d'être* of paramilitary groups and their post-conflict offshoots and ideologies.

This performative function can be comparatively easily delineated. In Derry City Cemetery, a masked gunman dressed in military garb looms above the gravestones. The stone on which the icon stands lists INLA members killed during the Troubles and commemorates the ten republican prisoners who died during the 1981 hunger strikes. The main textual inscription quotes the Irish socialist and revolutionary James Connolly and reads:

> Believing that the British government has no right in Ireland, never had any right in Ireland, and never can have any right in Ireland, the presence in any one generation of Irishmen of even a respectable minority ready to die to affirm that truth makes that government for ever a usurpation and a crime against human progress.

Another memorial in the heart of Belfast's Shankill commemorates Trevor King, William 'Frenchie' Marchant, and Davy Hamilton, all UVF men killed by the IRA and the INLA. King and Marchant were long-term and high-ranking UVF members implicated in a number of killings (Taylor, 1999; Cusack & McDonald, 1997). Marchant was one of the primary suspected masterminds of the Dublin and Monaghan bombings of 1974 that killed 33 civilians in the Republic of Ireland, the deadliest coordinated attack of the entire Troubles (Barron Report, 2003). Hamilton and King were killed in the same attack along with another UVF man, Colin Craig. Craig was once inscribed on the mural, but his inscription was removed after allegations emerged that he was an informer. Again, at this memorial the armed gunmen stand at attention, though this time next to a red poppy wreath and the red hand flanked by 'For God and Ulster', the motto of the UVF. The inscription reads: "These brave men were killed near this spot by the enemies of Ulster. No sacrifice is too great for one's country. They paid the ultimate sacrifice."

The inscriptions garlanding both memorials loudly proclaim the state of exception. Paramilitary inscription at republic and loyalist memorials in Northern Ireland exhibits a disturbing ideological, textual, and aesthetic standardisation. They seem to be almost etched with the help of pre-existing templates and nearly all justify the recourse to dehumanising force in the name of a constructed existential threat. This is reminiscent of what the anthropologist Alexei Yurchak (2005) refers to as a 'hegemony of form' rooted in 'semantic reproduction'. Yurchak's work is focused on the late Soviet era and how the constative meaning behind Soviet texts and symbols gradually became replaced with mere ritualised reproduction. The performance of the symbol or the text mattered far more than the literal meaning, which itself was simply lifted from what came before, akin to a template:

> With the increasing normalisation of all forms of authoritative discourse, the performative dimension of that discourse began to play a greater role than its constative dimension. It became more important to participate in the execution of the ritualised acts and the reproduction of ritualised texts of this discourse than to attend to their constative meanings.
>
> (Yurchak, 2005, pp. 59–60)

While Northern Ireland and late-Soviet Russia are certainly different contexts, Yurchak's insight suggests a compelling reason for the standardisation of paramilitary aesthetics and inscriptions. Like late-Soviet semiotics, what is important is reproducing the power of a bygone past, reinscribing the legitimating frameworks of the past in spite of the changing contexts in the present. In Northern Ireland, this means relentlessly reproducing the language of threat and exception to justify the ongoing relevance of the state of exception, without which paramilitary groups and their offshoots are sapped of their political and social legitimation.

The threat inscribed at both sites is quite clear. At the former it is 'The British government' and in the latter, the 'enemies of Ulster'. The Connolly quote goes even further, maintaining that even if support for the interpretation of republicanism inscribed at this site flags and wanes, the (ongoing) struggle of a 'respectable minority' is *still legitimate*. The term 'the enemies of Ulster' in turn makes a grasp at threat malleability. 'The enemies of Ulster' is quite semantically flexible and it can be interpreted or reinterpreted at a given moment to maintain the UVF's legitimacy. For example, the phrase could mean republicans or republicanism, or it could be far more broad, interpreted as anyone who supports or gives succour to republicans and their narratives, memories, and historiography, and finally, it might be anyone who opposes the original contractual identity of the Northern Irish entity famously proclaimed by its first Prime Minister James Craig: "A Protestant government for a Protestant people." The flexibility and malleability of the inscription provides ready access to the state of exception *in spite* of dynamic social change. Its seemingly endless aesthetic and semantic reproduction saturates the memory-space with a violent performance of paramilitary legitimation. Thus, in this sense, these sites of memory function as what Richard Schein (1997) calls 'discourse materialized': they are the material reproductions of the belligerent discourse that itself depends on maintaining the legitimating dialectic of the state of exception.

The second major, interrelated function of paramilitary public imagery is to help win the legitimation contests within their 'own' communities. There is a tendency, especially by those who look at Northern Ireland from the outside, to see paramilitary visual displays such as murals and parades as challenging and threatening to the other community(ies). However, as McCormick and Jarman

Figure 6.5 'You are now Entering Loyalist Sandy Row' Mural, Shaftesbury, Belfast. Removed June 2012. Source: Wikimedia Commons: en.wikipedia.org/wiki/Sandy_Row

(2005, p. 50) argue, "The murals are instruments in an ideological struggle for the hearts and minds within local communities." Sanctuary areas within Northern Ireland are not ideationally uniform, especially in the aftermath of the Good Friday Agreement, but maintaining the legitimacy of paramilitary groups tends to require that they be able to publicly portray themselves as the sole spokespeople for 'their' area, as we shall see. Consider the case of an (in)famous mural formerly located at the entrance to Belfast's PUL Sandy Row Estate (Figure 6.5). Although the mural was located at a peace line and proclaimed itself as demarcating a border, a closer look at the textual inscription reveals its more proximate function.

This is not Sandy Row, or unionist Sandy Row, or Protestant Sandy Row: it is loyalist Sandy Row, and the 'heartland of South Belfast Ulster Freedom Fighters', that is, the UDA. Through this mural the UDA seeks to define the interior of the community, not merely the exterior borders; it defines who lives there, what they believe, and who has the right to speak for them publicly.

Garnet Busby, a former UDA prisoner, claims that the Sandy Row mural was "held with fond memories for the community here and a lot of the community has mixed feelings about it going" (Rutheford, 2012).

There may be some reason to doubt the accuracy of that statement. The UDA has never elected a political representative to Stormont or to the Belfast City Council, despite numerous attempts to enter into mainstream politics. The

UVF has achieved a very small degree of success in electoral politics through the Progressive Unionist Party (PUP), but this may have been due to the political talent and personal charisma of its former leader David Ervine, who died in 2007. As of the date of writing, the party holds three seats on the 60-person Belfast City Council, but this is its only elected political representation. So the point must be made: if loyalist areas such as Sandy Row were indeed as uniform in their support of violent loyalism and the UDA as murals like the one in Figure 6.5 proclaim, then it stands to reason that the UDA should have been able to translate that into at least one political representative somewhere. As one blogger opines: "Once in the safety of a polling booth, Protestant people in South Belfast repeatedly rejected the political representatives of loyalist terrorism."[6]

There is a crucial difference between loyalist groups such as the UDA and the UVF and the mainstream republican party Sinn Féin. Sinn Féin of course has achieved unprecedented electoral success, becoming the largest CNR party in Northern Ireland and a significant force in the Southern Republic. This is in spite of the fact that its president Gerry Adams, who I cited to this effect in Chapter 3, has declared that the existential threat to CNR communities justifying the state of exception is over. Mitchell, Evans, and O'Leary (2009) argue that the unique circumstances of the Agreement facilitated Sinn Féin's rise; Sinn Féin essentially became the only option for a robust electoral expression of CNR identity politics and their transformation towards pragmatism on a variety of social and economic issues rendered them not only palatable to non-violent nationalism, but also a preferred electoral option. The fact that loyalist paramilitaries have not achieved comparable electoral success could also be due to the fact that the DUP occupies the political space of identity politics, sectarianism, and *threat replication*, which are necessary for such parties to form.

But Sinn Féin is engaged in its own intra-community legitimation battle, and it is fighting a battle on multiple fronts (Bean, 2007). From within its own ideological roots, Sinn Féin is challenged by dissident republicanism, which I define here as an ideology that feels the original state of exception *is still wholly intact*. But dissident republicanism is not necessarily a cohesive ideology as it is commonly portrayed in the media and as it exists in the public imagination (Bean, 2012). Some republican dissidents retain recourse to violent action, but others who self-identify as a dissident republican use the moniker to proclaim their opposition to Sinn Féin's monopoly of republican ideological space and do not support violence. Here, 'Colin' uses the moniker dissidentism to reject what he views as a Sinn Féin-orchestrated effort to wind down the Bloody Sunday March in the city of Derry/Londonderry in the aftermath of the Bloody Sunday Inquiry chaired by Lord Saville:

> I'm a dissident and I'm a proud dissident! I dissent from those who would take away my right to march! ... The dissident republicans, all of a sudden

6 Yourfriendinthenorth.blogspot.co.uk/2012/06/illusion-of-progress.html. Retrieved 9 December 2016.

> this scare of dissident republicans, I welcome any dissident republican on that march. And I welcome them on the platform where, if he wants to say something, the people can answer him ... Now there could be dissident republicans [participating in the march], I don't know them, I ain't in paramilitaries. I wasn't in the IRA, I was never in the IRA. Martin McGuinness was on that march manys the time and there wasn't a hew and cry about them!
>
> ('Colin', Derry)

'Colin' squarely rejects Sinn Féin's right to employ the bodies of those killed in Bloody Sunday to advance their own social and political narrative, as would have been Sinn Féin's relatively exclusive ability in the past (Conway, 2010; Dawson, 2007). He rather skilfully turns Sinn Féin's traditional violent memory-space back against them, outlining an intra-community legitimation battle over Derry's most resonant symbol, the bodies of those killed on Bloody Sunday.

The final function of belligerent public imagery I identify in Northern Ireland is what political geographers refer to as 'borderwork' (Rumford, 2008, 2013). Central to borderwork studies is the insight that borders are not just administrative creations and exercises of state power. They are also desired, created, and performed by ordinary citizens (and some non-citizens!).

> Borderwork is very much the business of citizens, of ordinary people. Citizens are involved in constructing and contesting borders throughout Europe: creating borders which facilitate mobility for some while creating barriers to mobility for others ... contesting the legitimacy and undermining the borders imposed by others.
>
> (Rumford, 2008, p. 3)

Borders define who and what lies within and who and what lies outside a bounded community. This community is usually territorial, but it can also be ideational or discursive, and it is always *performative*. Borders in the form of lines on a map may not change, but other borders change, contract, and pulse, and they may alter understandings of even staid lines on maps and the communities that surround them. In this sense, borders might be best visualised as what Hedetoft (2003, p. 152) calls, in a lovely image, "asymmetric membranes". Borders are performed into existence by the meanings and symbols citizens attach to then. For example, a highly visible part of the peace process in Northern Ireland has been the (administrative) elimination of the border between Northern Ireland and the Republic of Ireland. During the Troubles, the border was heavily militarised and all people attempting to cross into Northern Ireland were subject to stop and search at gunpoint. Now, however, the border in that sense has completely disappeared (though the 2016 Brexit vote threatens to return the border to prominence). At the time of writing, the border is not even marked on minor roads.

One of the paradoxes of the peace process is that while the border between Northern Ireland and the Republic of Ireland has been erased, the Agreement strengthened and calcified the constructed borders between the two communities in Northern Ireland (Borooah & Knox, 2015; Healy, 2006; Shirlow & Murtagh, 2006; Murtagh, 2002). As Rumford (2008) argues, borderwork is often the 'spatial politics of fear', the psychosocial attempt to create enclosed spaces of security, comfort, and familiarity. Populations that perceive themselves to be vulnerable to threats from outside their territorial zone of control will focus on creating or strengthening a border, a line of demarcation. Thus, where the state of exception remains resonant, we are likely to see entrenched and resonant borderlines and border zones.

A border is a made place, and like any other made place it requires regular maintenance. The performance of bordered micro-segregation in Northern Ireland requires regular revisiting. If the symbolic resonance of the border fades from inter-subjective cognition, the border fades into the background, not unlike the Northern Irish/Irish border pre-Brexit. But on the other hand, a growing sense of being close to a resonant borderline is often read as tenuous, dangerous, threatening. Protestants in close proximity to either side of the ROI/Northern Ireland border have historically felt a sense of dread and threat emanating from the borderline (Patterson, 2008). The same could be true for a member of any community near an interface in Belfast (Shirlow & Murtagh, 2006; Heatley, 2004). Fluctuations in asymmetric membranes, whether physical or ideational, have profound consequences for the people located in close spatial proximity to them. Thus, what I suggest here goes somewhat against the grain. Even if violent inscription is not citizens' preferred form of boundary maintenance, it may be acknowledged and tacitly accepted because the masked gunman or the body of the 'volunteer' constructs a zone of relative safety. They do so by separating the community from the other, the other which is potentially transgressive and potentially harmful. Shirlow and Murtagh (2006, p. 57) argue:

> For many residents of segregated places the borders between unionist/loyalist and republican/nationalist are not merely boundaries between communities but important instruments in the definition of discursively marked space.

For these authors, borders create distance. In the territorial sense of the word, they increase the time and effort needed to traverse space,[7] but in the ideational sense they "reduce contact with a lifestyle and cultural designation that is culturally,

7 For example, the Falls Road and the Shankill Road are located in close geographical proximity to one another in West Belfast, but I know of few locals who would cross that border. To travel by foot from a CNR sanctuary area such as the Falls Road to another CNR sanctuary area such as Ardoyne in North Belfast would be approximately 3–4 km via the fastest route, simply travelling north along an artery such as Woodvale Road, passing through the Shankill. But this route would simply not be considered by people living in the Falls Road. The trip would probably require a lengthy and circuitous route back to the City Centre before heading North in order to avoid PUL sanctuaries such as the Shankill. This would at least double the total length of the journey.

politically, and socially improper" (Shirlow & Murtagh, 2006, p. 57). As long as that impropriety remains, violent and violence-justifying public imagery will probably also remain, in spite of efforts by public and private actors to remove it.

In short, we can view the functions of violent inscriptions as reflecting and reproducing territorial and ideational distance in the form of borderwork and as semiotic tools used to maintain and replicate the state of exception. But these bordered places and spaces are also places of memory; they contain a sporadic, fractious, splintered record of the Troubles and the lives lost therein. The challenge for those who would resist violent inscription in Northern Ireland is who will be remembered in these spaces and how. Will the bodies of the dead, the spectral hauntings of place, be remembered primarily as complex human beings or as dehumanised political objects?

Resisting violent inscription

In Northern Ireland, resistance to violent inscription takes a number of forms. On one level, there are statutory bodies that partner with community organisations to alter visible inscriptions of violence and sectarianism. At a much more diffuse level, there are the myriad ways in which people seek acknowledgement, witnessing, and a semblance of justice for their loved ones who were lost by striving to create places of memory that can pass trial by space and thus alter the larger social imaginary.

But one important way in which violent inscription is resisted is through satire. A number of social media gadflies have sprung up in Northern Ireland in recent years that ridicule violent paramilitary imagery and narrative, often at real risk to themselves. The largest and most well known of these gadflies is Loyalists Against Democracy (LAD). These social media actors are deeply under-studied in the academic literature, especially as their satire fills a large gap in Northern Ireland's political landscape: the space of youthful, public, political non-sectarianism that has been afforded little to no formal political outlet (Spencer, 2013). In Figures 6.6 and 6.7, the LADs, as they are often known, skewer the aesthetic standardisation of paramilitary memory I discussed earlier. At the time of this writing (January 2017), LAD had 82,000 followers on Facebook and 23,000 on Twitter. In January 2014 LAD had 22,000 total followers on both platforms (Murphy, 2014) – a five-fold increase over 3 years, which suggests a rapid increase in public visibility.

But moving away from the social media sphere, a number of public organisations have provided funding and support for communities seeking to 're-image' their landscapes, remove visible signs of sectarianism, and promote inter-community tolerance and co-existence. Some of these organisations are the Northern Ireland Arts Council, the Northern Ireland Department of Social Development, the Northern Ireland Community Relations Council, the Northern Ireland Housing Executive, and the Republic of Ireland's Department of Foreign Affairs. I use the term 're-imaging' because perhaps the largest statutory programme aimed at

Figure 6.6 'LAD Opened the Fridge Door Too Quickly Last Night'. LAD, posted to Facebook 18 October 2013.

Figure 6.7 'Secrets of Shit Murals Revealed'. LAD, posted to Facebook 13 October 2013.

transforming violent memory-space in Northern Ireland was called 'Re-Imaging Communities', spearheaded by the Northern Ireland Arts Council.[8] The programme ended in 2015. Often, re-imaging means replacing violent paramilitary imagery with other public art that is supposedly more welcoming. One paramilitary mural subjected to re-imaging was the infamous 'You are Now Entering Loyalist Sandy Row' memorial (Figure 6.5) discussed previously. In 2012 the mural was replaced by an image of King William III. Altering the murals is an attempt to alter the imposed discourse rooted in the state of exception. It may also be read by communities themselves as undermining their secure border-places. Therefore, it is helpful to examine the re-imaging process to judge whether or not removing a prominent sign or marker constitutes the first step towards ameliorating a violent memory-space.

While the UDA claims to have spearheaded the Sandy Row mural's transformation, the reality is, as someone closely involved in the process told me, that a number of community actors, including small businesspeople and local residents, approached the statutory bodies listed above, who in turn reached out to representatives of community groups associated with the UDA ('Sally', Belfast). Removing paramilitary murals provokes varying degrees of resistance from within loyalist groups; generally, they are the ones who resist re-imaging, again, because it challenges their ability to maintain and replicate the state of exception. 'Sophie's' experience below is telling. She describes the difficulties her group encountered from the local UVF when they undertook re-imaging in a loyalist-defined community in County Derry and why she suspects the UVF may finally have given its consent to remove some of the violent imagery adorning her community:

> Well ... our-vice-chair ... she just happened to be friendly with the top [local UVF] man's wife, and she was the one who started the ball rolling and then we asked her to make tentative inquiries. And the next thing, myself and our vice-chair were called to his house. And he said, "What're youse on about? Tell me what you're on about?" And I think if it hadn't have been for her being friends with his wife we probably wouldn't have even got our foot in the door. And it didn't just stop there, there was people come up to visit us from Castlederg, Ballymena, Belfast, went right up the chain. It wasn't just local [UVF] people. And it took us two years.
>
> But see that was the difference from four years ago [when the initial conversations happened], the peace process had set in, the government had just been set up in Stormont in, what, 2008? And this was now 2009. So I suppose the whole thing had gone on where they were giving in their arms at that time and they wanted to show they were [*sic*] working for peaceful things.
>
> ('Sophie', County Derry)

8 See http://artscouncil-ni.org/the-arts/visual-arts1/re-imaging-communities. Retrieved 5 February 2017.

'Sophie's' experience suggests just how entwined paramilitary public displays and their ability to project legitimation and power are. Consider something that is fairly well known in Northern Ireland but can be somewhat shocking to those not from the province. Republicans and loyalists generally do not ask community members if they like the mural or the artwork displayed, or if they will volunteer their property to display it; they simply put it up, often on the walls of houses of people who are not asked for permission and then have no ability to alter it. 'Sophie' again here describes her experience, this time in relation to a particular UVF memorial in her community, one in which the names of UVF dead are inscribed:

> That's the [memorial] up there, but they've [the UVF] gone and repainted it now to take away the gunman. That wee thing's still there but they've redone it with all the poppies now. They got the money and did that all themselves, we had nothing to do with that at all. But that's on the side of somebody's bungalow. And they have a day every year where they come out … they do like this wee service and they lay a poppy wreath. They actually expect the person in this house to plug in the speaker for their loudspeaker. It's just people are afraid to say no.

Another illuminating case of re-imaging in Northern Ireland is the case of a memorial garden on Candahar Street in South Belfast, near the disputed Lower Ormeau Road interface area. Formerly a majority Protestant area, the Lower Ormeau Road has become majority Catholic in recent years with a significant number of foreign immigrants also settling the area.[9] Demographic shifts in disputed Belfast facilitate and entrench many in the PUL community's narrative of a state of siege and resurrect memories of being 'put out' of their homes by the other community during the Troubles. This can lead to retrenchment.

Candahar Street is located in the Annadale Flats area of Lower Ormeau and interfaces with the Catholic and external migrant-majority Haywood area. Like many interface areas in Belfast, there is a local cross-community organisation known as the Annadale–Haywood Residents Association (AHRA) that presumably would attempt to deal with interface issues or issues of relevance to both communities. It was this group that applied for funding from the Northern Irish Housing Executive (NIHE) to support a re-imaging programme and received £11,000 to erect a community memorial garden. The garden is not openly sectarian and is dedicated to the fallen of the First and Second World Wars; however, the poppy crosses, red hand of Ulster, and the decorative red, white, and blue, are clearly understood semiotic markers that connote bounded PUL memory-space,

9 The 2011 census lists the ethnoreligious composition of the two wards in question, Rosetta and Ballynafeigh, as 59 per cent and 57 per cent Catholic, and 31 per cent and 27 per cent Protestant, respectively. Census available at www.ninis2.nisra.gov.uk.

not unlike the imagery of King William of Orange at Sandy Row. Memory-spaces such as this are not 'shared' spaces, they are not neutral, and they represent to no small extent the limits of compromise with loyalist groups regarding public imagery. Figures such as King William, the use of the red poppy, the badge of the 36th Ulster Division, and even other figures such as the footballer George Best, are all means used to replace the masked gunman, but they are still sectarian in the sense that they all still connote an exclusivist display of PUL territorial ownership.

This leaves these sites of memory open to symbolic accretion, which I briefly discussed earlier, or the appending of commemorative elements to already existing sites of memory (Dwyer, 2004; Foote, 2003). Generally, symbolic accretion is intended to alter the symbolic narrative or appropriate the legitimised space of a prior site of memory to attach it to another strand of memory. Symbolic accretion is performed with the objects pilgrims leave at the Vietnam Veteran's Memorial (Haas, 1998; Wagner-Pacifici & Schwartz, 1991), at London's Cenotaph (Edkins, 2003), and other sites of memory of the First and Second World Wars (Winter, 1995). One extremely valuable study of symbolic accretion is Owen Dwyer's analysis of the figure of the Confederate General Nathan Bedford Forrest in the American South. Dwyer argues that accreting Forrest onto Confederate sites of memory challenges and attempts to alter the dominant southern patrician narrative symbolised by Robert E. Lee. But the uses of Forrest's body do not merely promote a 'working-class' narrative; rather, they are part and parcel with the rise of southern revisionist history (Dwyer, 2004). Also, in Northern Ireland, because the British state does not recognise the Troubles as a 'war', as I discussed in the previous chapter, security force personnel are denied a place in the highly resonant sites of British war memory across Northern Ireland. Therefore, the memory of those security force personnel who lost their lives are sometimes accreted onto existing war memorials maintained by the Royal British Legion as an implicit challenge to their exclusion (Switzer & Graham, 2009).

On 31 July 2014 loyalists paraded through the Lower Ormeau Road, ending up at the Annadale memorial garden. The parade was dubbed the Joe Bratty/Raymond Elder twentieth anniversary memorial parade and one of the bands participating, Lisburn's Pride of Ballymacash Flute Band, took to Twitter to write: "We are out tomorrow night in Belfast for the Joe Bratty/Raymond Elder memorial parade, pay respects to our fallen heroes!" (cited in Hughes, 2014). However, Bratty and Elder were notorious sectarian killers. Bratty was the leader of the South Belfast UDA until he was shot dead by the IRA in 1994. Raymond Elder was identified by eyewitnesses as one of the two gunmen in the Sean Graham's Bookmaker's massacre of 1992 that killed five Catholics and injured another seven. Elder was shot dead along with Bratty in 1994 on the Lower Ormeau Road by the IRA. The parade culminated at the memorial in Candahar Street with a UDA show of force. UDA and UFF flags were tacked onto the memorial garden and the paraders unveiled a banner displaying Bratty and Elder's faces on the wall of the garden (Hughes, 2014). Thus, the UDA reclaimed the site as a sectarian sanctuary and incensed the CNR community of the larger Lower Ormeau Road area, and they used a publicly funded and supposedly non-sectarian garden to do so.

Although the UDA imagery was rapidly taken down (at least on the garden – my visit to the area in 2015 revealed a number of other prominent UDA/UFF displays), it is difficult to escape the conclusion that in spite of the UDA and larger loyalism 'commitment' to the peace process, they are still in the business of expropriating public space for the promotion of their particular, violent, social memory and their performative reproductions of the state of exception. Though the larger 're-imaging' programme in Northern Ireland has had some qualified success stories (Independent Research Solutions, 2009), including 'Sophie's' County Derry/Londonderry community, both PUL and CNR communities in Northern Ireland (and apparently, the Northern Irish executive) are severely constrained in the types of narrative, ideational, and territorial challenges they can make to public displays of sectarianism. Loyalism and republicanism still exert the spatial power to drown out public challenges to how Troubles memory is represented, and this tends to drive challenges underground or shoulder them out of public space (Graham & Whelan, 2007).

But part of moving away from a sited approach towards a place-based approach is avoiding the temptation to accept that this is indeed 'loyalist Sandy Row', to accept that the scale, ferocity, and volume of certain forms of inscription are hegemonic. They are not, and appreciating the complexity of Northern Irish and other transitional memory-space requires scholars to listen to, seek out, and analyse those resistant voices, voices that are often confined to other modes of inscription, that are too terrified to paint over a mural. Even the highly ritualised, violent paramilitary inscription can provide some space for rehumanisation to creep back in, and with it, challenge the state of exception.

Chapter 7

It should never be lost

> It should never be lost that a 28-year-old man was murdered with his whole life ahead of him with children … and the impact that had on a small family … is extremely significant. And we need to come up with a way of commemorating the past that captures that human story, but isn't hamstrung by it … People should never be lost in the middle of it … to just become a statistic …
>
> … A 28-year-old man, at the end you get a paragraph or two in *Lost Lives*.
>
> (Niall Enright, interview with author)

Remembering loved ones

When I first began interviewing memory curators in Northern Ireland, I expected that those who 'had lost someone belonging to them' violently or those within the victims' communities who claimed to speak for them would employ a dominant narrative that tied a loved one's body in some way to a politicised utterance such as 'justice', 'innocence', or 'martyrdom'. As I have shown, these utterances and the narratives that surround them tend to be zero-sum, and as so many scholars have illustrated, so much of Troubles memory is zero-sum: valorising one body or one group is widely perceived as denigrating another (Brewer & Hayes, 2013; McEvoy & McConnachie, 2013; McDowell, 2008; Graham & Whelan, 2007). To test this presupposition, I asked every memory curator I spoke to that had 'lost someone belonging to them', "How would you prefer that your loved one is remembered?" The responses I collected proved that my initial supposition was somewhat misguided. Even those respondents who I believe can be implicated in the production of zero-sum public attitudes to victimhood, or those who view their loved one's bodies as inseparable from a larger political cause, or those for whom victimhood is a pronounced social identity, seem to demand that their loved ones be remembered as humans and in their humanity. As I discovered, when one is no longer speaking of a politicised object but a human body, the discourse is heartbreaking. Here, 'Colin' remembers his loved one killed on Bloody Sunday:

> We were sitting in [*sic*] bar in Derry … I didn't go out and drink much but that night we go out and we have one pint … and [my loved one] was sitting with a couple friends. The Salvation Army came into the [*sic*] bar selling the War Cry. And most people wouldn't have bought the War Cry, and at the time my judgements weren't that informed or formed … because I said, "You've hardly any [money] left, why'd you buy that thing?"
>
> "Let me tell you something, see when I was in London", he says, "The first two weeks I was in the hospital of the Salvation Army. You don't know the good work them people do. Every time you get a chance, you take that opportunity to support them …" And that's how I want [my loved one] remembered. Just a decent lump of a fella, who was a good [relative], a fairly good son, a man that met people as they are and accepted them.
>
> ('Colin', Derry)

Below, two respondents from County Tyrone return to defining facets of their loved ones' characters, small examples that tell larger human stories, and vividly illustrate a person still very much alive in their memory:

> How would I like to see him remembered? God, I don't know. Just as an ordinary fella … who was a really, really talented mechanic. [My relative] used to tell us when he was a kid, he'd sit on the edge of the vacuum cleaner while [my relative] pulled it around because he loved the burning of the engine, the burning noise. And he was just wile into cars, he was at the top of his game at cars, he only had to hear a noise and he could tell what the fault was … I don't need the world to remember. I'll always remember him.
>
> ('Erin', County Tyrone)

> Me mates at work used to call her the quiet woman … That's all she was interested in, knitting, sitting. She used to sit reading a book, Catherine Cookson or Agatha Christie books, and her knitting, like this [demonstrates] … I was into the sporting end, she hated football, but she had her knitting and that's what she was happy doing …
>
> The family has missed out. I have missed out … Seeing her face, especially the football [weeps]. She was a Fermanagh woman and me [relative] who flew the whole way from Australia for an all-Ireland final with Tyrone in it, missed seeing her face when Tyrone won its first all-Ireland final.[1] Missed

1 Even those not particularly interested in the two major Gaelic games (football and hurling) in Northern Ireland tend to feel a strong identification with their counties in the all-Ireland tournaments. I, for example, whilst not even quite understanding the rules and not being Irish, developed a strangely passionate and doomed attachment for perennial

> seeing her [*sic*] face that day ... There's always a missing link from that day, and nobody can replace that.
>
> ('Luke', County Tyrone)

Another common characteristic of the rehumanising anecdotes I recorded was comedy and humour. We have seen how 'Luke' intersperses laughter with tears above; Terry Enright's (who will be the subject of this upcoming section) family and friends did something similar in my interviews with them:

> And the thing is, Terry was a boxer and he was a hard man, but he done Irish dancing too, wasn't just the case of him doing all those hard things, he was involved in a lot of things. And he was a hard man but one time he was taking us up to Black Mountain and he jumped behind us and we said, "What's the matter?" and he said, "Oh, there's a cow." He was scared of a cow. Terry would knock that cow out. It was one of them things, *he was a human being, he wasn't a machine, he was most definitely a human being.*
>
> ('Conor', North Belfast, emphasis added)

> Me and Feargal, we could sit here and still have a laugh about our Terry. About the things he done, the mad things he done ... And I think that's the finest compliment anyone could give you when you're deceased is if you can make them laugh ... When people talk about our Terry in the [GAA] club, everybody has a funny story, everybody has a good memory.
>
> (Peter Hughes, West Belfast)

But these poignant, illustrative narratives sit side by side with a range of other body performances. To shift the context of the discourse even slightly will bring forth a far more politicised body performance. The dead are variegated, malleable containers and appreciating the unsettling complexity of a lost life requires witnesses to allow the space for a host of different constitutive performances, as my conversations with 'Colin', 'Benjamin', and 'Erin' all seem to demonstrate:

> And if we can prove 42 years on that [the British paratroopers] were involved in *murders*... because you don't murder a dog, you kill a dog, [my loved one] still is just 'killed', he was not, he was murdered, you follow me? So you deny [my loved one] his full humanity, 42 years later, if we can't have prosecutions for those that murdered him because *he ... was ... murdered.*
>
> ('Colin', Derry, original emphasis)

under-achievers County Galway during all-Ireland tournaments, as it was a place I grew up visiting. 'Luke' here is referring to a friendly in-family rivalry between his county, Tyrone, and his loved one's county, Fermanagh.

> You cannot forget that [my loved one] and the people in Enniskillen were murdered. They didn't die naturally, they didn't die in a road traffic accident, they were brutally, brutally murdered. And I think as the years go on people tend to forget about atrocities … you have to continue the memory of all the people that were murdered through terrorism.
>
> ('Benjamin', County Fermanagh)[2]

Below, I ask 'Erin' whether convicting the person(s) who killed her loved one in a court of law would provide a semblance of justice, or did she also require that person or persons to be punished. The question and her response depends on readers' understanding that, under the terms of the Agreement, conviction for Troubles-related offenses carries a minimal sentence:

> I remember my [relative] saying, [our loved one's] dead, so I want to kill a member of [the perpetrator's] family. I want a member of their family to die and let them suffer. Because killing them's not going to work. Because they're free from pain. Somebody that they really love. Of course it's all about punishment. If there's no deterrence we're just sowing the seed of more young people coming up through the ranks.
>
> ('Erin', County Tyrone)

Here we observe a different employment of bodies, markedly different in tone and more in tune with the politicised body narrative that the curators are seeking recognition for and acknowledgement of. Discursively linking the loved one's body to memory, and discursively linking the loved one's body to questions of 'justice' or 'accountability', provoke different performances, the latter practiced and politicised, the former impromptu and humanistic. Which performance is triggered tends to be directly related to the questions one asks. Questions of justice and accountability trigger responses that are politicised, and often practiced, which should not be surprising as I am certain many of my respondents have been asked those types of questions extensively by others besides myself. However, when we ask about the *person* the loved one was, how the person is remembered, respondents are often surprised and, at least initially, at a loss for words. They do not expect the question. Sometimes, the person's memory is recalled and narrated as 'standing for something', (i.e. a politicised object), but more often I found that the respondent, after some reflection, settled on

2 I wished to include 'Benjamin's' poignant illustration of his loved one as well in the section above, but because his testimony was so detailed and so personal and revealing, I could not find a way to extract it without compromising confidentiality. But in response to my question "How would you like to see your loved one remembered?", 'Benjamin' replied he wishes to see his love one remembered as a 'gentleman' who inspired respect in every one of his colleagues and as a warm, loving man who loved 'Benjamin' immensely.

illustrative and humanising anecdotes, anecdotes that flesh out the human, her life, and what they feel should never have been lost. The larger point here is that the type of dead-body performances that can be curated cannot be reduced to a single performance, a single narrative. Every bereaved survivor has a multiplicity of stories; every person who was lost is more than a single narrative or inscription. Individuals and social groups employ dead bodies to advance a social or political narrative, but even within a single individual, there is a dissonance between the essence of the ghost they wish to hold and remember and the political object they wish to deploy.

But what happens when the imperative to remember a loved one as a brother or sister, a father or mother, a wife, a husband, a friend, a lover, a child, a mentor, a companion, comes into direct contact with what we believe is *also* a political body, a body that can stand for something important, even profound? How can we keep alive the intricacies and contradictions of a deeply loved and deeply missed person while still positioning their killing within the context of a produced and practised political narrative? Can we?

Remembering Terry Enright

Terry Enright was shot dead at the age of 28 by gunmen from the short-lived loyalist death squad the LVF as he worked the door outside a nightclub in Talbot Street, Central Belfast. The official reason given for Terry's slaying was retaliation for the assassination of LVF leader Billy Wright in the Long Kesh/Maze Prison by the INLA under suspicious circumstances.[3] Terry left behind a young wife, two small children, three brothers, his parents Terry Senior and Mary Enright, and a wider Belfast community poleaxed with grief and confusion. At the time of Terry's killing, 11 January 1998, the Agreement was in sight, the promise of peace slowly creeping towards possibility in many people's minds, and Terry's killing must have seemed an indescribably brutal betrayal of those glimmers of hope.

Terry was born in 1969 and hailed from the Turf Lodge area of Upper Springfield, West Belfast, where he was an extremely popular youth worker, community worker, and amateur sportsman. The Enright family had quite a pedigree, not just within their own community, but across Belfast as well, McKittrick et al. (2008, p. 1423) describing Terry Senior as "one of the most respected community workers in Belfast". Terry Senior and Mary were involved in community and social activism throughout young Terry's whole life. The Enright family are a republican family but one who generally eschewed and eschews recourse to

3 Many in Northern Ireland believe that the British security services allowed Wright's killing in the Maze because Wright was about to reveal the extent of his collusive connections to the security services. Representatives of the INLA stridently denied that the British state either colluded in or looked the other way before, during, and after the assassination (Larkin, 2004).

violence in the service of republican political aspirations. Most of the respondents I spoke to referred to Terry Senior and Mary as 'mavericks': two people who possessed deeply help republican ideals but saw the republican struggle as encompassing more strands than merely the armed struggle and thus necessitating alternative foci and methods. Terry Senior (up until his passing) and Mary were involved in a number of causes long before they were 'fashionable', including environmental activism, specifically around Black Mountain conservation projects, the trade union movement, the women's movement, and beginning as early as the mid-1980s, Terry Senior especially seems to have developed cross-community contacts in the Shankill with men such as Billy Hutchinson, something relatively unheard of at that time, especially for a self-described republican activist. Terry Senior continued to leverage those contacts throughout the peace process, seeking to convince working-class loyalists that the equality provisions of the Agreement applied to them as well, were in their interest, and should not be deemed a threat.

Terry Enright was greatly influenced by his parents' example and began working with deprived youths fairly early in his life, mainly through probation referrals and various community projects. Terry did not finish school; I chose not to press my respondents on why that was specifically, but Terry's experience was not dissimilar to a large swathe of socially deprived youth in Belfast at the time.[4] However, Terry's lack of formal education did not seem to hamstring his own development as a youth worker; rather, it seems his own experience provided a highly empathic lens with which to view other youths struggling with issues of family disintegration, drug and alcohol dependency, violence, exclusion, and anti-social behaviour in the midst of the intense communal ruptures of the Troubles. We should also not be sanguine about the scope and scale of the risks to and pressures on such disaffected, excluded youths at that time. Paramilitary groups, as I discussed earlier, were the established force-wielders within the communities they purported to speak for. Young people engaging in drugs or anti-social behaviour were ruthlessly 'policed'; punishment beatings and punishment shootings were widespread (Lindsay, 2012; Monaghan, 2004; Knox, 2002; McEvoy & Mika, 2001). Within this context, Terry Enright presented disaffected youths with the possibility of another route for their life; Terry presented as someone who had lived their experience and come out the other end. One of the youths Terry worked with, who subsequently became a youth worker in his own community, describes Terry's example and the effect it had on his life:

> At the time, there were a lot of punishment attacks and a friend of mine who was actually on the course with Terry, he'd actually been shot twice at that stage, he's been shot once since … I suppose it was like an oasis once you're away with Terry, you were able to forget about any of the troubles

4 I do not possess the training nor the expertise to review the literature on Northern Irish education, educational disaffection, and social deprivation. I direct interested readers to Sutherland & Purdy (2006).

> you had back home, back in the street. And he was a good role model ... he was exactly the same as us. It wasn't just somebody coming in and telling us you're doing wrong here, you're doing wrong here, he just spoke to you like a human being and he gave you advice and he didn't tell you what to do. And we appreciated that as well ... He just treated you like, well, he pushed you, but he pushed you in a good way, in an encouraging way, in a challenging way. And I can tell you that through until Terry's death, we had a few years from '96 to '97 and then Terry was shot dead in '98, the amount of young people that he came into contact with then, seen him in the same way as I seen him, it is that positive role model that I have carried on into my own work with young people. And hopefully, I've had an impact on young people that I've been working with.
>
> ('Conor', North Belfast)

Other factors besides Terry's background contributed to his success as a youth worker. For one, Terry was what is generally referred to in Northern Ireland as a 'hard man'. For some from outside Northern Ireland, 'hard man' is coterminous with a paramilitary figure or gunman, and while the term certainly can describe the paramilitary figure, in Northern Ireland it is more generally used to refer to somebody whose body contains the potential for violence; someone who will not back down from a fight or 'knows how to handle himself'. Doormen at bars and nightclubs, for example, where Terry worked to gain a bit of extra money, would have been (and still mostly are) drawn from the ranks of such 'hard men'. It is important to note here that while Terry was a 'hard man', he was not involved in paramilitary activity, and the term needs to be understood in its more general sense. It also must be understood that to the youth population Terry worked with, a 'hard man' was to no small extent an aspirational figure. Terry's body, his skill at boxing, football, Gaelic games, and other outdoor pursuits would have resonated as a particular form of aspirational masculinity. But equally important, Terry's 'hard man' status was not the sum total of his appeal. Terry's younger brother Niall here describes the constellation of factors that he believes made Terry such an effective youth worker:

> I think there's just a lot of those things, particularly around young men, what young men relate to within those areas, these young, fit, macho guys, you know what I mean, that you can look up to, that you can aspire to ... So again, people liked that. He was big and strong and he was muscular and all those things. So there's a notion I suppose within particularly working-class male communities that that would be something to aspire to. And then obviously, young girls or young women would be going, there's an attractive big fella, he'll do us, that type of thing. So there are those personality and physical-type attributes that certainly helped him. But I suppose the other thing would have been genuine sincerity in terms of I understand what you're going through. Terry was a young person who left school with nothing and for all intents and purposes should have been unemployed despite the fact

> that he had loads of talents and could relate to young people lying in bed at twelve o'clock in the day with no hope. Could relate to young people standing on street corners drinking. Could relate to young people getting involved in paramilitary activity, for want of a better word. So he could relate to all those pressures that young people were under and could genuinely say, hand on heart, that I know what you're going through. Because I've been there.
>
> (Niall Enright, West Belfast)

But to truly understand Terry and the Enright family, as well as understanding the framing of Terry's life and death, one must also understand their own particular ethos of communitarian republicanism. For Terry Senior and Mary, the heads of the family, much of their work was rooted in their deeply held belief that their community, whether that be the CNR community of Northern Ireland, West Belfast, or the Upper Springfield area in particular, was unjustly deprived of their human, economic, and cultural rights as part of a conscious, programmatic campaign of repression by an occupational force backed up by local auxiliaries. This, perhaps, may be a relatively standardised republican understanding of Northern Ireland (see Chapter 3), but the Enright family's understanding varies, or perhaps deepens, in two very important ways. First, consider the ways in which Terry's brothers, Niall and Feargal, frame the conflict. We will hear from Feargal first:

> What actually happened is that there was a systematic policy of state collusion that involved people being killed who were combatants and people being killed who were non-combatants all the way back to the 1920s. Because the reality was you couldn't defeat someone who was fighting against you in an armed sense if you didn't terrorise the community that they lived in so the actual killing of civilians wasn't something that was mindless, it was something that was planned and coordinated. And it was logical. Doesn't mean right, it was totally wrong, it was brutal, it was evil, but it was logical and its why people were killed who were civilians.
>
> (Feargal Mac Ionnrachtaigh, West Belfast)

> The notion that as a people, as a community, we're mobile, we're moving forward and we're developing, so that notion, [*sic*] almost that the development of our community is where the justice will come … British state policy in Ireland is complex. You have the coercion, you have the consent, you have the manufacturing of the consent, you have the arm that kills you, that hits you over the head, that puts you in jail, you have the bit that funds you and that's all part of a holistic strategy. So ultimately [*sic*], the rising of the moon will be when justice comes. It's never-ending. It's that notion of progressing and moving towards it.
>
> (Niall Enright, West Belfast)

As we see from both brothers' testimony, in their perspective the British state policy in Ireland depended on keeping their community 'down', in the sense of trapping it in cycles of deprivation and dependence. Thus, and again for both brothers and undoubtedly for the Enright family as a whole, the best means to resist British state power lies in the development, regeneration, and betterment of their community, and not in armed violence. This narrow communitarianism risks myopia; it risks a too-inward focus that fails to view community empowerment pathways and obstacles outside of a larger context. But it seems that the Enright family, led by Terry Senior and Mary, actively counteracted that potential myopia by seeking out cross-community contacts and cross-community projects, and viewing the struggles faced by working-class communities in Northern Ireland as largely the same, regardless of ethnoreligious affiliation. For Terry Senior and Mary, it seems to have been not only an anti-colonial struggle, but an egalitarian struggle as well. Terry, later, would incorporate that ethos in his own youth work, regarding deprived loyalist youth as facing similar if not identical social pressures and barriers. This philosophy, learned no doubt from his parents, coupled with an almost brazen self-confidence rooted in the masculinised body, pushed Terry Senior and later young Terry across the divides and into the Shankill. Niall describes it thus:

> There's obviously major issues that divide the working class between Catholics and Protestants, people living in disadvantaged communities. But there's also a fair degree of commonality. A commonality around sincerity, and genuineness, and empathy ... The other thing was his confidence; he wasn't afraid so he would have been bold and brazen about going over to the Shankill ... I suppose the other thing, we would have all been brought up like that, you're brought up with a notion that you're not better than anybody and nobody's better than you.
>
> (Niall Enright, West Belfast)

To sum up, there are two aspects of the Enright family's particular republicanism that will be of great relevance when we turn towards examining the politics of inscribing Terry's body and Terry's memory. First and most importantly, the communitarian ethos discovers the best means of resistance to British rule in community empowerment, development, and regeneration and not in violence; and second, it views the deleterious effects of British rule as transcending well-established divisions, both ethnoreligious and territorial.

Immediately after his killing, Terry's body was subject to contestation over its ownership, over the rights to inscribe the meaning of his killing in a particular way. The first challenge seems to have come from the media, though the family suggests that the media may have been tipped some information about Terry that was not widely known in an effort to frame his death as that of a 'combatant', namely that Terry's wife is Gerry Adams' niece:

> So to us that was very obvious that was the justification. A person was murdered, then the state throws out a story, there's the justification. Gerry Adams' nephew was murdered ... [but] people wouldn't have made the link

> between them … so it was out of left field that one, when it went into the media right away, that Gerry Adams' nephew being murdered because it wouldn't have been common knowledge. It would have been something the families would have knew but in terms of the wider community, it wouldn't have been something you could have picked off the local taxi man, for example.
>
> (Niall Enright, West Belfast)

This attempted framing of his death engendered an immediate backlash with Terry's family, close friends, and larger community as they rapidly moved to reassert control over his body:

> The morning after Terry was killed … a reporter come over from the Irish press … and she says to me, "Did you know the deceased?" And I says, "I did, yeah." And I wasn't in good form to talk to a journalist or anything like that but the first thing she said to me was he was married to Gerry Adams' niece. I says, "What has that got to do with anything?! What has that got to do with this young fella that lost his life?!" And she started to get into a bit of nonsense talk, I said, "See before you start here now, are you here for the duration? Are you going to be here until this young man is laid to rest?!" … And I spoke to her at Terry's graveside when he was buried and I said to her, "And now do you understand the point I was trying to make to you? … Do you see the point I was trying to make to you?! Look round this graveyard, there's thousands of people, people from the unionist community, there's loyalist paramilitaries here, and you just wanted to make a point about Terry being married to Gerry Adams' niece?! Now how small do you feel?!"… And she apologised … But because of the reason I was there, it made me think, "I'm going to show this girl here. I'll show her when this lad gets buried, the amount of outpouring of grief in this community, the biggest civilian funeral West Belfast had ever seen!"
>
> (Peter Hughes, West Belfast)

The way the family describes it, the community backlash prevented the local and foreign press from adopting a tired and offensive framing, as did the spontaneous outpouring of grief from all sides of the community divide. The community rose up and refused to allow the media, perhaps led by misinformation from the British state, to dehumanise Terry's body, to reduce him to bare life:

> The whole outpouring of grief and the whole unveiling of who this guy actually was, nobody could have remembered that he was married to Gerry Adams' niece by the time it came to the other end of the funeral, such was the PR that came out of it … There were stories coming out about this and about that and about fifty things, and it hit the media across the world, it was in America, it was everywhere, and all of a sudden, that depersonalisation was

gone and this person as an individual in his own right was unveiled to the world in death, in terrible tragedy.

(Feargal Mac Ionnrachtaigh, West Belfast)

My search of relevant press articles from the time of Terry's killing suggests that the community was largely successful in their reclamation efforts (Clarity (1998) and Wynne-Jones (1998) are good examples of this).

In the first section of this chapter I described a dissonance between the loved one as a human whom those left behind wish to remember and the loved one as a politicised object that they often feel compelled to employ. In the case of people like 'Erin' and 'Luke', this dissonance can be especially acute because their loved one was not a politicised person in life and has become a highly politicised object in death. This dissonance is slightly less in Terry's body, because Terry was a thoroughly political person in life from a thoroughly political family, so employing his body as a tool in a constitutive, politicised narrative does not clash as much with the life he lived. But there is still dissonance, dissonance lying in the space between the complex human and simplified political narrative, and that dissonance can have a profound human toll.

The story the family wishes to tell, at least in part, is the story of Terry's death galvanising a deprived community to demand what they deserved, in the sense of no longer being socially, economically, and culturally excluded, and to stand for peace, largely through a Yes vote for the Agreement, but beyond that as well. The story is also of Terry as a transformative model, especially for deprived youth, a symbol of the possibility of a better life for young people. It is a story firmly in line with their vision of positive, communitarian republicanism. It is a story of relentless positivity, of putting aside or sacrificing, or even burying, one's own private grief in the service of political ideals. Niall, in a moment of deeply moving human candour, traces the origins of the story:

> There was a trajectory that this community had been on. There had been a realisation in the mid-80s that the conflict wasn't working, that the military conflict wasn't working. That the endless funerals wasn't working. So there was a trajectory that we needed to move away from violence and the notion I suppose that violence was violating everybody, it was brutalising us all ... But ... my dad was very political. He understood the politics of the day. *So the politics of the day was how can we transform Terry's murder into political capital for other social transformation? ... There was that notion of here's Terry's death and there's political capital to be gained. And my dad would have been* cold *enough to be able to go, "Right. We need to use this".*
>
> (Niall Enright, West Belfast, emphasis added)

In my interview with Feargal and Peter, perhaps feeding off one another, between the two of them they used some variation of either the adjective 'positive' or the nominalisation 'positivity' 25 separate times. They used it to describe Terry's character in life, the symbolism they believe is encapsulated in his memory performance, his (and their) hopes for their community, and to describe what they hoped his death, while indescribably tragic, still would represent. I never had the privilege of knowing Terry Enright the man in life, but I have no doubt that positivity and optimism in the face of adversity or disadvantage was an essential, integral part of his character and ethos. So the repetitive usage of the term is (emphatically!) not indicative of inauthenticity, but it is indicative of a narrative that has become practised, ritualised even, a presentation that has been communicated enough times to enough audiences that it has acquired to some degree a standardised lexicon:

> This French fella came … and he says, "Could you tell them the reason why [Terry's death] happened?" I says, "No really, I can't. I can tell you the positives that come out of it, but I couldn't tell you the reason why it was done …" I could tell people the positivity that came out of it.
>
> (Peter Hughes, West Belfast)

> Now I think one of the things Peter was talking about, my mother and father, their ideal was always that the revenge, if there's any, should be the laughter of our children. So the idea was that you'd keep somebody's memory alive in a positive sense … The fact that he's dead, can't be brought back, I mean that goes without saying. But the type of work that Peter's talking about, the type of work he was involved in, the type of unfolding positivity that had come out of his death, that's a revenge.
>
> (Feargal Mac Ionnrachtaigh, West Belfast)

They also use a variation on the term 'community' 114 times in a two-hour interview. Now I wish to stress that this type of content analysis (or just plain counting) is a blunt and not very illuminating analytic technique. 'Community' is a word I personally hear repeatedly in Northern Ireland (and a word I have employed repeatedly in this book), especially because so much of my research is done with and incorporating the perspectives of 'community workers'. It is also a fairly neutral and non-confrontational term to describe collectivities in Northern Ireland, collectivities that often object to other characterisations. But again, the repeated utterance bespeaks a practised discourse and a determined communitarian framing of Terry's life, death, and memory. Here Feargal describes the memorials to Terry Enright at the Gort na Mona GAA club. I reproduced one of the memorials in Chapter 1 (Figure 1.3); the other is reproduced in Figure 7.1. The murals were spearheaded and designed by local young people, something that the family and the GAA club takes a great deal of pride in:

> Kids were asking, "Well, who's this guy?" You see, they didn't know him, this happened in bygone years. "What did he do? And tell us a bit about him." So the idea was about creating kind of heroes within the club that

Figure 7.1 Terry Enright Memorial Mural, Gort na Mona GAA club, West Belfast. © Martin Melaugh and © CAIN. Used with permission. The top line reads: "Enright Park". The bottom line is difficult to translate exactly but essentially reads: "Praise the youth and they will prosper".

> young people could look up to as role models, people who were recognised within the community …
>
> The idea was that everyone was a success in their own way, not everybody can be an all-star hurler or Gaelic footballer but everybody has their own talents … that could make a contribution in some small way to the community here and that's why the mural project took place, the young people had found in a way, one of their own heroes. It wasn't somebody they see on TV, it wasn't a celebrity, it wasn't somebody who was a Premiership footballer, it was somebody just like them, who went to the same school as them, who played for the same GAA club as them, but somebody who made a special contribution that was recognised across Belfast. Why not have it recognised in our GAA club, why not have young people coming through and saying, "That's the type of guy I want to be?" *That's somebody positive, that's somebody who embodied what this community's all about.*
>
> (Feargal Enright, West Belfast, emphasis added)

After Terry's death, two major tributes to his memory were organised. The first was the naming of the Gort na Mona GAA pitch Enright Park. The second was the setting up of the Terry Enright Foundation, a foundation designed to work with deprived youths across working-class neighbourhoods of Belfast. The

Foundation sought, to the best of its ability, to carry on Terry's work and Terry's legacy around youth leadership, team-building, and cross-community understanding through the practices of adventure learning and outdoor pursuits:

> It was set up to continue the legacy of Terry, of the type of work that Terry was involved in … youth work, community work, centred in North and West Belfast. And then it widened out to Belfast-wide. The Terry Enright Foundation has always been about supporting potential, about supporting people coming through their communities.
>
> ('Conor', North Belfast)

The Foundation has now lasted for over 13 years but the Enright family and their friends and colleagues in the Terry Enright Foundation have taken the decision to wind it down. The reasons why illustrate in a deeply resonant way the uneasy, dissonant spaces between the public politics of inscription and the private spaces of grief and mourning:

> The family and the committee have made a decision that we're going to be wrapping up in 18 months. And I fully support it. And saying that, in 18 month's time, I'll be out of a job but I think it's what's needed. The Terry Enright Foundation has moved on from 2002, it'll be 14 years once we do wrap up. And I think it's a very positive legacy, throughout that time, all the young people we've worked with … they are the Foundation's legacy, they are Terry Enright's legacy …
>
> … You can end up warping your own [pause] … why you set up … You get veered off one direction to get a wee bit of funding, veered off in another direction, and by the time you finish up, ***you're just trying to keep an organisation afloat rather than an ideal.***
>
> ('Conor', North Belfast, emphasis added)

The difficulty that inevitably comes with the fusing of a human life, a human body, and an ethos or an ideal is that the body itself, and the name of that body, become subsumed into the material objects in which the narrative ideal is represented. It is a form of ***transubstantiation***, but this is a human body, not a divine body, nor a divinity in human form, like the body of Jesus Christ. The things, the objects that contain the circumscribed frames of community activism, youth empowerment, strength throughout adversity to which Terry's life is perhaps not reduced, but certainly simplified to (because all lives are too complex, too variegated, to ever be holistically represented in their entirety) become Terry's memory. And the material vestiges of Terry's memory, because they are human things and human creations, their human failings, or human difficulties, or human inconsistencies, assimilate into the memory, representation, and body of the loved one who has passed on. But this assimilation places a profound, almost indescribable psychological and social burden on its memory curators.

Every manifestation of the object becomes a manifestation of Terry and his memory: they bear his name, they bear his image, they bear the name of his father and mother, his brothers, his wife, and his children. And while they may take comfort in the knowledge of the positive, transformative narrative Terry's public representation certainly bespeaks, part of that necessarily circumscribed and politicised objectification always intrudes into the space of private grief. Terry's body can never be wholly buried, his ghost can never fully rest, as long as he is an object of public representation. But the dissonance is in so profoundly believing in the *perceived social or transformative value of the public representation* while at the same time knowing, somewhere, at the back of one's mind, that representation is colonising one's own private space of grief.

At this point in the story, I want to fade a bit into the background. It is time for Niall Enright to describe in his own words what I have interpreted, and while I have certainly selected which testimony to use, I feel it is important to yield the text to him:

> I was involved with the Terry Enright Foundation not from the first meeting, maybe the fourth or fifth meeting. And it played a lead role in a number of different community stuff, a lot of awards were named after Terry, in this area we run a youth achievement award, the main prize is the Terry Enright Award for young people who have overcome adversity and all those types of things. I suppose at a certain point, Joe, that takes its toll. And actually, it would've been taking its toll on my parents. That notion of the outward, resilient, strong, using good politics, at a certain point in time that takes its toll on you. And even conversations like these. Right in the aftermath, my ma and da would have been doing these regularly, maybe in the immediate aftermath, doing one a week. But then after, because you'd built up a bit of a reputation, then people were coming back to you at different times, so if somebody's killed, come back and talk to the family, decommissioning's going to happen, come back and talk to the family, IRA ceasefire, come back and talk to the family, Good Friday Agreement implemented, come back and talk to the family. And my da because of the politics was always willing to do it, "Let's get the message over the line", and blah, blah, blah. But after a while that takes its toll because the reality is that being strong and resilient and using Terry's death, there was also the personal end of that that suffers. And I suppose looking back at me da's own health, it suffered really, really badly because of that, that outward face of being strong and resilient and saying the right things and doing interviews and not saying a word out of place and being politically correct and then having to go back and I would have seen what he done, days after days of just withdrawing into himself, you'd have just seen the toll ....
>
> ... So with the Terry Enright Foundation, it's been the same, it's just taken its toll. It takes on a life of its own. You employ people. You do some good work, you do some bad work. You've staff issues. You've people you

can't get jobs. You have good workers, you have bad workers. You have project's you're proud of, you have projects you're not so proud of. *And in all this, your brother's name, and your name, is around it …*

… How do you do all this? All this, and you're sitting down and your brother's name is knocking about. So it came to a point where we were going, "I don't know if this is worth it …" All those different things that are going on and I suppose the notion came maybe four, five years ago, which was, "Look. Let's not just exist for existence's sake" *From a personal point of view, and this might sound strange, I want to bury Terry. I want to bury Terry. There's a notion that you haven't been able to …*[weeps]

… The notion is that we'll use the next three years to try and capture the learning in terms of what worked, what we did, what didn't work, and if there's other pieces of the work we can hand over to other people, we'll do that. *But they can't be depending on the Enright family no more. Me ma can't be coming along to give flowers every time there's an award*, we can't be there at every meeting, we can't be driving the thing …

… Because what happens is setting up the organisation becomes a harness for your grief and your motivation and your energy, but at some level, it's stopping you. At some level it's holding you back. Because you harness all this energy but ultimately, there's a thing you have to deal with. There's a big pain in the middle of you that you need to deal with. So it's very easy to go down the road of avoiding the trauma that you have to visit …

… I suppose from my perspective as a representative of the family, I was feeling that I had to get this right, not just from my perspective, but from Terry's kids' perspectives. It was getting this right for my ma and da, but also for Terry's kids and making decisions and going, "Am I making the right decision? And can I bring them with me?" …

… And again, every time you go to a meeting, probably you're having a normal meeting around HR and discipline and project reports, but it's an organisation set up in your brother's name, [*sic*], so it's here, he's here, all the time, [*sic*], Terry, he's never far from the table. So when you're talking about a programme succeeding or not, that's there, it's right there, right in front of your head, does this encapsulate what Terry's about? Does it not?

… I'm still a member of Gort na Mona. I'm still Gort na Mona's best ever player [laughs] … So again the pitch being named after Terry, that's a brilliant thing, that's a lovely thing, at the same time, and this is the other notion, our involvement in Gort na Mona, from the minute Terry was killed, and from the moment the pitch was named after him, it becomes more than just … it becomes more than that … The success or otherwise of Gort na Mona becomes something really, really important. And whether it's doing well or not doing well, it becomes at some level, not healthy I suppose … This was another living of legacy, but really it's a hobby. Gort na Mona is a social outlet. So at some point you have to go, is this a project? Isn't this supposed to be a fun thing? You bring your kids, you play Gaelic games, you have fun, you do all that. Ultimately, it's been a good thing, but there is that danger, there's always that danger.

(Niall Enright, West Belfast, emphasis added)

As I listen to Terry's family and friends and externalise and interpret the communitarian and empowering narratives that they present Terry's life and body as standing for, one message, one narrative of Terry's killing resonates above all else: *that it never should have happened.* I think that is the truest essence of what Feargal, Peter, 'Conor', and Niall, are saying. I am overwhelmed by the utter futility, utter stupidity of killing. I think about the 12 other people murdered within a month of Terry, many of them by the LVF as well. I think back to Walter Benjamin's (1992) storyteller and think that no matter how many muscles you have, how tough you are, we are but tiny, fragile human bodies unable to escape the spasmodic frenzy of hatred and violence. I think of my own culpability in asking the Enright family to curate the memory once more. I wonder how can Terry's death have been transformed into something so positive, so profound, but at the same time contain nothing positive or profound or meaningful or interesting at all? They just shot him and there was no purpose to that act, no meaning, no significance, except cruelty, futility, and pain. And I think this is what Niall means when he says, "It should never be lost". As much as Terry Enright's memory has been affixed into public inscription, subsumed into a political representation, affixed in places of memory that stand beyond or at least beside linear temporality, retained in the youths he influenced, the most heart-wrenching accusation of his killers and the state of exception still remains in the ghost-presence of Terry smiling, his daughter on his shoulders, or cleaning his hurling boots:

> He loved the hurling, and he was very fussy about his hurley [stick]. You'd have laughed at him, outside, cleaning it ... putting his colours and tapes all on it. And his boots! Very fussy about his boots. Had to have them all cleaned and polished and the other ones weren't a bit like that, they just threw their boots in the corner, but no, no, he went out and cleaned all his boots, put that Vaseline-stuff on them ....
>
> And I see him with [his daughter] on his shoulders, I have visions of that with him and with the kids, he loved playing with the kids and all ...
>
> And he bought our Feargal one of them things you box with ... you know the wee things on a stand ...
>
> And he was showing him how to do it. And even his youngest now, she only a year and ten months when he was murdered, he says, "Wait 'til you see her head-butting me [imitates her grand-daughter, laughs]". So you have all these visions of him that are very, very nice I have to say.
>
> (Mary Enright)[5]

5 Excerpted from an interview by Jude Collins with Mary Enright. Available at www.youtube.com/watch?v=idwt5YbZsN0.

Terry's places of memory, I argue, exhibit another, equally compelling aspect of dissonant memory and dissonant empathy. Terry's body and memory *are* politicised, they are objectified, but the control over the politics of inscription have largely remained with the family; it has not been taken from them, they have not been disowned, their rights to control and ownership over the body-presentation have been challenged, but those challenges have been largely defeated. Through the Terry Enright Foundation, through the massive outpouring of well-publicised, cross-communal grief, especially at his funeral, through the Gort na Mona GAA club murals, and through a host of other material and discursive avenues, Terry Enright's memory, in its preferred and controlled form, has passed trial by space. Yet the strain I perceive and interpret in talking to his family and his friends is real and is in addition to the trauma of his death, not because of it. The strain is in the curating of the memory itself, of constantly having to maintain the memory of a deeply loved human being as beyond human, as a political, communitarian, and transformative ideal. When Niall speaks of wanting to bury his brother, of how he has a sense he hasn't been able to, this is what he is referring to.

The materialised, public ideal of Terry may fade with the passage of time, with the changing of social and political contexts and backdrops. A young person who comes through Gort na Mona in ten years' time may find a slightly different inscription of Terry's body and memory awaiting them than a young person who comes through today. A troubled youth who works with 'Conor' may have a different experience than a youth who worked with Terry. But I believe what Niall and 'Conor' are saying is that it is important not to fight this inevitability, in a sense, not to seek to force a loved one's body and the message one purports to impart to it to never change or fade away. Because as long as we are able to hold onto the loved one's humanity, in the form of anecdotes, laughter, 'visions', smiles, faces, hands, we still retain the most powerful political statement of all: ***that they should never have been killed, their loved ones should never have had to suffer this agony, and nobody else should have to die or suffer like they did again.***

The danger is when the politicised object colonises the body entirely, and for whatever reason or whatever variety of reasons – political, social, or personal – forces the ghost to repeat, over and over again, the same ritualised narrative until the narrative takes over the body completely.

Chapter 8

We are all, potentially, *homines sacri*

The argument

In this book I have argued that the conflict in Northern Ireland was enabled and sustained by belligerent groups proclaiming the state of exception in response to a constructed existential threat. Like all social constructions, the threat was a complex interplay of pre-existing narratives and contemporaneous events that at different contextual junctures and in response to different events rendered the threat construction more or less resonant to a host community. I argue that belligerent groups and their supporters, tacit or active, to varying degrees internalised the performative reality of the state of exception and as such were able to legitimise the dehumanisation of bodies that could be cognitively conflated with the ongoing threat. To maintain and justify the state of exception, belligerents appropriated material and discursive space and inscribed within it places of violence-production.

But I also argue that even during the Troubles, the state of exception was never monolithic, never absolute. It had limits; and these limits were the product of a complex dialectic between violence-wielders and the communities and nascent political arrangements they purported to wish to produce or protect. Since the signing of the Agreement almost (at the time of this writing) 19 years ago, Northern Ireland has been essentially free of the type of widespread violence and killing that characterised the Troubles. The major paramilitary groups, and the majority of their former members, have declared the violent conflict over. In this context, the state of exception no longer possesses the degree of control it once had and, gradually, Northern Irish memory-space is splintering as individuals and social groups jockey to challenge or maintain the legitimacy of past killings, the rights of memory, and the framing of the past.

I have focused throughout this book on the narratives surrounding the political uses of dead bodies. I have suggested that dehumanising narratives and dehumanising political productions of dead bodies are implicated in and continue to be implicated in the ongoing replication of the brutal, tautological logic of the state of exception. They continue to trap Northern Ireland in this frame of reference; all arguments about the past, history, and memory are forced to engage with the logic of existential threat. Conversely, I have argued that rehumanising narratives, even those that may not be consciously political, seek to reinscribe the bodies, the human bodies, of the dead into Northern Irish memory-space and the material landscape, and in doing so, they challenge the state of exception itself. Rehumanisation argues that a body and the life it possessed are and were more than a political symbol, more than collateral damage, more than the product of their organisational status, their 'guilt' or 'innocence', their religion, their communal orientation, more than some palliative object to be wept over and jammed into a forced social catharsis, and most importantly, *more than the narrow symbolic production that suborns a complex human life to a politicised social narrative.*

Throughout this book I hope I have built a compelling case that memory in transitional societies is fundamentally dissonant in nature. Closely following the work of Primo Levi, I noted the necessity of maintaining a moral line between victim and perpetrator and the consequences, both individual and social, of erasing that line and sliding towards anarchic moral relativism (Levi, 1989). But I also noted how Levi brilliantly argues that the 'Grey Zone', that zone of terror, trauma, and abuse, to some extent implicates all those caught within it, and how it confounds and confuses our human attempts to judge and blame. I suggest that Levi forces his audience to hold two seemingly conflicting ideas at the same time and recognise, even embrace, the dissonance and confusion they produce in us. I suggest this dissonance, this confusion is an essential part of engaging with traumatic pasts, recognising the pain of others, and seeking somehow to bear witness to what has happened. Levi's challenge in turn is channelled by LaCapra's *empathic unsettlement*: how do we create the necessary space between victim and witness? How do we avoid subsuming ourselves or being subsumed into, the traumatised body? LaCapra (1998, 2001) argues that this space is necessary and must be maintained. It is necessary to facilitate an ongoing transactive, humanistic relationship and dialogue rooted in critical discussions about the nature of the act, the aesthetics of the object, and the memory of the offence. But these are obligations, perhaps, of the witness or the audience; the artist or the survivor may have similar, but mirror image obligations. These may be the obligation to resist the sometimes understandable desire to foreclose memory and to foreclose interpretation; to demand that witnesses and audiences only leave the experience with a right, proper, particular type of memory, a particular narrative perspective.

Thus we are left with a number of difficult and perhaps unanswerable questions. Is dissonant memory a social *Good* in transitional societies? Is it connected in some way to rehumanisation? Can societies prescribe or facilitate aesthetic forms and places of memory that might promote dissonant memory or would such programmatic top-down behaviour be imposing, even undemocratic? I confess I have no easy answers to these questions. But perhaps to provide a frame for exploring them further, I will examine two places of memory in Washington DC, USA: The United States Holocaust Memorial Museum (USHMM), opened in 1993, and the Vietnam Veterans Memorial (VVM), opened in 1982. The purpose of this brief discussion is to elucidate the ways in which the production of 'national' or large-scale places of traumatic memory can in fact *prevent* the type of dissonance and empathic unsettlement I have argued is crucial to facilitate an ongoing, critical reflection about the memory of the offence. However, in doing so I gloss over the holistic picture of these two places of memory – their unique histories, contexts, and positioning within the US scene. For those readers interested in a fuller picture of these two places of memory, I direct them to other sources which may challenge my readings and interpretations (for the USHMM, see Berenbaum & Kramer, 2006; Linenthal, 1995; Weinberg & Elieli, 1995; for the VVW see Haas, 1998; Ashabranner, 1989; Scruggs & Swerdlow, 1985).

Two places of memory in the United States

Peter Novick's (1999) acerbic look at Holocaust memory in the United States argues that the USHMM should be interpreted as part of an unfolding effort to present a particular political narrative of the Holocaust to a largely non-Jewish American audience. Novick notes how the Holocaust did not become such an integral facet of US memory and popular consciousness until the 1970s; in fact, he argues that during the years between the end of the Second World War and the 1970s, the Holocaust itself was generally not talked about, not discussed, and often marginalised in the larger public social memory of both American Jews and Gentiles. Even people who reject Novick's arguments (and Lopate's, discussed below) agree on this point. Rosenfeld (2002), for example, traces the burgeoning interest amongst American Jews in Holocaust remembrance to the 1967 Six Days War and its aftermath. Some explanation for this might be found in the assimilative priorities of American Jews and Jewish families in the United States; another might be found in the United States' international affairs of time, which focused on reconstructing (West) Germany to serve as a bulwark against Soviet expansionism. But remembering the Holocaust only became a ritualised 'civic duty' when powerful American Jews and Jewish organisations began to take an active interest in promoting it, often for political purposes:

> If, as many in Jewish organizations believed, Americans could be made more sympathetic to Israel, or to American Jews, through awareness of the Holocaust, efforts had to be made to spread that awareness through American society.
>
> (Novick, 1999, p. 208)

In this context, argues Novick, it is no coincidence that the original consultative group responsible for setting up the museum, the President's Commission on the Holocaust, was inaugurated under the administration of US President Jimmy Carter. Carter's political opponents in the Republican party had been increasingly seeking to make inroads into the critical political demographic of American Jews, and one strategy for doing so was to accuse the Carter administration of being too conciliatory towards the Palestinians in the larger Camp David Process. In no small regard, Novick writes, the drive of Holocaust memory curators led by Elie Wiesel dovetailed nicely with the Carter administration's fear that they could potentially alienate what had been up to then an overwhelmingly Democratic voting bloc and a consistent source of campaign funding: American Jews. And while only an irreparable cynic or an anti-Semite would suggest that Carter had no humanistic or moral reasons for creating the Commission and the larger attempt to institutionally memorialise the Holocaust, Novick marshals quite a bit of evidence to suggest that the Commission allowed Carter to burnish his pro-Jewish and pro-Israel credentials at the same time.

Jenny Edkins (2003) and James Young (1993) both argue that it is this larger political context that to no small extent dictated and shaped the aesthetic and narrative of the USHMM itself and other places of Holocaust memory in Europe. *The Holocaust had to be translated and synthesised for European and American, largely non-Jewish, consumption.* The site, therefore, was necessarily pedagogical; it had to 'instruct' Americans on how to remember the Holocaust, and the bodies of Holocaust victims had to be transformed from their socio-demographic realities. The victims of the Holocaust, a predominately poor, foreign, isolated, European Jewry, had to be transformed into a population that could representationally integrate and assimilate into the overwhelmingly Christian American and European audience. For the essayist Philip Lopate, this transformation is offensive, not just because it is inaccurate, but because it is manipulative. And not just because it is manipulative, but also because it presumes that Americans can only empathise with those bodies *that look like them*, or look like the people contained within the frame of the dominant social imagination:

> In so many books and movies of the Holocaust, I sense that I am being asked to feel a particular pathos in the rounding up of gentle, scholarly, middle-class, *civilized* people who are then packed into cattle cars, as though the liquidation of illiterate peasants would not be as poignant. The now-familiar news reel shot of Asian populations fleeing a slaughter with their meagre possessions in handcarts still reads to us a catastrophe involving 'masses', while the images of Jews lined up in their fedoras and overcoats tug at our hearts precisely because we see them as individuals.
>
> (Lopate, 2003, pp. 268–269, original emphasis)

As stated in the USHMM visitor guide, the museum has three objectives:

> The museum's primary mission is to advance and disseminate knowledge about this unprecedented tragedy, to preserve the memory of those who suffered, and to encourage its visitors to reflect upon the moral and spiritual questions raised by the events of the Holocaust as well as their own responsibilities as citizens of a democracy.
>
> (Cited in Edkins, 2003, pp. 154–155)

For Edkins (2003, p. 155), the narrative structure of the museum above all serves to "confirm American values by showing their opposite", namely the German or European values that led to the Holocaust, and their opposite being American values of freedom, democracy, and inclusion. The memorial certainly does that; but Edkins misses another crucial pedagogical imperative of the museum: the lesson it is trying to teach Americans about the perils of isolationism and bystanderism (Levy & Sznaider, 2002). The museum does not allow the visitor the freedom to choose his own path through the exhibits; rather, it forces visitors to follow a particular chronological and narrative pathway. It adopts this architectural and aesthetic choice because of its first imperative, to educate Americans about the Holocaust. But in forcing visitors into a pre-conceived, linear narrative, it forecloses any non-prescribed lessons about the Holocaust and Holocaust memory. The museum becomes a lecture and not a discussion. The memorial seemingly does not trust its viewers to come to their own conclusions. Teeger and Vinitzky-Seroussi (2007) argue that this is characteristic of sites of memory that produce a 'controlled consensus'. They argue that social memory on a macro scale in transitional societies tends to bifurcate into two types: consensus and fragmentation. The former "aims to enact and create consensus through a large degree of control in terms of both form and content" (Teeger & Vinitzky-Seroussi, 2007, p. 58), whereas the latter refers to a social memory incubated at multiple social nodes and aimed at different audiences within the same society.

The USHMM is firmly within the consensus-producing camp. This does not mean that diverse narratives and stories cannot find shelter under a consensual framework, but it does mean that narrative diversity must be subordinated to a larger controlling vision. James Young argues that one of the chief tensions in Holocaust memory is the tendency by non-Jews to want to 'universalise' the Holocaust, to present it in the form of a global struggle between 'good' and 'evil', characteristic of popular films such as *Schindler's List*, or to connect it to other mass atrocities or genocides, past and ongoing. This universalising drive conflicts with the tendency for Jews, and especially Israeli Jews, to 'particularise' the Holocaust, to see it as the unique culmination of centuries of bloody European anti-Semitism and to focus on Jewish suffering (Young, 1993). This tension can be seen even in one's choice of term: Holocaust (capital H) refers to Nazi Germany's programmatic elimination of suspect races and ideologies, predominately Jews of course, but also Roma, homosexuals, Slavs, the physically and intellectually disabled, those we would now term 'conscientious objectors', Jehovah's Witnesses, and even some Catholic and other Christian clergymen. The use of Holocaust in the lower case is highly controversial. I for one do not employ it, but those who do might suggest that Holocaust in the lower case would refer to any genocidal episode in history (see Finklestein, 1997). But the Hebrew term *Shoah*, in contrast, refers exclusively to the extermination of the European Jewry by Nazi Germany and its allies. The exclusivity of the term directly implies that the *Shoah* and the Jewish experience were unlike anything that ever came before or after. And again, we see this tension playing out in the USHMM's history, with memory curators led by Elie Wiesel resisting any attempt to expand the narrative scope of the USHMM to take in other genocides, such as the Armenian genocide (Novick, 1999). The USHMM, in its completed form, restricts the scope of victims to Jews and the Holocaust to the *Shoah*.

None of the preceding criticism should be taken to argue that the USHMM does not work to disrupt and confuse narratives and temporalities, but it does so only within the frame of *Shoah*. The complex 'pedagogical address' of the USHMM uses the forced disruption of linearity and temporality to approximate for Americans what the experience of forced dislocation, the shattering of families, and depersonalised mass death *must have been like* for the European Jewry (Ellsworth, 2002). But this effect depends on forcing visitors to stay on the prescribed path. Ironically, the USHMM attempts to disrupt one linearity by imposing another. There is a similar aesthetic imposed by the Memorial to the Murdered Jews of Europe (note the particularism) in Berlin, Germany. After experiencing the subterranean museum, visitors can take only one exit and are forced into a disorienting maze of black slabs for which they are given no guidance. The purpose once again is to force the visitor to experience the sense of dislocation and oppression that Jews must have felt.

Yet, as Edkins notes, "Despite the clear and somewhat disturbingly controlling intent of the exhibition designers, the story they had to tell didn't quite fit the linear narrative they wanted to impose" (Edkins, 2003, p. 157). For example, in the 'Tower of Faces' we see entrants to the camps posed for photographs. But these photographs were almost certainly taken by Jewish collaborators, by Primo Levi's *Sonderkommandos*, "just as hair was shaved, personal possessions removed and sorted, and the new arrivals abused and brutalized by their fellow victims" (Edkins, 2003, p. 160). But the casual viewer does not know this and no information is given to that effect. To do so would disrupt the memory that memorial is presenting and it would introduce empathic dissonance into a political narrative that is firmly rooted in producing particular narratives about the *Shoah* and how they should be understood by Americans. The narrative is one of uncritical Jewish victimisation and American virtue, rooted in the 'rescue' or 'liberation' of the remnants of the European Jewry, but it also a cautionary parable about what can happen if Americans succumb to the perils of non-interventionism. The United States, after all, stood on the sidelines as Hitler advanced across Europe, and still to this day, argues the narrative, many Americans fail to appreciate the existential threat that Jews continually live under. The generalisable denouement of the pedagogical narrative is a picture of Jews thriving in a powerful, militaristic state that can protect them or thriving as integral additions to American society and the American intellectual and social fabric; Jews who can reproduce that virtue so embedded in the American cultural fabric. It is a narrative that has become fairly ubiquitous in the United States. In Jersey City, New Jersey, a statue by the well-known sculptor Nathan Rapaport entitled 'Liberation' stares out of a small bay within the larger mouth of the Hudson River. The geographic placement is purposeful; it is meant to face directly across the bay at the Statue of Liberty and in its placement, it symbolically accretes itself to a larger American narrative of trauma, emigration, and rebirth.

In the statue, the American GI carries the body of an emaciated Jew, presumably rescued from a concentration camp. The healthy, robust figure of the GI and the skeletal figure of the Jew blend into one another and become inseparable, both physically and metaphorically. Liberation in the shadow of Lady Liberty; the end of the Holocaust is also the triumph of American values. But the cast-down, saddened face of the GI also implicates Americans as a whole in their failure to intervene sooner in the Second World War and their failure to acknowledge or understand the existential threat to Jews posed by anti-Semitism. Thus the triumph of American values also cautions against forgetting those values, which in this narrative is non-interventionism or bystanderism. But these narratives are not politically neutral. They can be easily implicated in the construction of a related narrative, a narrative that arguably undergirds ongoing American uncritical support for hyper-militaristic, proto-apartheid Israel. In no small sense, at both the USHMM and the 'Liberation' site, viewers are encouraged to experience both banal American patriotism and its mirror reflection, the guilt of a failure to intervene. In my reading, this is towards the dehumanising end of the spectrum because it employs the bodies of the victims of the Holocaust as tools in the construction of a political parable. This is not to suggest that the USHMM can be completely reduced to a dehumanising performance; it does present powerful human stories of Jewish suffering and the shattering effects of traumatic disruption. But the rehumanising power and potential of the site is muted by the carefully controlled consensus and by the political and pedagogical narrative that the site is intended to produce.

The Vietnam Veterans Memorial is not a 'narrative memorial' like the USHMM, but it would be facetious (and wrong) to claim that the artist, Maya Lin, and the chief political driver of the project, the veteran Jan Scruggs, did not inscribe a narrative field into the place of memory. But I argue that the chief difference between the narrative inscribed at the VVW and the USHMM is that the inscribed memory at the former does not overwhelm, shoulder out, or foreclose the specific narrative worlds, specific bodies of the dead, specific moralities, specific historiographies, or specific practices of grief and mourning that individuals bring with them to the site. The VVW is polysemic and polyphonic; the site itself (the sign) can produce multiple, interlocking fields of memory and meaning and it can do so in multiple voices. Yet at the same time the VVW also creates a controlling consensus, and I argue can be implicated in the foreclosure of empathic dissonance.

Unlike memorials to the Second World War and to a lesser degree the First World War, with the Vietnam War Americans were confronted for the first time with how to remember a war that the United States had lost, that half the populace had opposed, that was widely seen as unjust and even criminal, and that had provoked some of the most severe social ruptures since the American Civil War (Wagner-Pacifici & Schwartz, 1991). Scruggs ultimately arrived at a novel idea.

The memorial would be a veterans' memorial, not a war memorial; it would focus reverence on the bodies of soldiers and remain agnostic on the war itself (Scruggs & Swerdlow, 1985). As Scruggs stated, "In 1979, I had a dream that regardless of the controversy and divisiveness centered on Vietnam, the American people could come together to honor Vietnam vets" (Scruggs, 1981, n.p.). In line with Scruggs' vision, the aesthetic design of the memorial was put out to open competition with four requirements for an acceptable design: that the memorial be contemplative, that it harmonise with its surroundings, that it contain the names of every American soldier who died in Vietnam, and that it make no political statement about the war itself (Edkins, 2003, p. 74).

The winning entry was submitted by a young Chinese–American graduate student named Maya Lin. Lin's design intended to subvert the dominant war memorial form, to invert traditional phallocentrism, and to enable a "private awakening, a private awareness of loss". A sense of loss, and how individuals came to terms with loss, for Lin was wholly individual: "It is up to each individual to resolve or come to terms with loss. For death is in the end a personal and private matter, and the area contained within this memorial is a quiet place, meant for personal reflection and private reckoning" (cited in Savage, 2009, pp. 269–271).

The subsequent design reflected both Scruggs' and Lin's dovetailing imperatives. The Wall, instead of rising phallically into the air like cenotaphs, obelisks, plinths, and other traditional objects of war remembrance, descends into a gash in the earth. The gash is often interpreted as a metaphorical grave or a womb, perhaps both (McGirr, 2003). The two edges of the gash proceed in a 'V' until they meet at the apex, the deepest point of the gash, a feminised design that further inverts the traditional phallic memorial. Rather than evoking masculine ideals of heroism, virility, or courage, the aesthetic seems to coincide with Sara Ruddick's 'maternal thinking', emphasising quietude, peace, caring, and nurturing (Ruddick, 1989). As viewers enter the gash, the wall begins on each side at ground level but as they descend to the apex of the 'V', the wall reaches a height of 3.1 metres. The wall is constructed from reflective black material and the names of 58,272 American servicemen confirmed killed or missing in Vietnam are inscribed into the wall's 72 panels. The names are inscribed chronologically according to when the servicemen lost their lives. Perhaps the reflective surface is the most stunning feature of the design. As I can personally attest, seeing one's own face reflected back in the overwhelming, rising, disorienting cascade of names is a staggeringly effective aesthetic: a powerful personal rumination on war, death, and loss.

The immediate political reaction to Lin's winning design was vitriolic and intense, but perhaps what is most interesting is not the fact that such a reaction occurred, but how rapidly it dissipated. Pentagon official Thomas Carhart labelled the memorial "the black gash of shame and sorrow", a label which initially gained some traction in the conservative press. Other characterisations included "that degrading ditch", a "slap in the face" to veterans, and perhaps most hyperbolically, "A wailing wall for draft dodgers and New Lefters" (examples taken from Edkins, 2003 and Sturken, 1997). Critics also levelled not-so-subtle barbs at Lin herself, suggesting that Lin's race, youth, politics, and/or worldview were incommensurate with appropriate authorship. Critics even forced the inclusion of another memorial on the same site, one supposedly characteristic of traditional, 'respectful', and valorous modes of memory: Frederick Hart's sculpture 'Three Servicemen'.

Perhaps the major reason why the criticisms dissipated by the conclusion of the Reagan administration was the growing support the design received, not only from veterans' groups and the American military, but also from a panoply of diverse social and interest groups. As Haas (1998) argues, the Wall became a regular site of pilgrimage for groups and individuals from across the socio-political spectrum. Crucially, I argue here, this was only possible because of the polysemic and polyphonic design. The initial vision of Scruggs was largely realised; the memorial essentially stands aside and allows viewers the space to interact with the site on their own terms, with their own diverse memories, politics, and grief. The most visible example of the site's polysemy is the signs and artefacts brought by individual pilgrims and left at the wall. The outpouring of artefacts left at the wall surprised even Lin herself but reflect her desire to inject the site with the space for individual mourning. On one level, the gash is a mass, collective grave: the names soldered into the wall carry no individual markers; each name is listed as each before it and each after it, subsumed into a mass of bodies. It is up to the audience itself to mark their own loved ones and they have, with the dizzying and overwhelmingly diverse assortment of objects left at the wall ranging from the most common method of humanising a name – the photograph – to military dog-tags, letters, flowers, cards, medals, and other mementos that depend on a private understanding between the pilgrim, the object, and the ghost.

But for all its redolence and symbolic power, the VVW remains a product of its context, intentions, aesthetic, and its own particular form of political inscription. Its own particular polysemy is not a blueprint to be uncritically adopted by any society seeking an aesthetic form for remembering a difficult past (Kimmelman, 2002). The VVW is a product of a unique constellation of circumstances and though it has opened a space of shared grief for individuals and social groups from diverse political affiliations and backgrounds, I argue the VVW has largely failed to extend the empathic dissonance it rightly provokes beyond the context of US soldiers in US wars. Of course, this may simply be because neither Lin nor Scruggs wished it to do so, and the only way that such a unique place of memory could be produced at that time was to restrict the scope of allowable memory. But this hardly need go uncriticised.

From 1955 to 1975 over two million Vietnamese, Cambodian, and Lao violently lost their lives (this is a highly conservative estimate) (Hirschman, Preston, & Loi, 1995). It is impossible to parse those casualties or to speculate how many were a direct result of foreign intervention but the scope of the deaths suggests that what occurred in Southeast Asia during those years ranks as one of the worst episodes of sustained collective cruelty in recorded history (Appy, 2015). The bodies of those unnamed, faceless two million are absent from the VVW and absent from larger American social memory. The aesthetic of the VVW inscribes the traumatic experience of the Vietnam War as a traumatic experience that happened to Americans and American soldiers; this is a dubious and potentially offensive inscription (Sturken, 1997, pp. 82–83). The Vietnam War was a massive trauma inflicted on Southeast Asians by Americans, French, and other foreign powers, and to a much, much lesser degree on Americans and American soldiers. Yet, at one of the most symbolically resonant sites of memory in the entire United States, Americans gather to mourn and rehumanise their own dead, in the process displacing and dehumanising those who died as a consequence of American aggression. Is the VVW itself, and the grief enclosed there, implicated in the production of a new method of war, one in which the bodies of *our soldiers* function as a potent limit to political considerations, but the bodies of *their civilians* may be sacrificed with impunity? (Shaw, 2005). Has the VVW, as Sturken (1997, p. 82) argues, "catalysed a rewriting of history … primarily because its emphasis on war dead has allowed the themes of heroism, sacrifice, and honour to resurface?"

There is also the question of victimhood that has undergirded so much of this book. We have seen that the VVW promotes forgetting about American aggression and the killing of Southeast Asians, but another question must be asked: are the bodies of all American soldiers even *worthy of remembrance*? On 16 March 1968, approximately 100 American soldiers landed by helicopter near two hamlets known as Son My, later mistakenly recorded as My Lai. The two American platoons of Charlie Company proceeded to slaughter the civilian residents of the villages. They killed men and women working in rice fields, they herded women with babies into the town centre and slaughtered them with methods as diverse as bayonets to the head and indiscriminate machine-gun fire. They slaughtered people kneeling in prayer, burning incense, trying to run away (Belknap, 2002; Bilton & Sim, 1992). As one soldier later testified:

> I saw [fellow soldiers] shoot an M79 [grenade launcher] into a group of people who were still alive. But mostly it was done with a machine gun. They were shooting women and children just like anybody else. We met no resistance and I only saw three captured weapons. We had no casualties. It was just like any other Vietnamese village – old Papa-sans, women and kids. As a matter of fact, I don't remember seeing one military-age male in the entire place, dead or alive.
>
> (In Hersch, 1969, n.p.)

Only one man was ever convicted of the massacre, Lt. William Calley, who served three-and-a-half years in prison. The commanding officer, Ernest L. Medina, nicknamed 'Mad Dog' by his subordinates (the same deeply disturbing moniker adopted by Johnny Adair in Northern Ireland), was acquitted and never served a single day in prison. But let us take the admittedly extreme example of Sergeant Gary Roschevitz to make this point. Roschevitz killed at least ten separate unarmed civilians in at least three separate incidents. According to later testimony, as the massacre was winding down, Roschevitz herded a group of women together and ordered them to undress, with the intention of raping them. When they refused, he shot them (Yarborough, 2005, pp. 19–20). Let us consider that, as a hypothetical, Roschevitz would later perish in the war and become one of the 58,272 names on the wall. He did not, but it strains the boundaries of credulity to suggest that the VVW does not promote reverence for other American servicemen who committed vicious, sociopathic murders.

These objections are crucial to raise because they cut through Scruggs' and Lin's somewhat naïve belief that a memorial can transcend base politics, a prevailing understanding of the VVW widely reflected in both popular and academic literature. The VVW is a unique spatial and temporal phenomenon, its powerful and resonant design, aesthetic, and narrative rendered possible only by restricting the scope of inscribable bodies to American servicemen. In the bodies of American servicemen, conflated, depoliticised, and shorn of any authoritative performance save for the splintered and polyphonic voices of individual pilgrims, the VVW is both a product of, and helped to produce, a consensual means of remembering the Vietnam War in the United States. This consensus certainly speaks with a multitude of diverse voices, but those voices are bound by the limits of the politics of inscription imposed by the memorial itself and the limits of political discourse that undergirded the constraining design. The VVW forecloses who can be remembered and it forecloses how they can be remembered. There is no space to remember Southeast Asians and no space to adopt a position of anger, resentment, or injustice; these perspectives are rendered out of step with the imperative to produce quiet, reflective, hyper-individualised grief.

Both the USHMM and the VVW are two hugely important places of memory in the United States for remembering two episodes of mass trauma firmly burned into much of the collective American cultural psyche. But by illustrating their limitations, and the often unforeseen consequences of *any national site of memory*, or any attempt to produce a delineated social consensus over the nature of the past, I wish to suggest another, more complex reason to resist and even reject the appeal of Sir Kenneth Bloomfield with which I began this book. I wish to problematise the supposed necessity of 'shared grief' in transitional societies and the logical culmination of such 'shared grief' into a national place of memory, a national catharsis. Not only is such a catharsis unlikely any time in the near future of Northern Ireland, even positioning it as the end-point of a process of social restoration may be profoundly misguided.

A national memorial for Northern Ireland? The Long Kesh/Maze debacle

The Long Kesh/Maze Prison, located at a repurposed RAF base just outside the town of Lisburn, County Antrim, housed an estimated 25,000 republican and loyalist prisoners during its 29-year operational history (1971–2000). The Agreement signed in 1998 contains provisions for the release of all the prisoners accused of Troubles-related offences, and in September 2000 the last prisoner left the Long Kesh/Maze complex and the prison was officially closed. But questions remained about what to do with the 360-acre site, Northern Ireland's single largest redevelopable land parcel and a place rife with symbolic import.

For many republicans, the site is a primary repository of their particular conflict historiography. First, from 1971 to 1975, it housed the almost 2,000 Catholics rounded up during internment. Until 1976, internees and those convicted of Troubles-related offences were granted Special Status, a sort of unstated status as prisoners of war that afforded them special treatment and tacitly acknowledged the political aspects of their imprisonment (McEvoy, 2001). However, with the shift towards the policy of criminalisation in 1976, Special Status was revoked and republican and loyalist prisoners were treated as ordinary criminals. This led to a succession of protests by republican prisoners, culminating in the hunger strikes of 1981 when ten hunger strikers led by Bobby Sands starved themselves to death in protest over the conditions of their imprisonment. The hunger strikes and the uncompromising stance of the Thatcher government are, along with Bloody Sunday, arguably the two most central events in the modern republican historiography and the two most recognisable facets of their legitimation of the state of exception. The body of Sands especially, who was elected as an MP for the Fermanagh constituency as he lay starving to death, is for most republicans a sacred object. He is the Troubles' most visible and most recognisable martyr, and his image adorns countless gable walls across republican sanctuaries.

The Long Kesh/Maze site was transferred to the control of the Northern Irish executive in 2002, which in turn created a Maze Consultation Panel comprising representatives of the four main political parties (Sinn Féin, SDLP, UUP, DUP). In 2003 the republican ex-prisoner group Coíste na nIarchimí (hereafter, Coíste) proposed that the former prison site be preserved as a "heritage site for future generations" (Mac Gholla Minh, 2003, n.p.) Coíste argued that, at the very least, 5 per cent of the 360-acre site should be set aside for a museum devoted to the prison and its role in the Troubles. For unionists, however, Coíste's proposal was a non-starter because they tended to assume that such a museum would be a vehicle designed to promote a republican conflict narrative centred around Bobby Sands and the other hunger strikers, or for many unionists, terrorists. The Panel's draft report, issued in 2005, appeared to recognise the symbolic resonance of the site (and the potential economic windfall from conflict tourism), but proposed to replace Coíste's museum with an International Centre for Conflict Transformation (ICCT):

> It would be entirely fitting for the Long Kesh/Maze site, which was for so long a symbol of conflict, to become a symbol for the ongoing transformation from conflict to peace. We believe that the site would be an ideal location for an [ICCT] and as such has the potential to play an important role in promoting a shared society.
>
> (Cited in Graham & McDowell, 2007, p. 353)

But the Panel's report failed to alleviate the concerns of unionists and Northern Irish victims and survivors groups purporting to speak for victims and survivors of IRA violence. As Graham and McDowell argue, the term 'conflict transformation' is a term imbued with the same sort of 'constructive ambiguity' that characterised the Agreement's approach to victims and the past. Such ambiguity, coupled with the 'memory agnosticism' of both the British and Irish states, continues to provide the space for paramilitary groups to maintain and inscribe their particularistic conflict narratives rooted in the state of exception (Switzer & Graham, 2009; Graham & Whelan, 2007). And no group in Northern Ireland is better equipped than Sinn Féin to do exactly that. Sinn Féin remains the actor in Northern Ireland with the most well-developed, cohesive, and resourced historiographical programme (Murray & Tonge, 2005).

Coíste seems to have anticipated the backlash against their initial proposals and sought to couch them in the language of constructive ambiguity. They rhetorically ask themselves how they would respond to critics who fear they are interested in creating a 'shrine' to republicanism at the Long Kesh/Maze site:

> The key question here is whether this 'fear' is actually that people don't want the republican story told. We are not interested in a shrine – republicans are, in any case, political and not religious. If the question is a genuine one, it probably arises out of misapprehensions and misunderstandings, which are themselves the result of conflict, division, and decades of not talking to one another ... But an inclusive approach must emphasise that everyone has a right to tell their story. The dialogue and interaction of the various stories and how they are told will be an important conceptual 'exhibit' of the museum.
>
> (Mac Gholla Minh, 2003, n.p.)

On the surface, it seems that Coíste is proposing a curated space that all of Northern Ireland's various conflict narratives can share. And while there is no reason to disbelieve Coíste's intentions, Graham and McDowell (2007, p. 357) cite two Sinn Féin officials whose testimony seems to suggest another vision for the site:

> Long Kesh is on a standing with Robben Island, Auschwitz, and the Berlin Wall and we cannot afford to lose that history. It is one of the most famous and infamous buildings of the conflict. Everybody in Ireland knows of it as do many people around the world.
>
> [Long Kesh should be] recognized globally alongside Robben Island and Auschwitz. The site ... should now be recognized as a World Heritage Site, and we in Sinn Fein believe that such a submission should now be made.
>
> (Both cited in Graham & McDowell, 2007, p. 357)

I cannot but agree with Graham and McDowell that these sentiments represent a "myopic self-delusion" (2007, p. 357) on the part of Sinn Féin; but more to the point, sentiments such as these reveal the degree to which Sinn Féin is utterly ensconced within its own zero-sum production of Troubles memory and its particularistic narratives of victimhood. These two representatives implicitly claim that republican ex-prisoners belong on a similar moral plane to the murdered of Auschwitz and anti-apartheid activists imprisoned at Robben Island. And while perhaps some stretched comparisons can be made to the latter – after all the ANC and other anti-apartheid organisations did commit acts of terror, violence, and murder – to place Pat Magee or Gerry Kelly even rhetorically on the same moral plane as the victims of Auschwitz speaks volumes about the insularity and self-reinforcing capacity of Sinn Féin's politics of inscription.

To have a national memorial to violence, a shared place of traumatic memory, it seems that the minimum requirement must be at the very least a shared notion of just who gets to count as a victim. The USHMM and the VVW both confronted that problem in the United States. For the former, are acceptable victims of the Holocaust the 6 million plus Jews or the 11 million plus total victims of systematic Nazi persecution?[1] For Elie Wiesel, the *Shoah* is a Jewish, and only a Jewish genocide, and Wiesel and his supporters strenuously resisted (even to the point of threatening to leave Carter's Commission) the proposed inclusion of non-Jewish victims, such as victims of the Armenian genocide (Novick, 1999). This is not to say that Wiesel does not view the USHMM as part of a broader pedagogical tool to prevent other genocides, other atrocities, as evidenced by his remarks to then-US President Bill Clinton during the dedication of the USHMM (USHMM, 1993). But as I argued in the previous section, this is the narrative duality of American heroism/indifference (bystanderism) at work as embedded into the USHMM's fabric, and is not indicative of a predilection for inclusion within the USHMM's place of memory.

The USHMM and other sites of Holocaust memory in the United States were able to compromise, mainly by garlanding the exterior of sites with Wiesenthal's more inclusive 11 million figure, but devoting the internal area solely to the memory of Jewish victims. For example, at the New England Holocaust Memorial in Boston, MA, the initial inscription greets visitors with the 11 million figure, but the memorial itself is six glass obelisks shaped like smokestacks, each representing one million Jews. This is a hierarchy of victims; it elevates the Jewish victims over non-Jewish victims, and then again elevates Nazi victims over other victims whose innocence is not discursively taken for granted, for example the million plus civilian victims of the Allied bombing campaigns on German and Japanese cities, especially the firebombings of Hamburg, Dresden, and Tokyo and the nuclear obliteration of Hiroshima and Nagasaki.

1 Novick (1999) points out that the 11 million figure is an invention of Simon Wiesenthal and has no empirical basis.

The VVW is an even more interesting case. American soldiers became consensually acceptable objects of remembrance because, en masse, they could function as victims in a variety of different political narratives. In the traditional, hagiographical sense of war memorials common to right-wing, militaristic narratives in the United States, their bodies could stand for heroic patriotism and thus be worthy of deep reverence. But for left-wing, anti-militarist narratives of the sort that opposed the Vietnam War, they could also be framed as acceptable victims *of their own government*. Since the Vietnam War, a variety of well-known works of art have all portrayed the traumatic, dehumanising experience of American servicemen in Vietnam. From films such as *Platoon*, *Full Metal Jacket*, *Hamburger Hill*, *Born on the Fourth of July*, *Coming Home*, and *Apocalypse Now* to powerful, best-selling works of literature like Tim O'Brien's *The Things they Carried*, American soldiers in Vietnam are largely presented as victims of circumstance and politics that they lack any capacity to change. And the polyphonic capacity of Lin's sombre abstraction allows both narratives to share the same place of memory, but it restricts the appropriate subjects of memory to those whose appropriate victimhood has been discursively and politically established: American soldiers.

Consider, for example, another Academy Award-winning Vietnam War film, Michael Cimino's *The Deer Hunter*. Pauline Kael writes, "The Vietcong are treated in the standard inscrutable-evil Oriental style of the Japanese in the Second World War movies ... The impression a viewer gets is that if we did some bad things there, we did them ruthlessly but impersonally; the Vietcong were cruel and sadistic." Peter Arnett argues, "The central metaphor of the film is simply a bloody lie." War correspondent John Pilger argues as well that "Hollywood sensed a lot of money could be made with a movie that appealed directly to those racial insults that cause wars and allowed the Vietnam War to endure for so long" (all cited in Biskind, 2008, n.p.). The popularity and critical acclaim of *The Deer Hunter* seems very much bound up in the type of political inscription I am speaking of, one that reframes American servicemen as victims and the Vietnamese as the cruel oppressors.

In a republican conflict narrative, an IRA member locked up at Long Kesh is a victim of the British state's colonial oppression. But for many unionists and some nationalists, the IRA and loyalist paramilitaries were terrorist organisations; membership in such organisations was a crime, and because they committed crimes, members of such organisations were justifiably imprisoned. And while there are many conciliatory voices in Northern Ireland from both unionist and nationalist frames who might be prepared to acknowledge the deprived and/or socially unjust political and social circumstances that bred an impetus to join paramilitary organisations, to equate an IRA or a UVF man with the victims of Enniskillen or McGuirk's Bar is a bridge too far. 'Michael', a moderate unionist, perhaps articulates this best:

> I think in many ways and quite rightly, the Maze issue was very problematic for our constituency. I remember the debates being had around it at the time, about the need for a peace centre in Northern Ireland. And I remember

> going to one consultation session that was held with victims groups … and around that table were folks from a republican perspective, and each of their comments was very stark, it was "It must be the Maze. It must be the Maze." *It wasn't the fact of having a peace centre, it was the fact of having it tied ideologically to that site* ….
>
> … So I know a lot of people, looking externally, from outside, they'll feel it was a missed opportunity, that the site was unique in itself. But I don't know, especially within younger generations, somebody arrives to the Maze, they're not caring about Constable so-and-so. They want to hear about Bobby Sands … because there's a romanticism, there's a notoriety to that, whereas for a civilian or a member of the security forces who loses their life, in many ways they're just a statistic.
>
> ('Michael', County Fermanagh, emphasis added)

What 'Michael' is describing here is a discursive space where the politics of inscription are contested and ongoing. Consensus over who gets to count as a victim has not been achieved, nor has there been any larger consensus about the appropriate possibilities for inscribing these bodies. Contrary to many prevailing attitudes, I want to suggest that this is not necessarily a bad thing. I want to suggest that a fragmentary victimology and the splintering of memory that accompany it *prevent* the type of consensual, foreclosing narrative that we see in the case of the USHMM and the VVW. The fragmentation of memory-space in Northern Ireland has facilitated an ongoing, difficult conversation about the legacy of the Troubles and the causes and consequences of Troubles violence. This is not to say this conversation is always productive. There is a common Northern Irish acrid colloquialism for the state of political debate in Northern Ireland: 'Whataboutery'. Whataboutery refers to any claim for victimisation or collective trauma put forth by one community or individual being immediately being 'one-upped' by another, supposedly worse trauma inflicted on another community or individual, at some point in history. Whataboutery is a well-established system of dialogically evading any sort of responsibility for the causes and consequences of the Troubles. Whataboutery is generally accompanied by what a friend of mine refers to as 'mopery', 'MOPE' being an acronym for 'Most Oppressed People Ever'. Whataboutery and mopery are certainly products of fragmented memory-space in Northern Ireland, but I argue they are preferable to the rigid consensual frameworks often imposed by a consolidating transitional state or other 'victor'. Decoding Northern Ireland public debate and social dialogue often requires that we look beneath the well-publicised whataboutery and mopery that tend to fascinate the local and foreign media and all too often emanate from the ethnosectarian arrangement of Stormont. Beneath the whataboutery, as I have attempted to illustrate throughout this piece, there is a growing chorus of morally charged voices seeking new ways to remember and new ways to honour and house the ghosts of the past.

Thus, the problem with a peace centre or some sort of other national, shared place of memory is not necessarily rooted in the hierarchy of victims or the symbolically resonant topography of Long Kesh/Maze itself, though of course that site is particularly evocative and particularly implicated in the production of conflict narratives. It is rooted in the concern, as 'Michael' so clearly demonstrates, about a national political inscription so imposing that it will produce, eventually, a consensus. For 'Michael', this consensus will elevate figures like Bobby Sands to a place of prominence while shouldering out, forgetting, and marginalising attempts to remember others like the 'ordinary so-and-sos' who also lost their lives. 'Michael' and others view this as inscribing a public and pedagogical version of history into Northern Irish memory-space that will write out their traumatic experiences, and obscure the fact that their trauma and the trauma of their communities has an aetiology, namely, the IRA, Sinn Féin, and violent republicanism generally. A similar perspective would be advanced by those victimised by the British state, loyalists, or a collusion between the two. They fear a consensual public memory that will render them non-placed, render them placeless, eventually, if allowed to take hold. If the USHMM and the VVW are any indication, 'Michael' is right to worry, not necessarily about the potential for a dominant ascendancy of a purely republican historiography, that will likely always be publicly and vigorously challenged in Northern Ireland, but about the symbolic closure consensual memory necessarily implies.

But whataboutery is also a continuing and highly visible legacy of splintering memory. Whataboutery is rooted in the continuing inability of so many Northern Irish citizens, from all political and religious backgrounds, 'Michael' included, to problematise their particularistic notions of innocence or worthy and unworthy victimhood. For 'Michael' and others ensconced within an innocence/guilt dialectic, they simply cannot encounter other witnesses and other stories because innocence is so emotive that it cannot, in Butler's sense, adequately break down in the face of the other (McEvoy & McConnachie, 2012; Butler, 2006), even other 'innocents' like Eugene Reavey or the Bloody Sunday and Ballymurphy families. In the Lefebvrian sense, an attempt to make a place of memory on a national or provincial scale cannot pass trial by space because the ideational space for empathic dissonance simply does not yet exist. But depending on a national site of grief, mourning, and memory to facilitate the production of empathic dissonance is profoundly misguided. Even the most abstract, powerful, non-imposing site of memory in the United States, the Vietnam Veterans Memorial, *still depends on foreclosing who is worthy of commemoration and acceptable definitions of victimhood*, even if why they are victims or who victimised them remains in dispute.

Conclusion

For many, the splintered and difficult labours of memory in Northern Ireland reflect a society unable to cohere, unable to move on from the traumatic legacy of the past, unable to imagine a new society free from the sectarianism, atavism, and enclavement that continue to plague it. I disagree. To me, a splintering of memory is perhaps the best hope for a 'new' Northern Ireland. Splintering memory seems to suggest that Northern Ireland as a whole is becoming more polyphonic, but this unique social reality is being held back and muted by the consociational project, which normalised sectarian narratives, accepted the fictive historical pronouncement of the state of exception, and provided no formal political space for institutional challenges to the entrenched legacies of sectarianism that spawned both Sinn Féin and the DUP (Graham, 2011; Taylor, 2009; Tonge, 2004). As such, those wishing to challenge the consociational political reality and its acceptance of sectarianised memory-space have been pushed outwards, towards other nodes of political inscription and other means to reclaim the bodies of the dead. From these emergent, multi-nodal sites of inscription, they seek to effect in some way the production of a wider social imaginary. But denied the right to dominant public space and dominant public discourses by the twin silencers of paramilitarism and 'moving on', they are socially and spatially isolated and misunderstood, which in turn invites retrenchment, whataboutery, and a failure to transformatively encounter the other.

Given the calcification of Northern Irish political discourse and the ongoing quasi-institutionalised segregation of Northern Irish territory and society, the diversification of control over the bodies of the dead perhaps represents the best hope to eventually alter zero-sum victimhood and the dominance over public memory-space enjoyed by paramilitary groups and their violent surrogates. To continue to advocate for or demand a 'shared' place of memory seems to me to be indicative of a desire to finally put the Troubles to bed, to return the ghosts to their graves, to 'get on' with the larger neoliberal economic agenda that will, like the Wizard at the end of the *Wizard of Oz*, loudly proclaim that visitors, tourists, and the nouveau-elite should merely 'ignore that man behind the curtain'. But as Till (2005) suggests in relation to Berlin and Switzer and McDowell (2009) point out in relation to Belfast, simply piling layers of sediment (or 'investment', or 'urban renewal') on top of them will not keep the ghosts down. Worse, it will slowly mute the ongoing critical conversation about why they had to die, and who or what proclaimed and still seeks to proclaim the state of exception that allowed them to be killed.

Albert Camus writes in *The Rebel* that being able to cognitively justify the reduction to bare life and killing of another human being also justifies another killing: one's own. "Absurdist reasoning cannot defend the continued existence of its spokesman, and, simultaneously, accept the sacrifice of others' lives" (Camus, 1956, p. 7). By this Camus means that the same dehumanising logic that an actor employs to accept and institutionalise the state of exception can just as easily be applied to the actor him/herself. If we reduce and de-realise others to 'bare life', we can, in turn, all be so reduced and rendered unreal. Derek Gregory echoes Camus when he applies the state of exception to the infamous image of the hooded man in the Abu Ghraib Prison (see Figure 8.1):

Figure 8.1 'Hooded Man', Abu Ghraib Prison, Baghdad, Iraq. Source: Wikimedia Commons: https://en.wikipedia.org/wiki/Abu_Ghraib_torture_and_prisoner_abuse#/media/File:AbuGhraibAbuse-standing-on-box.jpg

> There has never been a greater need to untwist the separations between 'us' and 'them' than the present moment of danger. For as the viral 'war on terror' proliferates across the globe, and as regimes around the world invoke national security to suppress human rights, we are all, potentially, *homines sacri*. Our vulnerability is differentially distributed – scored by class, gender, sexuality, 'race', and other markers – but it is also shared. We could all end up on other boxes in other prisons, arms outstretched and wires attached to our trembling bodies.
>
> (Gregory, 2007, pp. 229–230).

The picture of the hooded man is especially redolent in Northern Ireland, where men have been tortured and hooded as well (Whyte, 2014; Amnesty International, 1971; see also Figure 8.2). I have heard one of them, Francie McGuigan, describe the same techniques of torture employed by the British military and security alters radically. Apparently pre-designatedpersons were arrested and not mal-treated until processed and transferred to a special interrogation centre, where they were then subjected to severe beatings and physical tortures in the nature of being forced to stand in a "search position" (legs apart, hands against wall) for hours at a time. When they would collapse, severe beatings were again administered. This pattern was followed by prolonged interrogation, often over several hours. The prisoners were offered money to give information relating to Irish Republican Army activities in Northern Ireland. During these tortures, the prisoners were first stripped naked, their heads covered with an opaque cloth bag with no vent-ilation. They were then dressed in large boiler suits (one-piece coverall garments). They were forced into the search postition in a room filled with the high pitched whining sound of an air compressor or similar device. This went on in some cases for 6 to 7 days. Many prisoners felt they were on the brink of insanity - one alleges he prayed for death, another that he tried to kill himself by banging his head against some metal piping in the room.

In short, the allegations are of such a nature as to provide a prima facie case of brutality and torture in contravention of Article 5 of the Universal Declaration of Human Rights and Article 3 of the European Convention on Human Rights. These statements conjure a familiar picture of activities employed by

Figure 8.2 Excerpt from Amnesty International Report of 8 August 1971 on the 'ill-treatment' of those arrested under the Special Powers Act.

services as were employed by the Japanese military and security services, as were employed by the Argentinian military and security services, as were employed by the American military and security services. Everyone who has been tortured was tortured for different 'reasons', but all were able to be tortured because they were not or no longer were human beings. If we accept that another's life is bare, then we have also accepted that our own lives are bare as well and we all, at some point and for some 'reason', could be *homines sacri*.

We as scholars of transitional societies need a greater understanding of how the state of exception has been and is being resisted, and all the complex and often culturally dependent forms that resistance can take. Too often, I argue, we accept and, intentionally or not, reify the state of exception by focusing our work on pronouncements, discourses, and aesthetics that are louder, more prominent, more visible, and neglect the muted voices of subaltern subjects, subjects who are out of place, who do not speak from a hegemonic/counter-hegemonic, dominant/contrapuntal place, who do not speak in genres we necessarily expect. We need a more complex, nuanced understanding of places of memory and how such places can perform resistance to or replication of the state of exception, why some places come to be integrated into a social imaginary and some merely fade to the peripheries of memory-space. As Gregory so brilliantly writes, we are all of us vulnerable to the state of exception. The imperative to challenge and resist does not merely rest with those populations *over there*, those 'others': it rests in us all.

Bibliography

Abdullah, O. (2016). Approaching hysteria through an Irigarian perspective in Fay Weldon's praxis. *European Scientific Journal*, 12(11), pp. 341–9.

Acorn, A. (2004). *Compulsory compassion: A critique of restorative justice.* Vancouver: UBC Press.

Adams, G. (1989). *A scenario for peace.* Dingle, IE: Brandon Books.

Adams, G. (2005). Gerry Adams addresses the IRA. *An Phoblacht.* Online Edition. First published 7 April 2005. Retrieved 8 December 2016 from www.anphoblacht.com/contents/13274.

Agamben, G. (1998). *Homo sacer: Sovereign power and bare life.* Stanford: Stanford University Press.

Agamben, G. (2005). *State of exception.* Chicago: University of Chicago Press.

Aiken, N. (2010). Learning to live together: Transitional justice and intergroup reconciliation in Northern Ireland. *International Journal of Transitional Justice*, 4(2), pp. 166–88.

Alderman, D. (2003). Street names and the scaling of memory: The politics of commemorating Martin Luther King Jr. within the African American community. *Area*, 35(2), pp. 163–73.

Alderman, D. (2010). Surrogation and the politics of remembering slavery in Savannah, Georgia (USA). *Journal of Historical Geography*, 36(1), pp. 90–101.

Alderman, D. & Campbell, R. (2008). Symbolic excavation and the artifact politics of remembering slavery in the American South: Observations from Walterboro, South Carolina. *Southeastern Geographer*, 48(3), pp. 338–55.

Alderman, D. & Inwood, J. (2013). Street naming and the politics of belonging: Spatial injustices in the toponymic commemoration of Martin Luther King, Jr. *Social & Cultural Geography*, 14(2), pp. 211–33.

Alderman, D., Butler, D., & Hanna, S. (2016). Memory, slavery, and plantation museums: The River Road Project. *Journal of Heritage Tourism*, 11(3), pp. 209–18.

Alexander, M. (2010). *The new Jim Crow: Mass incarceration in the age of colorblindness.* New York: New Press.

Allen, J. (2011). Powerful assemblages? *Area*, 43(2), pp. 154–7.

Amery, J. (1998). *At the mind's limits: Contemplations by a survivor on Auschwitz and its realities.* Bloomington, IN: Indiana University Press.

Amnesty International (1971). A report on allegations of ill-treatment made by persons arrested under the Special Powers Act after 8 August, 1971. Online Resource. Available at http://cain.ulst.ac.uk/events/intern/docs/amnesty71.htm.

Amster, R. (2003). Patterns of exclusion: Sanitising space, criminalising homelessness. *Social Justice*, 30(1), pp. 195–221.

An Crann/The Tree (2000). *Bear in mind: Stories of the Troubles.* Belfast: Lagan Press.

Anderson, B. (1991). *Imagined communities: Reflections on the origin and spread of nationalism.* London: Verso.

Appy, C. (2015). *American reckoning: The Vietnam War and our national identity.* New York: Viking.

Arthur, M. (1987) *Northern Ireland – soldiers talking.* London: Sidgwick & Jackson.

Arthur, P. (2009). How 'transitions' reshaped human rights: A conceptual history of transitional justice. *Human Rights Quarterly*, 31(2), pp. 321–67.

Ashabranner, B. (1989). *Always to remember: The story of the Vietnam Veterans Memorial.* New York: Putnam.

Ashplant, T., Dawson, G., & Roper, M. (2006). The politics of war memory and commemoration: Contexts, Structures, and Dynamics. In Ashplant, T., Dawson, G., & Roper, M. (eds), *Commemorating war.* New Brunswick, NJ: Transaction Publishers, pp. 3–86.

Assman, J. (2005). *Religion and cultural memory: Ten studies.* Stanford: Stanford University Press.

Augé, M. (1995). *Non-places: An introduction to an anthropology of supermodernity.* London: Verso.

Azaryahu, M. (1996). The power of commemorative street names. *Environment and Planning D: Society and Space*, 14(3), pp. 311–30.

Bakhtin, M. M. (1981). *The dialogic imagination: Four essays by M. M. Bakhtin.* Austin: University of Texas Press.

Bakhtin, M. (1984). *Problems of Dostoevsky's poetics.* Minneapolis: University of Minnesota Press.

Bal, M. (1999). Introduction. In Bal, M., Crewe, J., & Spitzer, L. (eds), *Acts of memory: Cultural recall in the present.* Hanover, NH: Dartmouth College Press.

Bal, M. (2002). *Travelling concepts in the humanities: A rough guide.* Toronto: University of Toronto Press.

Bardon, J. (2005). *A history of Ulster.* Belfast: Blackstaff.

Bar-On, D. (1989). *Legacy of silence: Encounters with children of the Third Reich.* Cambridge, MA; Harvard University Press.

Bar-On, D. (2006). *Tell your life story: Creating dialogues among Jews and Germans, Israelis and Palestinians.* Budapest: Central European University Press.

Barron Report (2003). *Report of the Independent Commission of Inquiry into the Dublin and Monaghan bombings.* Dublin: Houses of the Oireachtas–Joint Committee on Equality, Defence and Women's Rights.

Bar-Tal, D., Chernyak-Hai, L., Schori, N., & Gundar, A. (2009). A sense of self-perceived collective victimhood in intractable conflicts. *International Review of the Red Cross*, 91, pp. 229–58.

Basso, K. (1996). *Wisdom sits in places: Landscape and language among the Western Apache.* Albuquerque, NM: UNM Press.

Bauman, Z. (2013). *Collateral damage: Social inequalities in a global age*. Cambridge: Polity.
BBC News (2002). Belfast's divisions 'even greater'. Online Edition. First published 4 January 2002. Retrieved 11 December 2016 from news.bbc.co.uk/2/hi/uk_news/northern_ireland/1742276.stm.
BBC News (2005). Sinn Féin rejects on-the-run bill. Online Edition. First published 20 December 2005. Retrieved 11 December 2016 from news.bbc.co.uk/2/hi/uk_news/northern_ireland/4546648.stm.
BBC News (2009). 'UDA involved' in McDaid murder. Online Edition. First published 26 June 2009. Retrieved 2 May 2017 from http://news.bbc.co.uk/2/hi/uk_news/northern_ireland/foyle_and_west/8120284.stm.
BBC News (2013a). Husband of Shankill bomb victim dismissed bomber's apology. Online Edition. First published 21 October 2013. Retrieved 8 December 2016 from www.bbc.com/news/uk-northern-ireland-24609436.
BBC News (2013b). Police to investigate 'UVF gangsterism'. Online Edition. First published 3 October 2013. Retrieved 2 May 2017 from www.bbc.com/news/uk-northern-ireland-24391243.
BBC Panorama (2015). Britain's secret terror deals. Television Programme. BBC. First aired 28 May 2015.
BBC Panorama (2017). The spy in the IRA. Television Programme. BBC. First aired 11 April 2017.
BBC Spotlight (2016). Clandeboye: Community in fear. Television Programme. BBC. First aired 16 March 2016.
Bean, K. (2007). *The new politics of Sinn Fein*. Liverpool: Liverpool University Press.
Bean, K. (2012). 'New dissidents are but old Provisionals writ large?' The dynamics of dissident Republicanism in the new Northern Ireland. *Political Quarterly*, 83(2), pp. 210–18.
Beiner, G. (2008). In anticipation of a post-memory boom syndrome. *Cultural Analysis*, 7, pp. 107–12.
Belknap, M. (2002). *The Vietnam War on trial: The My Lai massacre and the court-martial of Lieutenant Calley*. Lawrence, KS: University of Kansas Press.
Bell, C. (2002). Dealing with the past in Northern Ireland. *Fordham International Law Journal*, 26, pp. 1095–147.
Benjamin, W. (1992). *Illuminations*. London: Fontana Press.
Bennett, Jill. (2005). *Empathic vision: Affect, trauma, and contemporary art*. Stanford: Stanford University Press.
Bennett, Jane. (2010). *Vibrant matter: A political ecology of things*. Durham, NC: Duke University Press.
Berenbaum, M. & Kramer, A. (2006). *The world must know: The history of the Holocaust as told in the United States Holocaust Memorial Museum*. Washington: USHMM.
Berger, P. & Luckmann, T. (1966). *The social construction of reality: A treatise in the sociology of knowledge*. New York: Anchor.
Berliner, D. (2005). The abuses of memory: Reflections on the memory boom in anthropology. *Anthropological Quarterly*, 78(1), pp. 197–211.
Bew, P. (2007). *Ireland: The politics of enmity 1789–2006*. Oxford: Oxford University Press.
Bilton, M. & Sim, K. (1992). *Four hours in My Lai*. New York: Viking.

Biskind, P. (2008). The Vietnam Oscars. *Vanity Fair.* Online Edition. First published March 2008. Retrieved 10 February 2017 from www.vanityfair.com/news/2008/03/warmovies200803.

Blanchot, M. (1995). *The writing of the disaster.* Lincoln: University of Nebraska Press.

Bloom, M. & Horgan, J. (2008). Missing their mark: The IRA's proxy bomb campaign. *Social Research,* 75(2), pp. 579–614.

Bloomfield, K. (1998a). *We will remember them: Report of the Northern Ireland Victims Commissioner, Sir Kenneth Bloomfield.* Belfast: Northern Ireland Office.

Bloomfield, K. (1998b). How should we remember? The work of the Northern Ireland Victims Commission. In Hamber, B. (ed.), *Past imperfect: Dealing with the past in Northern Ireland and societies in transition.* Derry/Londonderry: INCORE, pp. 50–5.

Blumer, H. (1986). *Symbolic interactionism: Perspective and method.* Berkeley, CA: University of California Press.

Bogdanov, K. (2012). The queue as narrative: A Soviet case study. In Baiburin, A., Kelly, C., & Vakhtin, N. (eds), *Russian cultural anthropology after the collapse of Communism.* London: Routledge, pp. 77–102.

Borooah, V. & Knox, C. (2015). Segregation, inequality, and educational performance in Northern Ireland: Problems and solutions. *International Journal of Educational Development,* 40, pp. 196–206.

Borzello, F., Kuhn, A., Pack, J. & Wedd, C. (2013). Living dolls and 'real women'. In Kuhn, A. (ed.), *The power of the image: Essays on representation and sexuality.* London: Routledge, pp. 9–18.

Bosco, F. (2004). Human rights politics and scaled performances of memory: Conflicts among the *Madres de la Plaza de Mayo* in Argentina. *Social & Cultural Geography,* 5(3), pp. 381–402.

Bourdieu, P. (1977). *Outline of a theory of practice.* Cambridge: Cambridge University Press.

Bourdieu, P. (1993). *The field of cultural production.* New York: Columbia University Press.

Bourdieu, P. (1994). *Language and symbolic power.* Cambridge, MA: Harvard University Press.

Bowcott, O. (2010). Claudy bombings: Father Chesney, the 'Provo Priest'. *The Guardian Online.* Retrieved 5 February 2017 from www.theguardian.com/uk/2010/aug/24/claudy-bombing-profile-father-chesney.

Brecht, B. (1964). *Brecht on theatre: The development of an aesthetic.* New York: Hill & Wang.

Breen-Smyth, M. (2013). Injured and disabled casualties of the Northern Ireland conflict: Issues in immediate and long term treatment, care and support. *Medicine, Conflict, & Survival,* 29(3), pp. 244–66.

Brewer, J. (2010). *Peace processes: A sociological approach.* Cambridge: Polity.

Brewer, J. & Hayes, B. (2013). Victimhood status and public attitudes towards post-conflict agreements: Northern Ireland as a case study. *Political Studies,* 61(2): 442–61.

Browning, C. (1992). *Ordinary men: Reserve Police Battalion 11 and the Final Solution in Poland.* New York: Penguin.

Bruce, S. (2007). *Paisley: Religion and politics in Northern Ireland.* Oxford: Oxford University Press.

Brüdholm, T. (2009). *Resentment's virtue: Jean Amery and the refusal to forgive.* Philadelphia: Temple University Press.

Burgess, J. (2011). *The Exodus.* Belfast: Nicholson & Bass.
Burgess, J. (2015). *Inconspicuous gallantry: Dramatising the lived experience of the UDR community in North and West Tyrone.* Derry: Blue Eagle Productions. Film.
Burk, A. (2003). Private griefs, public places. *Political Geography*, 22(3), pp. 317–33.
Burk, A. (2006). In sight, out of view: A tale of three monuments. *Antipode*, 38(1), pp. 41–58.
Butler, J. (1988). Performative acts and gender constitution: An essay in phenomenology and feminist theory. *Theatre Journal*, 40(4), pp. 519–31.
Butler, J. (1997). *Excitable speech: A politics of the performative.* New York: Routledge.
Butler, J. (2006). *Precarious life: The power of mourning and violence.* London: Verso.
Cadwallader, A. (2013). *Lethal allies: British collusion in Northern Ireland.* Cork: Mercier Press.
Campbell, L., Boyd, N. & Culbert, L. (2009). *A thousand dreams: Vancouver's Downtown Eastside and the fight for its future.* Vancouver: Greystone Books.
Camus, A. (1956). *The rebel: An essay on man in revolt.* New York: Alfred A. Knopf.
Canny, N. (2001). *Making Ireland British: 1580–1650.* Oxford: Oxford University Press.
Carothers, T. (2002). The end of the transition paradigm. *Journal of Democracy*, 13(1), pp. 5–21.
Caruth, C. (1996). *Unclaimed experience: Trauma, narrative, and history.* Baltimore: JHU Press.
Casey, E. (1996a). *The fate of place: A philosophical history:* Berkeley, CA: University of California Press.
Casey, E. (1996b). How to get from space to place in a fairly short stretch of time: Phenomenological prolegoma. In Feld, S. & Basso, K. (eds), *Senses of place.* Santa Fe, NM: School of American Research Press, pp. 13–52.
Cassel Report. (2006). *Report of the independent international panel on alleged collusion in sectarian killings in Northern Ireland.* Notre Dame, IN: Centre for Civil and Human Rights – Notre Dame Law School.
Castioradis, C. (1998). *The imaginary institution of society.* Cambridge, MA: The MIT Press.
Chin E. (2001). *Purchasing power: Black kids and American consumer culture.* Minneapolis: University of Minnesota Press.
Christie, N. (1986). The ideal victim. In Fattah, E. (ed.), *From crime policy to victim policy: Reorienting the justice system.* London: Palgrave Macmillan, pp. 17–30.
City of Vancouver (2013). Downtown Eastside area plan. Online Resource: Retrieved 5 February 2017 from http://vancouver.ca/files/cov/downtown-eastside-plan.pdf.
Clarity, J. (1998). Belfast buries apolitical victim of sectarian strife. *The New York Times Online.* First published 15 January 1998. Retrieved 9 February 2017 from www.nytimes.com/1998/01/15/world/belfast-buries-apolitical-victim-of-sectarian-strife.html.
Clarke, L. (2013). Martin McGuinness refuses to condemn IRA 'human bomb' attack in 1990 dubbed the 'work of Satan' by Catholic bishop. *Belfast Telegraph – Online Edition.* First published 7 November 2013. Retrieved 23 April 2014 from www.belfasttelegraph.co.uk/news/northern-ireland/martin-mcguinness-refuses-to-condemn-ira-human-bomb-attack-in-1990-dubbed-the-work-of-satan-by-catholic-bishop-29733940.html.
Cobain, I. (2012). UK accused of helping to supply arms for Northern Ireland loyalist killings. *The Guardian.* Online Edition. First published 15 October 2012.

Retrieved 8 December 2016 from www.theguardian.com/uk/2012/oct/15/uk-arms-northern- ireland-loyalist-massacre.

Cochrane, F. (2013). *Northern Ireland: The reluctant peace*. New Haven: Yale University Press.

Coetzee, J. M. (1983). *The life and times of Michael K.* Johannesburg: Raven.

Coetzee, J. M. (1999). *Disgrace*. London: Secker & Warburg.

Cohen, S. (2007). Winning while losing: The Apprentice Boys of Derry walk their beat. *Political Geography*, 26(8), pp. 951–67.

Collins, C., Hitte, K. & Joignant, A. (eds), (2013). *The politics of memory in Chile: From Pinochet to Bachelet*. Boulder, CO: Lynne Reiner.

Comaroff, J. & Comaroff, J. (2016). *Theory from the South: Or, how Euro-America is evolving towards Africa*. New York: Routledge.

Compton Report (1971). Report of the enquiry into allegations against the security forces of physical brutality in Northern Ireland arising out of the events of the 9 August 1971. Online Resource. CAIN. Retrieved 8 December 2016 from http://cain.ulst.ac.uk/hmso/compton.htm.

Conan Doyle, A. (1887/2016). *A study in scarlet*. Project Gutenberg. Online Resource. Retrieved 3 December 2016 from www.gutenberg.org/files/244/244-h/244-h.htm#link2HCH0002.

Connerton, P. (1989). *How societies remember*. Cambridge: Cambridge University Press.

Conservative Party of the United Kingdom (1979). Conservative general election manifesto 1979. Online Resource. Retrieved 8 December 2016 from www.margaretthatcher.org/document/110858.

Conway, B. (2009). Rethinking difficult pasts: Bloody Sunday (1972) as a case study. *Cultural Sociology*, 3(3), pp. 397–413.

Conway, B. (2010). *Commemoration and Bloody Sunday: Pathways of memory*. London: Palgrave Macmillan.

Coogan, T. P. (1996). *The Troubles: Ireland's ordeal, 1969–95, and the search for peace*. London: Hutchinson.

Coogan, T. P. (2000). *The IRA*. London: HarperCollins.

Correll, J., Urland, G., & Ito, T. (2006). Event-related potentials and the decision to shoot: The role of threat perception and cognitive control. *Journal of Experimental Social Psychology*, 42(1), pp. 120–8.

Cory, P. (2010). *The Cory Collusion Inquiry report*. Dublin: Irish Department of Justice.

Cowan, R. (2002). Does this letter prove a priest was behind IRA bombing? *The Guardian Online*. Retrieved 5 February 2017 from www.theguardian.com/uk/2002/sep/21/northernireland.ireland.

Crandell, J. (2005). *The Indian Island Massacre: An investigation of the events precipitated the Wiyot murders*. M.A. Thesis, unpublished. Humboldt State University, Arcata, CA.

Crawford, N. (2002). *Argument and change in world politics: Ethics, decolonisation, and humanitarian intervention*. Cambridge: Cambridge University Press.

Cresswell, T. (1996). *In place/out of place: Geography, ideology, and transgression*. Minneapolis: University of Minnesota Press.

Cresswell, T. (2014). *Place: A short introduction*. New York: John Wiley & Sons.

Cunningham, N. & Gregory, I. (2014). Hard to miss, easy to blame? Peacelines, interfaces and political deaths in Belfast during the Troubles. *Political Geography*, 40(1), pp. 64–78.

Curtis, J. (2014). *Human rights as war by other means: Peace politics in Northern Ireland.* Philadelphia: University of Pennsylvania Press.

Cusack, J. & McDonald, H. (1997). *UVF.* Dublin: Poolbeg.

Cusack, J. & McDonald, H. (2008). *UVF: The endgame.* Dublin: Poolbeg.

Darby, J. (1986). *Intimidation and the control of conflict in Northern Ireland.* Syracuse: Syracuse University Press.

Darby, J. (1997). *Scorpions in a bottle: Conflicting cultures in Northern Ireland.* Belfast: Minority Rights Publication.

Davis, M. (2005). Is Spain recovering its memory? Breaking the *pacto del olvido. Human Rights Quarterly,* 27(3), pp. 858–80.

Dawson, G. (2005). Trauma, place, and the politics of memory: Bloody Sunday, Derry, 1972–2004. *History Workshop Journal,* 59(1), pp. 151–78.

Dawson, G. (2007). *Making peace with the past? Memory, trauma and the Irish Troubles.* Manchester: Manchester University Press.

De Breadun, D. (1997). Tour of loyalists' devastated cells in Maze provides a picture of hell. *The Irish Times.* Online Edition. First published 15 August 1997. Retrieved 8 December 2016 from www.irishtimes.com/news/tour-of-loyalists-devastated-cells-in-maze-provides-a-picture-of-hell-1.96901.

De Brito, A. B., Aguilar, P., & González-Enríquez, C. (2001). Introduction. In De Brito, A. B., González-Enríquez, C., & Aguilar, P. (eds), *The politics of memory: Transitional justice in democratising societies.* Oxford: Oxford University Press, pp. 1–39.

Deleuze, G. & Guattari, F. (1987). *A thousand plateaus: Capitalism and schizophrenia.* Minneapolis: University of Minnesota Press.

Derrida, J. (1994). *Spectres of Marx: The state of debt, the work of mourning, and the new international.* New York: Routledge.

Derry Journal (2012). Remembering Stephen (11), shot by the British Army. *The Derry Journal.* Online Edition. First published 13 April 2012. Retrieved 5 February 2017 from www.derryjournal.com/news/remembering-stephen-11-shot-by-british-army-1-3733097.

Derry Journal (2014). Hain 'Sunday' views sparks parties dispute. *The Derry Journal.* Online Edition. First published 4 March 2014. Retrieved 11 December 2016 from www.derryjournal.com/news/hain-sunday-views-sparks-parties-dispute-1-5912458.

Dillon, M. (1999). *The Shankill Butchers: The real story of cold-blooded mass murder.* New York: Routledge.

Dorfman, A. (2002). *In case of fire in a foreign land: New and collected poems in two languages.* Durham, NC: Duke University Press.

Doss, E. (2010). *Memorial mania: Public feeling in America.* Chicago: University of Chicago Press.

Dreschler, H. (1980). *Let us die fighting: Namibia under the Germans.* New York: Lawrence & Hill Co.

Duras, M. (1959). Screenwriter. *Hiroshima mon amour. Film.* Paris: Pathé Films.

Dwyer, O. (2002). Location, politics, and the production of civil rights memorial landscapes. *Urban Geography,* 23(1), pp. 31–56.

Dwyer, O. (2004). Symbolic accretion and commemoration. *Social and Cultural Geography,* 5(3), pp. 419–35.

Dwyer, O. (2008). Putting the movement in its place: The politics of Civil Rights memorial landscapes. In Alexander, L. & Nieves, A. (eds), *'We will independent be': African*

American place making and the struggle to claim space in the United States. Boulder, CO: University of Colorado Press.

Dwyer, O., Butler, D., & Carter, P. (2013). Commemorative surrogation and the American South's changing heritage landscape. *Tourism Geographies*, 15(3), pp. 424–43.

Eakin, M. (2010). My little sister will always be eight, the age she was when I saw her murdered in Claudy. *Belfast Telegraph Online*. First published 30 August 2010. Retrieved 5 February 2017 from www.belfasttelegraph.co.uk/news/northern-ireland/my-little-sister-will-always-be-eight-the-age-she-was-when-i-saw-her-murdered-in-claudy-28557573.html.

Eames, R. & Bradley, D. (2009). *The report of the consultative group on the past.* Belfast: Northern Ireland Office.

Edkins, J. (2003). *Trauma and the memory of politics.* Cambridge: Cambridge University Press.

Edwards, A. & McGrattan, C. (2011). Terroristic narratives: On the (re)invention of peace in Northern Ireland. *Terrorism and Political Violence*, 23(3), 357–76.

Eichstedt, J. & Small, S. (2002). *Representations of slavery: Race and ideology in southern plantation museums.* Washington DC: Smithsonian Books.

Ellsworth, E. (2002). The U.S. Holocaust Museum as a scene of pedagogical address. *Sympoke*, 10(1–2), pp. 13–31.

Elster, J. (2004). *Closing the books: Transitional justice in historical perspective.* Cambridge: Cambridge University Press.

Ely Centre (2016). Memorial project information brochure. Online resource. Retrieved 3 November 2016 from www.elycentre.com/Media/Default/Documents/Memorial%20Project%20Info%20Brouchure-1.pdf.

Erll, A., Nunning, A., & Young, S. (eds), (2008). *Cultural memory studies: An international and interdisciplinary handbook.* Berlin: de Gruyter.

Escobar, A. (2001). Culture sits in places: Reflections on globalism and subaltern strategies of localisation. *Political Geography*, 20(2), pp. 139–74.

Fassin, D. & Rechman, R. (2009). *The empire of trauma: An inquiry into the condition of victimhood.* Princeton: Princeton University Press.

Feldman, A. (1991). *Formations of violence: The narrative of the body and political terror in Northern Ireland.* Chicago: University of Chicago Press.

Felman, S. & Laub, D. (1992). *Testimony: Crises of witnessing in literature, psychoanalysis, and history.* New York: Routledge.

Finklestein, N. (1997). Daniel Jonah Goldhagen's 'crazy' thesis: A critique of Hitler's Willing Executioners. *New Left Review*, I/224, pp. 39–87.

Finlay, A. (2001). Defeatism and Northern Protestant 'Identity'. *Global Review of Ethnopolitics*, 1(2): 3–20.

Fitzduff, M. (2002). *Beyond violence: Conflict resolution processes in Northern Ireland.* Tokyo: UN Press.

Fitzpatrick, D. (2013). Ethnic cleansing, ethical smearing, and Irish historians' 'history'. *History*, 98(329), pp. 135–44.

Fitzpatrick, L. (2015). Gender and affect in testimonial performance: The example of 'I Once Knew a Girl'. *Irish University Review*, 45(1): 126–40.

Flynn, B. (2009). *Soldiers of folly: The IRA Border Campaign 1956–1962.* Cork: Collins Press.

Foote, K. (2003). *Shadowed ground: America's landscapes of violence and tragedy, revised and updated.* Austin: University of Texas Press.

Forest, B., Johnson, J., & Till, K. (2004). Post-totalitarian national identity: Public memory in Germany and Russia. *Social & Cultural Geography*, 5(3), pp. 357–80.

Forgiveness Project (2010). Stories: Jo Berry and Pat Magee. Online Resource. First published 29 March 2010. Retrieved 8 December 2016 from http://theforgivenessproject.com/stories/jo-berry-pat-magee-england/.

Foucault, M. (1977). *Language, counter-memory, practice: Selected essays and interviews.* Ithaca, NY: Cornell University Press.

Foucault, M. (1984). Of other spaces: Utopias and heterotopias. *Architecture, Mouvement, Continuite.* Online resource. Retrieved 15 January 2017 from web.mit.edu/allanmc/www/foucault1.pdf.

Foucault, M. (1994). *The order of things: An archaeology of the human sciences.* London: Vintage, Reissue Edition.

Foucault, M. (2004). *Security, territory, population: Lectures at the Collège de France, 1977–1978.* London: Picador.

Freud, S. (1896/1999). The Aetiology of Hysteria. In Strachey, J. (ed.), *The standard edition of the complete psychological works of Sigmund Freud, vol. III.* New York: Vintage, pp. 189–224.

Freud, S. (1899/1999). Screen Memories. In Strachey, J. (ed.), *The standard edition of the complete psychological works of Sigmund Freud, vol. III.* New York: Vintage, pp. 301–20.

Freud, S. (1917a/1999). Mourning and melancholia. In Strachey, J. (ed.), *The standard edition of the complete psychological works of Sigmund Freud, vol. XIV.* New York: Vintage, pp. 237–58.

Freud, S. (1917b/1999). From the history of an infantile neurosis. In Strachey, J. (ed.), *The standard edition of the complete psychological works of Sigmund Freud, vol. XVII.* New York: Vintage, pp. 3–104.

Fulbrook, M. (1999). *German national identity after the Holocaust.* Cambridge: Polity.

Gallagher, E., Hamber, B., & Joy, E. (2012). Perspectives and possibilities. Mental health in post-agreement Northern Ireland. *Shared Space: A Research Journal on Peace, Conflict and Community Relations in Northern Ireland*, 13, pp. 63–78.

Gambetta, D. (1996). *The Sicilian mafia: The business of private protection.* Cambridge, MA: Harvard University Press.

Goffman, E. (1959). *The presentation of the self in everyday life.* New York: Anchor Books.

Goldhagen, D. (1996). *Hitler's willing executioners: Ordinary Germans and the Holocaust.* New York: Knopf.

Goodwin, R., Wilson, M., & Gaines, S. (2005). Terror threat perception and its consequences in contemporary Britain. *British Journal of Psychology*, 96(4), pp. 389–406.

Graham, B. (1998). Contested images of place amongst Northern Irish Protestants. *Political Geography*, 17(2): 129–44.

Graham, B. (2004). The past in the present: The shaping of identity in loyalist Ulster. *Terrorism and Political Violence*, 16(3), pp. 483–500.

Graham, B. (2011). Sharing space? Geography and politics in post-conflict Northern Ireland. In Meusberger, P., Heffernan, M., & Wunder, E. (eds), *Cultural memories: The geographic point of view.* Berlin: Springer, pp. 87–100.

Graham, B. & McDowell, S. (2007). Meaning in the Maze: The heritage of Long Kesh. *Cultural Geographies*, 14(3), pp. 343–68.

Graham, B. & Whelan, Y. (2007). The legacies of the dead: Commemorating the Troubles in Northern Ireland. *Environment and Planning D*, 25(3), pp. 476–95.

Graham, L. (2014). The 'innocent' victims of the Troubles and the enduring impediment to peace in Northern Ireland. *Shared Space: A Research Journal for Peace, Conflict, and Community Relations in Northern Ireland*, 17(1), pp. 37–54.

Gramsci, A. (1971). *Selections from the prison notebooks*. New York: International Publishing Co.

Gray, P. (2014). Famine and the land, 1845–1850. In Jackson, A. (ed.), *The Oxford handbook of modern Irish history*. Oxford: Oxford University Press, pp. 544–61.

Gregory, D. (1994). *Geographic imaginations*. New York: Wiley-Blackwell.

Gregory, D. (2004). *The colonial present: Afghanistan, Palestine, Iraq*. New York: Wiley-Blackwell.

Gregory, D. (2007). Vanishing points: Law, violence exception in the global war prisons. In Gregory, D. & Pred, A. (eds), *Violent geographies: Fear, terror, and political violence*. New York: Routledge.

Grossman, D. (1996). *On killing: The psychological cost of learning to kill in war and society*. Boston, MA: Back Bay Books.

Grosz, E. (1994). *Volatile bodies: Towards a corporeal feminism*. Sydney: Allen & Unwin.

Guattari, F. (1995). *Chaosmosis: An ethico-aesthetic paradigm*. Sydney: Power Books.

Haas, K. (1998). *Carried to the wall: American memory and the Vietnam Veterans memorial*. Berkeley, MA: University of California Press.

Habermas, J. (1984). *Theory of communicative action, volume I: Reason and rationalisation of society*. Boston, MA: Beacon Press.

Hackett, C. & Rolston, B. (2009). The burden of memory: Victims, storytelling and resistance in Northern Ireland. *Memory Studies*, 2(3), pp. 355–76.

Hain, P. (2014). Peter Hain: 'I have nothing to hide'. *The Telegraph*. Online Edition. First published 2 March 2014. Retrieved 11 December 2016 from www.telegraph.co.uk/news/uknews/terrorism-in-the-uk/10669760/Peter-Hain-I-have-nothing-to-hide.html.

Halbwachs, M. (1925/1992). *On collective memory*. Chicago: University of Chicago Press.

Hamber, B. & Wilson, R. (2002). Symbolic closure through memory, reparation, and revenge in post-conflict societies. *Journal of Human Rights*, 1(1): 35–53.

Hamilton, J., Hansson, U., Bell, J., & Toucas, S. (2008). *Segregated lives: Social division, sectarianism, and everday life in Northern Ireland*. Belfast: Institute for Conflict Research.

Hart, P. (1998). *The I.R.A. and its enemies: Violence and community in Cork, 1916–1923*. Oxford: Oxford University Press.

Haskins, E. (2011). Russia's postcommunist past: The Cathedral of Christ the Savior and the reimagining of national identity. In Philips, K. R. and Mitchell Reyes, G. (eds), *Global memoryspaces: Contesting remembrance in a transitional age*. Tuscaloosa: University of Alabama Press, pp. 46–79.

Harvey, D. (2009). *Social justice and the city, revised edition*. Athens, GA: University of Georgia Press.

Healy, J. (2006). Locality matters: Ethnic segregation and community conflict: The experience of Protestant girls in Belfast. *Children & Society*, 20(2), pp. 105–15.

Heaney, S. (1975). *North*. London: Faber & Faber.
Heatley, C. (2004). *Interface: Flashpoints in Northern Ireland*. Belfast: Lagan Books.
Hedetoft, U. (2003). *The global turn: National encounters with the world*. Aalborg: Aalborg University Press.
Hedges, J. (2015). Coalition for reconciliation is essential, Declan Kearney tells Westminster audience. *An Phoblacht*. Online Edition. First published 14 July 2015. Retrieved 11 December 2016. from www.anphoblacht.com/contents/25173.
Herman, J. (1992). *Trauma and recovery: The aftermath of violence – from domestic violence to political terror*. New York: Basic Books.
Herman, E. & Chomsky, N. (1988). *Manufacturing consent: The political economy of the mass media*. New York: Pantheon Books.
Hersch, S. (1969). Eyewitness accounts of the My Lai massacre. *The Cleveland Plain-Dealer*. Online Resource. First published 20 November 1969. Retrieved 10 February 2017 from www.cleveland.com/plain-dealer-library/index.ssf/2009/11/eye_witness_account_of_the_my_lai_massacre_story_by_ seymour_hersh_nov_20_1969.html.
Hills, J., Le Grand, J., & Piachaud, D. (eds), (2002). *Understanding social exclusion*. Oxford: Oxford University Press.
Hilyard, P., Kelly, G., McLaughlin, E., Patsios, D., & Tomlinson, M. (2003). *Bare necessities: Poverty and social exclusion in Northern Ireland, key findings*. Belfast: Democratic Dialogue.
Hirsch, M. (1997). *Family frames: Photography, narrative, and postmemory*. Cambridge, MA: Harvard University Press.
Hirsch, M. & Smith, V. (2002). Feminism and cultural memory: An introduction. *Signs*, 28(1), pp. 1–19.
Hirsch, M. & Spitzer, L. (2011). *Ghosts of home: The afterlife of Czernowitz in Jewish memory*. Berkeley, MA: University of California Press.
Hirsch, M. & Spitzer, L. (2016). Small acts of repair: The unclaimed legacy of the Romanian Holocaust. *Journal of Literature and Trauma Studies*, 4(1), pp. 13–42.
Hirschman, C., Preston, S., & Loi, V. (1995). Vietnamese casualties during the American War: A new estimate. *Population and Development Review*, 21(4), pp. 783–812.
Hirst, W. & Echterhoff, G. (2012). Remembering in conversations: The social sharing and reshaping of mmeories. *Psychology*, 63(1), pp. 55–79.
Hoare, Q. & Smith, G. (1971). General Introduction. In Gramsci, A., *Selections from the prison notebooks*. New York: International Publishing Co., pp. 22–130.
Hobbes, T. (1651/2001). *Leviathan*. New York: Bartleby.
Hobsbawm, E. & Ranger, T. (eds), (2012). *The invention of tradition (reissue edition)*. Cambridge: Cambridge University Press.
Hoelscher, S. (2003). Making place, making race: Performances of whiteness in the Jim Crow South. *Annals of the Association of American Geographers*, 93(3), pp. 657–86.
hooks, b. (1989). *Talking back: Thinking feminist, thinking black*. Boston, MA: South End Press.
hooks, b. (1990). *Yearning: Race, gender, and cultural politics*. Boston, MA: South End Press.
Holland, J. (2001). *The American connection, revised: US guns, money, and influence in Northern Ireland*. New York: Roberts Rinehart.
Horgan, J. (2013). *Divided we stand: The strategy and psychology of Ireland's dissident terrorists*. Oxford: Oxford University Press.

Hoskins, E. (2011). Russia's postcommunist past: The Cathedral of Christ the Savior and the reimagining of national identity. In Phillips, K. & Reyes, M. (eds), *Global memoryscapes: Contesting remembrance in a transnational age*. Tuscaloosa, AL: University of Alabama Press, pp. 46–79.

Hughes, B. (2014). Anger over memorial to UFF men linked to mass killing. *The Irish News*. Published 1 August 2014.

Hughes, J. & Donnelly, C. (2003). Community relations in Northern Ireland: A shift in attitudes? *Journal of Ethnic and Migration Studies*, 29(4), pp. 643–61.

Humphrey, M. & Valverde, E. (2008). Human rights politics and injustice: Transitional justice in Argentina and South Africa. *International Journal of Transitional Justice*, 2(1), pp. 83–105.

Husanovic, J. (2009). The politics of gender, witnessing, postcoloniality, and trauma: Bosnian feminist trajectories. *Feminist Theory*, 10(1), pp. 99–119.

Hutcheon, L. (1987). Beginning to theorise postmodernism. *Textual Practice*, 1(1), pp. 10–31.

Huyssen, A. (1994). *Twilight memory: Marking time in a culture of amnesia*. New York & London: Routledge

Huyssen, A. (2003). *Present pasts: Urban palimpsests and the politics of memory*. Stanford: Stanford University Press.

Ignatieff, M. (1993). *Blood and belonging: Journeys into the new nationalism*. New York: Farrar, Strauss, & Giroux.

Independent Monitoring Commission (2008). Twentieth report of the Independent Monitoring Commission. London: The Stationery Office. Online Resource. Retrieved 2 May 2017 from: https://web.archive.org/web/20081218015532/ http://www.independentmonitoringcommission.org/documents/uploads/Twentieth%20Report.pdf.

Independent Research Solutions (2009). Evaluation of the Re-Imaging Communities Programme: A report to the Arts Council of Northern Ireland. Belfast: Arts Council NI.

Irigaray, L. (1985). *This sex which is not one*. Ithaca, NY: Cornell University Press.

Irwin-Zarecka, I. (1994). *Frames of remembrance: The dynamics of collective memory*. New Brunswick, NJ: Transaction Publishers.

Jackson, A. (ed.) (2014). *The Oxford handbook of modern Irish history*. Oxford: Oxford University Press.

Jackson, M. (2002). *The politics of storytelling: Violence, transgression, and intersubjectivity*. Copenhagen: Museum Tusculanum Press.

Jackson, R. (2005). *Writing the war on terror: Language, politics, and counter-terrorism*. Manchester: Manchester University Press.

Jamieson, R. (2016). Framing blame and victimhood in post-conflict Northern Ireland. In McGarry, R. & Walklate, S. (eds), *The Palgrave handbook of criminology and war*. London: Palgrave Macmillan, pp. 169–87.

Janoff-Bullman, R. (1992). *Shattered assumptions: Towards a new psychology of trauma*. New York: Free Press.

Jarman, N. (1997). *Material cultures: Parades and visual displays in Northern Ireland*. Oxford: Berg.

Jarman, N. (1998). Painting landscapes: The place of murals in the symbolic construction of urban space. In Buckley, A. (ed.), *Symbols in Northern Ireland*. Belfast: Institute of Irish Studies, Queens University Belfast.

Jeffrey, L. & Candea, M. (2006). The politics of victimhood. *History and Anthropology*, 17(4), pp. 287–96.
Jelin, E. (2003). *State repression and the struggles for memory.* London: Latin American Bureau.
Jelin, E. (2007). Public memorialisation in perspective: Truth, justice and memory of past repression in the Southern Cone of South America. *International Journal of Transitional Justice*, 1(1), pp. 138–56.
Jonker, J. & Till, K. (2009). Mapping and excavating spectral traces in post-apartheid Cape Town. *Memory Studies*, 2(3): 303–35.
Jorgensen-Earp, C. & Lanziotti, L. (1998). Public memory and private grief: The construction of shrines at sites of public tragedy. *Quarterly Journal of Speech*, 84(2), pp. 150–70.
Jowitt, K. (1992). *New world disorder: The Leninist extinction.* Berkeley, MA: University of California Press.
Kaye, H. (1991). *The powers of the past: Reflections on the crisis and the promise of history.* Minneapolis: University of Minnesota Press.
Kelly, B. (2012). Neoliberal Belfast: Disaster ahead. *Irish Marxist Review*, 1(2), pp. 44–59.
Kelly, G. (2005). *'Storytelling' audit: An audit of personal story, narrative and testimony initiatives related to the conflict in and about Northern Ireland.* Belfast: Healing Through Remembering.
Kimmelman, M. (2002). Art/architecture: Out of minimalism, monuments to memory. *The New York Times.* Online Edition. First published 13 January 2002. Retrieved 10 February 2017 from www.nytimes.com/2002/01/13/arts/art-architecture-out-of-minimalism-monuments-to-memory.html.
Knox, C. (2002). 'See no evil, hear no evil': Insidious paramilitary violence in Northern Ireland. *British Journal of Criminology*, 42(1), pp. 164–85.
Knox, C. (2011). Cohesion, sharing, and integration in Northern Ireland. *Environment and Planning C: Government and Policy*, 29(3), pp. 548–66.
Kofman, S. (1998). *Smothered words.* Evanston, IL: Northwestern University Press.
Korstanje, M. (2015). The anthropology of airports: Criticism to non-place theory. *Advances in Hospitality and Tourism Research*, 3(1), pp. 40–58.
Kristeva, J. (1982). *Powers of horror: An essay on abjection.* New York: Columbia University Press.
LaCapra, D. (1998). *History and memory after Auschwitz.* Ithaca, NY: Cornell University Press.
LaCapra, D. (2001). *Writing history, writing trauma.* Baltimore: Johns Hopkins University Press.
Langenbacher, E. & Eigler, F. (2005). Introduction: Memory boom or memory fatigue in 21st century Germany. *German Politics & Society*, 23(3), pp. 1–15.
Larkin, P. (2004). *A very British jihad: Collusion, conspiracy, and cover-up in Northern Ireland.* Belfast: Beyond the Pale.
Latham, A. & McCormack, D. (2004). Moving cities: Rethinking the materialities of urban geographies. *Progress in Human Geography*, 28(6), pp. 701–24.
Laub, D. (1992). Bearing witness, or the vicissitudes of listening. In Felman, S. & Laub, D.. *Testimony: Crises of witnessing in literature, psychoanalysis, and history.* New York: Routledge, pp. 57–74.

Laub, D. (1996). Truth and testimony: The process and the Struggle. In Caruth, C. (ed.), *Trauma: Explorations in memory.* Baltimore: Johns Hopkins University Press, pp. 61–75.

Lawther, C. (2013). Denial, silence, and the politics of the past: Unpicking the opposition to truth recovery in Northern Ireland. *International Journal of Transitional Justice*, 7(1), pp. 157–77.

Le Bon, G. (1895/2009). *The crowd: A study of the popular mind.* Charleston, SC: Bibliolife.

Leebaw, B. (2008). The irreconcilable goals of transitional justice. *Human Rights Quarterly*, 30(1), pp. 95–118.

Lefebvre, H. (1991). *The production of space.* Oxford: Blackwell.

Lemarchand, R. (2005). The politics of memory in post-genocide Rwanda. Occasional papers, Center for Holocaust and Genocide Studies, University of Florida, pp. 25–54.

Lemarchand, R. (2006). Genocide, memory and ethnic reconciliation in Rwanda. *L'Afrique des Grands Lacs – Annuaire*, pp. 21–30.

Lemke. T. (2005). 'A zone of indistinction' – A critique of Giorgio Agamben's concept of biopolitics. *Outlines: Critical Practice Studies*, 7(1), pp. 3–13.

Lemm, C. (2006). Memory and promise in Arendt and Nietzsche. *Revista de Ciencia Politica*, 26(2), pp. 161–73.

Lerner, M. (1980). *The belief in a just world: A fundamental delusion.* New York: Plenum Press.

Levey, C. (2016). *Fragile memory, shifting impunity: Commemoration and contestation in post-dictatorship Argentina and Uruguay.* Oxford: Peter Lang.

Levi, P. (1989). *The drowned and the saved.* New York: Vintage.

Levi, P. (1995). *Survival in Auschwitz.* New York: Touchstone.

Levy, D. & Sznaider, N. (2002). Memory unbound: The Holocaust and the formation of cosmopolitan memory. *European Journal of Social Theory*, 5(1), pp. 87–106.

Lindsay, J. (1998). *Brits speak out: British soldiers' impressions of the Northern Ireland conflict:* Derry: Guildhall Press.

Lindsay, J. (2012). *No dope here? Anti-drugs vigilantism in Northern Ireland.* Derry/Londonderry: YES! Publications.

Linenthal, E. (1995). *Preserving memory: The struggle to create America's Holocaust Museum.* New York: Viking.

Lipset, S. (1996). *American exceptionalism: A double-edged sword.* New York: Norton.

Lister, D. & Jordan, H. (2005). *Mad Dog: The rise and fall of Johnny Adair and 'C' Company.* Edinburgh: Mainstream Publishing.

Lloyd, D. (1993). *Anomalous states: Irish writing and the post-colonial moment.* Durham, NC: Duke University Press.

Loftus, E. (1996). *Eyewitness testimony.* Cambridge, MA: Harvard University Press.

Lopate, P. (2003). *Getting personal: Selected writings.* New York: Basic.

Lowenthal, D. (1975). Past time, present place: Landscape and memory. *Geographical Review*, 65(1), pp. 1–36.

Lowenthal, D. (1985). *The past is a foreign country.* Cambridge: Cambridge University Press.

Lundy, P. & McGovern, M. (2008). Whose justice? Re-thinking transitional justice from the bottom up. *Journal of Law and Society*, 35(2): 265–92.

Lyotard, J-F. (1984). *The postmodern condition.* Minneapolis: University of Minnesota Press.

McAuley, J. (1999). Still no surrender? New loyalism and the peace process in Ireland. In Harrington, J. & Mitchell, E. (eds), *Politics and performance in contemporary Northern Ireland*. Amherst: UMASS Press.

McAuley, J. (2010). *Ulster's last stand: Reconstructing Unionism after the Peace Process*. Dublin: Irish Academic Press.

McAuley, J. (2015). *Very British rebels? The culture and politics of Ulster loyalism*. London: Bloomsbury.

McAuley, J. & Ferguson, N. (2016). 'Us' and 'them': Ulster Loyalist perspectives on the IRA and Irish Republicanism. *Terrorism and Political Violence*, 28(3), pp. 561–75.

McAuley, J. & Spencer, G. (eds) (2011). *Ulster loyalism after the Good Friday Agreement: History, identity, and change*. London: Palgrave Macmillan.

McBride, S. (2014). My murder of two Catholics helped prevent united Ireland – PUP leader Billy Hutchinson. *The Belfast Newsletter*. Online Edition. First published 19 March 2014. Retrieved 8 December 2016 from www.newsletter.co.uk/news/my-murder-of-two-catholics-helped-prevent-united-ireland-pup-leader-billy-hutchinson-1-5945099.

McCann, E. (1993). *War and an Irish town*, 3rd edn. London: Pluto.

McCormick, J. & Jarman, N. (2005). Death of a mural. *Journal of Material Culture*, 10(1), pp. 49–71.

McDonald, H. (2016). Boston College ordered by US court to hand over IRA tapes. *The Guardian Online*. First published 25 April 2016. Retrieved 23 April 2017 from www.theguardian.com/uk-news/2016/apr/25/boston-college-ordered-by-us-court-to-hand-over-ira-tapes.

McDonald, H. & Bright, M. (2003). Top Army officer handed over IRA files to Adair. *The Guardian*. Online Edition. First published 27 April 2003. Retrieved 8 December 2016 from www.theguardian.com/politics/2003/apr/27/northernireland.northernireland.

McDonald, H. & Cusack, J. (2004). *UDA – Inside the heart of Loyalist terror*. Dublin: Penguin Ireland.

McDowell, S. (2007). Who are the victims? Debates, concepts and contestation in 'post-conflict' Northern Ireland. CAIN Online resource. Available at http://cain.ulst.ac.uk/victims/introduction/smcd07whoarethevictims.html.

McDowell, S. (2008). Commemorating dead 'men': Gendering the past and present in post- conflict Northern Ireland. *Gender, Place, & Culture*, 15(4), pp. 335–54.

McDowell, S. & Switzer, C. (2011). Violence and the vernacular: Conflict, commemoration, and rebuilding in the urban context. *Buildings & Landscapes: Journal of the Vernacular Architecture Forum*, 18(2), pp. 82–104.

McEvoy, K. (2001). *Paramilitary imprisonment in Northern Ireland: Resistance, management, and release*. Oxford: Oxford University Press.

McEvoy, K. & McConnachie, K. (2012). Victimology in transitional justice: Victimhood, innocence, and hierarchy. *European Journal of Criminology*, 9(5), pp. 527–38.

McEvoy, K. & McConnachie, K. (2013). Victims and transitional justice: Voice, agency, and blame. *Social & Legal Studies*, 22(4), pp. 489–513.

McEvoy, K. & Mika, H. (2001). Punishment, policing, and praxis: Restorative justice and non-violent alternatives to paramilitary punishments in Northern Ireland. *Policing & Society: An International Journal*, 11(3–4), pp. 359–82.

McGarry, J. & O'Leary, B. (eds) (2004). *The Northern Ireland Conflict: Consociational Engagements*. Oxford: Oxford University Press.

Mac Gholla Minh, C. (2003). Coiste proposes museum for Long Kesh. *An Phoblacht*. Online Edition. First published 12 June 2013. Retrieved 10 February 2017 from www.anphoblacht.com/contents/10102.

McGirr, P. (2003). The Vietnam Veterans Memorial: Landscape and gender in the twentieth century. In Rotman, D. & Savulis, E-R. (eds), *Shared spaces and divided places: Material dimensions of gender relations and the American historical landscape*. Knoxville, TN: University of Tennessee Press, pp. 62–85.

McGovern, M. (2000). Irish Republicanism and the potential pitfalls of pluralism. *Capital and Class*, 24(2), pp. 133–61.

McGovern, M. (2015). State violence and the colonial roots of col in Northern Ireland. *Race & Class*, 57(2), pp. 3–23.

McGovern, M. & Shirlow, P. (1998). Language, discourse and dialogue. Sinn Féin and the Irish peace process. *Political Geography*, 17(2), pp. 171–86.

McGrattan, C. (2013). *Memory, politics, and identity: Haunted by history*. New York: Palgrave Macmillan.

McGuinness, M. & Downey, G. (2000). *Creggan: More than a history*. Derry: Guildhall Press.

McIntyre, A. (2013). Short fuse. *The Pensive Quill*. Online Resource. First published 24 October 2013. Retrieved 8 December 2016 from http://thepensivequill.am/2013/10/short-fuse.html.

McKay, S. (2007). Disgusting justification for sectarian murders. *The Irish News*. First published 30 January 2007. Retrieved 27 January 2017 from cain.ulst.ac.uk/victims/docs/newspapers/irish_news/mckay_in_300107.pdf.

McKay, S. (2009). *Bear in mind these dead*. London: Faber & Faber.

McKay, S. (2015). The torture centre: Northern Ireland's 'hooded men'. *The Irish Times*. Online Edition. First published 25 July 2015. Retrieved 8 December 2016 from www.irishtimes.com/news/crime-and-law/the-torture-centre-northern-ireland-s- hooded-men-1.2296152.

McKee, L. (2014). In defence of Anthony McIntyre. *The Pensive Quill – Online Blog*. First published 24 May 2014. Retrieved 23 April 2017 from http://thepensivequill.am/2014/05/in-defence-of-anthony-mcintyre.html.

Mackenzie, A. (2004). Re-imagining the land, North Sunderland, Scotland. *Journal of Rural Studies*, 20(3), pp. 273–87.

McKittrick, D. & McVea, D. (2001). *Making sense of the Troubles: The story of the conflict in Northern Ireland*. Belfast: Blackstaff.

McKittrick, D., Kelters, S., Feeney, B., Thornton, C., & McVea, D. (2008). *Lost lives: The stories of the men, women and children who died as a result of the Northern Ireland troubles*. Edinburgh: Mainstream.

McLaren, L. (2003). Anti-immigrant prejudice in Europe: Contact, threat perception, and preferences for the exclusion of migrants. *Journal of Social Forces*, 81(3), pp. 909–36.

McLaughlin, G. & Baker, S. (2010). *The propaganda of peace: The role of media and culture in the Northern Ireland peace process*. Bristol: Intellect Books.

McMaster, J. (2011). *Ethical and shared remembering: Commemoration in a new context*. Derry: The Junction.

McMaster, J. & Higgins, C. (2014). *War and memory*. Derry/Londonderry: The Junction.

McMurtrie, B. (2014). Secrets from Belfast: How Boston College's oral history of the Troubles fell victim to an international murder investigation. *The Chronicle of Higher*

Education. First published 26 January 2014. Retrieved 23 April 2017 from www.chronicle.com/interactives/belfast.

McSmith, A. (2016). The Shankill Road bombing: The history of collusion between MI5 and the IRA. *The Independent* (online). First published 25 January 2016. Retrieved 23 October 2016 from www.independent.co.uk/news/uk/home-news/shankill-road-bombing-the-history-of-collusion-between-mi5-and-the-ira-a6833586.html.

Magee, P. (2001). *Gangsters or guerrillas? Representations of Irish Republicans in 'Troubles fiction'*. Belfast: Beyond the Pale.

Malin, A. (1994). Mothers who won't disappear. *Human Rights Quarterly*, 16(1), pp. 187–213.

Mann, T. (1947/1999). *Dr. Faustus: The life of the German composer Adrian Leverkuhn as told by a friend*. New York: Vintage.

Mao, Z. (1937). The political problems of guerrilla warfare. In Zedong, M. *On Guerrilla Warfare*. Online Resource. Retrieved 8 December 2016 from www.marxists.org/reference/archive/mao/works/1937/guerrilla-warfare/ch06.htm.

Marschall, S. (2009). *Landscape of memory: Commemorative monuments, memorials, and public statuary in post-Apartheid South Africa*. Amsterdam: Brill.

Massey, D. (1994). *Space, place, and gender*. Minneapolis: University of Minnesota Press.

Massey, D. (2005). *For space*. Thousand Oaks, CA: SAGE.

Massey, D. & McDowell, L. (1994). A woman's place? In Massey, D., *Space, place, and gender*. Minneapolis: University of Minnesota Press.

Masson, J. (1984). The assault on truth: Freud's suppression of seduction theory. New York: Farrar, Strauss, & Giroux.

Minow, M. (1998). *Between vengeance and forgiveness: Facing history after mass violence*. Boston, MA: Beacon Press.

Misztal, B. (2003). *Theories of social remembering*. Maidenhead: Open University Press.

Mitchell, P., Evans, G., & O'Leary, B. (2009). Extremist outbidding in ethnic party systems is not inevitable: Tribune parties in Northern Ireland. *Political Studies*, 57(2), pp. 379–421.

Modlin, Jr., E. (2008). Tales told on the tour: Mythic representations of slavery by docents at North Carolina plantation museums. *Southeastern Geographer*, 48(3), pp. 265–87.

Moloney, E. (2002). *The secret history of the IRA*. New York: Penguin.

Moloney, E. (2008). *Voices from the grave: Two men's war in Northern Ireland*. London: Faber & Faber.

Monaghan, R. (2004). An imperfect peace: Paramilitary punishments in Northern Ireland. *Terrorism & Political Violence*, 16(3), pp. 439–61.

Monaghan, R. & Shirlow, P. (2011). Forward to the past? Loyalist paramilitarism in Northern Ireland since 1994. *Studies in Conflict & Terrorism*, 34(8), pp. 649–65.

Moriarty, G. (2016). Boston College subpoenaed for Anthony McIntyre interviews. *The Irish Times Online*. First published 25 April 2016. Retrieved 23 April 2016 from www.irishtimes.com/news/ireland/irish-news/boston-college-subpoenaed-for-anthony-mcintyre-interviews-1.2624190.

Moore, N. & Whelan, Y. (eds) (2007). *Heritage, memory, and the politics of identity: New perspectives on the cultural landscape*. Farnham: Ashgate.

Moxon-Browne, E. (1981). The water and the fish: Public opinion and the Provisional IRA in Northern Ireland. *Studies in Conflict & Terrorism*, 5(1–2), pp. 41–72.

Mullins, J. (1999). Terror of farmer named by Paisley as IRA Killer. *The Guardian Online*. First published 12 February 1999. Retrieved 27 January 2017 from www.theguardian.com/uk/1999/feb/12/6.

Muñoz, J. (1997). Photographies of mourning: Melancholia and ambivalence in Van der Zee, Mapplethorpe, and Looking for Langston. In Stecopolous, H. & Uebel, M. (eds), *Race and the subject of masculinities*. Durham, NC: Duke University Press.

Murphy, B. (2005). Peter Hart and the Issue of Sources. *Irish Political Review*, 20(7), pp. 10–11.

Murphy, P. (2014). LAD: What next for Northern Ireland's new politics of the people? *The Huffington Post Online*. First published 24 January 2014. Retrieved 5 February 2017 from www.huffingtonpost.co.uk/philip-murphy/northern-ireland_b_4654049.html.

Murray, G. & Tonge, J. (2005). *Sinn Féin and the SDLP: From alienation to participation*. Dublin: The O'Brien Press.

Murray, R. (2004). *The SAS in Ireland*. Dublin: Mercier Press.

Murtagh, B. (2002). *The politics of territory: Policy and segregation in Northern Ireland*. London: Palgrave Macmillan.

Murtagh, B. (2017). Urban alternatives and collaborative economics in Belfast's contested space. In Zebich-Knos, M. & Grichting, A. (eds), *Between the lines: Social ecologies in border landscapes*. London: Anthem, Ch. 13 (forthcoming).

Nagle, J. (2009). Sites of social centrality and segregation: Lefebvre in Belfast, a 'divided city'. *Antipode*, 41(2), pp. 326–47.

Ní Aoláin, F. (2000). *The politics of force: Conflict management and state violence in Northern Ireland*. Belfast: Blackstaff.

Nietzsche, F. (1873/1997). *Untimely Mediations*. Cambridge: Cambridge University Press.

Nikulin. D. (ed.) (2015). *Memory: A history*. Oxford: Oxford University Press.

Nolan, P. (2014). *Northern Ireland peace monitoring report: Number three*. Belfast: Community Relations Council.

Nora, P. (1989). Between memory and history: Les lieux de mémoire. *Representations*, 26(1), pp. 7–24.

Nora, P. (1996). *Realms of memory: The construction of the French past*. New York: Columbia University Press.

Novick, P. (1999). *The Holocaust and collective memory: The American experience*. London: Bloomsbury.

O'Connor, F. (1993). *In search of a state: Catholics in Northern Ireland*. Belfast: Blackstaff.

O'Connor, R. & O'Neill, S. (2015). Mental health and suicide risk in Northern Ireland: A legacy of the Troubles? *The Lancet Psychiatry*, 2(7), pp. 582–4.

Ó Dochartaigh, N. (1997). *From civil rights to armalites: Derry and the birth of the Troubles*. Cork; Cork University Press.

O'Dowd, L. & Komarova, M. (2011). Contesting territorial fixity? A case study of regeneration in Belfast. *Urban Studies*, 48(10), pp. 2013–28.

Offe, C. (1996). Varieties of transition: The East European and East German Experience. Cambridge: Polity Press.

O'Leary, B. & McGarry, J. (1993). *The politics of antagonism: Understanding Northern Ireland*. London: Athlone Press.

Olick, J. (1999). Collective memory: The two cultures. *Sociological Theory*, 17(3), pp. 333–48.

Olick, J. & Robbins, J. (1998). Social memory studies: From 'collective memory' to the historical sociology of mnemonic practices. *Annual Review of Sociology*, 24, pp. 105–40.

Olick, J., Vinitzky-Seroussi, V., & Levy, D. (2011). *The collective memory reader*. Oxford: Oxford University Press.

Olusoga, D. & Erichsen, C. (2010). *The Kaiser's Holocaust: Germany's forgotten genocide and the colonial roots of Nazism*. London: Faber & Faber.

O'Mahoney, B. with McGovern, M. (2000). *Soldier of the Queen*. Dingle, Ireland: Brandon Books.

Onishi, N. (2014). In California, saving a language that predates Spanish and English. *The New York Times*. Online Edition. First published 12 April, 2014. Retrieved 3 December 2016 from www.nytimes.com/2014/04/13/us/in-california-saving-a-language-that-predates-spanish-and-english.html.

O'Tuama, S. (1998). Judging the victims. *An Phoblacht* (Online), n.p. Retrieved 2 November 2016 from www.anphoblacht.com/contents/3512.

Passerini, L. (1987). *Fascism in popular memory: The cultural experience of the Turin working class*. Cambridge: Cambridge University Press.

Patterson, H. (2008). War of liberation or ethnic liberation? IRA violence in Fermanagh during the Troubles. In Bowden, B. & Davis, M. T. (eds), *Terror: From tyrannicide to terrorism*. St Lucia, Australia: University of Queensland Press.

Payne, L. (2008). *Unsettling accounts: Neither truth nor reconciliation in confessions of state violence*. Durham, NC: Duke University Press.

Perry, R. J. (2005). *"Wipe out the plague spots": The expulsion of the Chinese from Humboldt County*. M.A. Thesis, unpublished. Humboldt State University, Arcata, CA.

Perry, R. (2013). *Revisionist scholarship and modern Irish politics*. Farnham: Ashgate.

Phelan, P. (1993). *Unmarked: The politics of performance*. London: Routledge.

Phelps, T. (2005). *Shattered voices: Language, violence, and the work of truth commissions*. Philadelphia: University of Pennsylvania Press.

Police Ombudsman for Northern Ireland (2010). Public statement by the Police Ombudsman under Section 62 of the Police (Northern Ireland) Act 1998: Relating to the RUC investigation of the alleged involvement of the late Father James Chesney in the bombing of Claudy on the 31st July 1972. Belfast: Office of the Police Ombudsman for Northern Ireland.

Popular Memory Group (1982). Popular memory: theory, politics, and method. In Johnson, R., Mclennan, G., Schwartz, B., & Sutton, D. (eds), *Making histories: Studies in history making and politics*. London: Hutchinson, pp. 205–52.

Porter, N. (2003). *The elusive quest: Reconciliation in Northern Ireland*. Belfast: Blackstaff.

Potter, J. (2001). *A testimony to courage: The history of the Ulster Defence Regiment, 1969–1992*. Barnsley: Pen & Sword Books.

Potter, M. (2014). *Review of gender issues in Northern Ireland*. Belfast: Northern Ireland Assembly, Research and Information Service.

Powell, J. (2009). *Great hatred, little room: Making peace in Northern Ireland*. New York: Vintage.

Primoratz, I. (ed.) (2007). *Civilian immunity in war*. Oxford: Oxford University Press Press.

Proust, M. (1913/1981). *In search of lost time, Vol. I*. New York: Random House.

Radstone, S. (2008). Memory studies: For and against. *Memory Studies*, 1(1), pp. 31–9.

Rankine, C. (2015). The condition of black life is one of mourning. *The New York Times*. Online Edition. First published 22 June 2015. Retrieved 3 December 2016 from www.nytimes.com/2015/06/22/magazine/the-condition-of-black-life-is-one-of-mourning.html?_r=0.

Rea, T. & Wright, J. (1998). *Ireland: A divided island.* Oxford: Oxford University Press.

Regan, J. (2010). Irish public histories as an historiographical problem. *Irish Historical Studies*, 37, pp. 265–92.

Regan, P. (2010). *Unsettling the settler within: Indian residential schools, truth telling, and reconciliation in Canada:* Vancouver & Toronto: University of British Columbia Press.

Relph, E. (1976). *Place and placelessness.* London: Pion.

Richardson, J. (2008). Nietzsche's problem of the past. In Dries, M. (ed.), *Nietzsche on time and history.* Berlin: de Gruyter.

Roht-Arriaza, N. (2006). The new landscape of transitional justice. In Roht-Arriaza, N. & Mariezcurrena, J. (eds.). Transitional justice in the twenty-first century: Beyond truth versus justice. Cambridge: Cambridge University Press, pp. 1–16.

Roht-Arriaza, N. & Mariezcurrena, J. (eds) (2006). *Transitional justice in the twenty-first century: Beyond truth versus justice.* Cambridge: Cambridge University Press.

Rolston, B. (2002). Assembling the jigsaw: Truth, justice, and transition in the North of Ireland. *Race & Class*, 44(1), pp. 87–105.

Rolston, B. (2006). Dealing with the past: Pro-state paramilitaries, truth and transition in Northern Ireland. *Human Rights Quarterly*, 28(3), pp. 652–75.

Rosenfeld, A. (2002). The assault on Holocaust memory. *KulturPoetik*, 2(1), pp. 82–101.

Rosland, S. (2009). Victimhood, identity, and agency in the early phase of the Troubles in Northern Ireland. *Identities: Global Studies in Culture & Power*, 16(3), pp. 294–320.

Rothberg, M. (2009), *Multidirectional memory: Remembering the Holocaust in the age of decolonisation.* Stanford: Stanford University Press.

Rowan, B. (2016). Northern Ireland's violent past remains unresolved. *The Irish Times*. Online Edition. First published 16 January 2016. Retrieved 8 December 2016 from www.irishtimes.com/news/politics/northern-ireland-s-violent-past- remains-unresolved-1.2498749.

RTÉ Investigations Unit (2014). *The torture files.* Television Programme. First aired 4 June 2014.

Ruane, J. & Todd, J. (1996). *The dynamics of conflict in Northern Ireland: Power, conflict, and emancipation.* Cambridge: Cambridge University Press.

Ruddick, S. (1989). *Maternal thinking: Towards a politics of peace.* Boston, MA: Beacon Press.

Rumford, C. (2008). Introduction: Citizens and borderwork in Europe. *Space & Polity*, 12(1), pp. 1–12.

Rumford, C. (2013). *The globalisation of strangeness.* Basingstoke: Palgrave Macmillan.

Rutheford, A. (2012). Sandy Row erases infamous UFF terror mural. *Belfast Telegraph*. Online Edition. First published 26 June 2012. Retrieved 5 February 2017 from www.belfasttelegraph.co.uk/news/northern-ireland/sandy-row-erases-infamous- uff-terror-mural-16177246.html.

Said, E. (1978). *Orientalism.* New York: Pantheon.

Said, E. (1993). *Culture and Imperialism.* London: Vintage.

Sands, B. (1981). *Prison Diary.* Online Resource: The Bobby Sands Trust. Retrieved 8 December 2016 from www.bobbysandstrust.com/writings/prison-diary.

Savage, K. (1996). *Standing soldiers, kneeling slaves: Race, war, and monument in nineteenth-century America*. Princeton: Princeton University Press.

Savage, K. (2009). *Monument wars: Washington, D.C., the National Mall, and the transformation of the memorial landscape*. Berkeley, CA: University of California Press.

Scarry, E. (1985). *The body in pain: The making and unmaking of the world*. Oxford: Oxford University Press.

Schein, R. (1997). The place of landscape: A conceptual framework for interpreting the American scene. *Annals of the Association of American Geographers*, 87, pp. 660–80.

Schmitt, C. (1922/1985). *Political theology. Four chapters on the concept of sovereignty*. Chicago: University of Chicago Press.

Schwartz, B. (1996). Introduction: The expanding past. *Qualitative Sociology*, 9(3), pp. 275–282.

Scruggs, J. (1981). Statement at Commission of Fine Arts meeting, 13 October 1981. Document archived at Lehigh University Digital Library, exhibit entitled: "The Vietnam Wall Controversy". Retrieved 10 February 2017 from http://digital.lib.lehigh.edu/trial/vietnam/r3/october/.

Scruggs, J. & Swerdlow, J. (1985). *To heal a nation: The Vietnam Veterans Memorial*. New York: Harper & Row.

Senehi, J. (2009). The role of constructive, transcultural storytelling in ethnopolitical conflict transformation in Northern Ireland. In Carter, J., Irani, G., & Volkan, V. (eds), *Regional and ethnic conflicts. Perspectives from the front lines*. London: Routledge, pp. 227–38.

Shackel, P. (2003). *Memory in black and white: Race, commemoration and the post-bellum landscape*. Lanham, MD: Altamira.

Shanahan, T. (2009). *The Provisional Irish Republican Army and the morality of terrorism*. Edinburgh: Edinburgh University Press.

Shared City Project & Omagh Self-Help & Support Group (2011). *Remembering the past and looking to the future*. Self-published pamphlet.

Sharrock, D. (2001). Brighton deaths were justified, IRA bomber tells victim's daughter. *The Telegraph*. Online Edition. First published 11 December 2001. Retrieved 8 December 2016 from www.telegraph.co.uk/news/uknews/1364924/Brighton-deaths-were-justified- IRA-bomber-tells-victims-daughter.html.

Shaw, M. (2005). *The new western way of war*. London: Polity.

Shea, M. (2010). Whatever you say, say something: Remembering for the future in Northern Ireland. *International Journal of Heritage Studies*, 16(4–5), pp. 289–304.

Shirlow, P. (2006). Belfast: The 'post-conflict' city. *Space and Polity*, 10(2), pp. 99–107.

Shirlow, P. & Murtagh, B. (2006). *Belfast: Segregation, violence, and the city*. London: Pluto Press.

Simpson, K. (2009). *Truth recovery in Northern Ireland: Critically interpreting the past*. Manchester: Manchester University Press.

Sinn Féin (2016). Towards an agreed and reconciled future: Sinn Féin policy on reconciliation and healing. Sinn Féin: Dublin. Online Resource. Retrieved 11 December 2016 from www.sinnfein.ie/files/2016/Reconciliation_Policy_Ard_Fheis_2016.pdf.

Sluka, J. (1989). *Hearts and minds, water and fish: Support for the IRA and INLA in a Northern Ireland ghetto*. London: JAI Press.

Small, S. (2013). Still back of the big house: Slave cabins and slavery in Southern heritage tourism. *Tourism Geographies*, 15(3), pp. 405–23.

Smith, D. (2000). The mirror image of the present: Freud's theory of retrogressive screen memories. *Psychoanalytische Perspectieven*, 39, pp. 7–29.

Smith, N. (1996). *The new urban frontier: Gentrification and the revanchist city.* New York: Routledge.

Smith, N. (2008). *Uneven development: Nature, capital, and the production of space, 3rd edn.* Athens, GA: University of Georgia Press.

Smyth, J. (2000). Introduction: The 1798 rebellion in its eighteenth-century contexts. In: Smyth, J. (ed.), *Revolution, counter-revolution, and union: Ireland in the 1790s.* Cambridge: Cambridge University Press, pp. 1–20.

Smyth, M. (1995). Population movement: The statistics. In *Aspects of sectarian division in Derry Londonderry – Third public discussion: The changing population balance and Protestant drift.* Online Resource. CAIN. Retrieved 8 December 2016 from http://cain.ulst.ac.uk/issues/segregat/temple/discus3.htm.

Smyth, M. (1998). Remembering in Northern Ireland: Victims, perpetrators, and hierarchies of pain and responsibility. In Hamber, B. (ed.), *Past imperfect: Dealing with the past in Northern Ireland and societies in transition.* Derry/Londonderry: INCORE, pp. 31–49.

Southern, N. (2007). Protestant alienation in Northern Ireland: A political, cultural, and geographical examination. *Journal of Ethnic and Migration Studies*, 33(1), pp. 159–80.

Sparke, M. (2005). *In the space of theory: Postfoundational geographies of the nation-state.* Minneapolis: University of Minnesota Press.

Spencer, B. (2013). Loyalists Against Democracy – Unmveiling and assailing sectarianism. Online Blog. Retrieved 12 April 2017 from http://eamonnmallie.com/2013/10/loyalists-against-democracy-unveiling-and-assailing-sectarianism/.

Spencer, G. (2008). *The state of loyalism in Northern Ireland.* London: Palgrave Macmillan.

Spillman, L. & Conway, B. (2007). Texts, bodies, and the memory of Bloody Sunday. *Symbolic Interaction*, 30(1), pp. 79–103.

Spivak, G. (1988). Can the subaltern speak? In Nelson, C. & Grossberg, L. (eds), *Marxism and the interpretation of cultures.* Urbana, IL: University of Illinois Press.

Stan, L. (2013). *Transitional justice in post-communist Romania: The politics of memory.* Cambridge: Cambridge University Press.

Stedman, R. (2003). Is it really just a social construction? The contribution of the physical environment to sense of place. *Society & Natural Resources*, 16(8), pp. 671–85.

Steuter, E. & Wills, D. (2009). *At war with metaphor: Media, propaganda, and racism in the war on terror.* Lanfield, MD: Lexington Books.

Stevenson, R. (2008). Omagh marks tenth anniversary of deadly bombing. *The Guardian* (online). Retrieved 3 November 2016 from www.theguardian.com/uk/2008/aug/15/northernireland.uksecurity.

Stone, D. (1999). The domestication of violence: Forging a collective memory of the Holocaust in Britain. *Patterns of Prejudice*, 33(2), pp. 13–29.

Sturken, M. (1997). *Tangled memories: The Vietnam War, the AIDS epidemic, and the politics of remembering.* Berkeley: University of California Press.

Sturken, M. (2001). Absent images of memory: Remembering and re-enacting the Japanese Internment. In Fujitani, F., White, G., & Yoneyama, I. (eds), *Perilous images: The Asia-Pacific War(s).* Durham, NC: Duke University Press.

Sturken, M. (2007). *Tourists of history: Memory, kitsch, and consumerism from Oklahoma City to Ground Zero.* Durham, NC: Duke University Press.

Sutherland, A. & Purdy, N. (2006). *Attitudes of the socially disadvantaged towards education in Northern Ireland: Research report.* Belfast: Department of Education Northern Ireland.

Sutton, M. (2001). Malcolm Sutton: An Index of Deaths from the Conflict in Ireland. Online Resource: CAIN. Retrieved 8 December 2016 from http://cain.ulst.ac.uk/sutton/.

Switzer, C. & Graham, B. (2009). 'From thorn to thorn': Commemorating the Royal Ulster Constabulary in Northern Ireland. *Social & Cultural Geography*, 10(2), pp. 153–71.

Switzer, C. & McDowell, S. (2009). Redrawing cognitive maps of conflict: Lost spaces and forgetting in the centre of Belfast. *Memory Studies*, 2(3), pp. 337–53.

Taylor, C. (1994). *Multiculturalism.* Princeton: Princeton University Press.

Taylor, P. (1998). *Provos: The IRA and Sinn Féin.* London: Bloomsbury.

Taylor, P. (1999). Loyalists. London: Bloomsbury.

Taylor, R. (2009). The injustice of a consociational solution to the Northern Ireland problem. In Taylor, R. (ed.), *Consociational theory: McGarry and O'Leary and the Northern Ireland conflict.* London: Routledge, pp. 309–30.

Teeger, C. & Vinitzky-Seroussi, V. (2007). Controlling for consensus: Commemorating apartheid in South Africa. *Symbolic Interaction*, 30(1): 57–78.

Teitel, R. (2002). *Transitional justice.* Oxford: Oxford University Press.

Teitel, R. (2003). Transitional justice genealogy. *Harvard Human Rights Journal*, 16, pp. 69–94.

Thelen, D. (1989). Memory and American history. *The Journal of American History*, 75(4), pp. 1117–29.

Thomas, M. (2005). Girls, consumption space and the contradictions of hanging out in the city. *Social & Cultural Geography*, 6(4), pp. 587–605.

Thomson, A. (1994). *Anzac memories: Living with the legend.* Oxford: Oxford University Press.

Till, K. (2005). *The new Berlin: Memory, politics, place.* Minneapolis: University of Minnesota Press.

Till, K. (2006). Memory studies. *History Workshop Journal*, 62, pp. 325–41 (Review).

Till, K. (2012). Wounded cities: Memory work and a place-based ethics of care. *Political Geography*, 31(1), pp. 3–14.

Tomlinson, M. (2016). Risking peace in the 'war against the poor'? Social exclusion and the legacies of the Northern Ireland conflict. *Critical Social Policy*, 36(1), pp. 104–23.

Tonge, J. (2004). *The new Northern Irish politics.* London: Palgrave Macmillan.

Trouillot, M-R. (1997). *Silencing the past: Power and the production of history.* Boston, MA: Beacon Press.

Tuan, Y-F. (1975). Place: An experiential perspective. *Geographical Review*, 65(2), pp. 151–165.

Tuan, Y-F. (1977). *Space and place: The perspective of experience.* Minneapolis: University of Minnesota Press.

Tuan, Y-F. (1979). Space and place: Humanistic perspective. In Gale, S. & Olsson, G. (eds), *Philosophy in Geography.* Dordrecht: Reidel, pp. 387–427.

Turner, V. (1988). *The anthropology of performance.* Cambridge, MA: PAJ Press.

Turner, V. & Turner, E. (1978). *Image and pilgrimage in Christian culture: Anthropological perspectives.* Oxford: Blackwell.

Tutu, D. (1999). *No future without forgiveness: A personal overview of South Africa's Truth and Reconciliation Commission.* London: Rider.

United States Holocaust Museum & Memorial (USHMM) (1993). President Clinton and Elie Wiesel's remarks on Bosnia troops. Online resource: Available at www.ushmm.org/educators/lesson-plans/holocaust-unit/resources/handout-1. Retrieved 2 May 2017.

Verdery, K. (1999). *The political lives of dead bodies: Reburial and postsocialist change.* New York: Columbia University Press.

Vietnam Veterans Against the War (1972). *The winter soldier investigation: An inquiry into American war crimes.* Boston, MA: Beacon Press.

Vinitzky-Seroussi, V. (2002). Commemorating a difficult past: Yitzhak Rabin's memorial. *American Journal of Sociology*, 97(2), pp. 376–420.

Volkan, V. (1997). *Bloodlines: From ethnic pride to ethnic terrorism.* New York: Farrar, Strouss & Giroux.

Vollhardt, J. (2012). Collective victimization. In: Tropp, S, (ed.), *The Oxford handbook of intergroup conflict.* Oxford: Oxford University Press, pp. 136–57.

Vonnegut, K. (1969). *Slaughterhouse-five: Or the children's crusade.* New York: Delacorte.

Wagner-Pacifici, R. & Schwartz, B. (1991). The Vietnam Veterans Memorial: Commemorating a difficult past. *American Journal of Sociology*, 97(2): 376–420.

Walzer, M. (1977). *Just and unjust wars: A moral argument with historical illustrations.* New York: Basic.

Weber, M. (1919). Politics as vocation. Online resource. Retrieved 15 January 2017 from http://anthropos-lab.net/wp/wp-content/uploads/2011/12/Weber-Politics-as-a-Vocation.pdf.

Weinberg, J. & Elieli, R. (1995). *The Holocaust Museum in Washington.* New York: Rizzoli.

Weschler, L. (1995). A miracle, a universe: Settling accounts with torturers (Foreword and Afterword). In Kritz, N. J. (ed.), *Transitional justice: How emerging democracies reckon with former regimes, Vol. I: General considerations.* Washington DC: USIP.

West, H. (2003). Voices twice silenced: Betrayal and mourning at colonialism's end in Mozambique. *Anthropological Theory*, 3(3), pp. 343–65.

White, G. (2006). Landscapes of power: National memorials and the domestication of affect. *City & Society*, 18(1), pp. 50–61.

Whyte, L. (2014). "Britain taught the world how to torture": Northern Ireland's hooded men take new evidence back to court. *Vice News Online.* First published 24 December 2014. Retrieved 10 February 2017 from https://news.vice.com/article/britain-taught-the-world-how-to-torture-northern-irelands-hooded-men-take-new-evidence-back-to-court.

Williams, J. (2016). *A roof over my head: Homeless women and the shelter industry.* Boulder, CO: University of Colorado Press.

Wilson, J. (2000). The Brighton Bomber thinks again. *The Guardian.* Online Edition. First published 27 August 2000. Retrieved 8 December 2016 from www.theguardian.com/uk/2000/aug/28/northernireland.jamiewilson.

Wilson, R. (2005). Collective memory, group minds, and the extended mind thesis. *Cognitive Processing*, 6(4), pp. 227–36.

Winter, J. (1995). *Sites of memory, sites of mourning: The Great War in European cultural history*. Cambridge: Cambridge University Press.

Winter, J. (2001). The memory boom in contemporary historical studies. *Raritan*, 21(1), pp. 52–66.

Winter, J. & Sivan, E. (1997). *War and remembrance in the twentieth century*. Cambridge: Cambridge University Press.

Wood, I. (2003). *God, guns, and ulster: A history of Loyalist paramilitaries*. Edinburgh: Edinburgh University Press.

Wood, I. (2006). *Crimes of loyalty: A history of the UDA*. Edinburgh: Edinburgh University Press.

Wright, T. (1997). *Out of place: Homeless mobilisations, subcities, and contested landscapes*. Albany, NY: SUNY Press.

Wynne-Jones, R. (1998). Terry wasn't a player, but they killed him anyway. *The Independent*. Online Edition. First published 25 January 1998. Retrieved 9 February 2017 from www.independent.co.uk/news/terry-wasnt-a-player-but-they-killed-him-anyway-1140734.html.

Yarborough, T. (2005). *Surviving twice: Amerasian children of the Vietnam War*. Washington DC: Potomac Books.

Young, J. (1993). *The texture of memory: Holocaust memorials and meaning*. New Haven: Yale University Press.

Yurchak, A. (2005). *Everything was forever, until it was no more: The last Soviet generation*. Princeton: Princeton University Press.

Žižek, S. (1989). *The sublime object of ideology*. London: Verso.

Žižek, S. (1991). *For they know not what they do*. London: Verso.

Zola, E. (1898). *Letter to the President of the Republic: I accuse!* Online resource. Retrieved 11 December 2016 from www.marxists.org/archive/zola/1898/jaccuse.htm.

Index

For Product Safety Concerns and Information please contact our EU
representative GPSR@taylorandfrancis.com
Taylor & Francis Verlag GmbH, Kaufingerstraße 24, 80331 München, Germany

www.ingramcontent.com/pod-product-compliance
Ingram Content Group UK Ltd.
Pitfield, Milton Keynes, MK11 3LW, UK
UKHW020011200926
475702UK00014B/1823

* 9 7 8 0 3 6 7 1 9 1 7 4 0 *